To Preserve The Nation

To Preserve The Nation

*In the Tradition of the
Founding Fathers
American Government
Lecture Series*

SCOTT N. BRADLEY

COPYRIGHT © 2009 BY SCOTT N. BRADLEY.

LIBRARY OF CONGRESS CONTROL NUMBER:		2008904704
ISBN:	HARDCOVER	978-1-4363-4548-4
	SOFTCOVER	978-1-4363-4547-7

All rights reserved. No part of this book may be reproduced or transmitted in any form or by any means, electronic or mechanical, including photocopying, recording, or by any information storage and retrieval system, without permission in writing from the copyright owner.

This book was printed in the United States of America.

Freedom's Call

To order additional copies of this book, contact:
Xlibris Corporation
1-888-795-4274
www.Xlibris.com
Orders@Xlibris.com
46596

CONTENTS

Preface 9

Introductory Lecture 13

1. America's Spiritual Foundation 21
2. Individual Liberties and American Government 43
3. American Principles of Federalism 75
4. American History Time Line 100
5. Overview of the United States Constitution 137
6. The Bill of Rights and Other Amendments 150
7. Modern-Day Offenses (Unremitting Betrayals) 164
8. Of Money and Economics 201
9. The Moral Imperative 214
10. The Right to Keep and Bear Arms 225
11. Of Education and Freedom 240
12. Washington's Farewell Address 259
13. The Communist Manifesto 275
14. All Revolutions Are Not Created Equal (The American Revolution vs. Subsequent Revolutions) 289
15. George Washington: "The Elegant Exercise of Power"— a Study in the Rare, Pure Exercise of Mortal Authority 308
16. Our Sacred Honor: Our Modern Duty to Preserve Our Liberties 336

Appendix A:	Pledge of Allegiance	363
Appendix B:	Mayflower Compact	364
Appendix C:	Declaration of Independence	366
Appendix D:	Preamble to the Constitution	371
Appendix E:	The United States Constitution	372
Appendix F:	The Bill of Rights	384
Appendix G:	U.S. Constitution Amendments 11-27	387
Appendix H:	George Washington's Farewell Address	394
Appendix I:	George Washington's Farewell Address Vocabulary Words	405
Appendix J:	Communist Manifesto	465
Appendix K:	Brief Biographical and Philosophical Sketches	498

John Locke	499
Baron de Montesquieu	502
Sir William Blackstone	505
St. George Tucker	509

Selected Bibliography	513
Index	517

This book
is a
companion
to a
series of seventeen lectures
To Preserve the Nation:
In the Tradition of the Founding Fathers
by
Scott N. Bradley

(This series of lectures is available in both DVD video format and in audio formats)

This study course requires *both* this book
and the lecture presentations to be complete.

Each chapter in this book correlates with a lecture in the series. Together, they present the marvelous principles upon which the United States of America was established. The material is taught from the perspective of the Founding Fathers' "original intent." The lecture series, with this companion book, applies the wisdom of the American Founding Fathers to the study of United States history and the sound principles of proper government that were brought forth as this nation was established. In this series, the words of the founders are carefully reviewed, and the student is given the opportunity to not only understand the priceless principles of liberty, but also to know how to apply those timeless truths today so the blessings of liberty may be preserved for themselves and their posterity.

To receive a *free* DVD copy of the introductory lecture and pricing for the complete lecture series, visit

http://www.ToPreserveTheNation.com.

This seventeen lecture series and companion study guide book, with recommended reading list for expanded study by the serious student, may be ordered at http://www.ToPreserveTheNation.com.

Preface

Prior to the American Revolutionary War, concerned patriots throughout the American colonies organized "committees of correspondence" to ensure that vital information about their liberty and the political state of affairs was widely distributed so that all who cared could stay informed.

This lecture series has a similar focus and is part of what will be an ongoing effort to awaken again an understanding throughout America of the cause of liberty and proper government. In a modern-day setting, these lectures are intended to perform a similar function as the communications that were generated through the efforts of the committees of correspondence during the Revolutionary War. Each lecture touches upon information that is critical to the preservation of the liberty and proper government that was established at such great cost as this nation was founded. The intention of these lectures is to foster an understanding of how modern challenges that face the United States may be addressed using the wisdom and original intent of those who founded America. The words of this nation's founders in regard to the current challenges are the core message of each lecture. The principles espoused by America's founders are timeless, and this effort is intended to foster a return to the foundation principles upon which the United States was established so that it may again enjoy the fullness of liberty and proper government, which was created under the inspiration of God.

The current state of American politics and the unremitting betrayal of foundation principles bear solemn testimony that the need for this information has not diminished, but has become even more desperate.

Consequently, this lecture series and lecture book are offered as a guide that may be applied to assist in the effort to bring America back to the foundation that made it the freest, most prosperous, most respected, and happiest nation on earth.

The inspired men who established this nation wrote and spoke prolifically. In the written record they left, they explained and defined in acute detail the formula for the government they created under God's inspiration. When we return and study the Constitution "in the tradition of the Founding Fathers," it is, in many ways, like going to the wellspring and partaking of clean, pure, sweet water, which is so thirst-quenching and satisfying.

Much of what is currently written, said, and promoted by revisionists and detractors contradict the principles upon which America was founded. Consequently, there is generally a lack of understanding of many concepts that are critically important to the survival of the nation. Also, widely held beliefs often contradict the fundamentals that were defined and embraced as the nation was established. Each lecture could easily comprise an entire book, but by design, the series is not comprehensive in its review of each of the subjects. It is intended to briefly and succinctly give the student a sound understanding of the issues in the words of those who established this nation. I hope it will be a resource to assist the serious student to become an ally in the battle to restore the individual God-given rights that are the foundation of true liberty. The final chapter, "Our Sacred Honor," is something of a capstone. It is designed to reiterate many of the concepts that were previously touched upon in earlier lectures and to motivate students to recognize their personal responsibility to uphold the principles and standards of liberty vouchsafed to us through the Declaration of Independence and the United States Constitution.

If America is to remain free, each upcoming generation must come to know something of the bedrock principles upon which this nation was founded in order that we might enjoy the blessings of liberty that we cherish today. I hope each new generation will come to value liberty and seek diligently to preserve the principles upon which it is founded. Perhaps those who hear and read the words of the American founders will come to love these principles. This lecture series is offered to help those who will become the self-motivated leaders of the next generation, and I hope they will do the right things for the right reasons.

I hope all who participate in this educational process will resolve that, from this day forward, they will hold dear the great principles upon which this nation was founded and upon which it has been preserved. Each must come to understand that the philosophy that ignores the Constitution and the framework it established or allows the plain and pure meaning of its words to be twisted and modified by the whims of those who hold the reins of government debases the Constitution. Such a position ultimately removes the foundation of the nation and has the same inevitable result as though we had no constitution at all.

If the words of the Constitution may mean anything we (or the Supreme Court, the president, Congress, a judge, a police officer, a bureaucrat, or anyone else) say they mean, or mean nothing at all, then those who hold power hold limitless power, and tyranny will surely follow. The *written* constitution we enjoy may be read and plainly understood by all who will take the time to study it. Great strength, stability, and confidence may be derived by having that firm bedrock upon which to build and maintain our proper government. If this great nation is to be preserved, we must come to understand that those whom we select to hold office are constrained to act only within the constitutional scope of their office, and therefore, they are precluded from going beyond the bounds that have been set within the Constitution.

If this understanding becomes widespread, perhaps then we may be confident that America will always be safe and free.

PREFACE

Original Intent Defined
by
Thomas Jefferson

Thomas Jefferson

As he assumed the office of president of the United States, Thomas Jefferson confirmed the importance of keeping the Constitution within the bounds of original intent, saying,

> The Constitution on which our Union rests shall be administered by me according to the safe and honest meaning contemplated by the plain understanding of the people of the United States at the time of its adoption—a meaning to be found in the explanations of those who advocated, not those who opposed it . . . . These explanations are preserved in the publications of the time.[1]

It is from this perspective that this lecture series is delivered.

Scott N. Bradley

---

[1] Albert Ellery Bergh, *The Writings of Thomas Jefferson*, 10:248. Edited by Albert Ellery Bergh. Washington: Thomas Jefferson Memorial Association, 1907.

Introductory Lecture

RECOMMENDED RESOURCES FOR THE SERIOUS STUDENT:

The Children's Story by James Clavell

    The United States of America is indeed a choice land. It is a land blessed with abundant natural resources. Our rich and fertile farm and ranch lands have fed much of the world for many decades. Our mineral and energy stores are not as yet fully recognized and developed. Our people are industrious and hardworking as they labor to support their families and better their lives. The beauty and majesty of the land from sea to shining sea cannot be overstated. And yet this perspective does not capture the essence of why the United States has excelled all nations in goodness and prosperity.

    Many other nations are also abundantly blessed with natural resources, rich lands, and people who desire to succeed. But many of these other resource-rich nations languish in poverty or struggle through their daily existence. Something made the United States different.

    That something, I believe, may be discovered in the principles upon which this wonderful nation was founded.

    An honest and exhaustive study of the people and events that culminated in the birth of this nation leads the sincere truth seeker to the unequivocal conclusion that, if there is a single foundation principle upon which this nation was established, it is that God's hand was the sustaining influence overarching and under girding every significant event that led to the nation's establishment and that the founders recognized that influence and gave God their thanks and faith. Those who founded this nation, with few exceptions, were godly people who sought, to the best of their ability, to know God's will and to serve Him.

    With that faith-based foundation, those who established this nation recognized God as the source of their rights, and they embraced the principle that the purpose of government was to protect, preserve, and defend those unalienable God-given rights.

    They saw government not as a source from which rights are dispensed, for if government is powerful enough to grant rights, it is also powerful enough to destroy rights. They recognized that government must be constrained to act within a specific, limited scope if it was to fulfill its duty and yet be prevented from becoming a tyranny.

TO PRESERVE THE NATION

In light of these truths, it should not be surprising that the charter they established for the nation created a limited government that was granted power to act in only specific and well-defined areas. In addition, they divided and subdivided the power they granted to the national government in an effort to preclude any element of the government from stepping beyond the limits of proper government.

Those who founded this nation considered the Constitution to be a written, binding contract between those who were hired, or selected to hold office, and the citizens of the nation. All who hold office are required to take an oath to abide by the Constitution. In many ways, the Constitution is the job description of the officeholder. The Constitution grants specific power and withholds all other power[2] from the national government.

As this grand experiment in mankind's dream for freedom was launched at the end of the eighteenth century and beginning of the nineteenth century, there was great hope for its success in the hearts of the people, but there was also much trepidation. Was it possible for a people to govern themselves and maintain the liberty that had been won at such great cost and sacrifice?

The answer was astounding to the entire world. As these principles were applied, the nation blossomed almost overnight into a great beacon of hope for all mankind.

Within the framework of a properly limited and established government, people enjoyed the fruits of their labor and creativity. The abundance of the nation overflowed. The world stood in awe at the magnificence of a nation so blessed, and other wise nations sought to duplicate our success by attempting to adopt our success formula within their lands.

Unfortunately, for many years now, those who lead this nation, and we who are citizens of this great land, have failed to apply the foundation principles upon which this nation was established and upon which we became the freest, most prosperous, and happiest nation on earth. We have strayed far, and the greatness of this nation is being called into question.

I believe that a return to the foundation principles, which are tried and true, will result in a return to the conditions in which all that is of most worth in mortality may be restored to the individuals and families of this land.

However, this will only be possible if the individuals and families of this nation again step forward and vigorously insist that their representatives uphold the United States Constitution and abide by their oath to that document. We all have a duty to become constitutionalists who know that our freedoms will remain secure only if those who govern are constrained to act only within the powers granted to them.

This lecture series covers a broad spectrum of everything American. The lectures and this book are intended to give the student a foundation of sound "Americanist" principles

---

[2.] See Amendments 9 and 10.

upon which to build and, hopefully, assist in the effort to restore those principles and allow the American dream to continue.

The lectures and this book are companions in this effort. The book provides key reference material that is touched upon in the lectures, and the lectures often provide much in the form of background material that enhances what is found in the book.

Prior to reviewing the brief outline of what is included in the lectures of this series, the student is admonished to read the book that is recommended for this introductory lecture. The book is James Clavell's *The Children's Story.* The book is a fictional account of when America has been captured by a foreign power. The story takes place in a second-grade classroom and depicts how, in about twenty minutes, the new teacher unseats the values, attitudes, and beliefs of the children using gentle, insidious techniques that pull the children from their belief in God, family, and country. It depicts how a people that does not understand the meaning of the words behind their beliefs are in danger of losing what they hold so loosely.

In this lecture, the real-life story is told about a South Vietnamese family after the capture of that country by the communist revolutionary forces; how reeducation classrooms and camps are used in that country and in other countries that are captured by modern revolutionary means; how real-life families are faced with losing their traditionally held values, attitudes, and beliefs; and how efforts are made through insidious reeducation techniques to pull them away from their God, their family, and their country that they loved.

In light of this, the student is encouraged to firmly understand the principles of liberty, individual God-given rights, and the purpose of proper government as established by the Founding Fathers of the United States. That is the purpose of this lecture series.

The following is a brief overview or outline of each of the sixteen lectures that follow this introductory lecture:

Lecture 1: America's Spiritual Foundation

In spite of decades of effort by revisionist historians to unseat the truth, America, first and foremost, was a spiritual nation. Many today believe that America is a "commercial" nation, based solely upon economics. While people came to America for a lot of reasons (including economics), the under girding foundation was of a spiritual nature. This lesson will review much of the evidence that supports this truth.

Lecture 2: Individual Liberties and American Government

Where do liberties come from? Are they granted by government? The Founding Fathers of the United States clearly understood that if government is the grantor of liberties, it may also withdraw liberties. Individual God-given rights form the basis and purpose of government as understood and established by this nation's founders.

Lecture 3: American Principles of Federalism

In America, government power is divided and subdivided. Even sources of power are kept separate. This is designed to prevent government from accruing and consolidating power to the point it may become a tyranny. The principles established for the American government were designed to prevent the common tendency recognized in human nature to accrue and then begin to abuse power. Not only were powers granted to the national government divided and subdivided, they were also specifically listed so the limits of the power would be clearly understood and checks and balances between the different branches of government were created to ensure that the branches were kept within the bounds set within the Constitution.

Lecture 4: American History Time Line

A whirlwind tour of American history, from the voyage of Columbus forward to the modern era. This lecture is not intended to be a comprehensive examination of all that has occurred in those five hundred plus years, but to set a context for much of what the nation is experiencing today.

Lecture 5: Overview of the United States Constitution

The straightforward form and substance of the United States Constitution is reviewed. The student will recognize that its plain English words are easily understood and that every American of normal intelligence has not only the ability to understand the Constitution but also the duty to understand the document and demand that the leaders of the nation abide by it.

Lecture 6: The Bill of Rights and Other Amendments

The Bill of Rights were written and ratified to prevent the national government from misconstruing or abusing the powers that were granted to the national government, adding "further declaratory and restrictive clauses" to the Constitution to ensure that individual God-given rights were not infringed upon. Some of the more recent amendments were not so well conceived and will undoubtedly pose challenges to the nation as it moves forward.

Lecture 7: Modern-Day Offenses (Unremitting Betrayals)

In a manner similar to the review done within the Declaration of Independence, wherein the offenses of the king were reviewed to justify the action that was being taken, this lesson reviews some of the current violations of constitutional principle that are common in this modern era. While this lecture is not a comprehensive compilation of all modern violations, the student will be able to confidently begin to identify areas where the leadership of the United States strays from their oath to uphold the charter of the nation, the United States Constitution.

Lecture 8: Of Money and Economics

A proper financial foundation is critical to the freedom of the people of a nation. The Founding Fathers clearly understood these principles and unequivocally incorporated them into the form of government they created for the United States. The nation has strayed far from those principles, and the financial foundation of the nation is crumbling. A restoration of the foundation is possible, but only if the people of the nation are willing to first understand the correct principles, and then insist that the original principles be applied.

Lecture 9: The Moral Imperative

In spite of strenuous efforts by many today to foster the concept that there is no linkage between morality and liberty, the founders of the United States clearly understood that a moral people was required for a nation to be truly free. A virtuous people is necessary for freedom to reign. The liberty of the nation requires a moral foundation. Liberty, as envisioned by the founders of the nation, was not licentiousness, nor is it based upon license to violate baseline principles of morality that have been clearly defined for most of history. In the beginning, the people of the nation, by and large, bound themselves to those moral principles not because of draconian legislation, but because they firmly believed that each individual would ultimately face their God and be judged by the works they performed while in mortality.

Lecture 10: The Right to Keep and Bear Arms

The Second Amendment to the United States Constitution has generated a great deal of controversy in modern times. Many promote the idea that this right to bear arms is not an individual's right, which is protected by the Constitution. The clear and well-spoken views of the Founding Fathers will be reviewed to dispel this misconception.

Lecture 11: Of Education and Freedom

The Founding Fathers of the United States were unequivocally committed to the necessity of an educated populace in order to preserve liberty throughout the nation. However, the education process must confirm in the hearts and minds of the people of the nation the sound, firm principles upon which liberty and proper government are based. False philosophies that undermine or destroy the correct principles will facilitate the destruction of the nation's freedom.

TO PRESERVE THE NATION

This lecture will review the approach to education that was used as this nation was established and compare and contrast that approach with modern educational paradigms that promote false educational ideas to the detriment of the preservation of the nation. *The Humanist Manifestos* and the philosophies contained therein will be considered at length in this lecture.

Lecture 12: George Washington's Farewell Address

Published in 1796 as George Washington neared the completion of his second presidential term, this marvelous document reflects the love and devotion manifested by George Washington's forty-five selfless years of service to his nation. In this address, he offers timeless, priceless advice to his nation, pleading with America to stay the course that had been established under the United States Constitution. If American leadership had unerringly applied his counsel, or if they would begin again to vigorously abide by it, the nation would be quickly restored to its place as the freest, most prosperous, happiest, and most respected nation upon the earth. This lecture encourages all to become familiar with Washington's sound counsel and again insist that it be applied by American leadership. Approximately five hundred vocabulary words selected from George Washington's Farewell Address are included in the appendix of this book. The definitions of these words, taken from Noah Webster's 1828 publication, *An American Dictionary of the English Language*, are included so students may clearly understand and learn the words as they were understood by the Founding Fathers of the nation. This will facilitate future studies of the founding documents of the United States of America.

Noah Webster

INTRODUCTORY LECTURE

Lecture 13: The Communist Manifesto

Understanding *The Communist Manifesto* is critically important so the student may understand the concepts that are contained therein and how they are diametrically opposed to the concepts upon which the liberty of this nation and its proper government are based. The student will see how the false philosophies contained within *The Communist Manifesto* threaten all that is of worth to humanity. Americans need to clearly understand what the adversaries of freedom believe and what they promote so appropriate measures may be taken to defeat their efforts.

Lecture 14: All Revolutions Are Not Created Equal (The American Revolution vs. Subsequent Revolutions)

The American Revolution and French Revolution were contemporary with each other, but the basis of each were diametric opposites. Subsequent revolutions will also be reviewed, and the student will come to understand that virtually all modern-day revolutions are descendants of the false philosophies and tyranny imposed by the French Revolution. In spite of vigorous efforts by many in media, government, and education to convince Americans that other subsequent revolutions are simply reflections of the American Revolution, the student will receive the foundation to compare and contrast so they may understand the truth.

Lecture 15: George Washington: "The Elegant Exercise of Power"—a Study in the Rare, Pure Exercise of Mortal Authority

George Washington was one of those rare mortals who could be handed power but would not abuse it. He would be no tyrant, in any way, shape, or form—ever. Throughout his life, power was thrust upon him by those who would have him lead. He constantly made efforts to deflect power from himself, but the nation insisted, and he had power imposed upon him by a nation that desperately needed a leader to bring liberty to them. George Washington was the indispensable man in the establishment of the United States. He fulfilled his assignments with gracious humility, and each time his assignment was complete, he divested himself of the power he had been granted as quickly as he could. Numerous examples of Washington's character and how he elegantly handled power without being corrupted by it are reviewed in this lecture.

Lecture 16: Our Sacred Honor: Our Modern Duty to Preserve Our Liberty

This lecture is a sort of "capstone" lesson that compares the sacrifices of the founders of this nation and our modern-day duty to preserve the liberties and proper government that were bequeathed to us and our posterity at such great cost. What the Founding Fathers of the United States did, they did largely for their posterity. Many knew when they made the efforts that established the liberty of America that they, personally, would probably not

TO PRESERVE THE NATION

live to see a complete fulfillment of their dream of liberty for this land, but they saw in the nation they were establishing a great hope for their posterity. In like manner, those modern Americans who inherit this land have a similar duty to restore and preserve the blessings of liberty for their posterity. This lecture encourages this generation to step forward and measure up to this duty.

1.

AMERICA'S SPIRITUAL FOUNDATION

RECOMMENDED RESOURCES FOR THE SERIOUS STUDENT:

The Mayflower Compact—appendix
The Pledge of Allegiance—appendix
The Bulletproof George Washington
Commentaries on the Laws of England, Sir William Blackstone
The New England Primer
The Spirit of Laws, Montesquieu
A Basic History of the United States, vol. 1, by Dr. Clarence Carson
George Washington: A Collection, edited by Allen
America's Godly Heritage (video) by David Barton

QUOTES, ARTICLES, AND ORIGINAL SOURCES:

John Jay

TO PRESERVE THE NATION

In a letter dated February 28, 1797, to Jedidiah Morse, first chief justice of the United States Supreme Court, John Jay, wrote,

> It is to be regretted, but so I believe the fact to be, that except the Bible there is not a true history in the world.[3]

This statement reflects the deep religious foundation that sustained the most senior leadership of the United States as the nation was established.

A RELIGIOUS AND A MORAL PEOPLE

Modern revisionists have sought diligently to cast the Founding Fathers as godless and immoral men, bent on fostering a self-aggrandizing agenda for the nation they were creating. It would seem that these revisionists tell the grossest of lies in an effort to excuse and condone the vile behavior of current officials. Perhaps an even more sinister purpose of this effort is found in their dedication to destroy the principles upon which this nation was founded. By undermining the character of the men they denigrate, these revisionists promote the destruction of the principles the founders stood for, subverting the foundation of the nation and accelerating the merging of this nation into the godless, globalist, socialist supranation envisioned by modern elitists.

It would require volumes to fully expose the truth in the matter, but the good news is that there *are literally* volumes of evidence proving the utter falsehood of assertions being made by those who seek to destroy the founders and the nation that they established. A thorough evaluation of the words and writings of the founders of the nation reveals that they recognized the hand of God in every event that led to the successful founding of the United States, and they were quick to not only recognize that influence but also give thanks for it.

Though the founders had knowledge of and studied the perverse philosophy that we call "secularism" today, they rejected it, considered it repulsive, and looked to the God of Abraham, Isaac, and Jacob as their deity. The godless philosophies were unquestionably foreign to the beliefs of the nation and were rejected en masse by leaders and people alike.

The religious and moral roots of this nation were well-known a few generations ago, but in recent generations, that sure knowledge has been subverted by conspiring individuals with dishonorable intentions.

[3.] William Jay, *The Life of John Jay* (New York: J. & J. Harper, 1833), 2:280; Henry P. Johnston and Burt Franklin, eds., *The Correspondence and Public Papers of John Jay* (New York: Harper Brothers, 1890), 4:225; and quoted in Norman Cousins, *In God We Trust* (New York: Harper Brothers, 1958), 362.

AMERICA'S SPIRITUAL FOUNDATION

Mayflower

Few Americans today know that the "first American state document," the Mayflower Compact, began with the words "In the name of God, amen," indicating the sacred covenant the signers were entering into as they disembarked onto the shores of America. They bound themselves together in the name of God as they established their new government. In the Mayflower Compact, the Pilgrims documented the purposes for which they came to America. In part, they wrote,

> In the name of God, Amen. We whose names are underwritten . . . having undertaken, for the glory of God, and advancement of the Christian faith . . . a voyage to plant the first colony in the Northern parts of Virginia, do by these presents solemnly and mutually in the presence of God, and one of another, covenant and combine ourselves together into a civil body politic, for our better ordering and preservation and furtherance of the ends aforesaid.

Signing of Mayflower Compact

TO PRESERVE THE NATION

The twenty thousand Puritans who followed the Pilgrims to America between 1630 and 1640 were motivated almost solely by a desire to be free to worship and serve God according to the dictates of their conscience.

Pilgrims Debark Mayflower

It is interesting to note that the book used by these early settlers of America to teach reading skills was very strongly linked to the Holy Scriptures. The book was called *The New England Primer*. It was published in 1690, and for about a century and a half, it was the primary book used to introduce children to reading. The book draws upon words in the scriptures to not only teach reading skills but also teach great principles of life and character. Wonderful values were also instilled in the learner. In lecture 11 ("Of Education and Freedom"), a more in-depth review of the importance of principled education will occur.

The immortal words of the Declaration of Independence recognize God four times, crediting Him as the originator of mankind's rights, acknowledging Him as the Supreme Judge, and expressing a firm understanding that only by His divine protection would the pledge of the signers' lives, fortunes, and sacred honor be upheld. In the first two paragraphs of the Declaration, "the Laws of Nature and of Nature's God" is mentioned, as is the "Creator."

> When in the Course of human events, it becomes necessary for one people to dissolve the political bands which have connected them with another, and to assume among the Powers of the earth, the separate and equal station to which the Laws of Nature and of Nature's God entitle them, a decent respect to the opinions of mankind requires that they should declare the causes which impel them to the separation. We hold these truths to be self-evident, that all men are created equal, that they are endowed by their Creator with certain unalienable Rights, that among these are Life, Liberty and the pursuit of Happiness. That to secure these rights, Governments are instituted among Men.

And in the final paragraph, the "Supreme Judge" and "Divine Providence" are called upon.

> Appealing to the Supreme Judge of the World . . .

> And for the support of this Declaration, with a firm reliance on the protection of Divine Providence, we mutually pledge to each other our Lives, our Fortunes and our sacred Honor.

Many today who promote the godless philosophies of secularism promote the idea that the references in the Declaration to the "Laws of Nature and of Nature's God," and "Supreme Judge of the World," and "Divine Providence" are figures of speech that do not reference our Divine Creator—the God of Heaven. This position is nonsense! All of the American founders had studied William Blackstone's *Commentaries on the Laws of England*. Within those four volumes, Blackstone uses these terms and clearly defines them. In fact, the words within the Declaration can be directly tied into the phrases and words that Blackstone wrote in the *Commentaries*. This fact is confirmed in the following brief review of Blackstone's references out of volume 1 of his *Commentaries:*

Sir William Blackstone

Speaking "Of the Nature of Laws in General," Blackstone wrote,

> Rule of action, which is prescribed by some superior, and which the inferior is bound to obey . . . Supreme Being formed the universe . . . . Man, considered

> as a creature, must necessarily be subject to the laws of his Creator, for he is entirely a dependent being.[4]

So the God of the universe created mankind, and mankind is not only dependent upon Him, but is subject to His laws.

> As man depends absolutely upon his Maker for everything, it is necessary that he should in all points conform to his Maker's will.[5]

Man is bound to abide in his Maker's will because all mankind are absolutely dependent upon the Maker. Mankind is therefore obligated to obey Him.

> This will of his Maker is called the law of nature. For as God, when He created matter, and endued it with a principle of mobility, established certain rules for the perpetual direction of that motion; so, when He created man, and endued him with free will to conduct himself in all parts of life, He laid down certain immutable laws of human nature, whereby that free will is in some degree regulated and restrained, and gave him also the faculty of reason to discover the purport of those laws.
>
> Considering the Creator only a Being of infinite power, He was able unquestionably to have prescribed whatever laws He pleased to His creature, man, however unjust or severe.[6]

According to Blackstone, the will of the Maker is called "the law of nature." God has all power and could have given whatever laws He chose to give. The laws could have been unjust, severe, or even harsh, but Blackstone went on to say,

> But as he is also a Being of infinite wisdom, He has laid down only such laws as were founded in those relations of justice, that existed in the nature of things antecedent to any positive precept. These are the eternal, immutable laws of good and evil, to which the Creator Himself in all his Dispensations conforms.[7]

---

4. William Blackstone, *Commentaries on the Laws of England*, 4 vols. (England: Claredon Press, 1765-1769). 1:39.
5. Blackstone, *Commentaries*, 1:39.
6. Blackstone, *Commentaries*, 1:39-40.
7. Blackstone, *Commentaries*, 1:40.

Blackstone points out the basis of justice, and good and evil, and proposes that God Himself conforms to these eternal concepts that have existed even before the action that was taken to create earth and mankind.

> And which He has enabled human reason to discover, so far as they are necessary for the conduct of human actions. Such, among others, are these principles; that we should live honestly, should hurt nobody, and should render to everyone his due.[8]

God has enabled mankind to discover some of the baseline principles that are in accordance with His wise plan, including honesty, integrity, etc. Correlation could be made to the most basic laws of God in regard to human interaction, as are found in the Ten Commandments.

> This law of nature, being coeval with mankind and dictated by God Himself, is of course superior in obligation to any other. It is binding over all the globe in all countries, and at all times; no human laws are of any validity, if contrary to this.[9]

This term "law of nature" in regard to the concepts of godly principles recurs often in Blackstone's writings, and it is easy to correlate this phrase into the Declaration and other writing of the founders! These laws, as declared by God, are superior to all other laws—over the entire world! Mankind's laws are to conform to God's laws, or they are not valid.

> And such of them as are valid derive all their force, and all their authority, mediately or immediately, from this original . . . . Upon these two foundations, the law of nature and the law of revelation, depend all human laws; that is to say, no human laws should be suffered to contradict these.[10]

All of mankind's laws must conform to God's revelations, or they are of no valid force or authority. Mankind's laws, if they are to be just, must not contradict God's will. Blackstone reinforces this principle with the following example:

> To instance in the case of murder; this is expressly forbidden by the divine, and demonstrably by the natural law; and from these prohibitions arises the true unlawfulness of this crime.[11]

---

[8]. Blackstone, *Commentaries*, 1:40.
[9]. Blackstone, *Commentaries*, 1:41.
[10]. Blackstone, *Commentaries*, 1:41-2.
[11]. Blackstone, *Commentaries*, 1:42.

The law against murder conforms to God's expressed will, and therefore, mankind's laws against murder are just and proper. Therefore, the foundation of proper law and proper government was established by reviewing and understanding the revealed word of God and then seeking to establish mankind's law based upon the expressed will of God.

As the newly created United States went forward after declaring their independence from England, there were many great challenges! The outcome of the effort was many times called into question by the dire circumstances the nation faced.

In light of all these difficulties, it is well documented that the nation often resorted to calling upon God for assistance and delivery. There are many instances of record wherein the various state legislatures, and even the United States Congress, decreed days of fasting and prayer on behalf of the nation and the cause of liberty.

An example of such an event is found in Thomas Jefferson's writings:

> The Legislature of Virginia happened to be in session . . . The House of Burgesses, thereupon, passed a resolution, recommending to their fellow-citizens, that that day should be set apart for fasting and prayer to the Supreme Being, imploring him to avert the calamities then threatening us, and to give us one heart and one mind to oppose every invasion of our liberties.[12]

The United States Continental Congress also regularly admonished the new nation to exercise fasting and prayer in order to obtain their liberties. The following is a general order issued to the army by General George Washington in obedience to instructions he received from Congress:

> The Continental Congress having ordered Friday to be observed as a day of 'fasting, humiliation and prayer, humbly to supplicate the mercy of Almighty God . . .—the General commands all officers and soldiers to pay strict obedience to the orders of the Continental Congress, and by their unfeigned and pious observance of their religious duties, incline the Lord, and Giver of Victory, to prosper our arms.[13]

In light of this, we should not be surprised to note that in his writings, George Washington recognized God's hand over sixty times in the preservation of the nation as the struggles of the revolution unfolded.

It is interesting to note that after the revolutionary victory was accomplished and as the United States set out on its journey as a free nation, they passed ordinances regarding

---

[12] Bergh, *Thomas Jefferson*, 1:181.
[13] John C. Fitzpatrick, ed., *The Writings of George Washington from the Original Manuscript Sources, 1745-1799*, 39 vols. (Washington: United States Government Printing Office, 1931-44), 5:43.

their governance and how other states could join with the nation and become part of the United States. In 1787, the Congress passed the Northwest Ordinance of 1787, defining the terms under which new states could join the union as equal partners with the original thirteen states. After the new United States Constitution was ratified, Congress passed the ordinance again to make certain that there was no question the ordinance still applied under the new constitution. That ordinance recognized the importance of religion and morality in maintaining a free nation. Article 3 of that ordinance said,

> Religion, morality, and knowledge, being necessary to good government and the happiness of mankind, schools and the means of education shall forever be encouraged.

Many today would be shocked to see religion, morality, good government, and schools linked together in an ordinance passed by the national congress, but that was the original intent of the leaders who founded this nation! Indeed, it would appear they felt religion in school was essential to the survival of the nation. It is also of interest to note that the same Congress that re-passed the Northwest Ordinance, in which religion is fostered as an official policy, passed the First Amendment to the Constitution, in which the national government is prohibited from interfering with the God-given individual right of free exercise of religious expression. Modern courts have perverted this philosophy into a doctrine of a government bias or antagonism against religious expression. In reality, the founders intended to prevent the establishment of a particular religious denomination as the official tax-supported, government-sanctioned religion, such as existed in the case of the Church of England in England. The founders intended to prohibit the establishment of an official national religion, but did not force government to avoid formal recognition of God, nor did they diminish the right of the people to expect the government to recognize and preserve their God-given individual rights.

Lecture 2 will discuss in greater detail the founder's perspective that mankind's rights were obtained from God and that it is the purpose of government to preserve those God-given rights, as noted in the Declaration of Independence.

As the Constitutional Convention of 1787 met in Philadelphia and sought to write a charter for the nation that would preserve the nation and establish a national government, which would be constrained to operate within bounds that would allow God-given rights and individual liberty to flourish, there were many challenging times, and the risk of failure seemed to always hang in the balance as the great debates boiled. In his writings, James Madison notes that he saw and documented God's hand in the vicissitudes and trials experienced during the formulation of the Constitution of the United States during the Constitutional Convention. An example may be noted in Benjamin Franklin's pleadings with the delegates to the convention that they must seek God's will through prayer as they deliberated the momentous decisions they were making, saying,

TO PRESERVE THE NATION

Benjamin Franklin

I have lived, sir, a long time; and the longer I live, the more convincing proofs I see of this truth, that God governs in the affairs of men. And if a sparrow cannot fall to the ground without his notice, is it probable that an empire can rise without his aid? We have been assured, sir, in the sacred writings that 'except the Lord build the house, they labor in vain that build it.' I firmly believe this; and I also believe that, without His concurring aid, we shall succeed in this political building no better than the builders of Babel . . . .

I therefore beg leave to move that, henceforth, prayers imploring the assistance of heaven and its blessings on our deliberations be held in this assembly every morning before we proceed to business.[14]

[14.] Quoted in James Madison, *Journal of the Federal Convention*, 1:59-60.

AMERICA'S SPIRITUAL FOUNDATION

James Madison

James Madison was known as the "Father of the Constitution." He played a major role in the 1787 Constitutional Convention and wrote a number of the Federalist Papers in the effort to gain ratification of the Constitution. As the new constitution was placed in operation, he served in Congress and was instrumental in the creation and passage of the Bill of Rights. Afterward, he served as the United States secretary of state and later as president of the United States. In Federalist Paper no. 37, he wrote of the hand of the Almighty in the victory of the Revolutionary War and in the bringing forth of the new constitution:

> The real wonder is that so many difficulties should have been surmounted, and surmounted with a unanimity almost as unprecedented as it must have been unexpected. It is impossible for any man of candor to reflect on this circumstance without partaking of the astonishment. It is impossible for the man of pious reflection not to perceive in it a finger of that Almighty hand which has been so frequently and signally extended to our relief in the critical stages of the revolution.

As has been noted, George Washington was quick to recognize the divine intervention that the nation enjoyed and to ask for its continuance. In his first inaugural address, Washington said,

TO PRESERVE THE NATION

George Washington Inauguration

In tendering this homage to the great Author of every public and private good . . . No people can be bound to acknowledge and adore the invisible hand, which conducts the affairs of men, more than the people of the United States. Every step, by which they have advanced to the character of an independent nation, seems to have been distinguished by some token of providential agency.[15]

John Adams

---

15. James D. Richardson, comp., *A Compilation of the Messages and Papers of the Presidents* (New York: Bureau of National Literature, 1897), 1:44-5.

And John Adams, the nation's first vice president and second president, captured the concept of the importance of religion to the nation most succinctly when he said,

> Our Constitution was designed only for a moral and religious people. It is wholly inadequate for the government of any other.[16]

The recognition of God's hand in the affairs of the nation continued throughout the early years of the new republic, so we may unequivocally know that this perspective was the original intent of the founders. An example may be cited in the Day of Thanksgiving, which the Congress instructed George Washington to proclaim. The following is the proclamation issued by George Washington in fulfillment of Congress's wishes:

PROCLAMATION.

A NATIONAL THANKSGIVING.

[From Sparks's Washington, Vol. XII, 119.]
Messages and Papers of the Presidents, George Washington, vol. 1, 56

Whereas it is the duty of all nations to acknowledge the providence of Almighty God, to obey His will, to be grateful for His benefits, and humbly to implore His protection and favor; and

Whereas both Houses of Congress have, by their joint committee, requested me "to recommend to the people of the United States a day of public thanksgiving and prayer, to be observed by acknowledging with grateful hearts the many and signal favors of Almighty God, especially by affording them an opportunity peaceably to establish a form of government for their safety and happiness:"

Now, therefore, I do recommend and assign Thursday, the 26th day of November next, to be devoted by the people of these States to the service of that great and glorious Being who is the beneficent author of all the good that was, that is, or that will be; that we may then all unite in rendering unto Him our sincere and humble thanks for His kind care and protection of the people of this country previous to their becoming a nation; for the signal and manifold mercies and the favorable interpositions of His providence in the course and conclusion of the late war; for the great degree of tranquillity, union, and plenty which we have since enjoyed; for the peaceable

---

[16]. Charles Francis Adams, ed., *The Works of John Adams* (Boston: Little, Brown & Co., 1851), 4:31.

and rational manner in which we have been enabled to establish constitutions of government for our safety and happiness, and particularly the national one now lately instituted; for the civil and religious liberty with which we are blessed, and the means we have of acquiring and diffusing useful knowledge; and, in general, for all the great and various favors which He has been pleased to confer upon us.

And also that we may then unite in most humbly offering our prayers and supplications to the great Lord and Ruler of Nations, and beseech Him to pardon our national and other trangressions; to enable us all, whether in public or private stations, to perform our several and relative duties properly and punctually; to render our National Government a blessing to all the people by constantly being a Government of wise, just, and constitutional laws, discreetly and faithfully executed and obeyed; to protect and guide all sovereigns and nations (especially such as have shown kindness to us), and to bless them with good governments, peace, and concord; to promote the knowledge and practice of true religion and virtue, and the increase of science among them and us; and, generally, to grant unto all mankind such a degree of temporal prosperity as He alone knows to be best.

Given under my hand, at the city of New York, the 3d day of October, A. D. 1789.

GO. WASHINGTON.

This devoted recognition of the hand of God and its importance to the nation continued throughout Washington's administration and is restated in his Farewell Address, which he offered as he concluded his second presidential term. After forty-five years of dedicated, selfless, devoted service, George Washington departed public life, offering a loving plea to the nation to "stay the course" established in the beginning. A major portion of his monumental Farewell Address was dedicated to the critical role religion and morality were to play in the preservation of the nation:

> Of all the dispositions and habits, which lead to political prosperity, Religion, and Morality are indispensable supports.—In vain would that man claim the tribute of Patriotism, who should labor to subvert these great pillars of human happiness, these firmest props of the duties of Men and Citizens.—The mere Politician, equally with the pious man, ought to respect and to cherish them.—A volume could not trace all their connexions with private and public felicity.—Let it simply be asked where is the security for property, for reputation, for life, if the sense of religious obligation desert the oaths, which are the instruments of investigation in Courts of Justice? And let us with caution indulge the supposition,

that morality can be maintained without religion.—Whatever may be conceded to the influence of refined education on minds of peculiar structure—reason and experience both forbid us to expect, that national morality can prevail in exclusion of religious principle.—

'Tis substantially true, that virtue or morality is a necessary spring of popular government.—The rule indeed extends with more or less force to every species of Free Government.—Who that is a sincere friend to it can look with indifference upon attempts to shake the foundation of the fabric?

Alexis de Tocqueville

Outside observers of the United States also recognized the religious nature and foundation of the United States. During his visit to the United States, French author, historian, and philosopher Alexis de Tocqueville observed many instances of the religious habit of the nation. He commented extensively upon his observations. Citing a few of his statements will suffice to make the point:

> Americans send out ministers of the Gospel into the new Western States to found schools and churches there, lest religion should be suffered to die away in those

remote settlements, and the rising States be less fitted to enjoy free institutions than the people from which they emanated.[17]

As America pushed back the frontiers and settled new lands, they took with them their national religious perspective. This practice ensured that as additional states joined the union, they would reflect the values, attitudes, and beliefs of their fellow Americans and preserve their God-given liberty with the same zeal as the original states. This was in complete conformance with the requirements of the aforementioned Northwest Ordinance of 1787. It would also help ensure that the new states would also have the same form of government that the rest of the nation had. All of the states were to be built on the same foundation.

Tocqueville continued in explanation of his above-noted statement:

> They will tell you that 'all the American republics are collectively involved with each other; if the republics of the West were to fall into anarchy, or to be mastered by a despot, the republican institutions which now flourish upon the shores of the Atlantic Ocean would be in great peril. It is, therefore, our interest that the new States should be religious, in order to maintain our liberties.'[18]

Tocqueville also noted that in the United States, it was legal to do almost anything, but the innate religiosity of the American populace prevented licentiousness. While the law was not onerous upon the people to keep them in check, most Americans believed that they would ultimately face their God in a final judgment, which would consider their obedience to His will. Consequently, Americans, in general, self-regulated their behavior, and society was peaceful and stable. In noting this American perspective, Tocqueville wrote,

> Thus whilst the law permits the Americans to do what they please, religion prevents them from conceiving, and forbids them to commit, what is rash or unjust . . . .
>
> Religion in America takes no direct part in the government of society, but it must nevertheless be regarded as the foremost of the political institutions of that country; for if it does not impart a taste for freedom, it facilitates the use of free institutions . . . they hold it to be indispensable to the maintenance of republican institutions. This opinion is not peculiar to a class of citizens or to a party, but it belongs to the whole nation, and to every rank of society.[19]

[17.] Alexis de Tocqueville, *Democracy in America*, 12th ed, 2 vols. (New York: Vintage Books, 1945).
[18.] Tocqueville, *Democracy*.
[19.] Tocqueville, *Democracy*.

AMERICA'S SPIRITUAL FOUNDATION

The spiritual roots of America allowed the preservation of liberty.

It is also interesting to note that as he traveled about America visiting and viewing all aspects of American life, Tocqueville also visited American courts. In one of those visits, he witnessed an event that today seems almost impossible to imagine.

> Whilst I was in America, a witness, who happened to be called at the assizes of the county of Chester (State of New York), declared that he did not believe in the existence of God, or in the immortality of the soul. The judge refused to admit his evidence, on the ground that the witness had destroyed beforehand all the confidence of the Court in what he was about to say. The newspapers related the fact without any further comment.[20]

Americans held that a belief in an afterlife judgment was a great inhibitor to prevent injustice. As previously mentioned, Washington said in his Farewell Address, "Let it simply be asked where is the security for property, for reputation, for life, if the sense of religious obligation desert the oaths, which are the instruments of investigation in Courts of Justice?" The people relied upon this concept in obtaining justice, and in the case observed by Tocqueville, they distrusted an individual who felt he would never face God and His judgment if he lied in court, so he was not allowed to testify.

A common position that was widely held in America's early days was that the United States was a sort of a modern Israel—a covenant people before God. There was a belief that the nation had a divine destiny that was tied to that covenant. That perspective was often expressed in political writings and speeches in the early days of the nation. An example may be noted in a July 4, 1798, address given by Yale president Dr. Timothy Dwight. He spoke at length about the duty of Americans and preserving the liberty of the nation.[21] One of his main points was that if America is to remain strong and free, it must honor and sustain the Sabbath Day. As noted in numerous Old Testament scriptures,[22] the Sabbath Day had been a sign of the covenant between God and ancient Israel. In Dwight's view, if America was truly God's modern covenant people, America must abide in the sign of that covenant.

---

20. Tocqueville, *Democracy.*
21. See Ellis Sandoz, ed., *Political Sermons of the American Founding Era, 1730-1805* (Indianapolis: Liberty Fund, 1990), 1365-94.
22. For example, see Ez. 20:12-13, 15-17, 20.

TO PRESERVE THE NATION

Dr. Timothy Dwight

And that concern for the religious spirit of the nation was reflected even in the actions take by the United States Congress. For example, in an action that must seem astounding in light of more recent modern behavior in the U.S. Congress, on Christmas Day 1804, John Hargrove, at the request of Congress, delivered an address before the jointly assembled House and Senate of the United States. His assigned topic was "A Sermon, on the Second Coming of Christ, and on the Last Judgment."[23] Religious principles were truly at the core of the foundation of the United States in its early years!

This nation faces perilous times ahead. Perhaps more that any other time, we face a moral crisis—in our leadership, in the general apathy of the people of the nation, in our nation's widespread acceptance of the godless philosophies of secular humanism, and in the pervasive perversions that are embraced without thought by such a broad spectrum of our population. Under the goading of godless leaders that hold little sacred, and under the influence of a ubiquitous education system that teaches principles devoid of God, we have strayed far from the foundation principles of the nation. It would seem that the nation is forsaking God, and as a consequence, we must ask ourselves, is He forsaking the nation?

[23.] See Sandoz, *Political Sermons*, 1573-96.

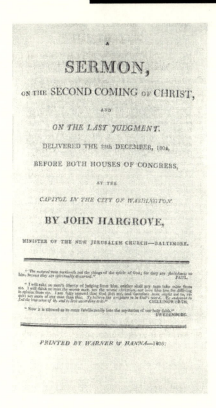

If this nation is to survive the challenges it faces, it must, first and foremost, return to that God who made it free. It must recognize His hand in all things and become obedient to His commandments. We must begin again to hold our national, state, and local leadership to a standard that reflects the godly principles upon which the nation was built.

The scope and magnitude of our nation's current moral turpitude cannot be underestimated, nor can the urgency of our return to God be overstated. During the Constitutional Convention of 1787, George Mason stated, "As nations cannot be rewarded or punished in the next world, they must be in this. By an inevitable chain of causes and effects, Providence punishes national sins by national calamities."[24] We must pray that we, as a nation, have not passed the point of no return, and we now face only the imminent justice of an offended God!

The following are additional interesting quotes regarding this topic and their references:

---

24. Madison, *Journal*, vol. 2, Wednesday August 22, 1787

TO PRESERVE THE NATION

RELIGION AND MORALITY

United States Constitution First Amendment: "Congress shall make no law respecting an establishment of religion, or prohibiting the free exercise thereof."

Thomas Jefferson

Thomas Jefferson, on living a virtuous and moral life, letter to his nephew Peter Carr, written from Paris, France, August 19, 1785:

> Pursue the interests of your country, the interests of your friends, and your own interests also, with the purest integrity, the most chaste honor. The defect of these virtues can never be made up by all the other acquirements of body and mind. Make these, then, your first object. Give up money, give up fame, give up science, give the earth itself and all it contains, rather than do an immoral act. And never suppose, that in any possible situation, or under any circumstances, it is best for you to do a dishonorable thing, however slightly so it may appear to you. Whenever you are to do a thing, though it can never be known but to yourself, ask yourself how you would act were all the world looking at you, and act accordingly. Encourage all your virtuous dispositions.[25]

Thomas Jefferson

> The God who gave us life, gave us liberty at the same time.[26]

[25.] Bergh, *Thomas Jefferson*, 5:82.
[26.] Bergh, *Thomas Jefferson*, 1:211.

Thomas Jefferson, 1782

> And can the liberties of a nation be thought secure when we have removed their only firm basis, a conviction in the minds of the people that these liberties of the gift of God? That they are not to be violated but with His wrath?[27]

George Washington Resigns His Commission at the Close of the Revolutionary War, 1783

> "I consider it as an indispensable duty to close this last act of my official life by commending the interests of our dearest country to the protection of Almighty God, and those who have the superintendence of them to His holy keeping."[28]

Benjamin Franklin, 1787

> "Let me add that only a virtuous people are capable of freedom. As nations become corrupt and vicious, they have more need of masters."[29]

Benjamin Franklin summarizing his view on universal religious truths in a letter to President Stiles of Yale University:

> "I believe in one God, the Creator of the universe. That he governs it by his providence. That he ought to be worshiped. That the most acceptable service we render to him is in doing good to his other children. That the soul of man is immortal, and will be treated with justice in another life respecting its conduct in this."[30]

Thomas Jefferson's letter to the Danbury Baptists, 1802 (In a private response to their letter expressing their concern that a national official religion might be established, Jefferson put their fears to rest, assuring them that it was impossible for a specific denomination to be established as the national "official" church. In the modern era, the phrase from this letter, "wall of separation between church and state," is frequently taken out of context and used as justification for creating an official government position that is adversarial or antagonistic to religious expression. In this letter, Jefferson quotes the phrase from the First Amendment that ensures that the national government is prevented from interfering with religious expression. The wall of separation he spoke of was a barrier to prevent government encroachment upon this great God-given right to worship.)

---

[27]. Bergh, *Thomas Jefferson*, 2:227.
[28]. Cited in William Gordon, *America*, 3:312.
[29]. To the Abbes Chalut and Arnaud, 17 April 1787, in Albert Henry Smyth, ed., *The Writings of Benjamin Franklin*, 10 vols. (New York: Macmillan Co., 1905-7), 9:569.
[30]. To Ezra Stiles, 1790, in Smyth, *Benjamin Franklin*, 10:84.

"Believing . . . that religion is a matter which lies solely between man and his God, that he owes account to none other for his faith or his worship, [and] that the legislative powers of government reach actions only, and not opinions, I contemplate with sovereign reverence that act of the whole American people which declared that their legislature [i.e., Congress] should "make no law respecting an establishment of religion, or prohibiting the free exercise thereof," thus building a wall of separation between church and state. Adhering to this expression of the supreme will of the nation in behalf of the rights of conscience, I shall see with sincere satisfaction the progress of those sentiments which tend to restore to man all his natural rights, convinced he has no natural right in opposition to his social duties."[31]

Alexis de Tocqueville

"The empire of religion is never more surely established than when it reigns in the hearts of men unsupported by aught beside its native strength. Religion is no less the companion of liberty in all its battles and its triumphs; the cradle of its infancy, and the divine source of its claims. The safeguard of morality is religion, and morality is the best security of law and the surest pledge of freedom."[32]

"In the United States the influence of religion is not confined to the manners, but it extends to the intelligence of the people. Amongst the Anglo-Americans, there are some who profess the doctrines of Christianity from a sincere belief in them, and others who do the same because they are afraid to be suspected of unbelief. Christianity, therefore, reigns without any obstacle, by universal consent; the consequence is, as I have before observed, that every principle of the moral world is fixed and determinate . . .

"The Americans combine the notions of Christianity and of liberty so intimately in their minds, that it is impossible to make them conceive the one without the other; . . .

"Despotism may govern without faith, but liberty cannot. Religion is much more necessary in the republic which they set forth in glowing colors than in the monarchy which they attack; . . . How is it possible that society should escape destruction if the moral tie be not strengthened in proportion as the political tie is relaxed? and what can be done with a people which is its own master, if it be not submissive to the Divinity?"[33]

[31.] Bergh, *Thomas Jefferson*, 16:281.
[32.] Tocqueville, *Democracy*, 1:43.
[33.] Tocqueville, *Democracy*, 1:309-313.

2.

INDIVIDUAL LIBERTIES AND THE AMERICAN GOVERNMENT

REPUBLICS VS. DEMOCRACIES

Recommended Resources for the Serious Student:
The Law by Frederick Bastiat
View of the Constitution of the United States by St. George Tucker
American Political Writing During the Founding Era, edited by Hyneman/Lutz
The Declaration of Independence
The United States Constitution
Colonial Origins of the American Constitution, edited by Lutz

QUOTES, ARTICLES, AND ORIGINAL SOURCES

The foundation of *American liberty* is built upon the concept of *individual rights*. This concept is unique in that it is different from the general perspective that is reflected in most governments, which foster the philosophy that rights come from government and that rights are collective in nature.

The Founding Fathers of this nation clearly understood that our *rights come from God* and were not created by and dispensed from government. This nation's founders knew that mankind's rights preexisted before any form of government and that it is the purpose of government to preserve those God-given rights. They sought most vigorously to establish a government that recognized and *preserved these concepts*.

Consequently, they established a government with enough power to sustain those rights within the framework they established and was limited in power to only the powers granted.

As we begin this review, it is important that the student understand that there are *several forms of government* that have become common throughout the history of the world, which may be categorized into a few general types. The following are simple definitions and brief commentary that will help clarify understanding as we proceed with this lecture:

Monarchy: Government by one, generally by birth or succession. The American founders had come to despise this form of government and considered it absurd that an individual or family held ascendancy over their fellow humans. The American founders rejected this form of government.

Oligarchy: Government of a few, generally a small group of "elite" leaders. This form is often closely related to monarchy. These elite leaders promote the idea that somehow they know better than their other more common fellow humans know, and therefore, they should, by right, govern and direct the mass of mankind. In spite of modern examples of American political leaders who seek to govern perpetually, and by their actions have seemingly assumed the mantle of elitists, the American founders rejected this form of government.

Anarchy: No government, mob rule—every man for himself. There are countless examples throughout history of how destructive mobs can become to individual God-given rights! Consequently, the American founders rejected this form of government also. It is interesting to note how closely related anarchy becomes to democracy when it comes to destroying God-given rights when the majority can be swayed to act in a manner that does not recognize the rights of the minority.

Democracy: Government by group; majority rule; mob rule. The people create legislation by majority vote.

Socrates

INDIVIDUAL LIBERTIES AND AMERICAN GOVERNMENT

An example of how democracy works can be found in ancient Greece. Socrates was put on trial for questioning the pantheon of gods that were worshiped throughout the land. He was tried before a three-hundred-man jury: 180 found him guilty, 120 found him innocent. It would seem from this that there was a fairly strong evidence that he was not guilty and, therefore, not eligible to be sentenced to death. But with the "majority rules" conviction, he was sentenced to death. If thirty-one more had found him innocent, he would have been set free. But in democracy, the concept is "majority rules."

Some people describe democracy as "a pack of wolves and a lone sheep deciding what was going to be for dinner."

Most Americans, and most people in the world today, think that the American founders created the United States as a democracy. Nothing could be farther from the truth, as we shall shortly discover. Majority rule can quickly become mob rule and anarchy. The rights of the minority are always at risk in such an environment. Such a government can quickly become a "tyranny of the masses," and the American founders sought to prevent such a disaster.

Republic: Elected representatives create legislation *within the scope and limits of government power that had been previously defined within the constitution*. It is government by law. The legislature, indeed, the entire government, is constrained to act within constitutionally delegate authority and may not encroach into areas that are not authorized. Elected officials are allowed to operate only within their defined boundaries and are not allowed to act on matters outside those boundaries. These limits are designed to protect the rights of all citizens, whether in the majority or in the minority. This is the type of government that was created for the *United States by the United States Constitution*.

The necessity of limits on government, if it was to be prevented from becoming a tyranny, was clearly understood by the Founding Fathers of the United States. Their views were clearly and eloquently stated and shall be reviewed at length during this lecture series. Others throughout the world have recognized the wisdom of the American founders in the matter of limits upon the power of governments and have spoken of their admiration as they have sought to prevent tyranny from engulfing their nations. In the mid-nineteenth century, the tyranny of socialist-communism was sweeping Europe. In 1850, a Frenchman named Frederic Bastiat wrote a magnificent little book titled *The Law*. In it, he applied the principles espoused by the American founders in an effort to contain government within bounds, which would allow God-given rights to survive and thrive. He spoke of the necessity of preventing government from destroying basic rights and becoming an instrument of plunder for the benefit of others who were fortunate enough to have the power of government in their hands.

Bastiat's book, *The Law,* is highly recommended reading! The following are excerpts from Bastiat's book that are mentioned in the lecture. They capture the essence of why governments are created and why they must be limited to prevent destruction of rights.

> Life, liberty, and property do not exist because men have made laws. On the contrary, it was the fact that life, liberty, and property existed beforehand that caused men to make laws in the first place.[34]

Frederic Bastiat

Bastiat agreed with the American founders that government and law were properly created to protect life, liberty, and property. Bastiat continues,

> What, then, is law? It is the collective organization of the individual right to lawful defense.

> Each of us has a natural right—from God—to defend his person, his liberty, and his property. These are the three basic requirements of life, and the preservation of any one of them is completely dependent upon the preservation of the other two. For what are our faculties but the extension of our individuality? And what is property but an extension of our faculties?[35]

[34.] Fredric Bastiat, *The Law* (Irvington-on-Hudson, New York: Foundation for Economic Education, 1974, 1998), 2.
[35.] Bastiat, *Law,* 2.

These rights are God-given. Each of these rights is essential to the preservation and enjoyment of the other rights. Remove or destroy one of these rights and the others fall also. The necessity of private property to liberty is often not understood in modern societies that have become steeped in the socialistic traditions espoused by educators, political leaders, and mass media, but application of a little common sense and logic will bring the honest truth seeker to the understanding that if one lacks the means *and* control of production and distribution (property, tools, transportation, etc.) to support and sustain one's self and one's family, that person is not truly free. In such a condition, they may exist only by compliance to the will of the holder of those means and to the sufferance of that holder to allow the use of those means. Alexander Hamilton captured the essence of the matter succinctly, writing,

Alexander Hamilton

In the general course of human nature, a power over a man's subsistence amounts to a power over his will.[36]

In the main it will be found that a power over the man's support is a power over his will.[37]

[36.] Alexander Hamilton, Federalist no. 79.

[37.] Hamilton, Federalist no. 73.

A lack of private ownership results in a form of serfdom reminiscent of the squalid conditions under which most people lived during the so-called Dark Ages, or Middle Ages. In spite of efforts to draw fine distinctions between that form of tyranny and modern government ownership or control of the mean of production or distribution found in the current variations of socialistic systems, an honest evaluation will reveal that the modern socialistic philosophies differ little from the ancient system of feudal ownership or control that ensured slaves for an aristocracy.

Bastiat went on to explain the purpose of government as the extension of the individual right to protect God-given rights; thus,

> If every person has the right to defend even by force—his person, his liberty, and his property, then it follows that a group of men have the right to organize and support a common force to protect these rights constantly. Thus the principle of collective right—its reason for existing, its lawfulness—is based on individual right.[38]

Therein is found the reason individuals and groups of individuals in society agreed to create governments—to preserve those essential liberties. If all mankind accepted their God-given rights with gratitude and sought to uphold and preserve those same rights for all of their fellow man, all would be well and just. However, Bastiat went on to point out a fatal tendency that seems to plague a great portion of mankind:

> Self-preservation and self-development are common aspirations among all people. And if everyone enjoyed the unrestricted use of his faculties and the free disposition of the fruits of his labor, social progress would be ceaseless, uninterrupted, and unfailing.
>
> But there is also another tendency that is common among people. When they can, they wish to live and prosper at the expense of others.[39]

Unfortunately, many wish to live and prosper at the expense of others. They wish to plunder the fruits of the labors of others and use this unearned wealth and prosperity for their own benefit. Bastiat then pointed out how some seek to manipulate the government and the laws created under their government for their own benefit so they may plunder without risk to themselves (because they use their government agents and the power of the law to confiscate and deliver the desired goods to themselves) while still reaping the

---

[38]. Bastiat, *Law*, 2.
[39]. Bastiat, *Law*, 5.

INDIVIDUAL LIBERTIES AND AMERICAN GOVERNMENT

benefit. This causes conflict regarding efforts by different groups to seize and then retain government power. He puts people into two categories:

1. The kind who wish to participate in the legal plunder

2. The kind who wish to prevent legal plunder (and wish to return to individual rights and true liberty)

> When plunder is organized by law for the profit of those who make the law, all the plundered classes try somehow to enter—by peaceful or revolutionary means—into the making of laws. According to their degree of enlightenment, these plundered classes may propose one of two entirely different purposes when they attempt to attain political power: Either they may wish to stop lawful plunder, or they may wish to share in it.[40]

Law is force, legalized. Bastiat then explains the great danger that faces society when the instrument of law is changed into an instrument of plunder:

> It is impossible to introduce into society a greater change and a greater evil than this: the conversion of the law into an instrument of plunder.
>
> What are the consequences of such a perversion? It would require volumes to describe them all. Thus we must content ourselves with pointing out the most striking.
>
> In the first place, it erases from everyone's conscience the distinction between justice and injustice.[41]

When the law becomes perverted and becomes an instrument of plunder, people in general lose the ability to see where justice has been dethroned, and they then seek to obtain all that they can obtain through the unjust use of government power to plunder from others. They become partakers of the system of spoils.

Bastiat then gives a simple definition by which citizens may know if the proper purposes of their government have become polluted:

> But how is this legal plunder to be identified? Quite simply. See if the law takes from some persons what belongs to them, and gives it to other persons to whom

---

[40]. Bastiat, *Law*, 7.
[41]. Bastiat, *Law*, 8.

it does not belong. See if the law benefits one citizen at the expense of another by doing what the citizen himself cannot do without committing a crime.

Then abolish this law without delay, for it is not only an evil itself, but also it is a fertile source for further evils because it invites reprisals. If such a law—which may be an isolated case—is not abolished immediately, it will spread, multiply, and develop into a system.[42]

An honest evaluation of what has happened in most modern governments, including, unfortunately, the United States, will reveal how widespread this systematized legalized plunder has become. Different groups gain power or status, which help politicians gain and hold the power they desire, and they, in turn, create laws that assist their power base to plunder some benefit from the general population. It seems that almost everyone, at one time or another, is "on the take" and party to the plunder. Tragically, law and justice are dethroned and replaced with a mob of self-serving benefit seekers who are eager to participate in a feeding frenzy of legalized plunder.

In summary: Mankind has a right to protect the inherent "God-given" rights and, therefore, a right to create government to ensure those rights. The problem arises with governments when they assume powers beyond those proper purposes for which the government was established and they become instruments of plunder—legalizing plunder in the name of government—which is the most powerful mortal force on earth.

Another little book that is highly recommended is Henry Grady Weaver's *The Mainspring of Human Progress*. The premise of this book is that the mainspring of human progress is *individual rights*. The right to choose leads people to do good things, and therefore, society in general progresses. In his book, Weaver quotes Isabell Paterson's book, *The God of the Machine* (34-35), noting,

> Most of the major ills of the world have been caused by well-meaning people who ignored the principle of individual freedom, except as applied to themselves, and who were obsessed with fanatical zeal to improve the lot of mankind-in-the-mass through some pet formula of their own . . . . it is highly presumptuous of any mortal man to assume that he is endowed with such fantastic ability that he can run the affairs of all his fellow men better than they, as individuals, can run their own personal affairs . . . THE HARM DONE BY ORDINARY CRIMINALS, MURDERS, GANGSTERS, AND THIEVES IS NEGLIGIBLE IN COMPARISON WITH THE AGONY INFLICTED UPON HUMAN BEINGS BY THE PROFESSIONAL "DO-

---

[42]. Bastiat, *Law*, 17.

GOODERS", who attempt to set themselves up as gods on earth and who would ruthlessly force their views on all others—with the abiding assurance that the end justifies the means.

Of course, in a most succinct manner, the United States Declaration of Independence clearly and unequivocally states the position of the Founding Fathers of the United States in regard to these principles. By these words, we may know the original intent of the American founders. The Declaration states,

> We hold these truths to be self-evident, that all men are created equal, that they are endowed by their Creator with certain unalienable Rights, that among these are Life, Liberty and the pursuit of Happiness.—That to secure these rights, Governments are instituted among Men, deriving their just powers from the consent of the governed,—That whenever any Form of Government becomes destructive of these ends, it is the Right of the People to alter or to abolish it, and to institute new Government, laying its foundation on such principles and organizing its powers in such form, as to them shall seem most likely to effect their Safety and Happiness.

Mankind's rights come from God. Government is created to protect those God-given rights. When government fails to protect and uphold those rights, it is the right of the people to alter or abolish the government. The position is clear, concise, and unequivocal. That is a fundamental foundational principle upon which the United States came into being and the purpose for which it continues to exist.

In spite of the aforementioned evidence to the contrary, politicians, educators, and the mass media promote the concept that the United States was created as a democracy and that the redistribution of wealth is an acceptable action under the American form of government. That misconception renders advisable the following review to reinforce the truth that the United States Constitution created a constitutional republic, wherein powers are few and defined to allow the fulfillment of responsibilities specific to the national government—and no more. Lecture 3 will review additional details in regard to the baseline fundamental principles of American federalism.

THE DEMOCRACY DECEPTION

About sixty years after the 1787 Constitutional Convention in Philadelphia, Karl Marx sought to foster democracy to promote the philosophies he wrote of in *The Communist Manifesto*:

> We have seen above that the first step in the revolution by the working class is to raise the proletariat to the position of ruling class, to win the battle of democracy.

TO PRESERVE THE NATION

Karl Marx

Shortly after Marx's scurrilous political pamphlet was published, Frederic Bastiat wrote his marvelous treatise, *The Law*, as a counterpoint to the doctrines proposed by Marx. In *The Law*, Bastiat wrote of the dangers of majority rule and the ability to use that concept to legalize plunder. Some years later, United States president Woodrow Wilson and his "alter ego" Edward Mandell House (founder of the Council on Foreign Relations [CFR]) popularized the concept of democracy as the American political form of government and its value for the entire world (as justification for involving the United States in World War I, Wilson and House coined the term: "We must make the world safe for democracy"). Since that time, there has been an unremitting effort on the part of the socialist-globalist cabal to universalize the false philosophy that the United States of America was established originally as a democracy and that that form of government continues to be the ideal of this nation, as well as the goal of all nations that would be free.

Edward Mandell House and Woodrow Wilson

INDIVIDUAL LIBERTIES AND AMERICAN GOVERNMENT

TYRANT'S VIEWS ON DEMOCRACY

As previously noted, in *The Communist Manifesto* Karl Marx wrote of the necessity of implementing democracy to achieve his proposed despotism. Democracy was seen by Marx as progress toward full-blown communism.

Lenin

Perhaps it is more than coincidence that about the time the aforementioned Wilson/House combination canonized their catchphrase fostering democracy, Lenin, the communist revolutionary who enslaved Russia, recognized democracy as a tool for his purposes, writing,

> Democracy is also a form of state which must disappear when the state disappears, but this will only take place in the process of transition from completely victorious and consolidated socialism to complete communism . . . . It would be a fundamental mistake to suppose that the struggle for democracy can divert the proletariat from the socialist revolution . . . . On the contrary, just as socialism cannot be victorious unless it introduces complete democracy, so the proletariat will be unable to prepare for victory over the bourgeoisie unless it wages a many-sided, consistent and revolutionary struggle for democracy.[43]

[43.] V. I. Lenin, "The Socialist Revolution and the Right of Nations to Self Determination" (theses, editorial board of Social-Democrat, Central Organ of the R.S.D.L.P., Published in German in April 1916 in *Vorbote*, no. 2; published in Russian in October 1916 in *Sbornik Sotsial-Demokrata*, no. 1. Printed according to the Sbornik text. Written in January–February 1916.

TO PRESERVE THE NATION

In 1938 and 1939, the future communist dictator of mainland China, Mao Tse-tung, following the lead of Karl Marx and Lenin, explained,

Chairman Mao Tse-tung

Education in democracy must be carried on within the Party so that members can understand the meaning of democratic life, the meaning of the relationship between democracy and centralism, and the way in which democratic centralism should be put into practice. Only in this way can we really extend democracy within the Party and at the same time avoid ultra-democracy and the laissez-faire that destroys discipline.[44]

Taken as a whole, the Chinese revolutionary movement led by the Communist Party embraces the two stages, i.e., the democratic and the socialist revolutions, which are two essentially different revolutionary processes, and the second process can be carried through only after the first has been completed. The democratic revolution is the necessary preparation for the socialist revolution, and the socialist revolution is the inevitable sequel to the democratic revolution. The ultimate aim for which all communists strive is to bring about a socialist and communist society.[45]

From the perspective of those who seek to subjugate humanity under their bloody yoke, implementing democracy is a necessary preliminary step.

[44.] Mao Tse-tung, "The Role of the Chinese Communist Party in the National War" (October 1938), from *Selected Works*, 2:205.

[45.] Mao Tse-tung, "The Chinese Revolution and the Chinese Communist Party" (December 1939), from *Selected Works*, 2:330-31.

INDIVIDUAL LIBERTIES AND AMERICAN GOVERNMENT

HISTORICAL WARNINGS AGAINST DEMOCRACY

Wise philosophers and statesmen from earlier history have recognized the dangers inherent in democracy and have warned society. American Founding Father John Adams understood well the shortcomings of democracy:

> Remember, democracy never lasts long. It soon wastes, exhausts, and murders itself. There never was a democracy yet that did not commit suicide.[46]

John Adams

During the founding era of America, historian Alexander Tytler is said to have explained at least part of the reason why a democracy tends to destroy itself:

> A democracy cannot exist as a permanent form of government. It can only exist until [a majority of] the voters discover they can vote themselves largesse [gifts] from the public treasury. From that moment on the majority always votes for the candidate promising the most benefits from the public treasury, with the result that a democracy always collapses over loose fiscal policy [taxing and spending], always followed by a dictatorship. The average life of the world's greatest civilizations has been two hundred years.[47]

---

[46]. To John Taylor, 15 April 1814, in C. F. Adams, *John Adams*, 6:484.

[47]. Quoted in Laurel Hicks et al., *American Government and Economics* (Pensacola, Fla.: Becka Book Publication, 1984), 37. Although this oft-quoted historically accurate statement has been attributed to Tytler for many years by prominent statesmen and leaders, it cannot be unequivocally verified as a Tytler statement by tracing it to an unimpeachable original source. Many secondary sources reference the statement to Tytler.

Alexander Hamilton also raised his voice in warning against democracy:

> It has been observed, by an honorable gentleman, that a pure democracy, if it were practicable, would be the most perfect government. Experience has proved that no position in politics is more false than this. The ancient democracies, in which the people themselves deliberated, never possessed one feature of good government. Their very character was tyranny; their figure, deformity.[48]

G. K. Chesterton

And nearly one hundred years ago, the great English philosopher and statesman G. K. Chesterton recognized the violent revolutionary tendencies of democratic movements, observing,

> You can never have a revolution in order to establish a democracy. You must have a democracy in order to have a revolution.[49]

MODERN "ADOPTION" OF DEMOCRACY

Today the term "democracy" is used almost exclusively as a form of government—the form of government that its promoters would say governs the United States. While this

---

[48.] Jonathan Elliot, *Debates in the Several State Conventions on the Adoption of the Federal Constitution*, 5 vols. (Philadelphia, J.B. Lippincott Co., 1901), 2:253.

[49.] G. K. Chesterton, *Tremendous Trifles* (1909), chapter 12, p. 63.

is a totally false concept, it has been made almost universally accepted as true. Presidents, governors, senators, congressmen, media moguls, teachers, etc. embrace and promote democracy as America's form of government. Indeed, based upon the ubiquitous and universal nature of the effort, it would seem appropriate to term the movement to redefine the nation as a democracy an organized "campaign." Because of this, it is critically important to remind ourselves that the United States is a republic. It was created as a republic by well-thought, purposeful action. It was specifically *not* created as a democracy. In fact, before the Seventeenth Amendment, the only *national* representatives who were elected democratically were the members of the House of Representatives. The United States Constitution also specifically states that the respective states of the nation are required to be republics.[50]

THE NATION'S FOUNDERS CREATED THE UNITED STATES AS A REPUBLIC

The republic created by the United States Constitution established the limits and bounds of the power of government and protected the God-given rights of both the majority and the minority. The majority does not have the power through majority vote to destroy the God-given rights of the minority—the supreme law of the land prevents it. The supreme law of the land, the United States Constitution, controls the evil tendency of democracy.

At the close of the Constitutional Convention on September 17, 1787, as Benjamin Franklin left the hall in Philadelphia, he was asked, "What kind of government have you given us, Dr. Franklin?" He replied, "A republic, if you can keep it."[51]

The first American dictionary, which was published in 1828 by Noah Webster (who is considered to be one of the Founding Fathers), gave the following definitions:

> **Republic**: A state in which the exercise of the sovereign power is lodged in representatives elected by the people. In modern usage, it differs from a democracy or democratic state, in which the people exercise the powers of sovereignty in person.[52]

> **Democracy**: Government by the people; a form of government, in which the supreme power is lodged in the hands of the people collectively, or in which the people exercise the powers of legislation. Such was the government of Athens.[53]

---

[50]. See U. S. Constitution, article 4, section 4.
[51]. Papers of Dr. James McHenry on the Federal Convention of 1787, in Charles C. Tansill, comp., *Documents Illustrative of the Formation of the Union of the American States* (Washington: U.S. Printing Office, 1927), 952.
[52]. Noah Webster, *An American Dictionary of the English Language* (1828).
[53]. Webster, *American Dictionary*.

So in a republic, the elected representatives create legislation within the framework established by the nation's charter; and in a democracy, the people create the legislation directly by majority vote. The founders saw many dangers inherent in a democracy, and they rejected it as a dangerous form of government, prone to a kind of "mob rule" mentality. They established a republic and, as shall be seen, placed limits upon the power of the legislature by which they could create laws, thus seeking to prevent tyranny.

The founders of this nation understood well the different forms of government and consciously created a republic, rather than a democracy. They understood that democracy was based upon "majority rules," and recognized that every democracy bears within its structure the basis for its ultimate destruction. A nation that ebbs and flows based upon the emotions, which can be brought to bear upon the "masses," will sooner or later destroy itself because principles will be compromised to meet the whims of the majority. In a democracy, unpopular or weak segments of society will eventually lose to the demands of the majority. For example, a democracy could decide to take the wealth or possessions from some and redistribute those properties to others based upon a majority vote.

On the other hand, the basis of a republic is law—law that applies to all, is limited to a specific scope, and protects all equally. The republic established by those who founded this nation is based upon the principle of *limited government*, government that has defined powers. All individuals and agencies within the government are to operate within the bounds established in the nation's charter—the United States Constitution.

And because it was recognized that unless the individual states within the United States were similarly organized under the principles of limited republican government, there would be seeds of destruction sown within the nation that would ultimately destroy the entire nation. Therefore, it is noteworthy that the Constitution specifies that every state in the United States was to have a republican form of government: "The United States shall guarantee to every State in this Union a Republican Form of Government."[54]

Interestingly, the fundamental differences between republics and democracies, and the superiority of a republican form of government for maintaining freedom, were generally well understood by the nation until relatively recently in the United States. The 1928 *U.S. Army Training Manual* (which was used by all of the men in uniform), gave this very accurate definition of democracy:

> A government of the masses. Authority derived through mass meeting or any form of "direct" expression. Results in mobocracy. Attitude toward property

---

[54.] U.S. Constitution, Article 4, Section 4

is communistic—negating property rights. Attitude toward law is that the will of the majority shall regulate, whether it be based upon deliberation or governed by passion, prejudice, and impulse, without restraint or regard to consequences. Results in demagogism, license, agitation, discontent, anarchy.

Tragically, throughout the twentieth century and continuing with even greater intensity during the twenty-first century, the movement to "institutionalize" the concept that democracy is the American and best form of government has gained even more acceptance. Even the military training establishment has contributed to the demise of correct understanding. In contrast to the 1928 *U.S. Army Training Manual*, noted above, by 1952 the army field manual had been rewritten and published as *The Soldiers' Guide*. The following is the "new" definition of democracy as promoted in *The Soldiers' Guide*:

> Meaning of democracy. Because the United States is a democracy, the majority of the people decide how our government will be organized and run—and that includes the Army, Navy, and Air Force. The people do this by electing representatives, and these men and women then carry out the wishes of the people.

Those who are familiar with the writings of Lenin and Mao Tse-tung will be shocked to recognize that this description of the national government and the manner in which the military is structured more closely parallels the drivel published by those communist leaders than the words of the American founders.

There continue to be vestiges of more correct understanding about the republic that was established, though those hints of truth are becoming more scarce because of the concerted effort to redefine the United States as a democracy and to obfuscate the true meaning, form, and structure of the republic that was originally created as the United States. Those who foster the agenda to redefine our government have also been largely successful at creating in the minds of the public the perception that a republic is "bad" because republics are only presented as part of the phrase "Peoples Republic of _____" (fill in the blank with the latest Marxist-based tyranny). Fortunately, for those who retain the willingness to think independently, when the Pledge of Allegiance to the United States flag was created by American patriots during the early part of the twentieth century, it correctly recognized the form of government under which this nation is established:

> I pledge allegiance to the flag of the United States of America, and to the **Republic**, for which it stands.

And thankfully, "The Battle Hymn of the Republic" has not yet been perverted into "The Battle Hymn of the Democracy"!

TO PRESERVE THE NATION

LIMITS ON GOVERNMENT POWER INHERENT IN THE FOUNDERS' CONSTITUTION

THE
FEDERALIST:
A COLLECTION
OF
ESSAYS,
WRITTEN IN FAVOUR OF THE
NEW CONSTITUTION,
AS AGREED UPON BY THE FEDERAL CONVENTION,
SEPTEMBER 17, 1787.

IN TWO VOLUMES.

VOL. I.

NEW-YORK:
PRINTED AND SOLD BY J. AND A. M'LEAN,
No. 41, HANOVER-SQUARE.
M,DCC,LXXXVIII.

Alexander Hamilton

John Jay

James Madison

The Federalist Papers were written and published in 1788 by Alexander Hamilton, James Madison, and John Jay for the purpose of debunking opposition to the new constitution. They accomplished this by thoroughly examining and explaining the new constitution and clarifying and identifying its intent and purpose as conceived by those who participated in the convention. This approach was taken to aid in its ratification. The scope and limits within which the United States national government was to operate under the United States Constitution was carefully explained by the authors of the Federalist Papers. Therein James Madison explains,

> The powers delegated by the proposed Constitution to the federal government are few and defined. Those which are to remain in the State governments are numerous and indefinite. The former will be exercised principally on external objects, as war, peace, negotiation, and foreign commerce; with which last the power of taxation will, for the most part, be connected. The powers reserved to the several States will extend to all the objects which, in the ordinary course of

INDIVIDUAL LIBERTIES AND AMERICAN GOVERNMENT

affairs, concern the lives, liberties, and properties of the people, and the internal order, improvement, and prosperity of the State.[55]

The Ninth and Tenth Amendments to the United States Constitution further emphasized the intent that the powers of the national government be limited to those specifically noted in the Constitution:

> The enumeration, in the Constitution, of certain rights, shall not be construed to deny or disparage others retained by the people.

> The powers not delegated to the United States by the Constitution, nor prohibited by it to the states, are reserved to the states, respectively, or to the people.

Defining the scope and magnitude of government power was key to maintaining individual God-given rights and allowing the people to remain a free and independent people. In the United States republic, the majority, regardless of their numbers and passion for democracy, are prevented from usurping the power of government and running roughshod over God-given liberty. All, including the nation's leaders, are bound to the limits of government. The following statements help us better understand the original intent of the nation's founders and how passionately they held the position that tyranny could only be avoided by clearly defining the limits of government and the areas in which it could operate:

> But what is government itself but the greatest of all reflections on human nature? If men were angels, no government would be necessary. If angels were to govern men, neither external nor internal controls on government would be necessary. In framing a government which is to be administered by men over men, the great difficulty lies in this: you must first enable the government to control the governed; and in the next place oblige it to control itself. A dependence on the people is, no doubt, the primary control on the government; but experience has taught mankind the necessity of auxiliary precautions.[56]

> If Congress can employ money indefinitely to the general welfare, and are the sole and supreme judges of the general welfare, they may take the care of religion into

---

[55]. Federalist no. 45
[56]. Federalist no. 51

their own hands; they may appoint teachers in every state, county, and parish, and pay them out of their public treasury; they may take into their own hands the education of children establishing in like manner schools throughout the Union; they may assume the provision for the poor; they may undertake the regulation of all roads other than post-roads; in short, every thing, from the highest object of state legislation down to the most minute object of police, would be thrown under the power of Congress; for every object I have mentioned would admit of the application of money, and might be called, if Congress pleased, provisions for the general welfare.

The language held in various discussions of this house is a proof that the doctrine in question was never entertained by this body. Arguments, wherever the subject would permit, have constantly been drawn from the peculiar nature of this government, as limited to certain enumerated powers, instead of extending, like other governments, to all cases not particularly excepted . . . .

In short, sir, without going farther into the subject, which I should not have here touched at all but for the reasons already mentioned, I venture to declare it as my opinion, that, were the power of Congress to be established in the latitude contended for, it would subvert the very foundations, and transmute the very nature of the limited government established by the people of America; and what inferences might be drawn, or what consequences ensue, from such a step, it is incumbent on us all to consider.[57]

When an instrument admits two constructions, the one safe, the other dangerous, the one precise, the other indefinite, I prefer that which is safe and precise. I had rather ask an enlargement of power from the nation, where it is found necessary, than to assume it by a construction which would make our powers boundless. Our peculiar security is in the possession of a written Constitution. Let us not make it a blank paper by construction.

I say the same as to the opinion of those who consider the grant of the treaty-making power as boundless. If it is, then we have no Constitution. If it has bounds, they can be no others than the definitions of the powers which that instrument gives. It specifies and delineates the operations permitted to the federal government, and gives all the powers necessary to carry these into

---

[57] Quoted in Elliot, *Debates*, 4:428-9. James Madison, speech on the U.S. House floor regarding the limits on the powers granted to the national government by the United States Constitution, the importance of Congress operating within those bounds, and the dangers of using the so-called "welfare clause" as an excuse to violate those limits, 7 February 1792.

INDIVIDUAL LIBERTIES AND AMERICAN GOVERNMENT

execution. Whatever of these enumerated objects is proper for a law, Congress may make the law; whatever is proper to be executed by way of a treaty, the President and Senate may enter into the treaty; whatever is to be done by a judicial sentence, the judges may pass the sentence.[58]

When all government, domestic and foreign, in little as in great things, shall be drawn to Washington as the center of all power, it will render powerless the checks provided of one government on another, and will become as venal and oppressive as the government from which we separated.[59]

If, then, the right to raise and appropriate the public money is not restricted to the expenditures under the other specific grants according to a strict construction of their powers, respectively, is there no limitation to it? Have Congress a right to raise and appropriate the money to any and to every purpose according to their will and pleasure? They certainly have not. The Government of the United States is a limited Government, instituted for great national purposes, and for those only. Other interests are committed to the States, whose duty it is to provide for them. Each government should look to the great and essential purposes for which it was instituted and confine itself to those purposes.[60]

In short, the people, through their delegates to the Constitutional Convention of 1787, granted to the national government *only* certain, specified powers and retained *all* other powers. The power to encroach upon individual God-given rights and property was never intended to be left in doubt or to be usurped by majority rule or eroded by those selected to fulfill positions within the government. The limits of the national government were known and defined to those specifically enumerated in the United States Constitution. This concept of defined power and "foundation principles" by which all (including those who held government office) would be bound was to be protected by the concept of a republican government, wherein the exercise of government would be contained within the bounds established by the national charter, the United States Constitution.

DEMOCRACY REJECTED FROM THE BEGINNING OF THE CONVENTION

As the Convention of 1787 gathered together, the perspective and intention of a limited, non-democratic government was held from the very beginning of their discussions

---

[58]. Bergh, *Thomas Jefferson*, 10:418-19.
[59]. Bergh, *Thomas Jefferson*, 15:331.
[60]. James Monroe, in Richardson, *Messages and Papers*, 1:736.

on the form of government that they had been tasked to organize. On May 31, 1787, at the beginning of the constitutional convention, Edmund Randolph told his fellow delegates that the purpose of the convention was "to provide a cure for the evils under which the United States labored; that in tracing these evils to their origin, every man had found it in the turbulence and follies of democracy."[61]

FEDERALIST PAPERS IDENTIFY FLAWS OF DEMOCRACY AND HOPE OF REPUBLIC

In his defense of the outcome of the Convention of 1787, James Madison, the "Father of the Constitution," eloquently expressed the fundamental concerns about democracy and the protections of a republic:

> Either the existence of the same passion or interest in a majority at the same time must be prevented, or the majority, having such coexistent passion or interest, must be rendered, by their number and local situation, unable to concert and carry into effect schemes of oppression. If the impulse and the opportunity be suffered to coincide, we well know that neither moral nor religious motives can be relied on as an adequate control. They are not found to be such on the injustice and violence of individuals, and lose their efficacy in proportion to the number combined together, that is, in proportion as their efficacy becomes needful.
>
> From this view of the subject *it may be concluded that a pure democracy, by which I mean a society consisting of a small number of citizens, who assemble and administer the government in person, can admit of no cure for the mischiefs of faction. A common passion or interest will, in almost every case, be felt by a majority of the whole; a communication and concert results from the form of government itself; and there is nothing to check the inducements to sacrifice the weaker party or an obnoxious individual.* **Hence it is that such democracies have ever been spectacles of turbulence and contention; have ever been found incompatible with personal security or the rights of property; and have in general been as short in their lives as they have been violent in their deaths**. Theoretic politicians, who have patronized this species of government, have erroneously supposed that by reducing mankind to a perfect equality in their political rights, they would at the same time be perfectly equalized and assimilated in their possessions, their opinions, and their passions.

[61.] James Madison, *Journal of the Federal Convention*, 1:81.

INDIVIDUAL LIBERTIES AND AMERICAN GOVERNMENT

A republic, by which I mean a government in which the scheme of representation takes place, opens a different prospect and promises the cure for which we are seeking. Let us examine the points in which it varies from pure democracy, and we shall comprehend both the nature of the cure and the efficacy which it must derive from the Union.

The two great points of difference between a democracy and a republic are: first, the delegation of the government, in the latter, to a small number of citizens elected by the rest; secondly, the greater number of citizens and greater sphere of country over which the latter may be extended.

The effect of the first difference is, on the one hand, to refine and enlarge the public views by passing them through the medium of a chosen body of citizens, whose wisdom may best discern the true interest of their country and whose patriotism and love of justice will be least likely to sacrifice it to temporary or partial considerations. Under such a regulation it may well happen that the public voice, pronounced by the representatives of the people, will be more consonant to the public good than if pronounced by the people themselves, convened for the purpose. On the other hand, the effect may be inverted. Men of factious tempers, of local prejudices, or of sinister designs, may, by intrigue, by corruption, or by other means, first obtain the suffrages, and then betray the interests of the people. The question resulting is, whether small or extensive republics are most favorable to the election of proper guardians of the public weal; and it is clearly decided in favor of the latter by two obvious considerations.[62]

FEDERALIST PAPERS FREQUENTLY REINFORCE THE COMMITMENT TO REPUBLICAN GOVERNMENT

Sprinkled throughout the Federalist Papers, almost like the leaven spoken of in the scriptures and which works such marvelous effect upon the bread, are numerous and constant reminders that the nation's founders consciously chose to establish the United States of America as a republic. They enumerated their reasons and expressed their concerns about the other forms of government, specifically and eloquently eschewing democracy because of its known defects and dangers. Of the numerous possible notations that could be made regarding statements within the Federalist Papers to the fact that the Constitution of the United States created a republican form of government for the nation, the following is a synopsis of a few brief contextual references that support and reinforce the fact that the United States was purposefully established as a republic.

---

[62]. Federalist no. 10; emphasis added

TO PRESERVE THE NATION

In Federalist no. 1, Alexander Hamilton proposes a series of papers designed to defend the proposed new constitution of the United States. Among his commitments is a promise to expose the new constitution as a republican form of government:

> I propose, in a series of papers, to discuss the following interesting particulars:—The utility of the UNION to your political prosperity—The insufficiency of the present Confederation to preserve that Union—The necessity of a government at least equally energetic with the one proposed, to the attainment of this object—The conformity of the proposed Constitution to the true principles of republican government—Its analogy to your own State constitution—and lastly, The additional security which its adoption will afford the preservation of that species of government, to liberty, and to property.

From the very outset, we see that the proposed new government is identified as a republican government.

Consequently, early in the sequence of papers devoted to the promotion of the proposed constitution, Alexander Hamilton addressed concerns which had been voiced by opponents in regard to ancient governments that purported to be republics by delineating the improvements devised and included in the new constitution, including separation of powers, the division of government departments, checks and balances, and the tenure of office proposed in the new constitution:

> But it is not to be denied that the portraits they have sketched of republican government were too just copies of the originals from which they were taken. If it had been found impracticable to have devised models of a more perfect structure, the enlightened friends to liberty would have been obliged to abandon the cause of that species of government as indefensible. The science of politics, however, like most other sciences, has received great improvement. The efficacy of various principles is now well understood, which were either not known at all, or imperfectly known to the ancients. The regular distribution of power into distinct departments; the introduction of legislative balances and checks; the institution of courts composed of judges holding their offices during good behavior; the representation of the people in the legislature by deputies of their own election: these are wholly new discoveries, or have made their principal progress towards perfection in modern times. They are means, and powerful means, by which the excellencies of republican government may be retained and its imperfections lessened or avoided.[63]

[63.] Federalist no. 9

INDIVIDUAL LIBERTIES AND AMERICAN GOVERNMENT

Montesquieu

Later in that same paper, Hamilton makes note of the fact that Montesquieu believed that a republic would preserve individual liberty.

After Hamilton opens the issue of republics, Madison takes up the topic and spends extensive time and portions of numerous papers, reviewing the matter in great detail. Madison's brilliant logic and crisp intellect conveys impeccable assurance that the republican form of government holds the greatest hope of preserving the liberty the Americans sought and that democracy was a certain path to tyranny. As previously quoted, Federalist no. 10 introduces a marvelous exposition of the topic.

Addressing the concern that republics could only succeed in a small geographic area, Madison sustains the choice of republican government while further denigrating democracy:

> The error which limits republican government to a narrow district has been unfolded and refuted in preceding papers. I remark here only that it seems to owe its rise and prevalence chiefly to the confounding of a republic with a democracy, and applying to the former reasonings drawn from the nature of the latter. The true distinction between these forms was also adverted to on a former occasion. It is that in a democracy the people meet and exercise the government in person; in a republic they assemble and administer it by their representatives and agents. A democracy, consequently, must be confined to a small spot. A republic may be extended over a large region.[64]

[64.] Federalist no. 14

Shortly thereafter, he seems almost prescient (particularly in light of the campaign in modern America) in foreseeing the tendency some have in confusing republics and democracies:

> Under the confusion of names, it has been an easy task to transfer to a republic observations applicable to a democracy only.[65]

He goes on to point out that (contrary to some modern wisdom—offered by some who promote democracy in America—that the form of government established originally by the founders is a blend of a republic and a democracy) the proposed constitution gives Americans an unmixed republic. Logic testifies that a government is either a republic or it is a democracy, but it cannot be both.

> America can claim the merit of making the discovery the basis of unmixed and extensive republics.[66]

Continuing in the same paper, as Madison makes the point that the founders set the boundaries of power for the national government and that the states retained their jurisdiction in areas not delegated to the national government, he again emphasizes that the government is a republic:

> In the first place it is to be remembered that the general government is not to be charged with the whole power of making and administering laws. Its jurisdiction is limited to certain enumerated objects, which concern all the members of the republic, but which are not to be attained by the separate provisions of any. The subordinate governments, which can extend their care to all those other objects which can be separately provided for, will retain their due authority and activity. Were it proposed by the plan of the convention to abolish the governments of the particular States, its adversaries would have some ground for their objection; though it would not be difficult to show that if they were abolished the general government would be compelled by the principle of self-preservation to reinstate them in their proper jurisdiction.[67]

In a later paper, Madison links republican government with liberty and stability and appropriate energy. He points out the fact that the convention gave careful consideration to the necessity of each element and the proper dose of each component. He notes the "genius of republican liberty" and how balance was considered and obtained:

[65.] Federalist no. 14
[66.] Federalist no. 14
[67.] Federalist no. 14

INDIVIDUAL LIBERTIES AND AMERICAN GOVERNMENT

Among the difficulties encountered by the convention, a very important one must have lain in combining the requisite stability and energy in government with the inviolable attention due to liberty and to the republican form. Without substantially accomplishing this part of their undertaking, they would have very imperfectly fulfilled the object of their appointment, or the expectation of the public; yet that it could not be easily accomplished will be denied by no one who is unwilling to betray his ignorance of the subject. Energy in government is essential to that security against external and internal danger and to that prompt and salutary execution of the laws which enter into the very definition of good government. Stability in government is essential to national character and to the advantages annexed to it, as well as to that repose and confidence in the minds of the people, which are among the chief blessings of civil society. An irregular and mutable legislation is not more an evil in itself than it is odious to the people; and it may be pronounced with assurance that the people of this country, enlightened as they are with regard to the nature, and interested, as the great body of them are, in the effects of good government, will never be satisfied till some remedy be applied to the vicissitudes and uncertainties which characterize the State administrations. On comparing, however, these valuable ingredients with the vital principles of liberty, we must perceive at once the difficulty of mingling them together in their due proportions. The genius of republican liberty seems to demand on one side not only that all power should be derived from the people, but that those intrusted with it should be kept in dependence on the people by a short duration of their appointments; and that even during this short period the trust should be placed not in a few, but a number of hands. Stability, on the contrary, requires that the hands in which power is lodged should continue for a length of time the same. A frequent change of men will result from a frequent return of elections; and a frequent change of measures from a frequent change of men: whilst energy in government requires not only a certain duration of power, but the execution of it by a single hand. [68]

In Federalist no. 39, Madison again reiterates the fact that the form of government proposed in the new constitution is strictly republican and that if the form were found to be anything but republican, it should be rejected by the nation:

The first question that offers itself is whether the general form and aspect of the government be strictly republican. It is evident that no other form would be reconcilable with the genius of the people of America; with the fundamental principles

---

[68]. Federalist no. 37

of the Revolution; or with that honorable determination which animates every votary of freedom to rest all our political experiments on the capacity of mankind for self-government. If the plan of the convention, therefore, be found to depart from the republican character, its advocates must abandon it as no longer defensible.

With a prescience that could apply in modern times, Madison then reviews examples of governments that are mistakenly called by some to be republics and the danger of not clearly understanding the true character of a republic. He then gives a definition of a republic:

> These examples, which are nearly as dissimilar to each other as to a genuine republic, show the extreme inaccuracy with which the term has been used in political disquisitions.
>
> If we resort for a criterion to the different principles on which different forms of government are established, we may define a republic to be, or at least may bestow that name on, a government which derives all its powers directly or indirectly from the great body of the people, and is administered by persons holding their offices during pleasure for a limited period, or during good behavior.

Shortly thereafter, Madison reinforces his position that the proposed government is republican by pointing out that the Constitution also requires that each state in the union also be dedicated to the republican form of government:

> Could any further proof be required of the republican complexion of this system, the most decisive one might be found in its absolute prohibition of titles of nobility, both under the federal and the State governments; and in its express guaranty of the republican form to each of the latter.

As he begins Federalist no. 49, Madison invokes the writings of Thomas Jefferson, noting Jefferson's fervent dedication to the republican form of government:

> THE author of the Notes on the State of Virginia, quoted in the last paper, has subjoined to that valuable work the draught of a constitution, which had been prepared in order to be laid before a convention expected to be called in 1783, by the legislature, for the establishment of a constitution for that commonwealth. The plan, like everything from the same pen, marks a turn of thinking, original, comprehensive, and accurate; and is the more worthy of attention as it equally displays a fervent attachment to republican government.

In Federalist no. 51, Madison extols the necessity of dividing and subdividing power and in checking power against power in order to prevent it from being abused by those who hold it. He speaks to the ways in which the proposed constitution addresses the issue, noting the

INDIVIDUAL LIBERTIES AND AMERICAN GOVERNMENT

republic to be a "compound republic" at both the national and state levels, as well as preventing the majority from going beyond the boundaries established within which government can act. Government is prevented from having the ability to abuse the minority—pointing out that true majority rule (democracy) could result in a tyranny of the masses:

> There are, moreover, two considerations particularly applicable to the federal system of America, which place that system in a very interesting point of view.
>
> First. In a single republic, all the power surrendered by the people is submitted to the administration of a single government; and the usurpations are guarded against by a division of the government into distinct and separate departments. In the compound republic of America, the power surrendered by the people is first divided between two distinct governments, and then the portion allotted to each subdivided among distinct and separate departments. Hence a double security arises to the rights of the people. The different governments will control each other, at the same time that each will be controlled by itself.
>
> Second. It is of great importance in a republic not only to guard the society against the oppression of its rulers, but to guard one part of the society against the injustice of the other part. Different interests necessarily exist in different classes of citizens. If a majority be united by a common interest, the rights of the minority will be insecure. There are but two methods of providing against this evil: the one by creating a will in the community independent of the majority—that is, of the society itself; the other, by comprehending in the society so many separate descriptions of citizens as will render an unjust combination of a majority of the whole very improbable, if not impracticable. The first method prevails in all governments possessing an hereditary or self-appointed authority. This, at best, is but a precarious security; because a power independent of the society may as well espouse the unjust views of the major as the rightful interests of the minor party, and may possibly be turned against both parties. The second method will be exemplified in the federal republic of the United States. Whilst all authority in it will be derived from and dependent on the society, the society itself will be broken into so many parts, interests and classes of citizens, that the rights of individuals, or of the minority, will be in little danger from interested combinations of the majority. In a free government the security for civil rights must be the same as that for religious rights. It consists in the one case in the multiplicity of interests, and in the other in the multiplicity of sects. The degree of security in both cases will depend on the number of interests and sects; and this may be presumed to depend on the extent of country and number of people comprehended under the same government. This view of the subject must particularly recommend a proper federal system to all the sincere and considerate friends of republican government, since it shows that in exact proportion as the territory of the Union may be formed

into more circumscribed Confederacies, or States, oppressive combinations of a majority will be facilitated; the best security, under the republican forms, for the rights of every class of citizen, will be diminished; and consequently the stability and independence of some member of the government, the only other security, must be proportionally increased, justice is the end of government. It is the end of civil society. It ever has been and ever will be pursued until it be obtained, or until liberty be lost in the pursuit. In a society under the forms of which the stronger faction can readily unite and oppress the weaker, anarchy may as truly be said to reign as in a state of nature, where the weaker individual is not secured against the violence of the stronger; and as, in the latter state, even the stronger individuals are prompted, by the uncertainty of their condition, to submit to a government which may protect the weak as well as themselves; so, in the former state, will the more powerful factions or parties be gradually induced, by a like motive, to wish for a government which will protect all parties, the weaker as well as the more powerful. It can be little doubted that if the State of Rhode Island was separated from the Confederacy and left to itself, the insecurity of rights under the popular form of government within such narrow limits would be displayed by such reiterated oppressions of factious majorities that some power altogether independent of the people would soon be called for by the voice of the very factions whose misrule had proved the necessity of it. In the extended republic of the United States, and among the great variety of interests, parties, and sects which it embraces, a coalition of a majority of the whole society could seldom take place on any other principles than those of justice and the general good; whilst there being thus less danger to a minor from the will of a major party, there must be less pretext, also, to provide for the security of the former, by introducing into the government a will not dependent on the latter, or, in other words, a will independent of the society itself. It is no less certain than it is important, notwithstanding the contrary opinions which have been entertained, that the larger the society, provided it lie within a practicable sphere, the more duly capable it will be of self-government. And happily for the republican cause, the practicable sphere may be carried to a very great extent by a judicious modification and mixture of the federal principle.

Madison makes multiple mention of the republican form of government proposed in the new constitution in Federalist no. 57, pointing out that several of the objections to the proposed government violate the desired republican form of government: "the principle of it strikes at the very root of republican government," "the characteristic policy of republican government," and "that violates the principles of republican government."

Are they not the genuine and the characteristic means by which republican government provides for the liberty and happiness of the people? Are they not the identical means on which every State government in the Union relies for the attainment of these important ends? What, then, are we to understand by the objection which this paper has combated? What are we to say to the men who profess the most flaming zeal for republican government, yet boldly impeach the fundamental principle of it; who pretend to be champions for the right and the capacity of the people to choose their own rulers, yet maintain that they will prefer those only who will immediately and infallibly betray the trust committed to them?

In writing of the powers of the president, and of his responsibilities, Hamilton notes that unlike the situation found in other forms of government, in a republic all who hold office can be held responsible for their actions:

> But in a republic where every magistrate ought to be personally responsible for his behavior in office.[69]

In concluding the Federalist Papers, Hamilton ties his final appeal for the ratification of the proposed constitution to the commitment he made at the beginning in Federalist Paper no. 1 and makes multiple references to the protections a republican form of government gives to the sacred liberties and property of those who are blessed to enjoy it. The safeguards of the proposed government are recapped, and the people are admonished to embrace it and begin to enjoy the fruits of a well-planned national charter:

> The additional security which its adoption will afford to republican government, to liberty, and to property.[70]

> The additional securities to republican government, to liberty, and to property, to be derived from the adoption of the plan under consideration, consist chiefly in the restraints which the preservation of the Union will impose on local factions and insurrections, and on the ambition of powerful individuals in single States who might acquire credit and influence enough from leaders and favorites to become the despots of the people; in the diminution of the opportunities to foreign intrigue, which the dissolution of the confederacy would invite and facilitate; in the prevention of extensive military establishments, which could not fail to grow out of wars between the States in a disunited situation; in the express guaranty of a republican form of government to each; in the absolute and universal exclusion of titles of nobility; and in the precautions against the repetition of those practices on the part of the State governments which have

---

[69]. Federalist no. 71
[70]. Federalist no. 85

undermined the foundations of property and credit, have planted mutual distrust in the breasts of all classes of citizens, and have occasioned an almost universal prostration of morals.[71]

Thus, we see that the evidence presented throughout the Federalist Papers, as well as countless other impeccable sources, is overwhelming and unimpeachable: The United States of America was established as a constitutional republic, not a democracy. By recognizing that great fact and seeking to preserve the foundation principles upon which this nation was founded, we may preserve the blessings of liberty for ourselves and our posterity. Those who have received knowledge of the "original intent" of those who founded this nation have a duty, a responsibility, even an obligation, to foster wider understanding of the truth in this matter. We must seek to make popular the sound and good principles that were ordained as this nation was established. We diminish our value in the cause of liberty if we adopt the lexicon of those who foster global democracy on the pathway to socialism. We allow our worth to be debauched if we become co-opted into unwitting shills for the cause of democracy (even if it is simply in the usage of the terms associated with that destructive movement) in order to obtain the praise of men and women who are not worthy to stand in the light of those who laid the foundation of this nation.

[71.] Federalist no. 85

3.

AMERICAN PRINCIPLES OF FEDERALISM

RECOMMENDED RESOURCES FOR THE SERIOUS STUDENT:

The United States Constitution
The Declaration of Independence
The Federalist Papers by J. Madison, A. Hamilton, J. Jay
The Spirit of Laws by Montesquieu
View of the Constitution of the United States by St. George Tucker

QUOTES, ARTICLES, AND ORIGINAL SOURCES

As we study the words that were written and spoken by the American Founding Fathers, it is important to know what the words meant when they were written and spoken. Today, many seek to modify the original meanings of the words in order to facilitate modifications in the form of government that was originally established for the United States. Fortunately, one of the American Founding Fathers wrote a comprehensive dictionary of the American language. In 1828, Noah Webster published his magnificent dictionary. Those who wish to know what the founders meant when they spoke the words they spoke may understand them by going to this dictionary and reading what the words meant when they were said. Since we are seeking to understand the original intent of the founders of this nation, it is imperative we understand what the words actually meant (particularly since we note a modern skewing of definitions, as noted in the last lecture regarding the concept of democracy).

In light of this, it is appropriate that we define the word "constitution." In Noah Webster's 1828 dictionary, *An American Dictionary of the English Language*, we discover what the Founding Fathers understood a constitution to be

> a system of fundamental rules, principles and ordinances for the government of a state or nation. In free states, the constitution is *paramount to the statutes or laws enacted by the legislature, limiting and controlling its power; and in the United States, the legislature is created, and its powers designated, by the constitution. (emphasis added)*

Paramount means *"of chief rank or importance; primary; foremost; superior."*[72] In other words, the Constitution is superior to and takes precedence over all enactments of any legislature. No act of the government may legally override the Constitution. Only those laws that are enacted under the terms defined by the Constitution are enforceable as legal. Every section of the established government is empowered to act only within the scope of power allowed within the charter of the Constitution. If an act of the legislature contradicts the Constitution, or if the legislature or any another department or agency of the government attempts to enact a "law," or exercise a power which goes beyond the powers defined and granted within the Constitution, the act is unconstitutional and, therefore, illegal, null, and void.

Of course, the Founding Fathers established a specific form of government for the United States. In the last lecture, we reviewed the fact that the United States Constitution created a *republican* form of government for this nation and defined the meaning of "republic." Specifically, however, the United States is called a *federal republic.*

To understand why the American government is called a federal republic, we should review the meaning of "federal," obtaining its definition from the Webster's 1828 dictionary, *An American Dictionary of the English Language.*

Webster notes the etymology of the word federal: from Latin—"a league"; from Hebrew—"to pledge." Then he defines it thus:

1. Pertaining to a league or contract; derived from an *agreement or covenant between parties.*
2. Consisting in a compact between parties, particularly and chiefly between states or nations; founded on alliance by contract or mutual agreement; as a federal government, such as that of the United States.

Knowing what a covenant is is important. Webster defined "covenant" as follows: Used as a noun it is defined as:

1. A mutual consent or agreement of two or more persons, to do or to forebear some act or thing; a contract; stipulation.
2. A writing containing the terms of agreement or contract between parties.

Used as a verb it indicates taking an action:

To enter into a formal agreement; to stipulate; to bind one's self by contract.

So a covenant is a binding contract. By examining these definitions, we come to understand that the United States Constitution may be considered a binding contract

---

[72.] Webster, *American Dictionary.*

that links the states together into a federal republic. It is interesting to note that at times, when the Founding Fathers wrote and spoke, they referred to the Constitution as a written, binding contract.

This lecture reviews four essential elements of the government established under the United States Constitution, discussing at length why each of the following components must be strictly adhered to if the nation is to retain its liberty.

First, in order to prevent power from being usurped and ultimately abused, the United States Constitution created a form of government that mandates a *separation of granted powers*. Granted powers are divided and subdivided along the following lines:

> The legislative is granted the power to make laws.
> The executive received the power to carry out and enforce laws.
> The judicial was assigned the power to judge in situations where the laws have
>   been broken, or when disagreements between citizens arise.

The second essential element is that the United States Constitution is a *written constitution*. Words have meaning, and the meaning of the words written in the Constitution may be known and understood, so all (both the leadership of the nation and the people) may clearly understand the exact scope, magnitude, and meaning of the Constitution and what the national government entails.

The third element involves *enumerated powers*. The powers granted to the national government were spelled out and listed in detail. The national government has no power to do what is not specifically listed in the Constitution.

The fourth critically important element included in the United States Constitution is that the powers granted to each department are restrained by *checks and balances* that are to be exercised by the other departments to ensure that each department operates only within the bounds established by the Constitution. Powers are distributed, powers broken up, and powers are shared in some instances, but in no instance does the Constitution allow encroachment between the departments of the national government that would allow power to grow into tyranny.

As considered in the previous lecture, those who founded the United States viewed God as the source of mankind's rights: "that they are endowed by their Creator with certain unalienable rights."[73]

They defined the purpose of government—to preserve God-given rights—and that it is the right of the people to alter or abolish a government that violates their rights.[74]

---

[73] See Declaration of Independence.

[74] "That to secure these rights, Governments are instituted among men, deriving their just Powers from the Consent of the Governed. That whenever any form of government becomes destructive of these ends, it is the right of the people to alter or abolish it." Declaration of Independence.

By incorporating the four essential elements listed above within the United States Constitution, the founders created a government with the intention of ensuring that the truths defined in the Declaration would be preserved and that future generations would be able to live under the principles espoused in the Declaration of Independence.

In a very eloquent manner, the Preamble to the United States Constitution succinctly captures and reviews the reasons the Constitution was set forth:

> We the People of the United States, in Order to *form a more perfect Union, establish Justice, insure domestic Tranquility, provide for the common defense, promote the general Welfare,* and *secure the Blessings of Liberty to ourselves and our Posterity,* do ordain and establish this Constitution for the United States of America. (emphasis added)

They sought to "form a more perfect Union." Under the first American constitution, the Articles of Confederation, the nation was on the verge of dissolution. The states were treating one another almost like separate nations. They lacked a cohesive foreign policy and lacked unity in almost innumerable ways. European powers were expecting the nation to dissolve and fragment and become fair game to again become their colonies.

The Articles of Confederation did not recognize a judicial system, and justice was often difficult to obtain. Equitable justice is essential to preserve liberty.

With an unstable government, domestic tranquility was often disturbed by riots and destruction created by disaffected members of society. Courts had been burned in some states where people felt justice had not been carried out. One of the complaints against the king, which was noted in the Declaration of Independence, was that he had allowed the miscarriage of justice.

In order to resist encroachments and offenses of foreign powers, the new states needed to unify their defensive powers and their posture in international affairs.

The concept of promoting the general welfare was understood and defined by the American founders in a manner completely different from how modern society defines "welfare"! Noah Webster's *An American Dictionary of the English Language* defined "welfare" as follows:

1. Exemption from misfortune, sickness, calamity or evil; the enjoyment of health and the common blessings of life; prosperity; happiness; *applied to persons.*
2. Exemption from any unusual evil or calamity; the enjoyment of peace and prosperity, or the ordinary blessings of society and civil government; *applied to states.*

The founder's definition of welfare indicated a general well-being or a general environment in society where peace and prosperity could thrive because people in general were confident in the stable progress of the future. They sought to create a proper government that would foster conditions in which the economy and society in general were predictable and not fraught with turmoil and doubt. Modern society commonly uses the term "welfare" in a manner that indicates some kind of government administered dole—a government handout. It is interesting to note that the term "welfare" was not used in that connotation as the United States was founded, having a vastly different definition than is applied today.

AMERICAN PRINCIPLES OF FEDERALISM

In creating the sound foundation of a national government that is based upon a clearly defined grant of powers, which were limited in scope and magnitude, the American founders wished to create a stable, safe, predictable society where individuals, families, and businesses could confidently move forward, knowing that the rules for liberty would allow them to succeed and that it was unlikely that something in the environment of society (such as government encroachment, war, civil unrest, monetary collapse, etc.) would dramatically change and destroy their peace, prosperity, and civil government. The Founding Fathers had suffered through the turmoil of an unstable society where the future was very unsure. For example, they had faced an economy that was based on a faulty money system, and they had found that it resulted in turmoil because no one knew if an investment would work because the value of money fluctuated dramatically in an environment of unbacked paper money and inflation caused by printing presses creating too much money and deflating its purchasing power. In creating the United States Constitution, they constitutionally precluded that flawed approach from encroaching upon the people's financial future. The Constitution was written to address the government-related circumstances that could have arisen to undermine the general welfare (by the definition in common usage in their day) of the nation.

Unfortunately, modern American leaders have greatly modified the original formula of proper government as constitutionally defined, changing not only the definition of the word "welfare" to mean redistribution of wealth through government mandated "entitlement" programs that define welfare as a dole or handout, but they have cast aside most of the other critical elements of the government established in the beginning of this great republic.

And the preamble closed with the grand hope that under the Constitution, the blessings of liberty would be preserved for themselves and their posterity. Many of the early American writers wrote of their hope that the freedom they sought so diligently to establish and preserve would be enjoyed by their unborn posterity. Many even recognized that it was unlikely they themselves would fully enjoy the full flower of their liberty, but they sought to build such a firm foundation of liberty and proper government that it would be unshakable and fully functional for the countless generations that would come after them.

PRIVATE PROPERTY

As discussed in lecture 2, the Founding Fathers of the United States clearly understood the necessity of preserving private property rights if freedom was to be preserved. Consequently, they established the nation with the full intention of preserving private property, stating that it is essential to individual liberty. The firm understanding they had of the necessity of private property was founded upon generations of evidence dating back to the Holy Scriptures. The following is a sampling of the logic and evidence that justified their position.

Exodus 20:15: "Thou shalt not steal." Remember the spiritual foundation lecture and how the scriptures were looked at as a source of God's wisdom for establishing proper government and how Blackstone used the example of "thou shalt not kill" to establish that principle as applying in society? The scriptures also established the validity of private property. The admonition against stealing presupposes the existence of private property.

Exodus 20:17: "Thou shalt not covet thy neighbour's house, thou shalt not covet thy neighbour's wife, nor his manservant, nor his maidservant, nor his ox, nor his ass, nor any thing that [is] thy neighbour's." *Covet*, in this case, means "To desire inordinately; to desire that which is unlawful to obtain or possess." That inordinate desire could, of course, lead to theft; therefore, we are admonished against that inordinate desire. The phrase "that [is] thy neighbor's" admits the existence of private property.

John Locke

John Locke in *Second Essay Concerning Civil Government* (pp. 30-31, par. 26-29): "Though the earth and all inferior creatures be common [as the gift from God] to all men, yet every man has a 'property' in his own 'person.' This, nobody has any right to but himself. The 'labor' of his body and the 'work' of his hands, we may say, are properly his. Whatsoever, then, he removes out of the state that Nature hath provided and left it in, he hath mixed his labor with it, and joined to it something that is his own, and thereby makes it his property." Locke goes on in his writing to discuss collecting acorns in the wild, thereby making the acorns private property by virtue of the labor to collect them.[75]

[75.] See appendix for a brief biographical sketch of John Locke and his philosophies.

John Locke, speaking of government, in *Second Essay Concerning Civil Government* (p. 57, par. 138): "The supreme power cannot take from any man any part of his property without his own consent. For the preservation of property being the end of government, and that for which men enter into society, it necessarily supposes and requires that the people should have property."

Sir William Blackstone

Sir William Blackstone, speaking of the rights of Englishmen, in *Commentaries on the Laws of England* (vol. 1, 125): "And these may be reduced to three principle of primary articles; the right of personal security, the right of personal liberty; and the right of private property."[76]

Sir William Blackstone in *Commentaries on the Laws of England* (vol. 1, 134): "The third absolute right, inherent in every Englishman, is that of property: which consists in the free use, enjoyment, and disposal of all his acquisitions, without any control or diminution, save only by the laws of the land. The original of private property is probably founded in nature."

Sir William Blackstone in *Commentaries on the Laws of England* (vol. 1, 135): "So great moreover is the regard of the law for private property, that it will not authorize the least violation of it; no, not even for the general good of the whole community."

[76.] See appendix for a brief biographical sketch of Blackstone and his philosophies.

Sir William Blackstone in *Commentaries on the Laws of England* (vol. 1, 135): When an individual's property is taken, it is only "by giving him a full indemnification and equivalent for the injury thereby sustained."

John Adams: "All men are born free and independent, and have certain natural, essential, and unalienable rights, among which may be reckoned the right of enjoying and defending their lives and liberties; that of acquiring, possessing, and protecting property; in fine, that of seeking and obtaining their safety and happiness."[77]

John Adams: "The moment the idea is admitted into society that property is not as sacred as the laws of God, and that there is not a force of law and public justice to protect it, anarchy and tyranny commence. Property must be secured or liberty cannot exist."[78]

Alexander Hamilton in Federalist no. 79: "In the general course of human nature, a power over a man's subsistence amounts to a power over his will."

Alexander Hamilton in Federalist no. 73: "In the main it will be found that a power over the man's support is a power over his will."

United States Constitution, Amendment 5: "No person shall . . . be deprived of life, liberty, or property, without due process of law; nor shall private property be taken for public use, without just compensation."

St George Tucker

[77.] George A. Peek Jr., ed., in *The Political Writings of John Adams* (New York: Liberal Arts Press, 1954), 96.

[78.] C. F. Adams, *John Adams*, 6:9, 280.

In summary of individual rights protected under the Constitution, St. George Tucker (perhaps the preeminent constitutional scholar of the American founding era), in his *View of the Constitution of the United States*, notes, "No person shall be deprived of life, liberty, or property, (and these are the objects of all rights) without due process of law . . . His private property shall not be taken for the public use without just compensation."[79]

James Madison noted, "Government is instituted to protect property of every sort . . . . This being the end of government, that alone is not a just government, . . . nor is property secure under it, where the property which a man has in his personal safety and personal liberty is violated by arbitrary seizures of one class of citizens for the service of the rest"[80]

CHECKING POWER WITH POWER

As noted at the beginning of this lecture, to make certain that power was not accrued to the point it could be abused, the founders implemented what we call "separation of powers," dividing and subdividing the power that was granted to the national government.

The American founders were exceptionally impressed and enlightened by Montesquieu's wisdom in the recommendation to separate and divide power to ensure that the considerable power inherent within government would not become abusive.[81] Montesquieu's views of the division of the departments of government into different "competing" and power-checking arms thankfully found their way into the miraculous constitution that was brought into being during the Convention of 1787. The concepts of executive, legislative, and judicial elements were also thoroughly introduced and reviewed in Montesquieu's *The Spirit of Laws*. And the system of separated and balanced powers came to be one of the most highly valued concepts as the Americans established their government.

While Montesquieu did not originate the concept of separation of powers, he had observed it, particularly in the style exercised in the English system of government, which was in existence during his lifetime. While Montesquieu found many faults within the English system of government, he had great praise for it because he perceived that the English had achieved freedom to a greater degree than most nations of that era had ever dreamed possible. In book 11, chapter 6 of *The Spirit of Laws*, he waxed eloquent in descriptions of freedom tied to the English system of government. He concluded that English freedom rested primarily on two pillars: the degree of separation that had been attained between executive, legislative,

---

[79]. St. George Tucker, *View of the Constitution of the United States with Selected Writings*. Edited by Clyde N. Wilson, (Indianapolis: Liberty Fund, 1999), 294-295. See appendix for a brief biographical sketch of Tucker and his philosophies.

[80]. Saul K. Padover, ed., *The Complete Madison* (New York: Harper & Bros., 1953), 267.

[81]. See appendix for a brief biographical sketch of Montesquieu and his philosophies.

and judicial power and the satisfactory mixture of monarchy, aristocracy, and democracy in the Crown, the House of Lords, and the House of Commons.

The following is a sampling of Montesquieu's "separation of powers" concepts that had such great sway in America and that ultimately were largely incorporated into the unique form of government the founders of the United States created:

Power Resisting Power

> To form a moderate government, it is necessary to combine the several powers; to rule, temper, and set them in motion; to give as it were, ballast to one, in order to enable it to resist another. This is a masterpiece of legislation, rarely produced by hazard, and seldom attained by prudence.[82]

Man's Tendency to Abuse Power

> Political liberty is to be met with only in moderate governments: yet even in these it is not always met with. It is there only when there is no abuse of power: but constant experience shews us, that every man invested with power is apt to abuse it; he pushes on till he comes to the utmost limit. Is it not strange, tho' true, to say, that virtue itself has need of limits?[83]

Power to Check Power

> To prevent the abuse of power, 'tis necessary that by the very disposition of things power should be check to power. A government may be so constituted, as no man shall be compelled to do things which the law does not oblige him, nor forced to abstain from things which the law permits.[84]

Requisite of Liberty

> When the legislative and executive powers are united in the same person, or in the same body of magistracy, there can be then no liberty; because apprehensions

---

[82] *The Spirit of Laws* V, 14 [30]. The first English edition was Thomas Nugent's translation (London: Nourse, 1750) References to *The Spirit of Laws* found herein are taken from this original translation, and notation reflects the original format of the text: book, chapter, paragraph—i.e. V, 14, [30] denotes Book V, chapter 14, paragraph 30.

[83] *Spirit of Laws* XI, 4, [1].

[84] *Spirit of Laws* XI, 4, [2].

may arise, lest the same monarch or senate should enact tyrannical laws, to execute them in tyrannical manner.[85]

Separation of Powers Fundamental

Again, there is no liberty, if the power of judging be not separated from the legislative and executive powers. Were it joined with the legislative, the life and liberty of the subject would be exposed to arbitrary control; for the judge would be then the legislator. Were it joined to the executive power, the judge might behave with all the violence of an oppressor.

Miserable indeed would be the case, were the same man, or the same body whether of the nobles or of the people, to exercise those three powers, that of enacting laws, that of executing the public resolutions, and that of judging the crimes or differences of individuals.[86]

Representative Government

As in a free state, every man who is supposed a free agent, ought to be his own governor; so the legislative power should reside in the whole body of the people. But since this is impossible in large states, and in small ones is subject to many inconveniencies; it is fit that the people should act by their representatives, what they cannot act by themselves.[87]

Local Self-Government

The inhabitants of a particular town are much better acquainted with its wants and interests, than with those of other places; and are better judges of the capacity of their neighbors, than of that of the rest of their countrymen. The members thereof of the legislature should not be chosen from the general body of the nation; but it is proper that in every considerable place, a representative should be elected by the inhabitants.[88]

---

[85]. *Spirit of Laws* XI, 6, [4].
[86]. *Spirit of Laws* XI, 6, [5,6].
[87]. *Spirit of Laws* XI, 6, [22].
[88]. *Spirit of Laws* XI, 6, [23].

Necessary Balance

Were the executive power not to have a right of putting a stop to the encroachments of the legislative body, the latter would become despotic; for as it might arrogate to itself what authority it pleased, it would soon destroy all other powers.

But it is not proper on the other hand that the legislative power should have a right to stop the executive. For as the execution has its natural limits, it is useless to confine it; besides the executive power is generally employed in momentary operations. The power thereof of the Roman tribunes was faulty, as it put a stop not only to the legislation, but likewise to the execution itself; which was attended with infinite mischiefs.[89]

Rights of the Legislative

But if the legislative power in a free government has no right to stay the executive, it has a right and ought to have the means of examining in what manner its laws have been executed.[90]

Executive Veto

The executive power, pursuant to what has been already said, ought to have a share in the legislature by the power of refusing, otherwise it would soon be stripp'd of its prerogatives. But should the legislative power usurp a share of the executive, the latter would be equally undone.[91]

A System of Checks and Balances

If the prince were to have a share in the legislature by the power of enacting, liberty would be lost. But as it is necessary he should have a share in the legislature for the support of his own prerogative, this must consist in the power of refusing.

The change of government at Rome was owing to this, that neither the senate who had one part of the executive power, nor the magistrates who were entrusted with the other, had the right of refusing, which was entirely lodged in the people.

[89.] *Spirit of Laws* XI, 6, [42,43].
[90.] *Spirit of Laws* XI, 6, [44].
[91.] *Spirit of Laws* XI, 6, [52].

Here then is the fundamental constitution of the government we are treating of. The legislative body being composed of two parts, one checks the other, by the mutual privilege of refusing. They are both checked by the executive power, as the executive is by the legislative.

These three powers should naturally form a state of repose or inaction. But as there is a necessity for movement in the course of human affairs, they are forced to move, but still move in concert."[92]

THE UNITED STATES CONSTITUTIONAL CONVENTION OF 1787

As the Founding Fathers of the United States met in the Constitutional Convention at Philadelphia through the long sweltering summer of 1787, they debated the structure of the government they were creating. All of the delegates had experienced or witnessed the siren call of power and had observed the deleterious effects of unrestrained or overreaching power. While all of them were students of the philosophies of government and many had personally participated in positions of responsibility within government, some of the participants (particularly James Madison) had deeply studied the issues in preparation for the solemn duty that faced them.

As the arduous debates and discussions extended from days to weeks to months, the structure of the government the delegates were creating emerged. It was a unique blend of the wisdom of the ages and the inspiration of God that rested upon the convention. In its final form, the new government was not a clone of any before-known government, but it clearly reflected the valuable concepts that Montesquieu had taught in his *The Spirit of Laws*. The founders carefully defined each element of government, delineating the areas of responsibility and the power held by each division (legislative, executive, judicial), respectively.

THE UNITED STATES CONSTITUTION ESTABLISHED A LIMITED GOVERNMENT WHOSE POWERS ARE FEW AND WELL DEFINED

THE CORRUPTING INFLUENCE OF POWER

The United States Constitution was written to address "human nature." The founders of the United States clearly understood human tendencies that lead to tyranny and improper government. It is interesting to note that many today seek to debunk the Constitution by

---

[92.] *Spirit of Laws* XI, 6, [53-56].

intimating that it is outdated because it was written during a horse-and-buggy agrarian period, so it could not possibly address the challenges of a modern society that is so steeped in technology. This position is falsely based. It does not matter what the level of technology is in society. What matters is that humans will hold office and power. The natural tendency of mankind to seek, obtain, then abuse power is what the Constitution was written to control. Regardless of technological advances, human nature is what leads to tyranny. The desire to obtain and then, ultimately, to abuse power have been almost universally recognized by thinking men throughout the ages.

The great statesman Lord Acton observed that "power corrupts, and absolute power corrupts absolutely."[93]

Daniel Defoe noted, "All men would be tyrants if they could."[94]

While the aforementioned men were not contemporary with the founders of this nation, the men who framed this nation's government recognized this—had experienced this—and sought to control this almost universal tendency to seek, obtain, and then abuse power.

Thomas Jefferson said, "In questions of power then let no more be heard of confidence in man; but bind him down from mischief by the chains of the Constitution."[95]

James Madison suggested the means to prevent this universal tendency to abuse power, saying,

> But the great security against a gradual concentration of the several powers in the same department consists in giving to those who administer each department the necessary constitutional means and personal motives to resist encroachments of the others. The provision for defense must in this, as in all other cases, be made commensurate to the danger of attack. Ambition must be made to counteract ambition. The interest of the man must be connected with the constitutional rights of the place. It may be a reflection on human nature that such devices should be necessary to control the abuses of government, But what is government itself but the greatest of all reflections on human nature?[96]

Madison also observed,

> The accumulation of all powers, legislative, executive, and judiciary, in the same hands, whether of one, a few, or many, and whether hereditary, self-appointed, or elective, may justly be pronounced the very definition of tyranny.[97]

[93.] Letter to Mandell Creighton, April 5, 1887, in Gertrude Himmelfarb, ed., *Acton, Essays on Freedom and Power* (1972), 335-6.
[94.] Daniel Defoe, *The Kentish Petition*, addenda, 11 (1701).
[95.] Kentucky Resolutions, in Bergh, *Thomas Jefferson*, 17:388.
[96.] Federalist no. 51
[97.] Federalist no. 47

Sources of Power

On numerous occasions throughout *View of the Constitution of the United States*, Tucker quotes other contemporary authors. In the following citation, he directly quotes Federalist no. 39. He apparently included it to point out that the new constitution not only divided and subdivided power, but it also gave consideration to ensure that the *sources* of power were never allowed to be consolidated, thus attempting to forestall the possibility that those seeking power could subvert the division of power by drawing the sources of power together for some nefarious purpose. The founders recognized mankind's tendency to seek and then abuse power, so they sought to make use of the tendency to jealously guard one's perceived power, exercise it in a manner that was beneficial to the power source, and protect it from encroachment by another. The Constitution divided the sources of power and assumed that each source of power would seek to keep the other sources from capturing their particular advantage.

The House of Representatives got their power from the people, the senators from the states, the president from a compound source involving a special (very temporary and single-purpose) blend of the states and the people's representatives. It is interesting how the Seventeenth Amendment destroyed this delicate balancing-of-power-sources act that was originally established and how current efforts to further pollute and ultimately destroy the electoral college would result in further erosion of this fundamental principle, greater abuse of power, and destruction of liberty!

> With regard to the sources from which the ordinary powers of government are to be derived. The house of representatives will derive its powers from the people of America, and the people will be represented in the same proportion, and on the same principle, as they are in the legislature of a particular state . . . The senate, on the other hand, will derive its powers from the states, as political and co-equal societies; and these will be represented on the principle of equality in the senate . . . The executive power will be derived from a very compound source. The immediate election of the president is to be made by the states, in their political character. The vote allotted to them are in a compound ratio, which considers them partly as distinct and co-equal societies; partly as unequal members of the same societies.[98]

From the beginning, the founders were concerned that some element of the government would usurp power beyond what was delegated and encroach beyond the boundaries that had been set, thus destroying the delicate balance of power that had been established.

[98.] Tucker, *View*, 97-98, quoting Federalist no. 39.

Jefferson spoke of his concerns in regard to this tendency, as did Washington:

> It has long . . . been my opinion . . . , that the germ of dissolution of our federal government is in the constitution of the federal judiciary; an irresponsible body (for impeachment is scarcely a scarecrow), working like gravity by night and by day, gaining a little today and a little tomorrow, and advancing its noiseless step like a thief over the field of jurisdiction, until all shall be usurped from the states, and the government of all be consolidated into one. To this I am opposed, because when all government, domestic and foreign, in little as in great things, shall be drawn to Washington as the center of all power, it will render powerless the checks provided of one government on another, and will become as venal and oppressive as the government from which we separated.[99]

> Toward the preservation of your Government and the permanency of your present happy state, it is requisite . . . that you *resist with care the spirit of innovation upon its principles, however specious the pretexts. One method of assault may be to effect in the forms of the Constitution alterations which will impair the energy of the system, and thus to undermine what can not be directly overthrown* . . . *Liberty itself will find in such a government, with powers properly distributed and adjusted, its surest guardian.*[100]

VALUE OF WRITTEN CONSTITUTION

The value of a written constitution is beyond measure. Words have meaning, and those meanings may be known. They are not open to arbitrary and unilateral interpretation or redefinition by those who would modify the Constitution to meet their whims. The words and the intended scope of the government were clearly established by those who framed the Constitution. There is an established and constitutional method for modifying the Constitution if it becomes necessary to do so. That process is defined in article 5 of the U.S. Constitution. There is no other way to legally modify it. Until it is modified legally (by the method defined within article 5 of the Constitution), it is obligatory upon all.

In recent years, a gross misunderstanding has become popular: that the Constitution may be modified upon the whim of the Supreme Court (some have called the Supreme Court a "constantly sitting constitutional convention") or by the decree of a president or by the vote of Congress. These philosophies defy all logic, reason, and firmly established constitutional principle. And yet this position is fostered today by those whom the founders of the nation warned against.

[99.] Bergh, *Thomas Jefferson*, 15:331.
[100.] George Washington, in Richardson, *Messages and Papers*, 1:210; emphasis added.

Tucker viewed the Constitution as a written contract, which was specific and exact, and from which variance was not legal:

> It is a written contract; . . . government was reduced to its elements; its object was defined, its principles ascertained; its powers limited, and fixed.[101]

SEPARATION/DIVISION OF POWER

In numerous statements throughout *View of the Constitution of the United States,* Tucker notes the wisdom of dividing and subdividing power to prevent its abuse. The separation of powers extends beyond the three branches of the national government, which the modern student normally considers the sum and substance of power separation. The states also retained their separate powers that fell within their jurisdiction in order to prevent abuse at that level of government. Each level and jurisdiction was to be held in check by the form of government that was established.

CONTROL OF POWER

In his review of the powers granted to the United States Congress (the House of Representatives and the Senate), Tucker addresses the common malady that afflicts the modern congress—that of extending their power beyond those specifically granted within the Constitution by means of interpretation and construction. He cites the Tenth Amendment as authority for his understanding of the intended prohibition of this practice.

> The powers vested in congress, the privileges of the members, and of each house, are severally enumerated in the constitution; . . . Consequently it would appear that they were not capable of extension, beyond the letter of the constitution itself. [Then he speaks of what is now the Tenth Amendment, saying that it] seems also not to favor a constructive extension of the powers of the federal government, or any department thereof.[102]

SEPARATION OF POWERS WITHIN THE NATIONAL GOVERNMENT

Tucker's view was that each element of the newly created national government was bound to limit their actions to the specific spheres allowed within the Constitution. The different departments are not allowed to encroach upon powers and responsibilities delegated to other

---

[101.] Tucker, *View*, 104.
[102.] Tucker, *View*, 146-147.

departments. The following statement by Tucker should be a warning to modern courts against the (now-common) practice of judicial "legislation." Of course, modern presidents commonly violate this crucial "prime directive" of the constitutional limits of power by issuing executive orders that are enforced upon the nation as though they had been legislated into existence by constitutional authority. Tucker said,

> All the powers granted by the constitution are either legislative, and executive, or judicial; to keep them for ever separate and distinct, except in the cases positively enumerated, has been uniformly the policy, and constitutes one of the fundamental principles of the American governments.[103]

Twentieth-century usurpers within the federal government have perversely twisted the so-called Commerce Clause of the United States Constitution to allow the national government jurisdiction over innumerable practices and acts that rightly fall within the power of the states or of individual choice. The intent of the Commerce Clause was to facilitate free and open trade between the states, which would encourage economic prosperity throughout the nation. Modern power-mongers have "interpreted" or constructed the Constitution to control areas that are not within their purview—such as civil rights, wage and price issues, contract matters, labor and management disputes, environmental concerns, etc. The national government was never intended to hold such powers, and Tucker is emphatic in his point that the national government certainly had no power to interfere with intrastate commerce.

> The constitution of the United States does not authorize congress to regulate, or in any manner to interfere with, the domestic commerce of any state.[104]

James Madison similarly captured the essence of the limits of the national government succinctly:

> The powers delegated by the proposed Constitution to the federal government are few and defined. Those which are to remain in the State governments are numerous and indefinite. The former will be exercised principally on external objects, as war, peace, negotiation, and foreign commerce; with which last the power of taxation will, for the most part, be connected. The powers reserved to the several States will extend to all the objects which, in the ordinary course of affairs, concern the lives, liberties, and properties of the people, and the internal order, improvement, and prosperity of the State.[105]

[103.] Tucker, *View*, 149.
[104.] Tucker, *View*, 193 footnote.
[105.] Federalist no. 45

As he continues his review of the powers granted to Congress, Tucker constantly reminds the reader that the power granted is specific and that the powers are very selectively granted.

In the following quotation, he notes that there are only very few offenses that Congress may either define or punish. Felonies not enumerated within the United States Constitution are, in Tucker's view, left within the jurisdiction of the state.

> The very guarded manner in which congress are vested with authority to legislate upon the subject of crimes, and misdemeanors. They are not entrusted with a general power over these subjects, but a few offenses are selected from the great mass of crimes with which society may be infested, upon which, only, congress are authorized to prescribe the punishment, or define the offense. All felonies and offenses committed upon land, in all cases not expressly enumerated, being reserved to the states respectively.[106]

WAR-MAKING POWERS

Contrary to blatant and grievous deviations that have occurred within the past fifty-plus years, the United States Constitution grants the power *solely* to Congress to take the nation into war. The executive does not have a shred of power granted to him in regard to this most momentous act.

> The power declaring war, with all its train of consequences, direct and indirect, forms the next branch of the powers confided to congress; and happy it is for the people of America that it is so vested. The term war, embraces the extremes of human misery and iniquity, and is alike the offspring of the one and the parent of the other. What else is the history of war from the earliest ages to the present moment but an afflicting detail of the sufferings and calamities of mankind, resulting from the ambition, usurpation, animosities, resentments, piques, intrigues, avarice, rapacity, oppressions, murders, assassinations, and other crimes, of the few possessing power! How rare are the instances of a just war! How few of those which are thus denominated have had their existence in a national injury! The personal claims of the sovereign are confounded with the interests of the nation over which he presides, and his private grievances or complaints are transferred to the people; who are thus made the victims of a quarrel in which they have no part, until they become principals in it, by their sufferings. War would be banished from the face of the earth, were nations instead of princes to decide upon their necessity. Injustice can never be the collective sentiment of a people emerged from barbarism. Happy the nation where the people are the arbiters of their own interest and their own conduct! Happy were it for the world, did the people of all nations possess this power.[107]

[106.] Tucker, *View*, 210-11.
[107.] Tucker, *View*, 211.

DELEGATION OF POWER PROHIBITED

Of course, modern congresses have blatantly disregarded their sole responsibility in the matter of war, lacking the courage to fulfill their constitutionally mandated duty in this regard. They have even failed in the natural tendency to jealously guard their sphere of influence. Dereliction of duty is the kindest definition that could be attached to the posture of Congress in this regard. Over the past fifty-plus years, Congress has made flimsy excuses as they have mumbled nonsense about "delegating" their authority in the matter of war to the president or blaming their impotence upon "treaties" that tie their hands and require (through entangling alliances) the United States to enter war. Constitutional protocol was well understood by those who founded this nation, and they knew that the authority that was assigned in the Constitution could not legally be delegated to another entity. The founders had diligently studied the works of John Locke. John Locke was emphatic in the matter of delegating constitutionally mandated authority:

> The legislative cannot transfer the power of making laws to any other hands, for it being but a delegated power from the people, they who have it cannot pass it over to others. The people alone can appoint the form of the commonwealth, which is by constituting the legislative, and appointing in whose hands that shall be. And when the people have said, "We will submit and be governed by laws made by such men, and in such forms," nobody else can say other men shall make laws for them; nor can they be bound by any laws but such as are enacted by those whom they have chosen and authorized to make laws for them. [108]

Tucker agreed with that position:

> A delegated authority cannot be transferred to another to exercise.[109]

EXPANSION OF POWER BY "CONSTRUCTION"

The modern nonsense of "implied" powers has resulted (through usurpation) in an infinite expansion of congressional power.

Many examples could be cited in which the Founding Fathers debunk the idea that the national government has authority to stray beyond the Constitution based upon "implied powers." One such citation by James Madison that shows their true intent will suffice:

---

[108]. John Locke, second essay from *Two Treatises of Government*.
[109]. Tucker, *View*, 219.

> I, sir, have always conceived—I believe those who proposed the Constitution conceived—it is still more fully known, and more material to observe, that those who ratified the Constitution conceived—that this is not an indefinite government, deriving its powers from the general terms prefixed to the specified powers—but a limited government, tied down to the specified powers, which explain and define the general terms.[110]

Tucker expanded this position further in regard to "construction" of powers granted within the Constitution, saying,

> Whenever, therefore, a question arises concerning the constitutionality of a particular power; the first question is, whether the power be expressed in the constitution? If it be, the question is decided. If it be not expressed, the next inquiry must be, whether it is properly an incident to an express power, and necessary to its execution. If it be, it may be exercised by congress. If it be not, congress cannot exercise it . . . And this construction of the "necessary and proper," is not only consonant with that which prevailed during the discussions and ratification of the constitution, but is absolutely necessary to maintain their consistency with the peculiar character of the government, as possessed of particular and defined powers, only; not of the general indefinite powers vested in ordinary governments.[111]

VIGILANCE REQUIRED TO PREVENT USURPATION

It has been said that it is human nature to accrue and then abuse power, especially within government. Tucker recognized this tendency even in the people of America and warned the nation to exercise vigilance in this matter:

> All governments have a natural tendency towards an increase, and assumption of power; and the administration of the federal government, has too frequently demonstrated, that the people of America are not exempt from this vice in their constitution. We have seen that parchment chains are not sufficient to correct this unhappy propensity; they are; nevertheless, capable of producing the most salutary effects; for, when broken, they warn the people to change those perfidious agents, who dare to violate them.[112]

Summarizing his view of the limits that are upon the national government, Tucker seemed to attempt to compress the matter into one sentence:

[110.] Quoted in Elliot, *Debates*, 4:428-9. Speech on the U.S. House floor, February 7, 1792.
[111.] Tucker, *View*, 227-8.
[112.] Tucker, *View*, 229.

The congress of the United States possesses no power to regulate, or interfere with the domestic concerns, or police of any state; it belongs not to them to establish any rules respecting the rights of property; nor will the constitution permit any prohibition of arms to the people; or of peaceable assemblies by them, for any purposes whatsoever, and in any number, whenever they may see occasion.[113]

PRESIDENTIAL POWER ALSO LIMITED

As he did in his review of the powers of the Congress, Tucker recognized the limited power granted to the president in article 2 of the Constitution, noting specifically that the president does not have the constitutional authority to "create" law. That authority was granted solely to the Congress.

> Thus, the part assigned to him by the constitution is strictly preventative, and not creative.[114]

Of course, to the immense erosion of the intended separation of powers, and to the detriment of liberty, this stipulation has been violated at will by every modern president as they "create" new laws through executive orders or by other means such as "administrative" law.

TREATY-MAKING POWER ADDRESSED

Another area that Tucker briefly touches upon in regard to the exercise of power is an area wherein the United States has strayed into dangerous territory in recent decades. It is the power to make treaties and the "interpretation" that the Constitution can be modified or amended simply by having the president agree to and the Senate ratify (as required in Articles 2 and 6 of the United States Constitution) treaties with other nations. Tucker is careful to note that such a position is wholly inconsistent with the intent and purposes specified within the Constitution and that such a position or action would subvert and completely destroy the deliberative amendment process that is outlined in article 5 of the Constitution. One of the prime foundational principles of the American experiment is found in the Declaration of Independence ("It is the Right of the People to alter or to abolish" their government), and the people would be left out of any constitutional modification if it were allowed to occur with actions taken solely by the president and the Senate.

In a lengthy review, Tucker addresses the logical limits of the treaty-making powers of the president and Senate and notes that it would be illogical to assume that the president and Senate have the power through treaties to go beyond the constitutional scope of their authority, saying,

---

[113.] Tucker, *View*, 253.
[114.] Tucker, *View*, 262.

> Let it be supposed, for example, that the president and senate should stipulate by treaty with any foreign nation, that in case of war between that nation and any other, the United States should immediately declare against that nation: Can it be supposed that such a treaty would be so far the law of the land, as to take from the house of representatives their constitutional right to deliberate on the expediency or inexpediency of such a declaration of war, and to determine and act thereon, according to their own judgment?[115]

It would seem today that Tucker's prediction of the nation being drawn into war without adhering to the constitutional requirement of a congressional declaration of war was almost prophetic—in view of the numerous modern instances of that mantra being the national justification in so momentous a matter!

Thomas Jefferson succinctly makes the point, saying,

> By the general power to make treaties, the Constitution must have intended to comprehend only those objects which are usually regulated by treaty and cannot be otherwise regulated . . . . It must have meant to except out of these the rights reserved to the states, for surely the President and Senate cannot do by treaty what the whole government is interdicted from doing in any way.[116]

And remember, Jefferson felt that the Constitution must be strictly held to the words written in the document, saying,

> Our peculiar security is in the possession of a written Constitution. Let us not make it a blank paper by construction.
>
> I say the same as to the opinion of those who consider the grant of the treaty-making power as boundless. If it is, then we have no Constitution. If it has bounds, they can be no others than the definitions of the powers which that instrument gives. It specifies and delineates the operations permitted to the federal government, and gives all the powers necessary to carry these into execution. Whatever of these enumerated objects is proper for a law, Congress may make the law; whatever is proper to be executed by way of a treaty, the President and Senate may enter into the treaty; whatever is to be done by a judicial sentence, the judges may pass the sentence.[117]

[115.] Tucker, *View*, 277.

[116.] "Manual of Parliamentary Practice," in Bergh, *Thomas Jefferson*, 2:442.

[117.] Bergh, *Thomas Jefferson*, 10:418-19.

TO PRESERVE THE NATION

As he debated the treaty-making power that was granted to the president and Senate as found in the Constitution, James Madison addressed the logical limits to the treaty-making power and made this statement,

> Does it follow, because this power is given to Congress, that it is absolute and unlimited? I do not conceive that power is given to the President and Senate to dismember the empire, or to alienate any great, essential right. I do not think the whole legislative authority have this power. The exercise of the power must be consistent with the object of the delegation.[118]

In spite of logic, reason, and the words of the Founding Fathers which indicate their original intent in the matter of treaties and the limited scope of their purpose and power, many American leaders in the twentieth and twenty-first centuries have insisted that the United States Constitution may be modified by international treaties which the president negotiates and the Senate ratifies. In 1951 Senator John W. Bricker first sponsored an amendment to the Constitution that would have closed this supposed loophole by recognizing the original intent of the American founders and limiting the treaty power of the United States government. While several versions of this amendment were put forth in an effort to appease critics and gain approval, the most direct and sound version of the proposed amendment stated:

> A provision of a treaty or other international agreement which conflicts with this Constitution, or which is not made in pursuance thereof, shall not be the supreme law of the land nor be of any force or effect.

It would seem that most thinking Americans would see in this amendment a solution to growing efforts to subvert the United States Constitution via the treaty process, and therefore this amendment would have passed immediately without opposition. Astonishingly, in 1954 the proposed Bricker Amendment failed to attain the two thirds vote threshold required for amendments in article 5 of the Constitution. Over the next few Congresses, subsequent rewritten diluted versions were offered, but always failed. The primary opposition to this amendment, which resulted in its defeat, came from the executive branch. President Eisenhower and his Secretary of State John Foster Dulles lobbied vigorously against its passage, and used all of the considerable power of their offices to defeat this amendment. Tragically, it would appear that they desired to continue to foster the false perception that the United States Constitution could be over-ridden by treaties negotiated by the president and ratified by the Senate. The danger of such a position should be readily apparent to all thinking Americans that value the liberty which is vouched safe in the United States Constitution!

[118.] Elliot, *Debates*, 3:514.

Conclusion

The statements by the founders noted within this lecture are simply a small sampling of what could be noted regarding their position on the constitutional limits and constraints placed upon the national government; they must suffice in support of the position that the powers delegated to the national government were sufficient to perform the duties delegated to the national government, but they were also few, specific, and constitutionally limited.

4.

OUTLINE OF AMERICAN HISTORY TIME LINE

RECOMMENDED RESOURCES FOR THE SERIOUS STUDENT:

A Basic History of the United States by Clarence Carson (six-volume set):
    Vol. 1-*The Colonial Experience: 1607-1774*
    Vol. 2-*The Beginning of the Republic: 1775-1825*
    Vol. 3-*The Sections and the Civil War: 1826-1877*
    Vol. 4-*The Growth of America: 1878-1928*
    Vol. 5-*The Welfare State: 1929-1985*
    Vol. 6-*America in Gridlock: 1985-2001*
    Teachers Guide
American Political Writing During the Founding Era by Hyneman/Lutz

A detailed review of over five hundred years of American history is not attempted herein. This lecture touches upon a basic time line and identifies key and recurring events that are reflected in challenges that currently face modern-day America. History has much to teach us if we are willing to learn from the experiences of those who went before and hear and heed their advice and counsel.

AMERICAN HISTORY TIME LINE

Quotes, Articles, and Original Sources

Patrick Henry

At the beginning of the American Revolution, the great patriot Patrick Henry stated, "I have but one lamp by which my feet are guided; and that is the lamp of experience. I know of no way of judging the future but by the past."[119]

William Shakespeare

In *The Tempest*, William Shakespeare (act 1, scene 1) observed "What's past is prologue," meaning, the experience of the past is but an introduction to that which is to come.

---

[119]. Patrick Henry, "Give me liberty or give me death" (speech to the Virginia Convention, Richmond, Virginia, March 23, 1775), quoted in William Wirt, *Sketches of the Life and Character of Patrick Henry*, 9th ed. (1836, reprinted 1970), 138-39; language altered to first person.

TO PRESERVE THE NATION

In many ways, history repeats itself. If we are willing to learn the lessons of history, perhaps the nation may avoid the mistakes of the past.

COLUMBUS'S VOYAGE

Christopher Columbus

We begin our review with the 1492 voyage of Columbus and the discovery of the American continent. Columbus set out to discover a shorter new trade route to the Far East and, in the process, discovered a continent that was not known at the time to the European peoples. The perspective that is held by many today that the people of Columbus's time believed the world to be flat is a misconception. It was generally known by those who considered such things that the world was spherical in shape, and while the size of the sphere was not clearly defined, and there was much that was yet unknown, the idea of a flat earth and that adventurous sailors would fall from the edge was not widely held. It is interesting to note that in his writings, Columbus reflect his perspective that he was led by the Holy Spirit in his voyages and that he believed that he followed a divine purpose in his discovery efforts. He sought to carry the name of Christ to the peoples he would meet as he sailed. In many ways, it was a spiritual voyage, and as we noted in the lecture that reviewed the spiritual foundation of the nation, that spiritual perspective was carried forward by subsequent migrations to the New World that Columbus discovered.

COLONIZATION OF THE ATLANTIC SEABOARD

Since this lecture series is focused upon the founding of the United States, it is appropriate that our brief review of history leap forward from the discovery of the new continent to the establishment of the European colonies on the eastern seaboard of America, which really began in earnest early in the 1600s.

Those who came to colonize America faced an arduous voyage across the ocean and subsequently had to carve out a living from the wilderness. They seemed to be uniquely qualified to overcome the hardships and rigors that faced them in this new land. They were a hardy, bold, and intrepid people. They did not shrink from the challenges and were vigorous in their efforts to subdue their new environment.

They came in little wooden ships (about one-thousandth the size of modern seagoing vessels), which were the normal mode of transportation to the New World. Very often, the goods that were necessary for their survival in their new location were spoiled during the two-month voyage from Europe.

And once they arrived here in America, their challenges had just begun! The new settlers faced the rigors of clearing the land, finding food, creating shelters, planting their crops, harvesting, dealing with hostile Indians (for example, the early history of colonization records a particularly tragic event in which 347 people were slaughtered by the Indians) and climate issues, etc.

In 1609, the Virginia settlement was established. Conditions were harsh in the new colony! The following narrative that was recorded by one of the early explorers notes the difficult conditions they faced in 1607 during an early settlement effort at a James River location and is reflective of the early circumstances faced by colonists. In June, 104 men had been left behind. Only forty-six survived until September:

> There were never Englishmen left in a foreign country in such misery as we were in this new discovered Virginia. We watched every three nights lying on the bare cold ground, what whether soever came . . . ; which brought our men to be most feeble wretches. Our food was but a small can of barley, sodden in water to five men a day. Our drink, cold water taken out of the river; which was at flood very salt: at low tide full of slim and filth, which was the destruction of many of our men. Thus we lived for the space of five months in this miserable distress, not having five able men to man our bulwarks upon any occasion.[120]

The arduous circumstances of the early colonists are reflected in a 1623 study that was made in Virginia. The study examined the Virginia population growth during the years 1607 through 1623. It documented immigration to Virginia, returns to England, numbers of deaths experienced in the colony, and the remaining population. It reflects the difficult conditions that faced the colonists:

        5,500 located to Virginia
-   300 returned to England
-   4,000 died
        1,200 living in Virginia in 1623[121]

As previously noted in lecture 1, in 1620 the Pilgrims arrived in America, and we have reviewed the Mayflower Compact, which documented their purposes for coming to

---

[120]. Quoted in Clarence B. Carson, *A Basic History of the United States* (Phoenix, AL: American Textbook Committee), 1:65.

[121]. Cited in Carson, *Basic History*, 1:66.

America—for the furtherance of the Christian faith. As also previously noted, due largely to unremitting religious wars in Europe, between 1630 and 1640 a great migration of Puritans to America occurred. During that period, over twenty thousand immigrated to America, almost exclusively in order to have religious freedom. Thus, religion played a major role in the migration to America. Immigrants wanted to worship according to the dictates of their own conscience but, interestingly, were often intolerant of other's desire to worship in their chosen way.

During the colonial period, the turmoil of European rivalry and monarchy were carried to the American colonies. With European powers holding claims in North America, it is not surprising that they sometimes clashed on the American continent. The French and Indian War (1754-1763) was a European war that spilled over to America. England and France were involved in one of their seemingly perpetual wars, and because the thirteen colonies were part of the British Empire, the Americans fought on the side of England. During this conflict, young George Washington gained valuable military experience and proved his mettle in combat.

The French and Indian War

SEEKING INDEPENDENCE

But the cost of unremitting European warfare heavily burdened the finances of the British Empire, and the king and the Parliament sought to fund many of their military encroachments by imposing onerous taxes upon their American colonies. Consequently, during the 1760s to 1770s numerous burdensome acts by the British government were imposed upon the American colonies. Due to the nature of these taxes and the manner in which they had been placed upon them, there was chaffing and growing discontent within the colonies, and Americans began to perceive themselves as "second-class citizens," having no representation in the British Parliament. In their resentment, they coined the term "no taxation without representation."

The Americans considered themselves freemen and had studied the works of men like William Blackstone, who documented the expectations of freemen. As they perceived growing infringement upon their unalienable rights as freemen, "Sons of Liberty" groups were organized to consider the cause of freedom in America. Committees of correspondence within each colony were organized to facilitate exchanges of information between the colonies and build unity regarding actions to ensure continuity among the colonies. American efforts at reconciliation with the king and his Parliament were generally rebuffed, and Americans became increasingly frustrated with British actions.

The Ride of Paul Revere

Battle of Lexington

By 1775, emotions and frustration on both sides of the Atlantic had reached a boiling point. The officers of the Crown decided to take precipitous action against the upstart colonists. The April 18, 1775, ride of Paul Revere and others was precipitated by hundreds of British troops marching from Boston to Lexington and Concord, Massachusetts, in an effort of the king's officers to disarm the colonists and capture Sam Adams and John Hancock. On the morning of April 19, the British troops confronted the local militia at Lexington and Concord, and the "shot heard round the world" was fired as hostilities commenced.

It was during this tumultuous period that Patrick Henry delivered his "Give me liberty or give me death" speech in Virginia.

Signing of Declaration of Independence

In light of all the developments, by July 1776, Americans felt that they had exhausted all of their peaceful options, and they prepared and signed their magnificent Declaration of Independence.

THE ILLUMINATI

Adam Weishaupt

It is interesting to note that as Americans sought to preserve their God-given rights and establish a government philosophy that recognized and preserved those rights, a movement based upon the antithesis of these concepts was founded. On May 1, 1776, a movement called the Illuminati was established by Adam Weishaupt in Europe. Its purpose was to abolish all religion, destroy all existing forms of government, and establish a new tyranny based upon a new order of rulers. As we shall discover in lectures 13 and 14, this event would ultimately adversely affect not only the new United States, but freedom-loving people all across the world. The following books, which were written and published during the American founding era, document official investigations of the Illuminati that were conducted in Europe:

Proofs of a Conspiracy (1798)
The History of Jacobinism (1798)

THE REVOLUTIONARY WAR

Revolutionary Soldiers

After the representatives of the people signed the Declaration of Independence, efforts were begun to create a constitution for the new United States. The efforts to write and ratify this new constitution, the Articles of Confederation, were long and frustrating, taking from August 1776 to 1781. The Articles of Confederation proved to be wholly inadequate to the governance of this nation. The Revolutionary War was nearly lost as it was fought under this flawed document.

As the Revolutionary War went forward, defeats were too many and victories were too few. The new nation struggled to find its way. The agonies and challenges of winters spent in Valley Forge and Morristown had to be faced. The Continental Army spent much of its time in retreat, trying to avoid a fatal defeat.

TO PRESERVE THE NATION

Washington Takes Command of American Forces

Toward the end of the Revolutionary War, George Washington was shocked, disappointed, and chagrined as he learned of efforts that were being made by disgruntled military officers to anoint Washington as the king of America through a military coup (this subject will be reviewed at some length in lecture 15). Washington vigorously opposed this effort and prevented it from happening.

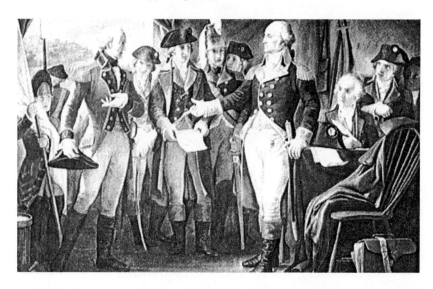

Surrender of Cornwallis

Finally, in spite of seemingly insurmountable challenges, on October 19, 1781, the American forces (with the assistance of French ships that blocked the Royal Navy from withdrawing their forces by sea) defeated British general Cornwallis at Yorktown, Virginia. The 1783 Treaty of Paris officially ended the Revolutionary War.

Yorktown

The United States Constitution

Signing of the U.S. Constitution

Although the war was over, the new nation began to unravel. The semblance of unity that had prevailed because of the common war effort disappeared, and the newly independent states began to bicker amongst themselves, almost treating one another as separate independent countries. European powers stood on the sidelines, expecting the new nation to dissolve and leave opportunity for new European colonies to be established.

Wise American statesmen saw that the Articles of Confederation lacked much that was needed to govern the nation and, consequently, called a constitutional convention to correct the deficiencies. The convention met behind closed doors in Philadelphia, Pennsylvania, from

May through September 1787 and (in spite of their charge to simply suggest changes and corrections to rectify the Articles of Confederation) created an entirely new constitution.

There were great difficulties experienced in the effort to obtain ratification of the new constitution, establish the new government under the new constitution, and frame a bill of rights to help ensure that God-given unalienable rights would be preserved, but finally the nation was able to step forward in the light of its divinely inspired freedom.

WARNINGS AGAINST ENTANGLING ALLIANCES

European powers continued to seek to manipulate the new United States for European purposes, but through the great leadership and efforts of wise American statesmen, the nation was able to avoid "entangling alliances" with foreign powers that would have undermined the nation's sovereignty. In light of developments in the twentieth and twenty-first centuries that violate the sound counsel given as the founder's original intent, the following are examples of admonitions on this subject that were given to the nation by those who stood at the head as the nation was established:

> Europe has a set of primary interests which to us have none or a very remote relation. Hence she must be engaged in frequent controversies, the causes of which are essentially foreign to our concerns. Hence, therefore, it must be unwise in us to implicate ourselves by artificial ties in the ordinary vicissitudes of her politics or the ordinary combinations and collisions of her friendships or enmities . . . .
>
> Why forego the advantages of so peculiar a situation? Why quit our own to stand upon foreign ground? Why, by interweaving our destiny with that of any part of Europe, entangle our peace and prosperity in the toils of European ambition, rivalship, interest, humor, or caprice?[122]
>
> I have ever deemed it fundamental for the United States never to take part in the quarrels of Europe. Their political interests are entirely distinct from ours. Their mutual jealousies, their balance of power, their complicated alliances, their forms and principles of government are all foreign to us. They are nations of eternal war.[123]
>
> I am for free commerce with all nations, political connection with none, and little or no diplomatic establishment. And I am not for linking ourselves by new treaties with the quarrels of Europe, entering that field of slaughter to preserve their balance, or joining in the confederacy of kings to war against the principles of liberty.[124]

[122.] George Washington's Farewell Address.
[123.] Bergh, *Thomas Jefferson*, 15:436.
[124.] To Elbridge Gerry, in Bergh, *Thomas Jefferson*, 10:77.

Commerce with all nations, alliance with none, should be our motto.[125]

I deem [one of] the essential principles of our government, and consequently [one] which ought to shape its administration, . . . peace, commerce, and honest friendship with all nations, entangling alliances with none.[126]

America has abstained from interference in the concerns of others, even when the conflict has been for principles to which she clings . . . . She goes not abroad in search of monsters to destroy. She is the well-wisher to the freedom and independence of all. She is the champion and vindicator only of her own.[127]

And in the inspired "Monroe Doctrine," we find James Monroe's great wisdom:

In the wars of European powers in matters relating to themselves we have never taken any part, nor does it comport with our policy so to do . . . . Our policy in regard to Europe . . . is, not to interfere in the internal concerns of any of its powers.

James Monroe

[125.] Paul Leicester Ford, ed., *The Writings of Thomas Jefferson*, 10 vols. (New York: G. P. Putnam & Sons, 1799), 7:374.

[126.] Thomas Jefferson's first inaugural address in Bergh, *Thomas Jefferson*, 3:321.

[127.] John Quincy Adams, address in Washington DC, July 4, 1821.

This position became the official policy of the United States and was largely followed until the twentieth century. The United States grew and prospered under it. And the nation avoided the almost constant bloodshed that was occurring throughout the rest of the world.

The War of 1812

In spite of the best efforts of great early American statesmen to avoid conflict, continued imperial actions by the British ultimately resulted in the War of 1812—which has been called by some the "We Really Mean We are Free and Independent" war.

The following is a summary of causes that resulted in the War of 1812:

—In spite of requirements established by the 1783 Treaty of Paris, England never really completely left U.S. territory after the Revolutionary War.

—Ongoing European conflicts (especially England vs. France) sought to involve and implicate the U.S.

—"Impressment" of American seamen by England. British naval vessels would stop U.S. ships and kidnap American seamen, claiming that they were British citizens who owed service to the British Navy.

—Seizure of U.S. ships by British war ships and interdiction of U.S. commerce on the high seas was a common practice of England.

The United States was poorly prepared for war and, initially the war, particularly on land, went poorly for the United States. The Atlantic coastline of the United States was subjected to attacks by the British. As Fort McHenry was shelled during the Battle for Baltimore, as he watched the spectacular British bombardment of the harbor through the night, and as the rockets red glare lit up the American flag that flew over the fort, Francis Scott Key wrote the words which became "The Star-Spangled Banner."

During the course of the war, the American army faced many defeats. Washington DC was seized by the British and the White House burned. However, the Americans enjoyed some notable sea victories, and the Battle of New Orleans (which was fought after war was over—due to poor/slow communications) was a resounding victory for the Americans.

Texan Independence and the Mexican War

In an event which ultimately affected United States history, Mexico became independent from Spain in 1821 and claimed most of the North American territory previously claimed by Spain. It would be fair to say that in so doing, Mexico "overreached" its dominion, lacking the ability to defend and preserve its claimed territory.

David Crockett

After some years of chafing under Mexican rule, Texas sought independence from Mexico. This independence effort led to armed resistance at the Alamo, from February to March 1836. One hundred fifty-seven men, who were joined by thirty additional volunteers, fought Santa Anna's Mexican army of four thousand. All 187 Texans and Americans at the Alamo died, including Davy Crockett (former U.S. congressman), Jim Bowie, and Will Travis.

James Bowie

TO PRESERVE THE NATION

William Barret Travis

In spite of the ultimate resounding defeat of the Mexican army by the Texans, Texan independence was never officially recognized by Mexico. Consequently, in 1845, when Texas accepted the offer to join the United States, the United States was drawn into a boundary dispute with Mexico.

Fall of the Alamo 1836

The Mexican-American War resulted from this boundary dispute as Texas joined the American Union. Prior to hostilities beginning, the United States made numerous attempts to negotiate a peaceful resolution through purchase of the disputed territory. The following is a brief summary of proposals that were offered:

- The United States proposed the Rio Grande as the boundary between Mexico and the United States
- The United States offered to assume and pay claims made by Americans against Mexico in return for what ultimately became Eastern New Mexico
- The United States offered $5 million to purchase the western half of what ultimately became New Mexico
- More than $20 million was offered to purchase California

Mexico refused all offers. Their logic for so doing was interesting: the Mexican government felt too weak to carry out any agreement due to the fact that revolutions to overthrow the Mexican government were virtually annual occurrences in that nation, and it was feared that subsequent governments would repudiate any agreement with the United States.

In response to an encroachment incident—Mexicans entered Texas—the United States declared war against Mexico on May 13, 1846. Mexico fought a largely defensive war. The U.S. actions against Mexico experienced challenges such as long supply lines and long marches as the United States took the war to Mexico. From the beginning, U.S. victory seemed a foregone conclusion. U.S. forces easily expelled Mexico from California, and on September 14, 1847, U.S. forces occupied Mexico City. The Treaty of Guadalupe Hildalgo was negotiated to conclude hostilities, and the U.S. Senate ratified the treaty in March 1848. Under the terms of the treaty are the following:

- The Rio Grande became the southern border of Texas.
- The United States *purchased* California and New Mexico (including territory which became other states) for $15 million, and the United States agreed to pay American citizens' claims against Mexico, up to $3.25 million.

These monetary arrangements were made in spite of the complete American military victory over Mexico. Later, the United States paid Mexico $10 million for the Gadsden Purchase, which included Southern portions of the states of Arizona and New Mexico, for use as future potential railroad routes.

THE COMMUNIST MANIFESTO

In keeping with our practice of sometimes noting world events that would prove of significance to the United States, we note at this time a concurrent world event that would ultimately effect the United States: *The Communist Manifesto* was published in 1848. The stated purpose of communism is to abolish all religion, destroy all existing forms of government, establish a new order of rulers. The similarities between the Illuminati and communism are more than uncanny and happenstantial. The linkage is unequivocal and will be discussed in future lectures.

TO PRESERVE THE NATION

THE CIVIL WAR

While the American Civil War deserves a greatly expanded review, it shall not be attempted here due to the "overview" perspective purpose of this lecture. The potential of dissolution of the American nation was a concern early in the nation's existence. In his monumental Farewell Address, George Washington foresaw the dangers of "sectionalism" within the nation and, in 1796, warned against regional antipathies. It is interesting to note that the Southern states were not the first to consider secession. Due to anger about the Republican movement under Thomas Jefferson (versus the Federalist movement under John Adams), Massachusetts first considered secession in the days of Jefferson's presidential administration.

The causes of the Civil War are complex, and while the slavery issue played a role, it was by no means the only cause (in spite of attempts by many historians to simplify the facts in this matter)! Competitive economic preeminence between the North and South certainly must be considered among the primary causes; and state rights versus a "centrist" government were also principle motivators.

Robert E. Lee

A principle participant in the war who deserves additional study is Robert E. Lee. He was a Virginian. Virginia was a Southern state and cast their lot with the secessionist cause. Lee's prowess as a military leader was universally recognized in America as the war loomed. Lincoln offered him the assignment of leading the Union Army against the South. Lee refused, acknowledging that he could never fight against his home state, and while he loved the United States, he could not find much joy in a Union which must be held together at the point of a bayonet. Lee's sterling character remained untarnished to the end of his life, and his principles and character are worthy of study and emulation by all Americans!

AMERICAN HISTORY TIME LINE

Stonewall Jackson

JEB Stuart

Southern generals Thomas J. "Stonewall" Jackson and J. E. B. Stuart are also worthy of study and emulation.

TO PRESERVE THE NATION

General Hooker

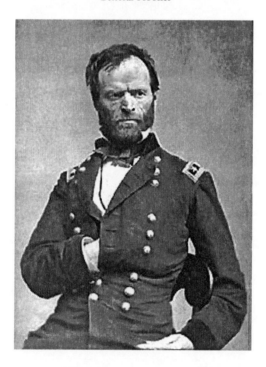

William T Sherman

Union generals such as Ulysses S. Grant, William T. Sherman, Ambrose Burnside, and Joseph Hooker should also be mentioned and studied, but for different reasons.

General U. S. Grant

While much ado is made of Lincoln's Emancipation Proclamation, it, in reality, is a strange anomaly in the war. The Proclamation declared that *only* slaves in the rebellious states that had seceded were declared as set free. It did nothing for the slaves who resided in states that had not left the Union. Had the Southern states succeeded in their efforts to secede, the Proclamation would have been of no effect because the Confederate States would be an independent nation and not subject to any edicts of the United States. It would appear that the Emancipation Proclamation was a tactic of the war designed to give the perception of a stronger moral basis to the actions of the Union and to create a state of rebellion among the "freed" slaves of the South, thereby confuting the war efforts of the South against the North.

General Burnside

Fortunately, the nation ultimately was not dissolved, and everyone throughout this great nation still may live under and enjoy the blessings of an inspired United States Constitution (albeit largely misunderstood today). Unfortunately, the costs of this war and schism were, and still are, terrible. Many of the foundational principles upon which this nation was established were forgotten or subverted. The delicate balance of power created under the "original intent" of the founders has been largely set aside, and the validity of the founder's fear of centralized power has been graphically demonstrated as the volume of usurped power at the national level has expanded exponentially through the years.

The "radical Republicans" who held power in the United States Congress in the years following the Civil War proved to be tyrants, indeed, as they "deconstructed" the South and set the stage for the growth of a leviathan national government that would vastly overstep the bounds originally established by the nation's founders.

From every perspective, the Civil War was a tragic event in American history. With Americans killing Americans, it (by far) is the most deadly and destructive war (from an American perspective) that the nation has been engaged in. Over six hundred thousand Americans died in the war, and the suffering of wounded and destruction of the nation's infrastructure and goodwill is untold. Not only did the American Civil War severely damage the nation's form of government, it also marked the beginnings of the modern concept of "total war" and foreshadowed the conflagrations that now engulf civilian and military populations alike throughout the world in modern "shock and awe" wars.

Diverging from the American Formula

With the progressive "unraveling" of proper government principle since the Civil War, America has faced many growing challenges that, increasingly, threatened the continued existence of the nation under the United States Constitution! Since the Civil War, increasingly aggressive efforts that undermine the sound national foundation that was created as the country was established have been foisted upon the nation. In this ongoing scheme, 1913 proved to be a very bad year for the United States! In 1913 the following actions created national problems that continue unabated:

— The Federal Reserve System was established, allowing a profit-driven private banking system that creates debt-based money out of thin air to largely control the nation's economy
— The Sixteenth Amendment—Income tax was implemented, allowing the national government to access the resources of the American people without involving the states
— The Seventeenth Amendment—Direct election of senators was ratified, removing representation of the states at the national level

Lecture 8 graphically demonstrates the deleterious effects of these actions on the American economy!

WORLD WAR I AND THE LEAGUE OF NATIONS

World War I followed shortly after the betrayals of 1913, accelerating the movement away from the Founding Fathers' original intent for the United States. Tragic events in Europe led up to and precipitated what should have been a very limited conflict:

- Bosnia and Herzegovina had been annexed by Austria in October 1908, and that action irritated the Serbs—they wanted those provinces for their Serbian empire.
- In June of 1914, the archduke of Austria, Franz Ferdinand, and his pregnant wife, Sophie, visited Sarajevo, the capital of Bosnia.

Archduke of Austria Assasinated

- Franz Ferdinand was the heir to the Austro-Hungarian throne, and a secret society of Serbian nationalists (called "the Black Hand" or "Union or Death") plotted his assassination. The Founding Fathers of the United States called conspirators such as this "secret combinations." (Secret combinations: a term coined by the American founders to describe conspiratorial efforts to usurp power or destroy liberty, subvert proper government, or pursue improper design—see lecture 11 for Noah Webster's definition).
- On June 28, 1914, a group of Serbs from this secret combination, which were closely aligned with many elements of the Serbian government, were successful in their attempt to murder the archduke and his wife.

- As a consequence of this action, Austria declared war on Serbia. Based upon treaties of alliance (entangling alliances) that required successive nations to come to the aid of offended nations with whom they were aligned, the rest of Europe quickly took sides. The world was well on the way to war within thirty days.
- Russia stepped forward to help Serbia, Germany responded on the side of Austria to counter Russia's involvement. Germany and Turkey had an alliance for defense in the event of war, consequently Russia declared war on Turkey, then Great Britain and France declared war on Turkey.
- Millions of lives were ultimately lost in the devastating trench warfare that followed, and millions more died as a result of the related pestilence.
- It would be difficult to conceive of a more senseless and tragic war, but it is even more inane to imagine any justification for the United States to enter the fray.
- Entangling alliances drew the world into this irrational conflagration, but at the time, the United States had no such alliances which placed demands on this nation to enter the war.

Efforts were quickly applied in an effort to pull the United States into a war that should never have been entered into:

- President Woodrow Wilson took a public position against U.S. involvement in the war, while privately seeking entrance into the war
- "Col." Edward Mandell House, Wilson's "alter ego," sought diligently on both sides of the Atlantic to precipitate U.S. involvement in the war. House had long entertained dreams of overthrowing the United States Constitution,[128] and House saw an opportunity to further his socialist views through involving the United States in World War I
- As they coined the term "Making the World Safe for Democracy," the Wilson/House efforts finally resulted in the United States entering the war in 1917
- America's involvement quickly turned the tide of the stalemated war, and Germany and his allies were defeated. The world was devastated and war weary. The nations of the world were desperate for a permanent solution and peace. President Woodrow Wilson and Edward Mandel House drew up a plan that would create a world body that would be the foundation of world government. They called it the League of Nations and sought to incorporate it into the peace treaty so it would have to be accepted if the peace treaty the world so desperately sought was signed

---

[128.] See Edward Mandell House's book *Philip Dru: Administrator*, which was first published in 1912 and which proposed a fanciful scenario in which a benevolent "elite" leader implements socialism in the United States.

The peace treaty that was to end World War I was called the Treaty of Versailles. It was not an agreement that was "negotiated" with the defeated nations. It was dictated and imposed upon Germany. The treaty was extremely punitive against Germany and set the stage for World War II. In the treaty are the following:

- Land was taken from Germany and given to France, Poland, and Czechoslovakia
- German colonies were confiscated, and trade sanctions against Germany were implemented
- Huge war reparations payments were required from Germany, which responded by printing huge volumes of unbacked (worthless) paper money, causing hyperinflation[129]

As previously noted, the League of Nations was incorporated into the Treaty of Versailles, and it was presented to the United States Senate as a "package deal" (meaning, peace would not be achieved, and the war would continue, if the Senate attempted to remove the League of Nations from the package) in an attempt to implement the United States into a collectivist/socialist world government (by subverting the United States Constitution). In violation of the Founding Fathers original intent, entangling alliances that required the United States to enter into future wars were an integral part of the League of Nations. Consequently, the treaty and league were rejected by U.S. Senate, and a separate peace treaty was ultimately negotiated between the United States and the belligerents.

Wilson at Versailles

---

[129]. See lecture 8.

TO PRESERVE THE NATION

House and Wilson were heartbroken by the Senate's rejection of the League of Nations. As a result of what he learned from this failed experience, House was convinced that additional "groundwork" was needed to prepare the United States to embrace future efforts to implement his plan. Consequently, he established the Council on Foreign Relations (CFR), an organization created to ultimately promote socialist world government and integrate the United States into that government through a long-term effort to "educate" the American public and its leaders. The Council on Foreign Relations is headquartered in New York City and boasts a membership including some of the most prominent Americans and national figures. Today, its members, though only about four thousand strong, fill a very high percentage of key government positions at both the national and state levels, as well as pivotal positions in the media, business, and education.

Edward Mandell House

Following World War I, there was a dramatic rise of what may be termed tyranny-promoting "isms" worldwide. Russia fell under communism as a result of the 1917 Communist Revolution. Fascism swept over in Italy the 1920s. National socialists (Nazis) seized the reins of power in Germany during the 1930s through the election process. Military imperialism blossomed in Japan. And the different forms of tyranny sought preeminence in struggles throughout the nations of the world as these tyrants vied for power. An example can be found in the Spanish Civil War, in which the communists and fascists sought to implement their form of poison over the peoples of that land. It was as though gangs of criminals sought to control nations.

World War II

While most of the citizens of the United States were apparently oblivious to the conspiratorial forces that were insidiously working to bring about a devastating war that would ultimately engulf the entire world and take the lives of approximately fifty-five million human beings, some (rare) inspired statesmen attempted to warn those who were wise enough to hear the watchmen on the tower. Former U.S. undersecretary of state J. Reuben Clark Jr. made the following statement regarding predictions of World War II in an address delivered in April 1937:

> Nevertheless there is strongest reason for believing that some of the most skilled, astute, and shrewd diplomats, politicians, and statesmen of all Europe are now planning to have the people of the United States finance the next European war either before the war begins or during its progress.
>
> Furthermore, certain of these same diplomats, politicians, and statesmen are planning to entice the United States into an offensive and defensive military alliance in order that we shall participate in that next world war by sending our young men to the battlefields of Europe. The argument they now plan to use to bring this about is that in this way only can the peace of the world be preserved. While this is a most profound fallacy, it will unfortunately find a sympathetic ear among many of the people of this country who do not fully understand international relations. It will require the wisest statesmanship on our part to prevent the United States from becoming again the victim of a world military catastrophe.[130]

About this time, Britain signed a mutual defense treaty with Poland. This entangling alliance required Britain to go to war in the event Poland was attacked. Other entangling alliances already existed that would quickly create another "domino" effect similar to what happened at the beginning of World War I, once the first shots were fired.

In August 1939, Hitler of Germany and Stalin of Russia signed their secret "nonaggression pact" in which they divided Europe into "spheres of influence"—Stalin was to take his chunk of Eastern Europe and Hitler staked out his territory. The next month they invaded Poland and divided the spoils, thus beginning World War II. Of course, before then we had English Prime Minister Chamberlain giving Hitler what was not his right to give and then promising the world peace.

[130.] Conference Report, April 1937.

Hitler

England and the host of entangling alliances in Western Europe promptly declared war on Germany as a result of Germany's Polish invasion. Germany responded by leashing the "blitzkrieg" (lightning) war on Western Europe and quickly destroyed Europe's defenses. When Hitler had secured his rear by subduing Western Europe, he turned his attention to the east, focusing on his real goal—Russia, and her wealth of natural resources.

Meanwhile, United States president Franklin Delano Roosevelt and Soviet operatives—such as Harry Hopkins, Alger Hiss, and Harry Dexter White—who were highly placed in the American administration, were seeking to get into the fray on the side of the Soviets, but they thought that they could only get away with a certain amount of overt aid without a declaration of war and a formal alliance with the Soviets.

Franklin DeLano Roosevelt

Japan's imperialistic actions, along with her (entangling) alliances with Germany and Italy, opened the way for Roosevelt. Through trade sanctions against Japan, he set up the scenario in which Japan was motivated to attack the United States. If Japan attacked the United States, the United States would declare war on Japan, precipitating reciprocal declarations of war on the United States by Japan and her allies, Germany and Italy. The United States would then declare war on Germany and Italy. These actions would instantly put the United States in the war on the side of Russia. In this, we find another perfect example of how entangling alliances work and why the American founders so passionately warned their nation against them.

There is excellent documentation regarding Roosevelt's prior knowledge of the pending attack on Pearl Harbor, but he did nothing to avert it or mitigate its devastation. He left our troops, sailors, civilian populations, ships, aircraft, etc. in their most vulnerable position as sitting ducks. It has been suggested that he needed a "day of infamy" that would rally all of America to a unified cry for war. If such were the case, he got what he wanted and slaughtered not only the thousands of Americans on December 7, 1941, but cost the lives of hundreds of thousands over the next four years—in the process, changing the nation in countless ways, from its family values, its morality, its view of government, its workforce, its economics, etc.

Stalin

By this means, America entered World War II on the side of Joseph Stalin and his godless communist government. A detailed study of U.S. efforts on behalf of Stalin and his communist regime is appalling and shocking. Stalin's depredations upon his own people should make God-fearing people weep. Is it, for example, worse to kill six million Jews as Hitler did or to kill ten million kulaks as Stalin did? Each is horrible and each will bring upon their perpetrators the judgments of God. In spite of this, the United States chose to sustain "Uncle Joe Stalin" when the chips were down. The United States sent over 490,000 vehicles to Stalin during the war, along with other countless tons of war material and billions of dollars of aid. Well-documented evidence indicates that the leaders of this nation often placed support of Stalin's war effort above support of our own troops in the field, allowing, at times, for our own troops to "go without" in order to provide material to Stalin.

Relatively early in the war, the United States military established a toehold in the Mediterranean from which we could have launched an attack against the "soft underbelly" of Europe, which would have allowed us to sweep north through Yugoslavia, Romania, and Hungary to quickly defeat Germany; but at Stalin's insistence, the Western Front, he demanded, had to be opened on the coasts of France. He wanted the oil fields and rich farmlands of Yugoslavia, Romania, and Hungary as his own prizes, and he feared that U.S. presence in that area would preclude his evil designs on the region, as well as ultimately threaten the borders of his debauched regime. So Roosevelt agreed to back up and launch the invasion from England—at great risk and expense to America.

The war in the Pacific was a series of murderously brutal "island-hopping" battles in which the valor of Americans was demonstrated countless times. It is reported that by February 1945, Japan made overtures to senior American leaders to surrender under terms similar to terms that ultimately ended the war in September, but those overtures were ignored and not acted upon. The bloody battles of Iwo Jima and Okinawa and others followed, and finally, in August, the United States dropped the atomic bombs on Hiroshima and Nagasaki, Japan, precipitating the unconditional surrender of Japan. It is of interest to note that in the days between the atomic bomb attacks on Hiroshima and Nagasaki, the Soviets had entered the war against Japan and, therefore, "earned" a "share" of the victory over Japan and a "toehold" in that region.

Churchill, Roosevelt, Stalin

The tales of Roosevelt's "concessions" to Stalin throughout the war are amazing, but few exceed the treachery of the agreements at Yalta and Teheran. In those agreements, Roosevelt basically conceded to Stalin the territories that Hitler and Stalin had agreed in their secret 1939 "nonaggression pact" for him to pillage, plunder, and enslave. In a manner similar to Chamberlain's betrayal of Czechoslovakia to Hitler, Roosevelt "gave away" sovereign peoples and nations to the man who is arguably the most wicked tyrant of the twentieth century. And then, Roosevelt apparently agreed to return to slavery those people who had fled the oppression of communism by migrating westward into Europe during the war. The number is not definitely known, but estimates range between two and five million people who were rounded up by American troops and, under force of arms, were returned to the chains of communist slavery. Several hundred thousand committed suicide rather than face again the repression they had suffered under the hands of the Soviet taskmasters. Those millions of people who were returned lived out their lives in slave labor camps, in many cases suffering a fate worse than death. This "operation" came to be termed Operation Keelhaul by the U.S. Pentagon and is well documented. General Dwight D. Eisenhower presided over this operation, but perhaps it could be said that he was "only following orders"—in much the same defense that was offered by those who participated in Hitler's Final Solution to the Jewish Problem.

THE FOUNDING OF THE UNITED NATIONS

UN Flag

With the war won, the way was open for another run at world government! Actually, prior to the end of the war, the plans were well underway for establishment of the United Nations. In fact, the term United Nations was commonly applied to the coalition of allies who opposed the Axis (Germany, Japan, and Italy) powers. Alger Hiss, as previously mentioned, was a man who had held high position in Roosevelt's administration and who later would be revealed as a Soviet operative, and he was chosen to preside over the creation of the organization that would be the successor of the League of Nations. When examining the makeup of those chosen to create the United Nations, it would be difficult to imagine the assembly of a body of individuals more dedicated to the destruction of traditional values of American government or a group more obsessed with the implementation of global socialism. That is one of the reasons many were so pained when, on September 11, 1990, in a speech before Congress, President George H. W. Bush stated, "Out of these troubled times, our fifth objective—a new world order—can emerge . . . . We are now in sight of a United Nations that performs as envisioned by its founders."

United Nations Building

In another tragic turn of events, as World War II closed out, the U.S. State Department arranged to deliver captured Japanese arms to the communist Chinese, who were led by Mao Tse-tung. In much the same manner as Fidel Castro of Cuba was presented a few years later, Mao was presented to the American public as an "agrarian reformer," not the communist tyrant he was.

Fidel Castro

Applying lessons learned during the failed attempt to ratify the League of Nations after World War I, in 1945 the promoters of the United Nations prevented extensive debate over the United Nations Charter as it was presented to the United States Senate to ratify the U.S. membership and received quick ratification with almost no opposition. Afterward, however, after they had carefully reviewed the treaty, astute and experienced statesmen voiced strong concerns about the United Nations Charter and purposes. Former U.S. Undersecretary of State J. Reuben Clark Jr. made the following statement on the UN after reviewing the charter:

> There is no provision in the Charter itself that contemplates ending war. The Charter is built to prepare for war, not to promote peace. The Charter is a war document, not a peace document (it doesn't) prevent future wars, it takes from us the power to declare them, to choose the side on which we shall fight, to determine what forces and military equipment we shall use in the war, and to control and command our sons who do the fighting.[131]

The United Nations Charter is structured as the framework of a world government, and while there are superficial parallels, there is nothing within that framework that would reflect true similarity to the structure that is contained within the United States Constitution. The UN is *not* designed to limit government power, recognize God-given rights, or preserve the form of government Americans cherish.

Subsets within the UN called "regional arrangements" are designed to facilitate governance by the United Nations and move the participating nations into compliance with the purposes of the United Nations. For example, careful review of the United Nations Charter and the North Atlantic Treaty Organization (NATO) charter reveal that they are mother and son. In the United Nations Charter, we read,

United Nations Charter
Chapter VIII
Article 52

1. Nothing in the present Charter precludes the existence of regional arrangements or agencies for dealing with matters relating to the maintenance of international peace and security as are appropriate for regional action, provided that such arrangements are consistent with the Purposes and Principles of the United Nations.
2. The members of the United Nations entering into such arrangements or constituting such agencies shall make every effort to achieve pacific settlement

---

[131] J. Reuben Clark Jr., *Selected Papers on International Affairs*, edited by David H. Yarn Jr. (Brigham Young University Press), 437-470. White paper review of the United Nations Charter.

of local disputes through such regional arrangements or by such regional agencies before referring them to the Security Council.
3. The Security Council shall encourage the development of pacific settlement of local disputes such as regional arrangements or by such regional agencies either on the initiative of the states concerned or by reference from the Security Council.
4. This Article in no way impairs the application of Articles 34 and 35.

Article 53

1. The Security Council shall, where appropriate, utilize such regional arrangements or agencies for enforcement action under its authority. But no enforcement action shall be taken under regional arrangements or by regional agencies without the authorization of the Security Council . . . .

In the NATO Handbook, we read,

NATO Handbook
February 1972

The signatory countries undertake, in conformity with the terms of the United Nations Charter . . . .
 The Treaty is an agreement between certain countries for their collective self-defense as provided for in Article 51 of the Charter of the United Nations.
 . . . it is a Treaty of alliance within the framework of the Charter of the United Nations . . .

And the NATO Treaty specifies,

The North Atlantic Treaty
Washington D.C., 4 April 1949

The parties to this Treaty reaffirm their faith in the purposes and principles of the Charter of the United Nations . . .

ARTICLE 1

The Parties undertake, as set forth in the Charter of the United Nations, to settle any international dispute in which they may be involved by peaceful means in such a manner that international peace and security and justice are not endangered, and to refrain in their international relations from the threat or use of force in any manner inconsistent with the purposes of the United Nations.

ARTICLE 5

The parties agree that an armed attack against one or more of them in Europe or North America shall be considered an attack against them all, and consequently they agree that, if such an armed attack occurs, each of them, in exercise of the right of individual or collective self-defense recognized by Article 51 of the Charter of the United Nations, will assist the Party or Parties so attacked by taking forthwith, individually and in concert with the other Parties, such action as it deems necessary, including the use of armed force, to restore and maintain the security of the North Atlantic area.

Any such armed attack and all measures taken as a result thereof shall immediately be reported to the Security Council. Such measures shall be terminated when the Security Council has taken measures necessary to restore and maintain international peace and security.

ARTICLE 7

This Treaty does not affect, and shall not be interpreted as affecting, in any way the rights and obligations under the Charter of the Parties which are members of the United Nations, or the primary responsibility of the Security Council for the maintenance of international peace and security.

The NATO treaty stipulates that an attack on one of the member nations requires other member nations to enter the conflict in defense of the attacked nation, just like the alliances of Europe prior to both World War I and World War II dragged the other nations into warfare and dramatically expanded what should have been at most a limited conflict.

In brief, the NATO treaty, of which the United States is a signatory member, which is simply a recognized subset of the United Nations organization, requires the United States to go to war if a member of NATO is ever attacked—in direct violation of the advice of the Founding Fathers to not involve the nation in entangling alliances. Of course, the United States has entered into numerous other similar United Nations-sanctioned "regional arrangements" that have similar requirements.

The nation's founders pled with the nation to avoid such entanglements and used impeccable logic to explain why such agreements must be avoided. The following statement by Tucker in his *View of the Constitution of the United States reinforces* the principle that constitutional protocol not be put aside by such foolish agreements. In 1803, Tucker foresaw the dangers that would face the nation if the nation's leadership violated the wise advice that had been given by the Founding Fathers:

> Let it be supposed, for example, that the president and senate should stipulate by treaty with any foreign nation, that in case of war between that nation and any other, the United States should immediately declare against that nation: Can

it be supposed that such a treaty would be so far the law of the land, as to take from the house of representatives their constitutional right to deliberate on the expediency or inexpediency of such a declaration of war, and to determine and act thereon, according to their own judgment?[132]

And in this lecture series, we discuss at length the fact that constitutional protocol prohibits a power that was constitutionally delegated by the people of the nation to Congress to be redelegated by Congress to another individual or body (foreign or domestic). Consequently, the power to involve the United States in war resides *only with the United States Congress and may not be constitutionally delegated (usurped) through treaty or any other means.*

OTHER MODERN ENTANGLING ALLIANCES

Since World War II, and the entrance of the United States into the United Nations and other UN-approved "regional arrangements," the United States has been engulfed in almost perpetual war. None of these wars were entered into via the *constitutional* processes, but were simply in fulfillment of stipulations of entangling alliances. The following examples could be cited:

— Korea (entered into based upon United Nations' directives)
— Vietnam (entered into based upon the Southeast Asia Treaty Organization [SEATO], another "regional arrangement" under the United Nations)
— Bosnia (the United Nations directed NATO to take over the "enforcement" process the UN had previously directly participated in)
— Kuwait (Gulf War I) (UN Resolutions used as justification and, as previously noted, President George H. W. Bush hoped the action would facilitate a more powerful and influential UN)
— Iraq (Gulf War II) (The October 2002 Congressional Iraq War Resolution that unconstitutionally delegated the congressional power to decide whether or not to go to war to the president justified the war based upon UN resolutions)

In addition to the tragic events noted to this point, the so-called "cold war" seems to have been fostered by actions taken by American leadership. While the serious student will be motivated to do further research in this field, perhaps a few examples will suffice in support of the proposition that in the cold war, the United States faced the best enemies money could buy:

— The Soviet Union. The U.S. offered diplomatic recognition (legal validation as a nation, and the recognition of the brutally tyrannical Soviet system as the

---

[132.] Tucker, *View of the Constitution*, 277.

representative of the subjugated peoples) in the 1930s when the Soviet system was on the verge of collapse and provided economic assistance from the 1930s through the current period. During World War II war material and funding from the United States sustained the repressive Soviet regime; U.S. technology transfers to the Soviet Union through the decades allowed the Soviet Union to maintain a semblance of military parity with the United States, etc.
— China. The United States armed Mao Tse-tung after World War II, provided economic assistance, granted the "most favored nation" status, provided critically important defense-related technology transfers, etc.
— Al-Qaeda (Osama bin Laden) was a U.S. "ally" (1979-1989) during the Afghanistan-Soviet conflict; U.S. funds constructed the "hardened" underground Tora Bora complex for bin Laden in Afghanistan, which later became the "hideout" of bin Laden.
— Saddam Hussein, infamous tyrant of Iraq, was a U.S. ally against Iran during Iraq-Iran conflict; the CIA participated in "intelligence sharing" with Saddam, etc.

The efforts to further entangle the United States in poorly conceived alliances continues, and there has been an acceleration in recent years to involve the United States with globalist organizations in an effort to facilitate the merger of the United States into global government at expense of the United States Constitution. Recent sovereignty-destroying agreements include the following:

—North American Free Trade Agreement (NAFTA)
—General Agreement on Tariffs and Trade (GATT)
—World Trade Organization (WTO)
—Central American Free Trade Agreement (CAFTA)
—Security and Prosperity Partnership (SPP) (an expansion of NAFTA seeking the merger/integration of the United States, Canada, and Mexico)

LESSONS OF HISTORY

In his day, Thomas Jefferson spoke of actions taken by those in power that were inconsistent with liberty and proper government, saying,

> Single acts of tyranny may be ascribed to the accidental opinion of a day; but a series of oppressions, begun at a distinguished period, and pursued unalterably through every change of ministers, too plainly prove a deliberate, systematical plan of reducing us to slavery.[133]

[133.] Bergh, *Thomas Jefferson*, 1:193.

And so we end this lecture in like manner as we began.

In volume 1 of *The Life of Reason*, we read,

> Those who cannot remember the past are condemned to repeat it . . . . This is the condition of children and barbarians, in whom instinct has learned nothing from experience.[134]

George Santayana

History has many lessons to teach us.

History teaches us that the future is in many ways cast by what has gone before. By studying history, we may often project future events. Hopefully, Americans of this generation will be wise enough to learn the lessons of history and avoid the liberty-destroying dangers we have been so eloquently warned against and that we are able to see so plainly threatening the nation.

[134.] George Santayana, *The Life of Reason* (1905), 1:284.

5.

Overview of the United States Constitution

(A brief, simplified synopsis and outline of the baseline principles found in the United States Constitution)

Recommended Resources for the Serious Student:

The United States Constitution
Declaration of Independence
The Federalist Papers by J. Madison, A. Hamilton, J. Jay

Quotes, Articles, and Original Sources

By the 1770s, the leadership of the United States had substantial experience writing constitutions. They had created numerous constitutions within their home colonies and states (see *Colonial Origins of the American Constitution*, ed. Donald S. Lutz). They recognized the importance of constitutions as charters that defined the legal framework of government, created the limits and bounds of the government entity, and were superior to any legislative enactments that could occur within that entity. Consequently, after declaring the nation's independence in 1776, the representatives of the United States drafted a constitution for the new nation. The new constitution was called the Articles of Confederation. It created a loosely knit confederation of states that had banded together to break away from England and fight against England's efforts to resubjugate them. It took years to finally get ratified although the states treated it as if it had been ratified during the years they pursued the successful outcome of the Revolutionary War.

TO PRESERVE THE NATION

First Flag at Independence Hall

The experience under the Articles of Confederation was as close to utter failure as it could be without experiencing utter failure. The newly created United States nearly lost the Revolutionary War under the Articles of Confederation. The document and its framework proved itself wholly inadequate for the new nation. The powers necessary for the administration of a nation were not included in the document, and after the conclusion of the war, the nation was in danger of dissolving into bickering independent nation-states. The European powers watched from the sidelines, eagerly anticipating the dissolution of the nation and expecting to be able to swoop in and reestablish colonies in North American as the American experiment failed.

Independence Hall

Wise leaders of the United States saw the dire straits of the nation and sought a solution. Initial attempts, such as the Annapolis Convention, were poorly attended and did not have the charge to address the challenges that the entire nation faced under the faulty Articles of

OVERVIEW OF THE UNITED STATES CONSTITUTION

Confederation. Congress was convinced that the Articles needed to be corrected if the nation was to survive and asked the states to send representatives to a convention in Philadelphia, beginning in May 1787, to suggest corrections to the Articles.

All of the states sent their legally authorized representatives, except Rhode Island, who refused to participate. As they gathered a quorum toward the end of May, the delegates recognized (in spite of their clearly defined and limited charge to suggest *only* corrections to the Articles) that as the legally authorized representatives of the states and people, they had authority to set aside the Articles and create an entirely new constitution.

Considering the fatal flaws inherent within the Articles of Confederation, they immediately set the Articles aside and began the arduous task of creating a new constitution. Fortunately, they were honorable, noble men who sought to preserve the God-given blessings of liberty for themselves and their posterity, and they created a new government that was unique among all governments heretofore established.

The men who created the new constitution were well-steeped in history and had studied the different forms of government that had existed throughout history. With the insight of hindsight, they were able to identify desirable characteristics of government and undesirable characteristics of government. They were able to both learn from the mistakes of the past and to build upon the successes of the past.

But the final form of government created by the convention was far more than a composite of former governments. It was (and is) unique among all known governments. Those who were present during the long hot debates of the 1787 Convention testified that they were aware of the "hand of God," or the "finger of God," in their efforts and that divine intervention resulted in a form of government that exceeded all expectations and all excellence. In spite of almost continuous efforts to undermine and destroy it, it has endured for more than two centuries and has been the most copied (but never duplicated) form of government in history.

Under this constitution, the people of the United States became the freest, most prosperous, most respected, happiest people on earth. Its principles are both timeless and priceless. Contrary to current efforts to subvert and destroy the Constitution by creating the false belief that the Constitution is "outdated" and written for a long-gone "agrarian" society, it was designed to address the flaws of human nature that are associated with power and recurring attempts by tyrants (or would-be tyrants) to bring others into subjection. The characteristic of mankind to seek, obtain, and then begin to abuse power is not dependent upon the technological circumstances of society. That flawed tendency can and has been exhibited throughout all history and is still rampant today. The Constitution was set forth with timeless principles that are designed to restrain that disposition inherent in virtually all mankind—that tendency to ultimately abuse power.

The United States Constitution grants to the national government the specific power necessary to fulfill its proper role and withholds all other power from the national government. And the power that it does grant to the national government it divides and subdivides to ensure (if we will abide in its clearly defined construction) that power will not be usurped and the people lose their liberty.

As previously presented, the United States Constitution embodies the following essential "Americanist" principles of liberty:

Separation of powers—divided powers (legislative, executive, judicial). Each department holds only specified powers.

Written constitution—words have plain English meanings that may be known.

Enumerated powers—powers delegated to the national government are limited to those listed and specified.

Checks and balances—the departments of government may exercise powers to restrain and prevent usurpation by other departments. Some certain specified powers are shared between departments.

The United States Constitution follows a very simple, straightforward form that is logically organized and that groups associated information in an easily understood fashion. It is considered a "job description" for those who are called to hold office at the national level. The following material should be studied while reviewing the complete text of the United States Constitution, which is found in the appendix.

The United States Constitution is organized in a sort of outline form. The main headings are called "articles." There are only seven articles in the Constitution. We give each of the articles a brief description, below, which identifies the topic that is reviewed in the article. Within most of the articles are subheadings called "sections." The sections review subtopics under the article. There are also clauses under the articles and sections that provide additional detail and explanation. This lecture is not intended to provide a detailed exposition of every element of the Constitution, but is, rather, a general introductory overview to assist in the effort to become familiar with the document and facilitate further detailed study.

The following are the seven articles and the scope that is defined therein:

Article I
Legislative

Article II
Executive

Article III
Judicial

Article IV
"Catch-all" article that reviews several important aspects that needed to be defined at the national level:
    Interactions between states and recognition of actions taken by states
    Rights of citizens from state to state

OVERVIEW OF THE UNITED STATES CONSTITUTION

Admission of new states to the Union
Disposal of U.S. property requires approval of both houses of Congress
Every state to be guaranteed a republican form of government
National government is required to protect the states from invasion

Article V
Amendment process defined (the *only* legal way to change the Constitution)

Article VI
Debts incurred under the previous constitution, the Articles of Confederation, would be honored and repaid.
The United States Constitution is defined as the "Supreme Law of the Land."
An oath to support the United States Constitution is required of *all* who hold office.

Article VII
The process required to ratify the Constitution is defined.
Signed 17 September 1787
In the "Year of Our Lord"
12th Year of Independence

Article I—Legislative

Section 1—All legislative powers herein granted shall be vested in a Congress of the United States, which shall consist of a Senate and House of Representatives.

[Constitutionally, *all* legislative power that is granted to the national government of the United States is granted to *only* the House and Senate. And, of course, the legislative enactments of the legislature must be kept within the scope of power and bounds granted within the Constitution. Remember, the Constitution is superior to all other legislative acts and may not be violated by usurpation carried out by any element of the government it created. No other part of the national government may in *any* way, shape, or form create a new law. *None* of the other departments may legislate. The judiciary cannot, the executive cannot, and neither can the numerous departments that fall under the executive.]

Section 2—House of Representatives
    Chosen (elected) every second year to fulfill a two-year term of office
    Power of the purse (the House originates all legislation dealing with money)
    Elected directly by the people of the states (people are the source of power)
    Age twenty-five or older
    Seven years a citizen of United States
    Representation is based upon population (as determined by a census that will be conducted every ten years)

Power of impeachment is held by the House (power to bring charges against officeholders; this is the power to bring an indictment, not power to conduct a trial and convict)

Section 3—Senate
Two senators per state (states are equally represented)
Originally state legislatures selected senators (changed by the Seventeenth Amendment—the people of each state now directly elect their senators)
Six-year term of office
Thirty years old or older
U.S. citizen for a minimum of nine years

Power to *try* impeachments is held by the Senate (when the House has brought impeachment charges, the Senate conducts the trial); when the president of the United States is tried, the chief justice of the Supreme Court presides over that trial.

If the person who has been impeached is found guilty (two-thirds must find the impeached person guilty if the charges are to be upheld), the person is removed from office, may not hold office again, and may be tried in criminal court after removal from office.

Section 7
Funding bills originate in the House of Representatives
Senate may amend funding bills
Process for approval of legislation between both houses is defined
Presidential veto process is reviewed (how a presidential veto is overridden)

Section 8
Enumeration (listing) of powers of Congress
"Congress Shall have Power To . . ."

- Collect authorized taxes
- Pay national debts
- Provide for the common defense and general welfare of the nation
- Establish uniform duties, imposts and excises throughout the United States
- Borrow money
- Regulate commerce with foreign nations/interstate commerce/Indian Tribes
- Regulate immigration and naturalization
- Establish national bankruptcy laws
- Coin money and regulate its value, and regulate foreign currency exchange
- Establish a national standard of weights and measures
- Punish counterfeiting
- Establish post offices and post roads

OVERVIEW OF THE UNITED STATES CONSTITUTION

- Copyright/patent authority
- Create federal courts below the Supreme Court
- Create laws to punish piracy and terrorism
- Declare war
- Grant letters of marque and reprisal (subcontract war)
- Determine handling of wartime captures
- Raise and support armies
- Provide and Maintain the navy
- Make rules to govern and regulate the U.S. military
- Power to call out the militia and determine their use, suppress insurrections and repel invasions
- Create the District of Columbia

This clause authorizes and defines the extent of federally held land

"Necessary and Proper" Clause

(Allows authority to carry out the mentioned powers, but does not grant power to usurp authority not necessary for the fulfillment of the Constitutionally enumerated powers or assignments)

Section 9

Writ of habeas corpus (a critical element in the preservation of freedom) may not be suspended except for the (presumably brief) period necessary to sort out the confusion associated with rebellions and invasions, as required for public safety.

[Habeas corpus is a protection for someone accused of a crime. It dates back in English legal practice at least to the Magna Carta, which was signed by King John in 1215, and it was included in the rights granted by King Charles II in 1679. It was well understood to be a basic unalienable right of free citizens. The concept behind habeas corpus is that an accused may not be picked up and put in jail and held indefinitely without a trial. It prevents arbitrary imprisonment. Habeas corpus basically means "bring the body." The accused must be brought before the court, and a judge must review the evidence and charges to see if there is justification for the accused to be held. When not bound by this concept, kings had made a practice of arresting individuals and keeping them imprisoned without any justification, and the American founders wanted to make certain that this never happened in the United States. It is interesting to note that this power is included under the enumerated powers of Congress, *not* the president. It is also interesting to note that in 1863, during the Civil War, President Lincoln and the military suspended habeas corpus. Chief Justice Taney of the Supreme Court found that action unconstitutional because the power to suspend habeas corpus was granted within the Constitution to the Congress, not the president. In an unconstitutional act, the

Congress promptly "redelegated" their authority to suspend habeas corpus to the president. Since then, the president has claimed the power to suspend habeas corpus.]

No bills of attainder are allowed in the United States.

[A bill of attainder is a law passed by a legislative body that, by the law, names an individual as an outlaw. A person so named became an outlaw simply because the law declared he was an outlaw. This had been a common practice of kings who wished to bring the power of the law to bear against someone, perhaps to give some color of justification for confiscating his property or for some other act of tyranny against the person. Such laws were a method of confiscation and control.]

No ex post facto laws are to be created in the United States.

[Ex post facto simply means "after the deed or fact." An ex post facto law is a law that is created after an act has already been committed, and that makes the act illegal retroactively and punishable under the newly created law. An ex post facto law would allow a punishment to occur for an act that was legal at the time the act was committed.]

Issues regarding taxes and handling of money are also addressed in this section.

In addition, this section prohibits creation of special classes of people.

[It is interesting to note that the founders wanted to make certain that no one was granted special consideration based upon class. Unfortunately, although not technically creating a titled class of nobility, modern efforts to legislatively identify "classes" or groups of people and to grant special legal or economic status to them are growing problems in the nation. This approach ultimately fosters the concept of "class conflict," which Marx encouraged in *The Communist Manifesto*.]

The section also seeks to prevent officeholders from being influenced by gifts or title granted by foreign powers.

Section 10
States are constitutionally prohibited from the following actions:

- Enter into treaty, alliance, compact, agreement, or confederation with another state or foreign entity
- Grant letters of marque and reprisal
- Coin money
- Make paper money (only gold and silver are legal money)
- Create bills of attainder
- Create ex post facto laws

-Impair contractual obligations
-Grant titles of nobility
-Establish taxes on trade (without Congressional approval and control)
-Engaging in war unless invaded and in imminent danger which will not permit delay

Article II—Executive
It is interesting to note that the authors of the United States Constitution were careful to create an executive office with a clearly defined set of responsibilities. They purposefully did not create a monarch with broad and all encompassing powers. A careful review of this article within the Constitution will reveal that the presidential powers granted within the Constitution are actually few and well defined. The office is bounded by constraints which are only exceeded by unconstitutional usurpation.

Section 1
President of the United States
    Term of Office: four years
    Elected by Electoral College
    The Electoral College is a special single-purpose legislature. Its *only* assignment: elect the president and vice president

The number of "electors" in the Electoral College is based upon the total number of senators and congressmen in the United States Congress (plus three for Washington DC). However, no Senator or Representative, or person holding an office of trust or profit under the United States may serve as an elector.

Current Electoral College numbers are based upon the following categories:

100 senators
435 congressmen
  3 Washington DC[135]
538 total presidential "electors"

538 total presidential "electors"/2 = 269 + 1 = 270 electoral votes necessary for a majority, which is required to elect the president

    -President must be a natural-born citizen of United States
    -Must be at least thirty-five years old
    -Must have been in the United States for at least fourteen years

---

[135.] See the Twenty-third Amendment.

Prior to assuming office after election, the president must take the Presidential oath of office:

> "I do solemnly swear (or affirm) that I will faithfully execute the Office of President of the United States, and will to the best of my Ability, preserve, protect and defend the Constitution of the United States."

Section 2
President is commander in chief of the army and navy, and of the militia, when called into the actual service of the United States

> Presidential power to grant reprieves and pardons, except in the case of impeachment

Presidential power to do the following:

> -Make treaties (with consent of two-thirds of the Senate)
> -Nominate ambassadors, other officials, Supreme Court judges, and other officers of the United States (with Senate consent)

Section 3
Presidential requirement to annually report the State of the Union to Congress

Section 4
Requirement to remove president, vice president, and all civil officers upon impeachment for, and conviction of, treason, bribery, or other high crimes and misdemeanors

Article III—Judicial

Section 1
> The Judicial power of the United States is vested in

>> -One supreme court
>> -Inferior courts established through congressional power

> Judges are allowed to hold office during good behavior

Section 2
Enumerates cases in which the Supreme Court shall have power to exercise "original jurisdiction"

> In cases not specifically mentioned within this section, the Congress has authority to make exceptions to the court's jurisdiction and limit the court from participation in cases that are identified by the Congress

Trial by jury is protected (except in cases of impeachment)

Section 3
Treason against the United States is defined as:

-Levying war against the United States
-Adhering to enemies of the United States
-Giving aid and comfort to U.S. enemies

Conditions and requirements are defined to obtain conviction of treason:

-Testimony of two witnesses of the same act
-Confession in open court

Punishment of Treason:

-Congressional power to declare punishment
-However, no attainder of treason shall work corruption of blood or forfeiture except during the life of the person attainted

[If a person is found guilty of treason and their property is confiscated as punishment for their treason, that property must be returned to their heirs after their death. The children are thereby not punished for the sins of their parents.]

Article IV

Section 1
Full faith and credit recognizes public acts of each state, in other states

-Acts
-Records
-Judicial Proceedings

Section 2

-Privileges and immunities of citizens shall apply from state to state
-Extradition of those accused of crimes between states

Article I Section 8, clause 4 (Legislative article) is tied to the Article IV "Full Faith and Credit" requirements between states. Article I Section 8, clause 4 states:

Congress shall have power . . . To establish an uniform rule of naturalization

[The United States Congress will (must) define how United States citizenship is obtained. The individual states were constitutionally precluded from defining citizenship requirements. That authority was retained at the national level. In Federalist no. 32, Alexander Hamilton makes brief comment regarding the necessity of this condition, and in Federalist no. 42, James Madison eloquently explains the dangers which would have been associated with allowing states to define citizenship rules—some states having a low standard, and other states having more stringent standards, and how that condition would adversely effect the states as immigrants sought easy citizenship through the states with the lower standard and then migrated to states which had established the higher standards.]

Section 3

>Congress makes rules and regulations regarding disposal of U.S. property and regarding U.S. territory or other property belonging to the United States

[*Both* houses of Congress must be involved in and approve the disposal of property owned by the United States. Such an act cannot be undertaken unilaterally by one of the houses—even if the attempt is made by treaty and approved by the Senate.]

Section 4

>-*Every* state must have a republican form of government

[*Not a democracy, monarchy, or other form of government*]

>-The national government shall protect each state from invasion

Article V
The amendment process defined

>Two-thirds of both houses of Congress may propose amendments to the Constitution
>   OR
>When two-thirds of the states request it, Congress *shall* call a constitutional convention

[To date, all amendments to the Constitution have occurred by the first process—two-thirds of both houses passing the amendment and then forwarding it to the states for ratification. The only constitutional convention that has happened occurred in 1787 and resulted in the setting aside of the existing constitution, the Articles of Confederation, and the writing of an entirely new constitution. If another constitutional convention is ever called, it is most likely that the current United States Constitution will be set aside and a new constitution written, just as it was in 1787. With the current general lack of understanding of the basic principles of individual God-given rights, proper government, property rights, government constrained to act only in limited specified areas, etc., a modern constitutional convention would be fraught with danger beyond measure for liberty-loving Americans.]

>Ratification process (after two-thirds of both houses propose and pass the amendment and forward the proposed amendment to the states for ratification):
>>three-fourths of state legislatures approve the proposed amendment
>
>>OR
>
>>three-fourths of conventions in states approve the proposed amendment
>
>(as it approves and submits the amendment for ratification, Congress defines whether it will be ratified by state legislatures or state conventions)

Article VI

>-Previous debts of the United States are to be honored and paid.
>-The U.S. Constitution is the "Supreme Law of the Land."
>-Treaties made under the Constitution shall be the "Supreme Law of the Land."

[This often misunderstood concept about treaties is reviewed in detail elsewhere in this lecture series. The original intent of the Founding Fathers is considered herein, and the founder's clear understanding was that a treaty could *not* amend the United States Constitution. Treaties do not modify the Constitution or set aside principles of proper government and individual God-given rights, which are protected under the form of government the Constitution created.]

>-*All* who hold office are *required* to take an oath to uphold the U.S. Constitution
>-No religious test may be required in order to hold office

Article VII

>-Ratification of nine states was required to establish this constitution as the new United States Constitution
>-All the states who were represented in the convention signed the new constitution
>-Signed "the Seventeenth Day of September in the Year of our Lord one thousand seven hundred and Eighty seven"
>-Twelfth Year of Independence of the United States of America

(Review the United States Constitution—see appendix)

6.

The Bill of Rights and Other Amendments

Recommended Resources for the Serious Student:

The United States Constitution
The Declaration of Independence
Federalist Papers by J. Madison, A. Hamilton, J. Jay
View of the Constitution of the United States by St. George Tucker

Quotes, Articles, and Original Sources

At the close of the Constitutional Convention of 1787, the convention passed the following resolution. The resolution outlined the process by which the new constitution was to go forward.

Resolution of the 1787 Constitutional Convention:

> Resolved,
>
> That the preceeding Constitution be laid before the United States in Congress assembled, and that it is the Opinion of this Convention, that it should afterward be submitted to a Convention of Delegates, chosen in each State by the People thereof, under the Recommendation of its Legislature, for their Assent and Ratification; and that each Convention assenting to, and ratifying the Same, should give Notice thereof to the United States in Congress assembled.

The Constitutional Convention of 1787 had been called to correct recognized deficiencies in the then-existing constitution, the Articles of Confederation. As the convention assembled and began its business in May 1787, they recognized that as the legal representatives of the states and the people, they had the authority to create an entirely new constitution. They immediately set aside the existing constitution and set about creating a new constitution.

THE BILL OF RIGHTS AND OTHER AMENDMENTS

The nation's experience between 1776 and 1787 had demonstrated that a fully functioning national government must have certain *specific* powers (*not* unlimited powers that are all-encompassing in scope and magnitude) in order to properly fulfill the responsibilities associated with a nation among nations.

Fortunately, the men who participated in the convention were honorable men who sought to create a new form of government that would preserve the blessings of liberty for themselves and their posterity while granting to the national government the power to perform that which a national government should properly perform. They sought to establish a government that lived up to the promise put forth in the Declaration of Independence in 1776 and kept government within its proper purpose—to preserve the God-given rights of mankind.

The convention met each day behind closed doors and made no "press release" statements on the front steps of the Constitution Hall each day as they adjourned. This approach allowed them to freely debate the issues that came before them and for each of them to weigh the issues and change their position as they came to realize the proper direction they should follow.

The debates through the long hot summer of 1787 were arduous and often emotional! But the appropriate solution gradually came forth, and the new constitution was adopted by the convention.

When the new constitution was signed and brought forth for the nation's approval, there was a shocked outcry! It was an entirely new constitution. It created a much stronger national government than the nation had experienced under the Articles of Confederation. It was a new form of government that had never been known before. And it did not include a bill of rights.

While there were a few who had participated in the convention who withheld their approval of the new constitution because it did not include a bill of rights, most of those who had participated in the convention felt that a bill of rights was not necessary and in fact could be dangerous from a legal perspective. If a list of rights (or a list of anything, in a legal view) was compiled, the list was considered to be comprehensive, and any rights that were inadvertently omitted would be considered purposely excluded. They felt that it would be dangerous to put forth a list of rights that would certainly be incomplete, because how could you possibly list *all* of mankind's God-given rights?

Besides, it was felt by the participants of the convention that they had not granted the national government sufficient power to abuse any rights of Americans (remember, they sought to specifically enumerate the powers granted, and the powers were limited to those specifically enumerated or listed in the Constitution).

Nevertheless, many prominent and influential Americans, including liberty-loving luminaries such as Thomas Jefferson and Patrick Henry insisted that a bill of rights was essential.

The debates regarding the ratification of the new constitution became arduous and, in many instances, rancorous. Some suggested scrapping the new constitution and calling a new convention to write another new constitution. Those who had participated in the 1787 Convention felt that such an effort could not possibly improve upon the document they had so carefully debated and created, and it was entirely likely that a new convention would result in failure and the ultimate failure of the nation.

Finally, it became apparent that the effort to ratify the new constitution was doomed without a commitment to create a bill of rights for the Constitution. The commitment was made that if the Constitution was ratified as presented, that the newly constituted national government would seek input from the states regarding suggestions for the bill of rights and that the Congress would immediately bring forth (through the constitutionally defined article 5 amendment process) a bill of rights for the states to examine and ratify.

With that commitment, the new constitution was ratified, the national government was formed, and Congress set about the effort to create a bill of rights. Many suggestions were submitted that identified rights that needed to be protected. Among the many suggestions were numerous duplicates that were simply variations on the same topic. Those duplicates were satisfactorily reconciled together by men such as James Madison and George Mason.

And the danger of "forgetting" to list all rights that needed to be protected (and the legalistic consequences mentioned above) did not go away! It is interesting to note that the Ninth and Tenth Amendments were included as "catch-all" amendments that basically reinforced the position that "if we forgot any rights, we still retain them, even if we did not list them!"[136]

The bill of rights amendment process that occurred after the Constitution was ratified:

* A total of 189 amendments were suggested to the Congress
* Those suggested amendments were boiled down to seventeen proposed amendments, which were presented to Congress
* Congress passed twelve amendments and forwarded them to the states for ratification

The following is an example of a suggested amendment that was rejected by Congress because it injected the national government into issues that the founders considered solely within the prerogative of the states: "No State Shall violate the Equal Rights of Conscience, or the Freedom of the Press, or the Trial by Jury in Criminal Cases."

The states ratified ten of the proposed amendments (which became the Bill of Rights); two of the proposed amendments that had been forwarded to the states by Congress failed to be ratified. It is interesting to note, however, that one of those failed proposed amendments was ultimately ratified in May 1992 and became the Twenty-seventh Amendment.

---

[136]. See the Ninth and Tenth Amendments and consider how they protected unmentioned rights and specifically denied the national government powers that were not specifically granted within the United States Constitution.

THE BILL OF RIGHTS AND OTHER AMENDMENTS

PREAMBLE TO THE BILL OF RIGHTS

"The conventions of a number of the states having, at the time of their adopting the Constitution, expressed a desire, in order to prevent misconstruction or abuse of its powers, that further declaratory and restrictive clauses should be added; and as extending the ground of public confidence in the government will best insure the beneficent ends of its institution."

This preamble is specific in expressing the purpose of the Bill of Rights: the national government was having further "declaratory and restrictive clauses" placed upon it to prevent any possibility of the national government expanding its power beyond the bounds established by the Constitution. The rights recognized within the Bill of Rights were rights of the people that were necessary to preserve their liberty.

Amendment I
Congress shall make no law establishing religion or prohibiting its free exercise
Or abridging free speech
Or freedom of the press
Or the right of the people to peaceably assemble
Or the right to petition the government for redress of grievances

[This amendment prohibited the establishment of a national religion and ensured that the national government would not interfere with the free exercise of the individual right to worship in accordance with personal conscience. It is interesting to note that at the time this amendment was brought forth, seven of the states had established state religions. And while the nation's founders hoped the states would someday eliminate those state sanctions, they made no attempt to force the matter with the states because it was considered a state's rights matter in which the national government had no jurisdiction. The fact is that the same Congress that passed this amendment also repassed the Northwest Ordinance, which admonished the connection of religion and morality in the education system to ensure that proper government could flourish. Unquestionably, the Founding Father's original intent in this matter was not antagonistic to religion. They simply wished to prevent a national tax-supported religion that would have the power and prominence to quash other religious denominations.

The wording in favor of freedom of speech has been perverted in modern America in favor of pornography and licentious expressions. The original intent of the founders was to ensure that the people had the right to speak their minds regarding matters of government—expressing discontent if need be—and having that right protected. That perspective has been greatly undermined in recent years as legislation has been passed by Congress that limits the ability to fully express political concerns, particularly during the election process.

The right to peaceably assemble, in many instances, is becoming more restricted by legislation in recent years, and careful consideration needs to be given to restoring this right.

The right of petition is a right that the founders felt had been largely denied to them as they attempted to take their grievances to the king prior to the Revolutionary War. This concern is even mentioned in the Declaration of Independence as one of the justifications for the revolution. Access to the political leaders of the nation is essential to keep the leaders on track with proper government. The people must be able to be heard before their chosen leaders.]

Amendment II

The right of the people to keep and bear arms shall not be infringed.

[The Second Amendment is the subject of lecture 10, so it will not be reviewed in detail in this lecture. As with the other amendments associated with the Bill of Rights, this right to keep and bear arms is an *individual* right that the founders intended to protect from encroachment. It is interesting to note that recent modern constitutions that have been written with the assistance of American representatives, such as the newly created Iraq constitution, do not contain protection of this individual God-given right, which is essential to the survival of liberty. This should be recognized as a red flag warning to all who mistakenly think that calling a new constitutional convention as allowed under article 5 of the current constitution and creating a new United States constitution that will better reflect the needs of a more "modern" society is a safe and advisable risk. Modern authors of constitutions, if given the opportunity, would undoubtedly "forget" a broad spectrum of mankind's unalienable rights and fail to preserve the limited government the founders gave America. Undoubtedly, the modern authors would also grant the new government powers to encroach upon God-given rights. The old saying "forewarned is forearmed" should alert freedom-loving Americans of this grave risk and motivate them to preserve and restore the current divinely inspired constitution!]

Amendment III

The people of the nation are protected from being compelled to house soldiers in their homes without their consent in time of peace, and it may be required only during war if Congress authorizes it through appropriate legislation.

[This amendment was an outgrowth of the irritation the colonists felt before the Revolutionary War as the king had stationed troops in the midst of the civilian populations and insisted that the troops be housed in the homes of the citizens. It would be difficult to imagine a more effective way to control the people and completely subjugate them! The soldiers had proven themselves to be a burden in many ways, and the Founding Fathers were certain they wanted to prevent the government from instituting this population-control method on the people.]

Amendment IV

The right of the people to be secure in their persons, houses, papers, and effects against unreasonable searches and seizures is recognized and protected.

THE BILL OF RIGHTS AND OTHER AMENDMENTS

Extreme specificity is required to obtain a warrant, including probable cause, an oath by an officer, detailed descriptions of place to be searched, and persons or things to be seized.

[This amendment, again, was an outgrowth of abuses that the colonists had experienced under the king prior to the Revolutionary War. The king's officers exercised search warrants called "writs of assistance." They were basically blank warrants that gave the officers permission to go anywhere, search anything they chose to search, and confiscate whatever they thought might be incriminating. The Founding Fathers had experienced this form of tyranny and wanted to place powerful constraints upon the government to prevent future tyranny. This amendment is under heavy attack in modern America. Unfortunately, it would seem that the philosophy of the concept of "writs of assistance" is returning to America. The current challenges associated with this diminishing right are reviewed in more detail in lecture 7.]

Amendment V

Requirement for indictment by grand jury before a person may be tried for a serious crime

No "double jeopardy" is allowed for the same offense, having once gone through trial process

Accused is not required to witness against self (self-incrimination)

"Due process" is required to take a person's life, liberty, or property

Fair price must be paid for private property taken for public use

[Before a person may be charged for a serious crime, a grand jury has to examine the evidence that the prosecutor holds, which would indicate if the person should be arrested and charged. Unfortunately, all too often, grand juries become largely a "rubber stamp," giving approval for virtually all requests that are placed before them. All too often they simply operate under the premise that the prosecutors would never ask for anything that is unwarranted or not fully supported by evidence. This requirement for examination of evidence was intended as a protection for the person that may be accused. Arrest and trial are generally extremely embarrassing and dramatically affect the life of the person who faces such a challenge. This protection was put into place to prevent such a burden on the charged person if the charges were unsubstantiated or flimsy.

Prior to the establishment of the United States, the king had often caused persons who had faced trial, but sufficient evidence had not been found to convict them, to be rearrested to face trial on the same charges, hoping that evidence would be found that would incriminate them. The "double jeopardy" protection was included in the Bill of Rights to prevent this abuse in America.

Accused persons cannot be compelled to witness against themselves. It is interesting that ancient Israel had a similar protection in their judicial code.[137] This concept is also important because it would invalidate self-incriminating statements that were obtained through torture of the accused.

The "due process" concept was originally intended to protect a person's life, liberty, or property from arbitrary heavy-handedness by government. It required a full and fair hearing to review the matter to ensure fairness. Historically, the courts (the judicial branch) were called upon to review and adjudicate such matters, but recent practice often has the organization (for example, perhaps a department of the executive branch) that could be accused of some self-serving action reviewing its own actions within the department and precluding the individual who may be at risk from seeking judicial review. Many consider this modern practice one that may result in insufficient review and impartiality to consider the merits and ensure fairness and in violation of other amendments that indicate the original intent to provide as much impartiality and fairness as possible through the jury process.

If property is taken for public use, its full market value must be paid to the individual losing the property. Many consider recent "takings" to be for arbitrary reasons that the Founding Fathers would find invalid, such as to improve tax collections for a municipality or to allow private developers to develop a project for profit. Lecture 3 reviewed many statements by the Founding Fathers and others that relate to their position on the sacred importance of preserving private property rights. In addition, lecture 13 reviews *The Communist Manifesto* and the position of the communists that private property should be abolished. Indeed, the first point of the ten points of *The Communist Manifesto* states, "Abolition of property in land and application of all rents of land to public purposes." Modern Americans must carefully guard against any insidious efforts to encroach upon private property, which is an essential element of liberty!]

Amendment VI
Right of accused to speedy and public trial
Right of accused to impartial jury
Right of accused to be tried in the local district in which the crime was committed

---

[137.] See Walter M. Chandler, in *The Hebrew Trial*, cited Maimonides (*Sanhedrin* 4:2), "We have it as a fundamental principle of our jurisprudence that no one can bring an accusation against himself. Should a man make confession of guilt before a legally constituted tribunal, such confession is not to be used against him unless properly attested by two other witnesses"; and Mendelsohn, in *Criminal Jurisprudence of the Ancient Hebrews* (133), "Not only is self-condemnation never extorted from the defendant by means of torture, but no attempt is ever made to lead him on to self-incrimination. Moreover, a voluntary confession on his part is not admitted into evidence, and therefore not competent to convict him, unless a legal number of witnesses minutely corroborate his self accusation."

THE BILL OF RIGHTS AND OTHER AMENDMENTS

Right of accused to know the charges
Right of accused to confront both accusers and witnesses
Right of accused to compel witnesses with favorable information to testify
Right of accused to have a defense attorney

[The speedy trial was intended to prevent an accused person from having to languish in jail for an extended period before being tried for a crime he may not have committed. The public trial was to prevent secret trials of questionable justice from being carried out against the citizenry by a tyrant.

The Founding Fathers considered the jury system to be essential to the maintenance of liberty and to prevent miscarriage of justice. The Declaration of Independence noted the king's violation of the jury trial process as one of the justifications of the revolution ("For depriving us in many cases, of the benefits of Trial by Jury"). Prior to the passage of the Bill of Rights, Thomas Jefferson express his hope that the jury system would be further protected and ensured, and in his first inaugural address, Jefferson stated,

> I deem [one of] the essential principles of our government, and consequently [one] which ought to shape its administration, . . . trial by juries impartially selected.[138]

Original intent also considered the ability of the jury to judge both the application of the law *and* the facts in the case before them as essential in obtaining justice. What this meant was that while the law may have prohibited an action that a defendant was charged with and the defendant had committed the act, but based upon circumstances involved in the specific case before them, the jury could decide to set the law aside and find the defendant "not guilty." Evidence of this power can be found in mid-1800s court cases regarding runaway slaves that had been caught, which the law required to be returned to their "owners," wherein juries exercised their legal right to judge the application of law. In many of those cases, juries refused to send slaves back to their owners. They said "yes" to justice, "no" to the law. That right was upheld by the Supreme Court. Due to the 1895 *Sparf v. United States* case[139] in which this power of the jury was denied, recent decades have found the court system reluctant to inform the jury of this power that they have historically held. It is interesting to note Thomas Jefferson's comment on this matter:

> It is in the power, therefore, of the juries, if they think permanent judges are under any bias whatever in any cause, to take on themselves to judge the law as well as the fact. They never exercise this power but when they suspect partiality in the judges; and

---

[138.] Thomas Jefferson's first inaugural address in Bergh, *Thomas Jefferson*, 3:321.
[139.] 156 U.S. 51

by the exercise of this power they have been the firmest bulwarks of English liberty. Were I called upon to decide whether the people had best be omitted in the legislative or judiciary department, I would say it is better to leave them out of the legislative. The execution of the laws is more important than the making [of] them.[140]

The importance the founders of this nation placed upon the jury is emphasized by the numerous times it is mentioned and protected in both the United States Constitution and the Bill of Rights.[141]

The accused was to be tried in the area where the crime was committed to ensure that the people closest to the matter would be able to judge the matter.

The accused was to be able to know and understand the charges—there were to be no surprises so an appropriate defense could be prepared.

The accused was to be able to confront the witnesses against him and to be able to cross-examine the witness under oath. This allowed full disclosure and prevented anonymous accusations that could not be refuted under cross-examination, as had often been the case under previous tyrannies.

The accused was also ensured the right to compel witnesses to attend the trial and testify that may have favorable evidence in the case. This ensures that even people who don't want to get involved because of inconvenience, fear, or any other reason could be required to testify in the case.

And of course, this amendment also ensures the right of the accused to be represented in court by defense counsel, even if they cannot afford to pay.]

Amendment VII

The right of jury trial in civil suits that involve more than $20 is protected

The facts or "findings" of a jury may not be set aside by the judge or by an appellate court

[The right to have a jury trial in civil lawsuits is protected by this amendment. In addition, the findings of the facts by the jury may not be changed by a judge if the decision is appealed.]

Amendment VIII

Excessive bail is prohibited

Excessive fines are prohibited

"Cruel and unusual" punishments are prohibited

[In cases where the nature of the crime and the accused are not considered dangerous to the community and the risk of escape is not high, bail must not be set so high as to prevent

---

[140.] Bergh, *Thomas Jefferson*, 7:422.
[141.] U.S. Constitution, article 3, section 2, clause 3; Amendments 5, 6, and 7.

THE BILL OF RIGHTS AND OTHER AMENDMENTS

the person from being allowed to be set free to assist in preparation of their defense and participating in other obligations such as continued employment and family affairs.

The king had historically used fines as a method of confiscation of property. The Magna Carta had precluded forfeiture in an attempt to prevent confiscation. Many recent legislative enactments require confiscation of the property of the accused upon conviction of certain crimes. Many consider some of the circumstances under which this occurs to be a miscarriage of justice because the value of the lost property far exceeds a "reasonable" fine. It is also of interest to note that in the fourth point of *The Communist Manifesto*, Karl Marx advocated the "confiscation of the property of all emigrants and rebels."[142]

Over the centuries, many cruel and unusual punishments had been used by government against criminals. Torture was common. Mutilation was often practiced wherein nostrils were split or ears cut off. Branding with hot irons was also common, as was drawing and quartering and disemboweling. These abuses are prohibited by this amendment—Americans are considered above these practices. It is interesting to note that some have sought to prohibit capital punishment (the death penalty) by application of this amendment. However, as a counterpoint to that position, it is also of interest to note that the United States Congress in the Coinage Act of 1792 mandated the death penalty for officers of the U.S. mint who debased the precious metal content of U.S. coinage for fraudulent purposes or embezzled the precious metal that was to be struck as coin. So it would seem that the original intent of this amendment did not prohibit the death penalty in certain justifiable cases.]

Amendment IX

Listing of certain rights in the Constitution shall not be interpreted to limit the rights of the people to those enumerated rights

[The people retain all rights, whether listed or not]

Amendment X

If a power was not specifically delegated within the Constitution to the national government, the national government does not posses that power
[Powers not specifically withheld from the states by the Constitution continue to be held by the states or the people]

[The Ninth and Tenth Amendments were "catch-all" amendments that were intended to address the legal concern that if rights were limited to those listed in the Bill of Rights, some of the rights may have been overlooked. There was a concern that the assumption would

---

[142]. See lecture 13.

be that they were overlooked purposefully and they were not intended to be retained as the rights of the people. Since it would be impossible to list every individual right, these two amendments basically said, "If we failed to mention any rights, we still retain them." In addition, the Tenth Amendment reiterated the fact that the intention was to grant to the national government *only* those powers specifically listed within the Constitution and that *all* other powers were retained by the people or the states.]

Amendment XI

Establishes the right of a state to not be sued by a citizen of another state without that state's permission

[This amendment was ratified after a citizen of South Carolina sued the state of Georgia in federal court.]

Amendment XII

Originally, the person receiving the most electoral votes became president and the one who received the next most votes became vice president (even if they were political rivals—as had been the case when John Adams was elected president and Thomas Jefferson was elected vice president)

This amendment requires the electors to vote specifically for president, then specifically for a vice president

Details in the presidential and vice presidential election process are specified in the event a majority of electoral votes are not received.

Washington DC Presidential Electors

The Twenty-third Amendment (ratified March 1961) is mentioned here out of order because it pertains to the presidential electoral voting process—allowing Washington DC to have presidential electors. The number of Washington DC electors is *not* to exceed the number of electors from the smallest state (the smallest state has two senators and one congressman (total of three electors); therefore, Washington DC is allowed three electors.

Amendment XIII

Slavery is abolished in the United States, except as a punishment for crime upon conviction

Amendment XIV

The Fourteenth Amendment is the most poorly written and vindictive amendment in the United States Constitution. It has resulted in the largest number of court proceedings and legislative actions of any of the amendments and has been used to severely impinge upon state rights. A full examination of this flawed amendment will not be attempted herein, but an example of the challenges created by the amendment is noted below:

Section 1 of the Fourteenth Amendment states, "All persons born or naturalized in the United States and subject to the jurisdiction thereof are citizens of the United States."

[The intention of this portion of the amendment was to make certain that those who had previously been held as slaves were citizens of the United States. Recent interpretations attempt to use this clause to justify granting U.S. citizenship to babies born in the United States to people who have entered the United States illegally. Court rulings that reviewed this amendment soon after it was passed never considered this interpretation! The following logic is offered to assist in the review of this position:

> If an ambassador from another nation was serving in the United States and had a baby while here, the baby would not be considered a citizen of the United States because the ambassador was not "subject to the jurisdiction" of the United States. Persons who enter the United States illegally, by definition, and by their every action, have attempted to avoid being "subject to the jurisdiction" of the United States. Therefore, a baby born to them should not logically be assumed to automatically be a citizen.

Section 5 of the Fourteenth Amendment grants the Congress authority to correct misunderstandings within the amendment: "The Congress shall have power to enforce, by appropriate legislation, the provisions of this article." Therefore, Congress has the authority to clarify and correct the many erroneous interpretations and applications of this amendment which the courts have inflicted upon the nation.

[Some of the vindictive aspects of this amendment were mitigated by President Andrew Johnson's 1868 pardon of Confederate soldiers.]

Amendment XV
In the United States, the right to vote may not be denied or abridged because of one's race, color, or previous condition as a slave.

Amendment XVI
This allows the national government to directly tax the nation's citizens rather than being constrained to financially operate the national government within the bounds established by the Founding Fathers.

[This amendment is the basis for the federal income tax. It is also of interest to note that in *The Communist Manifesto*, Karl Marx proposed that nations that were to embrace communism must implement "A heavy progressive or graduated income tax." (Point 2 of the ten points of *The Communist Manifesto*) The United States graduated federal income tax is in compliance with Marx's formula for the destruction of liberty and proper government.]

Amendment XVII
Previously, the states appointed their senators to the United States Senate.
This amendment establishes that the people of the state directly elect the senators who will represent their state

[This has resulted in costly special requests for federal funding by senators anxious to "buy" votes back home by currying favor with constituents back home by providing government largess to those voters; but which expenditures are not allowed under the powers granted to the national government by the United States Constitution. Examples would include:

-Federal medical/health care
-Federal welfare services for the poor
-Federal funding to education
-Federal subsidies to local law enforcement
-Federal resources for highway construction
-Federal aid for natural disasters
-Federally funded or guaranteed loans (domestic and international)]

Amendment XVIII
This amendment prohibits the manufacture, sale, or transportation of intoxicating liquors within the United States. It was called "Prohibition." This amendment was repealed by the Twenty-first Amendment nearly fifteen years later.

Amendment XIX
This amendment established the right to vote for women.
Prior to ratification of this amendment, several states had already recognized this right.

Amendment XX
Establishes the dates upon which presidential and congressional terms end
Establishes the date upon which congress shall assemble each year
Establishes terms and conditions under which the vice president elect acts as president
Describes the selection of president or vice president in the event of death

Amendment XXI
Repeals the Eighteenth Amendment (prohibition of intoxicating liquors)

Amendment XXII
No person shall be elected to the office of president more than twice.
No person who has acted as president for more that two years of a term to which someone else was elected shall be elected more than once.

THE BILL OF RIGHTS AND OTHER AMENDMENTS

Amendment XXIII

Grants to the District of Columbia (Washington DC) the number of electors for president and vice president it would be entitled to if it were a state (but no more than the least populous state)

Amendment XXIV

The right to vote in any election for president, vice president, electors for the president or vice president, or senators or representatives shall not be denied for reason of failure to pay any poll tax or other tax.

Amendment XXV

The vice president is to fill presidential vacancy upon death or resignation of the president or removal from office.

The president is to nominate a new vice president if the vice president office is vacant.

The proposed new vice president is to be confirmed by majority vote of the House and Senate.

Rules are defined for the transfer of power if the president is unable to perform duties or if deemed unable to perform duties.

Amendment XXVI

Right of citizens eighteen years or older to vote

Amendment XXVII

Senators and representatives may not receive pay increases they voted for themselves until after the next election of representatives (which occur every two years)

This amendment was one of the original twelve amendments that Congress passed as part of the Bill of Rights but was not ratified by the states at that time.

(Review the Bill of Rights and other *amendments*—see appendix)

7.

Modern-Day Offenses

Recommended Resources for the Serious Student:

The United States Constitution
The Declaration of Independence
The Federalist Papers by J. Madison, A. Hamilton, and J. Jay
View of the Constitution of the United States by St. George Tucker

Quotes, Articles, and Original Sources

>Much of the material that is included in this lecture is found in other lectures in this series. In an effort to facilitate the ease of study of these subjects within this lecture, to reinforce the position of the American Founding Fathers, and expose how the current practices diverge from the original intent expressed when the nation was established, the information is restated in this lecture.

As has been previously noted, the American Declaration of Independence captured the essence of many marvelous, timeless self-evident truths about the equality of all mankind before God and government, the source of mankind's rights, our proper relationship to government, the purpose of government, and the authority of the sovereign people over government. Government is a creature created by the people, and the creature is never intended to become the master of the people who created it. Let us briefly review the stirring words of the Declaration of Independence as we begin our review of "modern-day" offenses:

>We hold these truths to be self-evident, that all men are created equal, that they are endowed by their Creator with certain unalienable Rights.

And after brief mention of some of those rights, the Declaration goes on to specify the purpose of government, saying,

MODERN-DAY OFFENSES (UNREMITTING BETRAYALS)

> That to secure these rights, Governments are instituted among Men, deriving their just powers from the consent of the governed, That whenever any Form of Government becomes destructive of these ends, it is the Right of the People to alter or to abolish it, and to institute new Government, laying its foundation on such principles and organizing its powers in such form, as to them shall seem most likely to effect their Safety and Happiness.

Therein we note, in its most brief and succinct form, the definition of liberty and the constraints under which government is to operate.

The Founding Fathers of the United States were not wild-eyed radicals who sought to burn down society by their destructive actions. They were noble and honorable men who sought for the blessings of liberty to be obtained for themselves and their posterity. They were well-reasoned, and felt it their duty to honestly set forth their intentions for the examination of all mankind. As noted in the following paragraph from the Declaration, they sought to take their rightful place as a nation among nations, and wanted to explain to the world why they were taking the action they took:

> When in the Course of human events, it becomes necessary for one people to dissolve the political bands which have connected them with another, and to assume among the Powers of the earth, the separate and equal station to which the Laws of Nature and of Nature's God entitle them, a decent respect to the opinions of mankind requires that they should declare the causes which impel them to the separation.

After making that statement, and briefly but eloquently capturing the essence of the purpose and limits of government as already noted, the founders went on to explain the causes of their disaffection from their mother country:

> When a long train of abuses and usurpations, pursuing invariably the same Object evinces a design to reduce them under absolute Despotism, it is their right, it is their duty, to throw off such Government, and to provide new Guards for their future security... The history of the present King of Great Britain is a history of repeated injuries and usurpations, all having in direct object the establishment of an absolute Tyranny over these States. To prove this, let Facts be submitted to a candid world.

The Declaration goes on to enumerate the "offenses of the king," citing them as justification for the action they were taking in disassociating from the government of the king. The Declaration is quite direct and unequivocal in its indictment against the king!

We will note just a few of the king's offenses that may have some application in modern America:

TO PRESERVE THE NATION

From the Declaration of Independence (Offenses of the King):

> "He has refused his Assent to Laws, the most wholesome and necessary for the public good."

> "He has dissolved Representative Houses repeatedly, for opposing with manly firmness his invasions on the rights of the people."

> "He has obstructed the Administration of Justice."

> "He has erected a multitude of New Offices, and sent hither swarms of Officers to harass our people, and eat out their substance."

> "He has combined with others to subject us to a jurisdiction foreign to our constitution."

> "[He was] depriving us in many cases, of the benefits of Trial by Jury."

> "For transporting us beyond Seas to be tried for pretended offenses"

> "[He was] altering fundamentally the Forms of our Governments."

> "A Prince, whose character is thus marked by every act which may define a Tyrant, is unfit to be the ruler of a free people."

The Declaration of Independence declares God is the source of our rights, and proper government's purpose is to secure those rights. All of the other assumptions and usurpations in the name of government that violate that baseline principle ultimately become the basis of tyranny. That baseline principle of the purpose of government as defined within the Declaration of Independence became the basis for our national government. Therein we find what may be termed the "spiritual birth" of the nation. The Declaration of Independence was the "promise" of liberty, the United States Constitution was "born" to deliver that promise to those who would be blessed to live under its protection. Our national charter, the United States Constitution, was created to preserve that fundamental principle: God is the source of mankind's rights, and government is charged with the responsibility to preserve those rights, period.

That principle must be considered one of the most critically important concepts that must be understood if we are to understand and apply the precepts we would term the "original intent" of the American Founding Fathers.

Today, many detractors of the sound doctrine found within the United States Constitution claim that it is impossible to know how the plain English words of the Constitution are to be understood, claiming that the words may mean nearly anything they decide they mean in order to construe a meaning that fosters their un-American agenda. If it is true that the meanings of the words within the Constitution may be twisted into any perverse meaning, then the United States is left without a Constitution (for such a position means that the words mean nothing at all). If such is truly the condition, the nation faces the gravest and most dire consequences. Fortunately, words do have meanings, and those meanings may be known if we are willing to seek them out.

So what is meant by "original intent," and how may we know it?

As he assumed the office of president of the United States, Thomas Jefferson confirmed the importance of keeping the Constitution within the bounds of "original intent," saying,

> The Constitution on which our Union rests shall be administered by me according to the safe and honest meaning contemplated by the plain understanding of the people of the United States at the time of its adoption—a meaning to be found in the explanations of those who advocated, not those who opposed it . . . . These explanations are preserved in the publications of the time.[143]

It is from this perspective that we are seeking to understand the words of our national charter, and it is from this perspective that this information in this lecture is presented.

Those who founded this nation considered the United States Constitution to be a written, binding contract between those who were elected to hold office and the citizens of the nation. The founders were so serious in their intent that all government officials be bound to uphold the United States Constitution that they unequivocally required all who hold office to take an oath to abide by the Constitution. The Constitution is the "job description" of the officeholder. The Constitution grants specific power and withholds all other power[144] from the national government.

During this nation's founding era, oath taking was considered a serious and sacred matter. The gravity of taking an oath is reflected in the definition that is included in Noah Webster's *An American Dictionary of the English Language*.

OATH DEFINED

> A solemn affirmation or declaration, made with an appeal to God for the truth of what is affirmed. The appeal to God in an oath, implies that the person imprecates his vengeance and renounces his favor if the declaration is false, or if the declaration

---

[143.] Bergh, *Thomas Jefferson*, 10:248.
[144.] See Amendments 9 and 10.

is a promise, the person invokes the vengeance of God if he should fail to fulfill it. A false oath is called perjury.[145]

Unfortunately, those who currently hold the reins of power at the national level have largely forgotten the sound principles of proper government that are embodied in the plain English words of the United States Constitution, and consequently, we have strayed far into paths that undermine our liberty and our God-given unalienable rights.

Let us briefly look at a few blatant violations of "original intent" that are being rampantly carried out today, at great risk to the destruction of the principles of liberty, which the United States Constitution was written to preserve.

THE CONSTITUTIONAL SEPARATION OF POWERS

In Federalist no. 47, Madison observed,

> The accumulation of all powers, legislative, executive, and judiciary, in the same hands, whether of one, a few, or many, and whether hereditary, self-appointed, or elective, may justly be pronounced the very definition of tyranny.

Unfortunately, modern congresses have blatantly disregarded their responsibility in the matter of powers delegated solely to them, lacking the courage to fulfill their constitutionally mandated duty in this regard. They have failed in the natural tendency to jealously guard their sphere of influence. Dereliction of duty is the kindest definition that could be attached to the posture of Congress in this regard. Over the past several decades, Congress has made flimsy excuses as they have mumbled nonsense about "delegating" their authority in various issues (such as matters pertaining to war or international trade) to the president or to international bodies or blaming their impotence upon "treaties" that they incorrectly claim tie their hands and require (through entangling alliances) the United States to perform certain "obligations."

Constitutional protocol was well understood by those who founded this nation, and they knew that the authority that was assigned in the Constitution could not legally be delegated to another entity (foreign or domestic). The founders had diligently studied the works of John Locke. John Locke was emphatic in the matter of delegating constitutionally mandated authority:

> The legislative cannot transfer the power of making laws to any other hands, for it being but a delegated power from the people, they who have it cannot pass it over to others. The people alone can appoint the form of the commonwealth, which is by constituting the legislative, and appointing in whose hands that shall be. And

---

[145.] Webster, *American Dictionary*.

MODERN-DAY OFFENSES (UNREMITTING BETRAYALS)

when the people have said, 'We will submit and be governed by laws made by such men, and in such forms,' nobody else can say other men shall make laws for them; nor can they be bound by any laws but such as are enacted by those whom they have chosen and authorized to make laws for them.[146]

Thomas Jefferson agreed that delegated power cannot be redelegated:

> Our ancient laws expressly declare, that those who are but delegates themselves shall not delegate to others powers which require judgment and integrity in their exercise . . .
>
> [They cannot transfer] powers into other hands and other forms, without consulting the people . . .
>
> Necessities which dissolve a government, do not convey its authority to an oligarchy or a monarchy. They throw back, into the hands of the people, the powers they had delegated, and leave them as individuals to shift for themselves. A leader may offer, but not impose himself, nor be imposed on them.[147]

St. George Tucker also agreed that delegated power cannot be redelegated:

> A delegated authority cannot be transferred to another to exercise.[148]

For many years now, the nation has strayed from these sound principles. The carefully devised plan of the founders of this nation regarding the separation of powers is almost universally ignored. Those who hold a given constitutional power routinely allow others to encroach upon their authority and then reciprocate by usurping power not delegated to them. The price of such action is yet to be fully realized. If the liberties that were bequeathed to the nation are to be saved, we must immediately restore the foundation upon which the nation was established and built. Congress must again assume its duty in the matters delegated to them and wrest again their rightful power from the hands, both foreign and domestic, that have usurped the congressional constitutional responsibility.

In the review that follows, we must remember that *all* legislative authority granted by the Constitution is held by the United States House and Senate (No other organization or entity—foreign or domestic—may create legislation for the nation). Neither the

---

[146] Second essay from *Two Treatises of Government*.
[147] Bergh, *Thomas Jefferson*, 2:173-8.
[148] Tucker, *View*, 219.

president nor any part of the executive branch nor the judiciary or any international tribunal created by treaty, agreement, or usurpation may create legislation by which the people of this nation are bound. **The power to legislate may not be delegated by the legislature**. The U.S. Constitution, article 1 section 1, clause 1 states,

> All legislative Powers herein granted shall be vested in a Congress of the United States, which shall consist of a Senate and House of Representatives.

"TO REGULATE COMMERCE WITH FOREIGN NATIONS"

Keeping this foundational principle in mind, let us begin by briefly examining international commerce. Article 1, section 8, clause 1 of the United States Constitution delegates to Congress the authority to collect "Duties, Imposts and Excises, to pay the Debt and provide for the common Defense." In Federalist no. 45, James Madison indicated that the primary source of revenues for performing the responsibilities of the national government would be import taxes collected as foreign goods were brought into this country:

> The powers delegated by the proposed Constitution to the federal government are few and defined. Those which are to remain in the State governments are numerous and indefinite. The former will be exercised principally on external objects, as war, peace, negotiation, and foreign commerce; with which last the power of taxation will, for the most part, be connected.

Note the fact that it was the founder's original intent that taxes on imports were to be the primary source of revenue for the operation of the United States government. Consider this in light of information that is noted below regarding international so-called "free trade" agreements that eliminate the ability of the United States to collect import taxes under the goading of international bodies that do not follow the United States Constitution or have the best interests of the United States as their motivation.

The Commerce Clause of the United States Constitution *requires only* Congress (excluding *all* other entities, foreign and domestic) to create the laws and regulations pertaining to *foreign commerce*. Remember, that power *may not* be redelegated by Congress. The U.S. Constitution, article 1, section 8, clause 3 states,

"The Congress shall have Power to . . . regulate Commerce with foreign Nations."

The United States Constitution directs that the United States Congress is the body that is to regulate commerce with foreign nations. While constantly ignored today, as previously noted, constitutional protocol dictates that authority delegated to a legislative body cannot be "redelegated" by that body. Constitutional protocol was well understood by those who founded this nation, and they knew that the authority that was assigned within the Constitution could not legally be delegated to another entity.

In light of this, it is the sole responsibility of Congress to regulate commerce with foreign nations. Congress cannot constitutionally delegate that responsibility to any other

MODERN-DAY OFFENSES (UNREMITTING BETRAYALS)

organization, especially international bureaucracies that were not elected by the citizens of the United States!

In violation of this critically important principle, on numerous occasions Congress has unconstitutionally voted to delegate this power to international organizations. In recent years, by their actions in this area, Congress and the executive branch have consistently and methodically subverted the sovereignty of the United States. By their efforts, and in the name of "free trade," power to regulate our commerce with foreign nations has been passed to such organizations as the World Trade Organization (WTO), the North American Free Trade Agreement (NAFTA), the General Agreement on Tariffs and Trade (GATT), and the Central American Free Trade Agreement (CAFTA). Other so-called "free trade" agreements are pending and aggressively being fostered, such as the Free Trade Area of the Americas (FTAA) and the Security and Prosperity Partnership (SPP), which would effectively erase the borders between the United States and Mexico and Canada, and would effectively destroy the economic and political independence of the nation. Based upon the decades-long track record of American officials and their unelected globalist advisors, experience would predict that in the relative near term expanded efforts to merge the United States into Trans-Atlantic, Trans-Pacific, Asian, Middle Eastern and other economic/political arrangements will emerge. To add insult to injury, the United States generally provides the bulk of financial resources to these sovereignty-eroding organizations and has only one vote in these decidedly anti-American forums.

Approval of these agreements by our national leadership has allowed international nonelected bureaucracies to dictate numerous economic and domestic policies of the United States in a manner that should be solely the prerogative of the United States. Additionally, these agreements eliminate U.S. import fees that were constitutionally authorized as a revenue source to fund the nation's legal activities; and as this constitutionally authorized revenue source is eliminated, and in an effort to replace those lost revenues, additional burdens are placed upon the backs of American taxpayers, either through additional debt or through higher internal taxes. In addition, the foreign countries involved in these trade agreements generally retain trade barriers that prevent the United States from enjoying expanded profitable trade interactions with the foreign power. Of course, there are some large international companies that take advantage of cheap labor in these foreign nations, which in many instances verges upon slave labor, and then imports their goods into the United States without having to pay import taxes. The real beneficiaries of these trade deals are international corporations and senior leadership of the foreign powers while the common citizens of the United States and the other nations are left without benefit. In fact, many previously high-paying American jobs have been taken overseas by corporations that manipulate these agreements for their benefit and profitability. These job losses have harmed the American employment market and the American economy.

Of even greater concern is the demonstrable fact that these types of agreements lead, ultimately, to merger into regional governments that subvert national sovereignty. These agreements have far less to do with free trade between nations and far more to do with subverting the sovereignty of the United States to a globalist organization that does not uphold the principles vouched safe by the United States Constitution.

Just as the European common market has metastasized into a supranational regional government that dictates economic and domestic policy to the European nations that have joined it; these agreements are precursors to a regional arrangement that will ultimately subvert and destroy our inspired Constitution. As testimony of this, we have the European outcome unfolding right before our eyes, as well as the experience our own nation has had with subversive rulings from both NAFTA and WTO. We are foolish to think that these historical facts will not replicate themselves if we follow the exact path that brought about the European Union (EU).

We may learn valuable lessons from the glaring example of the history of the European Union, and from that example we may learn how regional governments that subvert national governments are born. We also have the painful history of many examples of where the actions taken under authority of NAFTA, GATT, and WTO have undermined the ability of the United States to act independently and to our national benefit. We must learn from these experiences. And wisdom would dictate that we modify our path to return to one that is both constitutionally sound and also protective of our national interests.

As Americans become more aware of the threat these supranational efforts pose to our priceless liberty and the God-ordained proper government which was established under the United States Constitution, it is likely that the public outcry against such efforts will magnify to the point that the promoters of these sovereignty-destroying programs will seek to obfuscate their efforts by simply changing the name(s) of their program(s), bringing forth new deceptive programs with seemingly innocuous purposes which further their goals, ignoring (or mocking) the groundswell of public concern, offering platitudes of assurance that they have the best interest of Americans in their hearts, denying their true purposes, or attempting to bring ridicule upon those who raise the voice of warning by resorting to ad hominem attacks against them. Perhaps all of these tactics, among others, will be employed but Americans must be wise enough to see through these schemes and redouble their efforts to derail these subversive programs.

It is imperative that the members of the United States Congress stand forth and exercise the most vigorous efforts possible within the proper authority of their respective offices to wrest from the clutches of foreign entities this critically important power and restore their constitutional responsibility to regulate commerce with foreign nations!

Entangling Alliances

Entangling alliances are closely related to these sovereignty-destroying trade agreements. Because they were astute observers of the workings of men and nations, the founders of this nation wisely admonished the nation to avoid relationships with foreign powers that would cause the nation to be drawn into international controversy and conflict. Their solemn admonition was to avoid what they termed "entangling alliances."

Many dozens of instances could be cited that would unequivocally establish the founder's position in this matter, but a few statements must suffice.

In his monumental Farewell Address, George Washington counseled us,

MODERN-DAY OFFENSES (UNREMITTING BETRAYALS)

George Washington

Europe has a set of primary interests, which have to us none, or very remote relation. Hence, she must be engaged in frequent controversies, the causes of which are essentially foreign to our concerns. Hence, therefore, it must be unwise in us to implicate ourselves, by artificial ties, in the ordinary vicissitudes of her politics, or the ordinary combinations and collusions of her friendships or enmities.

Why forego the advantages of so peculiar a situation? Why quit our own to stand upon foreign ground? Why, by interweaving our destiny with that of any part of Europe, entangle our peace and prosperity in the toils of European ambition, rivalship, interest, humor, or caprice?

Thomas Jefferson had much to say on the matter, stating, at various times,

> I know that it is a maxim with us, and I think it a wise one, not to entangle ourselves with the affairs of Europe.[149]

---

[149]. Ford, *Thomas Jefferson*, 4:483.

> The Constitution thought it wise to restrain the executive and Senate from entangling and embroiling our affairs with those of Europe.[150]
>
> Determined as we are to avoid, if possible, wasting the energies of our people in war and destruction, we shall avoid implicating ourselves with the powers of Europe, even in support of principles which we mean to pursue. They have so many other interests different from ours that we must avoid being entangled in them. We believe we can enforce these principles, as to ourselves, by peaceable means, now that we are likely to have our public councils detached from foreign views.[151]
>
> I have ever deemed it fundamental for the United States never to take part in the quarrels of Europe. Their political interests are entirely distinct from ours. Their mutual jealousies, their balance of power, their complicated alliances, their forms and principles of government are all foreign to us. They are nations of eternal war. All their energies are expended in the destruction of the labor, property, and lives of their people. On our part, never had a people so favorable a chance of trying the opposite system of peace and fraternity with mankind, and the direction of all our means and faculties to the purposes of improvement instead of destruction.[152]

And perhaps the following statement, which Jefferson made in his first inaugural address, most succinctly captures the essence of his position:

> I deem [one of] the essential principles of our government, and consequently [one] which ought to shape its administration, . . . peace, commerce, and honest friendship with all nations, entangling alliances with none.[153]

[150.] Jefferson's "Manual of Parliamentary Practice," in Bergh, *Thomas Jefferson*, 2:442.
[151.] To Thomas Paine, in Ford, *Thomas Jefferson*, 8:18:
[152.] To President Monroe, in Bergh, *Thomas Jefferson*, 15:436.
[153.] Jefferson's first inaugural address, in Bergh, *Thomas Jefferson*, 3:321.

MODERN-DAY OFFENSES (UNREMITTING BETRAYALS)

John Quincy Adams

Of course, there were other prominent founders who reinforced the official position of the United States, such as this statement that John Quincy Adams made in a July 4, 1821, speech:

> America has abstained from interference in the concerns of others, even when the conflict has been for principles to which she clings . . . . She goes not abroad in search of monsters to destroy. She is the well-wisher to the freedom and independence of all. She is the champion and vindicator only of her own.[154]

And, in the inspired "Monroe Doctrine" we find James Monroe's great wisdom:

> In the wars of European powers in matters relating to themselves we have never taken any part, nor does it comport with our policy so to do . . . . Our policy in regard to Europe . . . is, not to interfere in the internal concerns of any of its powers.

This position became the official policy of the United States and was largely followed until the twentieth century. The United States grew and prospered under it. And we avoided the almost constant bloodshed that was occurring throughout the rest of the world.

---

[154] John Quincy Adams, address delivered at the request of the Committee of Arrangements for the Anniversary of Independence at the city of Washington on the Fourth of July 1821 while he served as U.S. secretary of state. Published in pamphlet form, Cambridge; Printed at the Univ. Press, by Hilliard and Metcalf, sold by Cummings & Hilliard, No. 1 Cornhill, Boston, 1821.

In lecture 4, American History Time Line, we reviewed examples of how European nations have been drawn into bloody conflicts by their complicated treaties of alliance which required them to enter wars that lacked logical justification, and which resulted in tragic consequences for the nations so embroiled. During their era, the Founding Fathers of this nation had observed unending conflicts between European nations which were carried out in the name of international entangling alliances. They wisely pled with the leaders and people of the United States to scrupulously avoid entangling alliances and the dire consequences which they knew would follow.

Because the United States strayed from the founder's sound advice in this area nearly a century ago, and we continue to blatantly disregard this policy of eschewing entangling alliances, we, as a nation, now find ourselves constantly embroiled in the conflicts of belligerent nations around the world. This is because we have turned from the sound doctrines that were implemented as this nation was established. Our involvement in global conflict has become epidemic since the United States abandoned the advice of the nation's founders and entangled itself with international, globalist organizations: UN, NATO, SEATO, CENTO, etc. etc.

This nation must awaken and arouse itself to a sense of its awful situation; turn from the false entangling philosophies that have been so highly organized, so cleverly disguised, and so powerfully promoted for so many years; and return to the sound principles upon which this nation was founded, which allowed the nation to become the greatest, freest, most prosperous, most respected, and happiest nation on earth.

We must seek the withdrawal of the United States from this insidious effort to involve the United States in entangling alliances that constantly draw the nation into undeclared, unconstitutional international conflicts.

Immigration

As they wrote the United States Constitution, the founders of this nation delegated to the United States Congress the authority to deal with the issue of immigration and naturalization, saying,

> The Congress shall have Power . . . To establish an uniform Rule of Naturalization.[155]

Therefore, Congress must create legislation defining immigration and naturalization regulations and is not subject to agreements negotiated by the executive or the wishes of international organizations or populations.

In addition, the responsibilities of the national government in protecting the states from invasion are clearly defined within the United States Constitution:

[155.] U.S. Constitution, article 1, section 8, clause 4

MODERN-DAY OFFENSES (UNREMITTING BETRAYALS)

> The United States shall guarantee to every State in this Union a Republican Form of Government, and shall protect each of them against Invasion.[156]

Thomas Jefferson expressed his concerns with an "open" immigration policy. In regard to the dangers of foreign influence destroying our freedom through immigrants who lacked understanding of the Americanist principles of liberty, Jefferson stated,

> They will bring with them the principles of the governments they leave, imbibed in their early youth; . . . These principles, with their language, they will transmit to their children. In proportion to their numbers, they will share with us the legislation. They will infuse into it their spirit, warp and bias its directions, and render it a heterogeneous, incoherent, distracted mass.[157]

By any reasonable definition, the current illegal alien invasion must be considered an invasion, and Jefferson's statement regarding the dangers of foreign polluting political philosophies being injected into the nation's policies by immigration supports the possibility that the "republican form of government" of both the states and the nation may be in danger.

The integrity and protection of the international borders of the nation must be maintained. No "right of migration" exists for foreign nationals to enter the nation under terms other than those defined by Congress, and Congress has a duty to establish terms that protect the sovereignty of the nation and its *established* form of *limited* constitutional government.

History bears solemn witness that any nation that cannot or will not maintain the integrity of its borders will not long remain a sovereign nation. History abounds with numerous examples, both in ancient times as well as in modern times, of this unequivocal truth. If the United States is to remain a free and independent nation under the United States Constitution, it must immediately secure its international borders.

MONEY

Lecture 8, Of Money and Economics, extensively addresses the Founding Father's "original intent" regarding money and how the nation's current leadership has strayed from the sound money system the founders originally established for the nation. That lecture should be reviewed for a more detailed understanding of the concepts of money and the founders' "original intent."

The Constitution states,

[156.] U.S. Constitution, article 4, section 4
[157.] Bergh, *Thomas Jefferson*, 2:120-121.

Congress shall have power . . . To coin Money, regulate the Value thereof, and of foreign Coin, and fix the Standard of Weights and Measures.[158]

No State shall . . . coin money; emit Bills of Credit; make any Thing but gold and silver Coin a Tender in Payment of Debts.[159]

The Founding Fathers intended that the United States monetary system was to be based upon precious metals that have intrinsic value and that would back the nation's currency. "Unbacked" paper money (paper that is declared as money, but is not backed by precious metal) was rejected as extremely dangerous and, ultimately, destructive of the nation's economy. The current monetary policy violates every sound economic principle upon which this nation was originally established, threatens the financial viability of the nation, and the continued prosperity of the people of the land.

THE COURT SYSTEM

Congress (*not* the executive department or any other entity—foreign or domestic) has the power to create courts. The power to create courts may not be delegated to *any* other entity by Congress. United States Constitution, article 1, section 8, clause 9 states, "Congress Shall have power To . . . constitute Tribunals inferior to the supreme Court."

Efforts by the executive department to establish courts and tribunals are a violation of constitutionally delegated authority. The fact that the Congress has facilitated this usurpation by unconstitutionally delegating to the executive the authority to create courts and tribunals, regardless of the purpose, is an indictment against Congress. All congressional enactments which may be construed to delegate to the president this power must be rescinded.

There are also growing efforts to subvert the American judicial system to a world court system that would dictate that un-American "justice" be imposed upon citizens of the United States, denying them safeguards that most Americans take for granted and rarely consider, but which are essential to maintaining freedom. This movement must be exposed as an insidious effort to destroy the foundation of American liberty and destructive of the God-given individual rights which are vouched safe by the Constitution and our marvelous Bill of Rights. Under no circumstances should the American people allow their leaders to betray them to proposed international tribunal systems!

DEALING WITH TERRORISM

Congress (*not* the executive department or any other entity—foreign or domestic) has the power to create law and policies dealing with international terrorism. The power

---

[158.] Article 1, section 8, clause 5.
[159.] Article 1, section 10, clause 1.

to create law policies dealing with international terrorism may not be delegated to *any other entity by Congress.* United States Constitution, article 1, section 8, clause 10 states, "Congress Shall have power To . . . Punish Offenses against the Law of Nations."

The president has the authority, and the duty, to respond and defend the nation from immediately imminent attacks, but congressional responsibility takes preeminence in establishing anything beyond the immediate defense and response to an attack. In recent decades, the executive has usurped the constitutionally established congressional prerogative to establish policies and direct the nation's response to terrorism. And by the so-called Security and Prosperity Partnership (SPP) the executive is apparently fostering an expanded usurpation of constitutionally mandated congressional authority by establishing an international structure that will determine how the nation's security is maintained. This will be done by a presidential initiative which incorporates Canada and Mexico into the policy-making process by which the security of the United States is assured. Congress has a duty to reassert its responsibility in this area and deny the president's efforts to encroach upon their mandated authority.

CONSTITUTIONAL WAR-MAKING POWERS

The United States Constitution grants the power *solely* to Congress to take the nation into war. The executive (president) does not have a shred of power granted to him in regard to this most momentous act, nor does an entangling alliance with another nation have the power to automatically draw this nation into war. Article 1, section 8, clause 11 of the United States Constitution states, "Congress shall have Power . . . To declare War."

As noted elsewhere herein, in 1803, St. George Tucker, one of the preeminent constitutional scholars of the founding era of the United States, published his monumental work *View of the Constitution of the United States*. In that volume, he painstakingly reviews the form of government created by the United States Constitution, the powers granted within that document, and the scope and limits within which each component of the government is to operate. In regard to the matter of war, Tucker notes the following:

> The power declaring war, with all its train of consequences, direct and indirect, forms the next branch of the powers confided to Congress; and happy it is for the people of America that it is so vested. The term war, embraces the extremes of human misery and iniquity, and is alike the offspring of the one and the parent of the other. What else is the history of war from the earliest ages to the present moment but an afflicting detail of the sufferings and calamities of mankind, resulting from the ambition, usurpation, animosities, resentments, piques, intrigues, avarice, rapacity, oppressions, murders, assassinations, and other crimes, of the few possessing power! How rare are the instances of a just war! How few of those which are thus denominated have had their existence in a national injury! The personal claims of the sovereign are confounded with the interests of the nation over which he presides, and his private grievances or complaints are

transferred to the people; who are thus made the victims of a quarrel in which they have no part, until they become principals in it, by their sufferings. War would be banished from the face of the earth, were nations instead of princes to decide upon their necessity. Injustice can never be the collective sentiment of a people emerged from barbarism. Happy the nation where the people are the arbiters of their own interest and their own conduct! Happy were it for the world, did the people of all nations possess this power.[160]

During the debates of the Constitutional Convention of 1787, the delegates sought to build into their new constitution the greatest protection against frivolous or unjustified involvement of the nation in war. They sought to make the process for entering into war as deliberative as possible. They sought to place the responsibility for the decision as close to the people as possible since it would cost the blood and fortune of the people if it were entered into. They sought to remove the ability of one person, or office, to commit the nation to war. They debated and discussed the matter in excruciating detail before arriving at the solution they included in the final form of the Constitution.

Since the U.S. House of Representatives was to be the only department elected directly by the people and it is constitutionally the department with the power of the purse for the nation and thus most answerable to the people and since the U.S. Senate was originally appointed by the respective state legislatures (which would be responsible to pay for war by taxing their constituents), the decision was made to require the Congress to declare war if it was to be done.

The founders specifically withheld from the president of the United States the power to commit the United States to war. They did not want to allow conditions to arise under which some future president could act as the monarchs of the world had done in throwing their nations into unjustified war.

So Congress is to determine when the nation goes to war, and *only* Congress may declare war. The president is the commander of the military, but he has no power to determine when or if the nation goes to war; and Congress constitutionally retains numerous other powers and authority over the armed forces of the nation, including funding decisions, the power to make rules for the government and regulation of the military, the power to mobilize and deploy the militia, and other important influence. See the United States Constitution, article 1, section 8, clauses 11-16 for the actual delegation of war-making powers to the Congress.

So even during war, the president of the United States is subject to congressional restraint and does not possess "plenary" (full and absolute) powers as some have claimed.

James Madison, considered by many to be the "Father of the Constitution," was an active participant in the Constitutional Convention of 1787. During the debate regarding

---

[160]. Tucker, *View*, 211.

MODERN-DAY OFFENSES (UNREMITTING BETRAYALS)

the war-making powers, he made the following comment regarding the dangers associated with the circumstance of war, the tendency of power to accrue to the office of the executive during war, and the concerns he had that war may present opportunities to manipulate trickery and usurpation that would destroy the liberty of the nation:

> In time of actual war, great discretionary powers are constantly given to the Executive magistrate. Constant apprehension of war has the same tendency to render the head too large for the body. A standing military force, with an overgrown Executive, will not long be safe companions to liberty. The means of defense against foreign danger have been always the instruments of tyranny at home. Among the Romans it was a standing maxim, to excite a war whenever a revolt was apprehended. Throughout all Europe, the armies kept up under the pretext of defending, have enslaved, the people.[161]

During the Constitutional Convention of 1787, Thomas Jefferson was serving this nation on assignment in France. At the conclusion of the convention, Madison forwarded the new constitution to Jefferson. After he had reviewed the document, Jefferson noted the control placed upon the president in regard to war-making power and wrote to Madison, saying,

> We have already given, in example, one effectual check to the dog of war, by transferring the power of declaring war from the executive to the legislative body, from those who are to spend, to those who are to pay.[162]

James Madison continued throughout his life to hold concerns regarding the war-making powers of a nation, expressing his fears of an expanded executive power during a state of war, and the risks that unremitting war will destroy the freedom of the nation:

> Of all the enemies to public liberty war is, perhaps, the most to be dreaded, because it comprises and develops the germ of every other. War is the parent of armies; from these proceed debts and taxes; and armies, and debts, and taxes are the known instruments for bringing the many under the domination of the few. In war, too, the discretionary power of the Executive is extended; its influence in dealing out offices, honors, and emoluments is multiplied; and all the means of seducing the minds, are added to those of subduing the force, of the people . . . . No nation could preserve its freedom in the midst of continual warfare.[163]

[161.] Madison, *Journal*, 1:264-265.
[162.] Bergh, *Thomas Jefferson*, 7:461.
[163.] *Writings of Madison*, 4:491.

TO PRESERVE THE NATION

Unfortunately, modern congresses have blatantly disregarded their sole responsibility in the matter of war, lacking the courage to fulfill their constitutionally mandated duty in this regard. They have failed in the natural tendency to jealously guard their sphere of influence. They have even facilitated the usurpation of power by the executive branch, claiming that they may delegate their authority in the matter of war to the president or to please international organizations. Constitutional protocol was well understood by those who founded this nation, and they knew that the authority that was assigned in the Constitution could not legally be delegated to another entity. This matter of delegation was previously reviewed.

Congress (*not* the executive department, or any other entity—foreign or domestic) has the power to determine how war will be conducted if the nation enters a war. The power to determine how war will be conducted if the nation enters a war may not be delegated to *any* other entity by Congress. The United States Constitution, article 1, section 8, clause 11 states, "Congress Shall have Power To . . . Grant Letters of Marque and Reprisal."

Congress has the power to determine what forces will be used when the nation enters war, including "subcontracting" military action to forces other than the United States military through letters of Marque and Reprisal. Before the nation created the navy, letters of Marque and Reprisal were issued to ships captains who militarily engaged the enemy on behalf of the United States. With these official letters, if they were captured during battle, they could not be executed as pirates because they held official authorization to act on behalf of the United States.

Congress (*not* the executive department, or any other entity—foreign or domestic) has the power to determine how material and prisoners captured during war shall be dealt with. The power to determine how material and prisoners captured during war shall be dealt with may not be delegated to *any* other entity by Congress. The United States Constitution, article 1, section 8, clause 11 states, "Congress Shall have Power To . . . Make Rules concerning Captures on Land and Water."

In spite of congressional silence which indicates acquiescence to his actions, the president does not have the authority to create policy regarding prisoners of war (POWs). Congress must reassume the authority they have lost, and begin again to take their delegated authority seriously.

Congress (*not* the executive department, or any other entity—foreign or domestic) has the power to determine the rules and regulations of the United States military forces. The power to determine the rules and regulations of the United States military forces may not be delegated to *any* other entity by Congress. The United States Constitution, article 1, section 8, clause 14 states, "Congress Shall have Power To . . . Make Rules for the Government and Regulation of the land and naval Forces"

The president has largely usurped this congressional authority and, in an even more onerous development, many of the current leaders of the United States foster the idea that the nation's military forces may be assigned to international multi-national military organizations and operations, and have their activities directed by those foreign military commanders on behalf of actions which are not related to the proper purposes for which the United States military exists.

MODERN-DAY OFFENSES (UNREMITTING BETRAYALS)

The might of the United States military is to be used solely to protect the people of this nation from attacks against their lives, liberty, and property. The U.S. military is to remain strictly under U.S. command, and is not to be used to carry out the mandates of any international or foreign power, or to be used as "nation-builders", or "peace keepers" in disputes foreign to this nation.

For many years, the nation has strayed from this brief sampling of sound principles. If the liberties that were bequeathed to the nation are to be saved, we must immediately restore the foundation upon which the nation was established and built. Congress must again assume its duty in the matter of war and wrest the war-making power from the hands, both foreign and domestic, that have usurped the congressional constitutional responsibility!

FEDERAL LANDS

In regard to the power granted by the United States Constitution to the federal government to hold and control land within this nation, article 1, section 8, clause 17 of the United States Constitution states,

> Congress shall have power . . . To exercise exclusive Legislation in all Cases whatsoever, over such District (not exceeding ten Miles square), as may, by Cession of particular States, and the Acceptance of Congress, become the Seat of the Government of the United States, and to exercise like Authority over all Places purchased by the Consent of the Legislature of the State in which the Same shall be for the Erection of Forts, Magazines, Arsenals, dock-yards, and other needful Buildings.

By authority of this constitutional stipulation, Washington DC was created as a federally held jurisdiction, and (by consent of the state legislatures in which the lands were to be "federalized") the other authorized actions were carried out (forts were established, as were magazines, arsenals, dockyards, and other buildings). No other authority for permanently held federal lands is found within the United States Constitution.

The Tenth Amendment to the United States Constitution reinforces the intent of the founders that unless a power was specifically granted to the national government, it was withheld from the federal government and retained by the states or the people:

> The powers not delegated to the United States by the Constitution, nor prohibited by it to the States, are reserved to the States respectively, or to the people.

It was clearly understood by the founders of this nation that additional states would be admitted and become part of the new nation. Article 4, section 3 of the United States Constitution states,

> New States may be admitted by the Congress into this Union.

TO PRESERVE THE NATION

As the founders of this nation created the regulations that were to guide the admission of new states to the nation, they ensured that all new states would be admitted upon equal footing and status with the original thirteen states:

> And whenever any of the said States shall have sixty thousand free inhabitants therein, such State shall be admitted by its delegates, into the Congress of the United States, **on an equal footing with the original States, in all respects whatever**; and shall be at liberty to for a permanent constitution and State government: Provided, The constitution and government, so to be formed, shall be republican, and in conformity to the principles contained in these articles, and, so far as it can be consistent with the general interest of the confederacy, such admission shall be allowed at an earlier period, and when there may be a less number of free inhabitants in the State than sixty thousand.[164]

Certainly, by treaty and through purchase, the national government obtained additional land in the westward movement, but in the beginning, as quickly as these lands were obtained, efforts were undertaken to pass those lands into the hands of the states or to the people as the new states were admitted as states. This was one of the means by which the federal government sought to eliminate the national debt.

By observing their actions as they admitted new states east of the Mississippi River, we may deduce that the Founding Fathers of this nation intended that the national government *not* unconstitutionally withhold lands from the states and the people. Federal land holdings within the states east of the Mississippi varies between 1 to 3 percent in each of those states. In the West, the federal government has unconstitutionally retained ownership of vast tracks of land that should have passed to the states or the people. For example, in Utah, two-thirds of the land mass of the state is held by the federal government. Other Western states have a much higher percentage of their land held by the federal government.

Because true wealth and prosperity are inextricably interwoven to the land (raw materials—minerals, timber, energy sources, food, water, etc.—are all tied to land ownership), federal land ownership prevents a full measure of prosperity from being attained in the states that have been thus handicapped.

There is no constitutional justification for the federal government to be the largest landholder in this nation, and in fact, article 1, section 8, clause 17 of the Constitution states the original intention of founders that the land holdings of the federal government be

---

[164.] GOVERNMENT OF THE NORTHWEST TERRITORY 1787. An ordinance for the government of the territory of the United States northwest of the river Ohio. Article V. Emphasis added. This ordinance created the framework and process by which new states have been admitted to the Union since the founding of the nation. After the United States Constitution was ratified, this ordinance was again passed by Congress to ensure that it was clearly understood to apply under the new Constitution.

relatively small and constrained to specific purposes defined within the Constitution. And we may clearly see by their actions (East of the Mississippi River) that the founders carried out that intention as they administered the affairs of the nation.

The reality is we do not have too many people; we have too much government. The federal government should not hold ownership and power over the vast tracts of land that it currently does, and the nation must begin the effort to pass those lands into the control of the states and the people as is required by the United States Constitution and the legislative intent expressed and demonstrated by the Founding Fathers.

TREATY-MAKING POWER

In regard to treaties, the United States Constitution makes the following stipulations:

> No State shall enter into any Treaty, Alliance, or Confederation.[165]

> He [the president] shall have Power, by and with the Advice and Consent of the Senate, to make Treaties, provided two thirds of the Senators present concur.[166]

> The judicial Power shall extend to all Cases, in Law and Equity, arising under this Constitution, the Laws of the United States, and Treaties made, or which shall be made, under their authority;—to all cases affecting [the section goes on to enumerate the scope of the power granted].[167]

> This Constitution, and the Laws of the United States which shall be made in Pursuance thereof; and all Treaties made, or which shall be made, under the Authority of the United States, shall be the supreme Law of the Land.[168]

In his writings, St. George Tucker briefly touches upon the exercise of the treaty-making power, an area wherein the United States has strayed into dangerous territory in recent decades.

The danger lies in the false perception that by the power to make treaties, the Constitution can be modified or amended. This recent "interpretation" is that simply by having the president agree to and the Senate ratify treaties with other nations (as required in Articles II and VI of the United States Constitution), the United States Constitution may be modified as though it had been amended by the process defined in article 5 of the Constitution. Tucker is careful to note that such a position is wholly inconsistent with the intent and purposes specified within

---

[165.] Article 1, section 10
[166.] Article 2, section 2
[167.] Article 3, section 2
[168.] Article 6

the Constitution and that such a position or action would subvert and completely destroy the deliberative amendment process that is outlined in article 5 of the Constitution.

Article 5 states that amendments to the Constitution occur when two-thirds of *both* houses of Congress have agreed to a proposed amendment *and* three-fourths of all states agree to those changes. Thereby, Congress may not change the Constitution without the concurrence of the people.

One of the prime foundational principles of the American experiment is found in the Declaration of Independence ("it is the Right of the People to alter or to abolish" their government), and the people would be left out of any constitutional modification if it were allowed to occur with actions taken solely by the president and the Senate. George Washington touched upon this issue in his monumental Farewell Address, saying,

George Washington

> This Government, the offspring of our own choice, uninfluenced and unawed, adopted upon full investigation and mature deliberation, completely free in its principles, in the distribution of its powers, uniting security with energy, and containing within itself a provision for its own amendment, has a just claim to your confidence and your support. Respect for its authority, compliance with its laws, acquiescence in its measures, are duties enjoined by the fundamental maxims of true liberty. The basis of our political systems is the right of the people to make and to alter their constitutions of government. But the constitution which at any time exists till changed by an explicit and authentic act of the whole people is sacredly obligatory upon all. The very idea of the power and the right of the people to establish government presupposes the duty of every individual to obey the established government . . . .

> If in the opinion of the people the distribution or modification of the constitutional powers be in any particular wrong, let it be corrected by an amendment in the way which the Constitution designates. But let there be no change by usurpation; for though this in one instance may be the instrument of good, it is the customary weapon by which free governments are destroyed. The precedent must always greatly overbalance in permanent evil any partial or transient benefit which the use can at any time yield.[169]

Tucker quotes a contemporary congressional resolution pertaining to the treaty-making power of the president and Senate that notes their reservations to treaties that go beyond their view of the constitutional scope and that would appear to require constraint:

> That when a treaty stipulates regulations on any of the subjects submitted by the Constitution to the power of Congress, it must depend for its execution, as to such stipulations, on a law or laws to be passed by Congress; and it is the constitutional right and duty of the House of Representatives, in all such cases, to deliberate on the expediency, or inexpediency, of carrying such treaty into effect, and to determine and act thereon, as in their judgment, may be most conducive to the public good.[170]

Tucker proceeds to note the impeccable logic of such a congressional position:

> A contrary construction would render the power of the President and Senate paramount to that of the whole Congress, even upon those subjects upon which every branch of Congress is, by the Constitution, required to deliberate. *Let it be supposed, for example, that the President and Senate should stipulate by treaty with any foreign nation, that in case of war between that nation and any other, the United States should immediately declare against that nation: Can it be supposed that such a treaty would be so far the law of the land, as to take from the House of Representatives their constitutional right to deliberate on the expediency or inexpediency of such a declaration of war, and to determine and act thereon, according to their own judgment?*[171]

It would seem today that Tucker's prediction of the nation being drawn into war without adhering to the constitutional requirement of a congressional declaration of war was almost prophetic—in view of the numerous modern instances of that mantra being the national justification in so momentous a matter!

---

[169] In Richardson, *Messages and Papers*, 1:205-16.
[170] Resolution of the House of Representative, 6 April 1796, in Tucker, *View*, 277.
[171] Tucker, *View*, 277; emphasis added.

More succinctly, Thomas Jefferson makes the point:

> By the general power to make treaties, the Constitution must have intended to comprehend only those objects which are usually regulated by treaty and cannot be otherwise regulated.... It must have meant to except out of these the rights reserved to the states, for surely the President and Senate cannot do by treaty what the whole government is interdicted from doing in any way.[172]

Jefferson felt that the Constitution must be strictly held to the words written in the document:

> Our peculiar security is in the possession of a written Constitution. Let us not make it a blank paper by construction.

> I say the same as to the opinion of those who consider the grant of the treaty-making power as boundless. If it is, then we have no Constitution. If it has bounds, they can be no others than the definitions of the powers which that instrument gives. It specifies and delineates the operations permitted to the federal government, and gives all the powers necessary to carry these into execution. Whatever of these enumerated objects is proper for a law, Congress may make the law; whatever is proper to be executed by way of a treaty, the President and Senate may enter into the treaty; whatever is to be done by a judicial sentence, the judges may pass the sentence.[173]

As he debated the treaty-making power that was granted to the president and Senate as found in the Constitution, James Madison addressed the logical limits to the treaty-making power and made this statement:

> Does it follow, because this power is given to Congress, that it is absolute and unlimited? I do not conceive that power is given to the President and Senate to dismember the empire, or to alienate any great, essential right. I do not think the whole legislative authority have this power. The exercise of the power must be consistent with the object of the delegation.[174]

The Founding Fathers of this nation unquestionably felt that the power to make treaties did not embrace the power to modify the Constitution. In their view, the treaty-making power was a limited grant of power that could not undermine or destroy individual God-

---

[172.] Jefferson's "Manual of Parliamentary Practice," in Bergh, *Thomas Jefferson*, 2:442.
[173.] Bergh, *Thomas Jefferson*, 10:418-19.
[174.] Elliott, *Debates*, 3:514.

given rights or the structure or framework of the limited, carefully defined government they established.

It is astonishing that in recent decades efforts to destroy the sovereignty of the nation and the United States Constitution have been undertaken through the treaty process, and those efforts have been expanded through "executive agreements" that the president makes with foreign powers and with "trade agreements" such as NAFTA, GATT, WTO, CAFTA, which are not treaties (and which would have never passed the Senate by the required two-thirds vote had they been presented as treaties). None of these methods can modify the United States Constitution in any way, shape, or form, but they are treated by those in power as having done so. Tragedy will follow if the nation continues along this path.

The current false philosophy regarding treaty power, as promoted by those who would usurp authority within this nation, will lead to the destruction of the United States Constitution and result in the loss of our liberty if the citizens of this nation are not willing to expose and derail these attempts. While authority is not granted within the Constitution to deconstruct the constitutional authority of the land by treaty, an amendment similar to the one offered by Senator John W. Bricker (which was discussed near the conclusion of lecture 3) may be necessary to assure that future leadership does not seek to undermine the nation's charter through the treaty process.

ADDITIONAL CONSIDERATION OF MATTERS PERTAINING TO THE COURTS

The United States Constitution defines the scope and purpose of the judicial system it created. As with all other aspects of the government the founders of this nation framed, there were "checks and balances" established to ensure that the court system did not usurp power and destroy the liberty of the nation.

Article 1, section 8, clause 9 states, "Congress shall have power . . . To constitute Tribunals inferior to the Supreme Court."

Article 3 of the Constitution creates "one supreme Court" and reiterates that Congress has the authority to create lower courts, saying,

> Such inferior Courts as the Congress may from time to time ordain and establish.[175]

As already noted in this lecture, in recent modern times, the executive branch has ignored the constitutional stipulation that only Congress may create courts or "tribunals" and claimed to establish courts for various purposes. No authority is granted within the Constitution

---

[175] U. S. Constitution article 3, section 1, clause 1

for such action, and Congress is remiss if it fails to aggressively act within its constitutional prerogative to preempt such usurpation. And as also noted previously, in spite of recent actions to the contrary, Congress may *not* constitutionally delegate to another a power that was delegated to them by the people through the Constitution.

Article 3 of the Constitution defines the scope and power of the United States Supreme Court, noting specific cases in which the court has "original jurisdiction." Within the scope specifically defined within the Constitution, the Supreme Court can not be denied authority to act. However, the authors of the United States Constitution placed "checks and balances" within the Constitution on the court. Certainly, article 3, section 2, clause 2 of the United States Constitution defines a "check and balance" that was created to prevent the court system from usurping power. It states specifically,

> In all the other Cases before mentioned, the supreme Court shall have appellate Jurisdiction, both as to Law and Fact, with such Exceptions, and under such Regulations as the Congress shall make.

Regardless of opinions to the contrary, the United States Constitution actually states, "With such Exceptions, and under such Regulations as the Congress shall make." We often speak of the "checks and balances" that were so wisely written into the document to prevent power from being consolidated into tyranny, but almost no one recognizes this "check" that may be exercised to balance against a usurping court.

And of course, as previously noted, the Constitution delegates to the Congress authority over the existence of all federal courts inferior to the Supreme Court (see article 1, section 8, clause 9 and article 3, section 1). While article 3, section 2 of the United States Constitution delegates specific authority for Supreme Court involvement in certain specified instances, it seems certain that in cases not specifically enumerated within the Constitution that the United States Congress has the authority to rein in the rogue court system that currently exists by simple majority vote in both the House and Senate. By exercising this rarely used authority, the United States Congress could remove specific cases from the purview of the federal court system if the federal court system began to usurp authority in those cases.

An example of how this could be accomplished is found in the 1868 *Ex parte McCardle* case, which was taken to the Supreme Court by an individual seeking relief from an onerous act of Congress (but which act Congress had, under authority of article 3, section 2, clause 2 prohibited from being reviewed by the Supreme Court). The following is the relevant excerpt from the declaration the Supreme Court made when McCardle sought to bring the case to them for redress:

> We are not at liberty to inquire into the motives of the legislature. We can only examine into its power under the Constitution; and the power to make exceptions to the appellate jurisdiction of this court is given by express words . . . . It is quite clear, therefore, that this court cannot proceed to pronounce judgment in this case, for it has no longer jurisdiction of the appeal; and judicial duty is not less

fitly performed by declining ungranted jurisdiction than in exercising firmly that which the Constitution and the laws confer.

The irony is that this unanimous 1868 Supreme Court decision is a good decision upholding a repellent act of Congress.

While this approach has been rarely used, and some would deny that the authority of Congress to act in such a manner is granted within the Constitution, it is there for all to read and only awaits a courageous Congress to act upon it.

And in spite of contrary opinions, not only has article 3, section 2, clause 2 been successfully applied in the past by the United States Congress, it may easily be applied today if Congress could be brought to exercise it by the outcry of an informed electorate. The following is a generically worded resolution that could be used as a template suggesting how such an act may be worded in the required instances.

POSSIBLE WORDING OF CONGRESSIONAL ACT WHICH WOULD REMOVE CASES FROM THE JURISDICTION OF FEDERAL COURTS

> The appellate jurisdiction of the Supreme Court and the jurisdictions of the inferior federal courts shall not extend to hearing or determining the power of a state to *(Insert the issue or subject which is to be prevented from being reviewed by the federal court system)*. Such jurisdictions shall not extend to hearing nor determining the refusal of any state to give full faith and credit to any act regarding *(Insert issue or subject)* under the law of any other state.

This approach applies the United States Constitution "in the tradition of the Founding Fathers." It recognizes and applies the congressional authority over the courts as allowed and found in article 1, section 8, clause 9; article 3, section 2, clause 2; and article 4, section 1.

No "full faith and credit" complaints could be taken to the federal courts and the power to encroach into these matters would be kept out of the hands of the federal government. Each state would be responsible within their own realm before God for their actions in these matters.

AMENDING THE CONSTITUTION AND CONSTITUTIONAL CONVENTIONS

In regard to the process by which the United States Constitution is to be changed, article 5 of the United States Constitution states,

> The Congress, whenever two thirds of both Houses shall deem it necessary, shall propose Amendments to this Constitution, or, on the Application of the

> Legislatures of two thirds of the several States, shall call a Convention for proposing Amendments, which, in either Case, shall be valid to all Intents and Purposes, as Part of this Constitution, when ratified by the Legislatures of three fourths of the several States, or by Conventions in three fourths thereof, as the one or the other Mode of Ratification may be proposed by the Congress; Provided that no Amendment which may be made prior to the Year One thousand eight hundred and eight shall in any Manner affect the first and fourth Clauses in the Ninth Section of the first Article; and that no State, without its Consent, shall be deprived of its equal Suffrage in the Senate.

In brief, article 5 states that amendments to the Constitution occur when two-thirds of *both* Houses of Congress have agreed on a proposed amendment *and* three-fourths of all states agree to those changes.

The founders of this nation were good and wise and honest men who sought to establish a charter for this nation that would ensure the blessings of liberty for themselves and their posterity, but in their wisdom, they knew that they were mere mortals who were not omniscient. They knew that time and circumstances may ultimately dictate a need for changes in the Constitution. They were also firm in their conviction that the Constitution was a written, binding contract that all who hold office are required to obey. Washington stated in his Farewell Address, "The constitution which at any time exists till changed by an explicit and authentic act of the whole people is sacredly obligatory upon all."

If changes became necessary, they were not to occur through usurpation or by any means than by the process defined in the United States Constitution. The founders did not embrace the modern lie that the Constitution is a "living document" that can be changed by decree, in practice, or by any other means than the article 5 process.

In recent years, a gross misunderstanding has become popular: that the Constitution may be modified upon the whim of the Supreme Court (some have called the Supreme Court a "constantly sitting constitutional convention") or by the decree of a president or by the vote of Congress. These philosophies defy all logic, reason, and firmly established constitutional principle. And yet this position is fostered today by those whom the founders of the nation warned against.

The Founding Fathers of this nation were unequivocal in their position that the Constitution was binding upon all until changed by an authentic act.

In his Farewell Address, Washington warned that factions, groups, parties, or combinations would arise that would attempt to modify the foundation of the constitutional government that had been established and that those efforts could result in the overthrow of the freedom of the land, saying,

> All obstructions to the execution of the laws, all combinations and associations, under whatever plausible character, with the real design to direct, control, counteract, or awe the regular deliberation and action of the constituted authorities, are destructive of this fundamental principle and of fatal tendency . . . .

MODERN-DAY OFFENSES (UNREMITTING BETRAYALS)

> However combinations or associations of the above description may now and then answer popular ends, they are likely in the course of time and things to become potent engines by which cunning, ambitious, and unprincipled men will be enabled to subvert the power of the people, and to usurp for themselves the reins of government, destroying afterwards the very engines which have lifted them to unjust dominion. . . .
>
> Toward the preservation of your Government and the permanency of your present happy state, it is requisite not only that you steadily discountenance irregular oppositions to its acknowledged authority, but also that you resist with care the spirit of innovation upon its principles, however specious the pretexts. One method of assault may be to effect in the forms of the Constitution alterations which will impair the energy of the system, and thus to undermine what can not be directly overthrown.[176]

It is currently in vogue to suggest that the Constitution is somehow flawed and that recent usurpations by the federal government demonstrate the truth of that position, particularly in cases in which the Founding Fathers of this nation clearly intended that jurisdiction in a matter be withheld from the national government and left in the hands of the states. Those who hold the position that the Constitution is flawed are often quick to insist that constitutional amendments are desperately needed to correct the "flaws" they perceive. The real truth about "flaws" that are supposedly in the current United States Constitution is this: every single one of these so-called flaws have been brought about by usurpation of authority not granted by the Constitution. The flaw is not in the Constitution—it is in those who seek power and those who allow them to hold power. The key to stopping this is in a courageous Congress, not in scrapping the Constitution or in modifying it every time some tyrant seeks to usurp power not granted in God's inspired document. If we changed it for every whim of false philosophy that came along, we would have many thousands of amendments and not a real constitution.

Virtually all of the "flaws" that clamor for a constitutional amendment could be solved by the majority vote of a courageous congress to remove the matter from a runaway court system (as previously discussed). Logic, reason, and historical precedent testify that the task of obtaining a simple majority in Congress is much easier than getting two-thirds of both houses and three-fourths of all the states to bring amendments forth that aren't needed to begin with.

And the danger of seeking amendments in the many emotional issues that face the nation today is magnified by huge orders of magnitude if the "good and well-meaning people" of the land become so frustrated and angry with a congress that can't bring them an amendment they wish to pass that they demand a constitutional convention be called. Remember, article 5 of the Constitution *requires* Congress to convene a convention if two-thirds of the states call for one (the Constitution says they *"shall call"* a convention, not that they "may call" a convention). We are already dangerously close to that event, within only a few states.

---

[176]. Richardson, *Messages and Papers*, 1:209-10.

Of course, the only national constitutional convention we have had in the entire history of the United States resulted in what we would call today a "runaway convention." While those who attended the Convention of 1787 had been called together to suggest changes that would correct perceived flaws in the existing constitution, the Articles of Confederation, they immediately saw within the purview of their authority as duly elected representatives of the people and states to set aside the existing constitution and write another one. That is exactly what they did, and they even changed the unanimous consent required by the Articles of Confederation to a lesser level to ensure easier ratification of the new constitution. Fortunately, God had raised up men for this very purpose, and the results were endorsed by God. Where are such men today? In light of the dangers associated with a constitutional convention, one must ask one's self: among the prominent leaders of this nation, is there even one who could hold a candle to the inspired works of those whom we call the Founding Fathers of this nation? The risk for such an action today cannot be measured.

Virtually all of the rights recognized and protected within the Bill of Rights are under assault today. Only a few examples will be cited herein.

The Preamble to the Bill of Rights expresses the purpose of the Bill of Rights. The Bill of Rights did not "create" new rights; it simply recognized preexisting God-given rights and made clear that additional restrictive clauses that applied to the national government were being added to the United States Constitution to ensure there was a clear understanding that the national government did not have powers granted that would infringe upon individual God-given rights. The Ninth and Tenth Amendments were all-encompassing and made certain to protect all unmentioned rights and prevent the national government from assuming any rights not specifically granted (enumerated or listed) within the Constitution.

> The conventions of a number of the states having, at the time of their adopting the Constitution, expressed a desire, in order to prevent misconstruction or abuse of its powers, that further declaratory and restrictive clauses should be added.[177]

THE RIGHT TO KEEP AND BEAR ARMS

This topic is the subject of an entire lecture (lecture 10). Consequently, only the briefest mention is made at this point regarding the attacks that are currently carried out against this critically important right.

The United States Constitution Second Amendment states,

> A well regulated Militia, being necessary to the security of a free State, the right of the people to keep and bear Arms, shall not be infringed.

---

[177]. Preamble to the Bill of Rights

Without exception, those we refer to as the "Founding Fathers" of this nation studied Blackstone's *Commentaries* prior to the Revolutionary War. Therein, Blackstone notes the right of self-defense as one of mankind's unalienable rights:

> [Self-defense is] justly called the primary law of nature, so it is not, neither can it be in fact, taken away by the laws of society.[178]

In keeping with that wisdom, the Second Amendment was included in this nation's bill of rights to ensure the future protection of this individual God-given right.

In spite of the Second Amendment, there is an unprecedented effort underway today in our nation to disarm the people of this nation.

PROTECTIONS AGAINST UNREASONABLE SEARCHES AND SEIZURES

The Fourth Amendment to the United States Constitution was created, at least in part, due to the abuses the Founding Fathers had suffered as the king's officers had exercised blanket search warrants called "writs of assistance" during the colonial period. These writs were completely open-ended and allowed the officers to search anything, at any time, without judicial oversight in regard to legal justification. This personal, painful experience led to this amendment becoming part of the Bill of Rights, as additional restriction upon the power of the national government. The Fourth Amendment requires extreme specificity, the taking of an oath by the requesting officer, and judicial oversight. Search warrants are not to be issued without strict adherence to the requirements defined by this amendment:

> Upon probable cause, supported by Oath or affirmation, and particularity describing the place to be searched, and the persons or things to be seized.

In the frenzied weeks following the tragic attacks of September 11, 2001, the United States Congress passed a bill titled the USA PATRIOT Act of 2001. The name is an acronym for "Uniting and Strengthening America by Providing Appropriate Tools Required to Intercept and Obstruct Terrorism." This enormous bill was introduced, passed, and signed by the president within a four-day period. The document was not even available for the members of Congress to read prior to the vote. It conveys wide and sweeping powers to the national government. A careful reading of the act reveals grave concerns about the potential of those powers being someday abused.

[178.] Sir William Blackstone, *Commentaries on the Laws of England*, vol. 3, 4 [1765-1769]

A full review of concerns with the USA PATRIOT Act would require a document that would exceed the size of the act itself. Perhaps a few examples will suffice to demonstrate how it is at odds with the foundation principles of the nation and how the seeds of tyranny are perceived by many to be found within its pages.

While much ado has been made about the supposed possible violations that individuals may experience if bookstores or libraries were asked to provide records that would reveal something about an individual's reading habits, this is really a "red herring" that is designed to divert the public mind from other deeper and more onerous dangers.

As examples, only a few specific citations will be directly quoted from the act. They are written in the legal jargon, so they do not read like great prose.

A few general concerns about the USA PATRIOT Act would have to include the following sample statements:

- The act *requires* judges to issue a search warrant or wiretap upon application by a federal agent. The act requires none of the specificity required by the Fourth Amendment, but simply states, for example, "Upon an application made pursuant to this section, the judge **shall** enter an ex parte order as requested, or as modified, approving the release of records if the judge finds that the application meets the requirements of this section" (Sec. 501).

The section has no requirements for specificity as required by the Fourth Amendment. By the wording, judges are required to issue a warrant based only upon the request, without further stipulations as required by the Fourth Amendment.

- Clauses throughout the act create the specter of "*secret orders.*" For example, the clauses following the "shall" issue statement just noted state the following: "(2) An order under this subsection shall not disclose that it is issued for purposes of an investigation described in subsection (a). (d) No person shall disclose to any other person (other than those persons necessary to produce the tangible things under this section) that the Federal Bureau of Investigation has sought or obtained things under this section."

Wording throughout the act is very broad and absolutely could be applied to circumstances broader than terrorism, and in fact, we must assume that the broadness of the statements was purposeful. In fact, in many places the act begins to sound hauntingly like the blanket "writs of assistance" we have previously mentioned. Examples of these concerns can be found in the following quotation found within the act:

- Upon application . . . , the court shall enter an ex parte order authorizing the installation and use of pen register or trap and trace device **anywhere within the United States**, if the court finds that the attorney for the Government has certified to the court that the information likely to be obtained by such installation and use is *relevant to an ongoing criminal investigation.* The order, upon service of that order, shall apply to any person or entity providing wire or electronic communication service in the United States whose assistance may facilitate the execution of the order. Whenever such an order is served on any person or entity not specifically named in the order, upon request of such person or entity, the attorney for the Government or law enforcement or investigative officer that is serving the order shall provide written or electronic *certification that the order applies to the person or entity being served.* (Sec. 216)

Did you catch that? In order to get an order, all an agent must do is "certify to the court that the information likely to be obtained by such installation and use is *relevant to an ongoing criminal investigation."* Such orders are good anywhere in the United States and apply to anyone the officer serves (as long as the officer certifies that it applies to that person).

The original version of this act said that such orders could not be challenged in court, but one of the superficial changes that was made upon the reauthorization of the act (to supposedly protect the liberties of Americans) was that the orders could be challenged in court *after one year.*

Beyond these specific statements, a few general concerns about the USA PATRIOT Act would have to include the following broad statements:

- The act places many onerous burdens upon businesses that are charged with the responsibility of being de facto agents of the government in reporting to the government business transactions, particularly financial transactions, of law-abiding American citizens. These reporting requirements not only violate the historical privacy of Americans in their lives and financial matters, but they also add costs and other burdens to the business that is required to collect and transmit information regarding activities that Americans should never have to report to anyone.

- The act dramatically expands federal government powers of surveillance, search, and arrest and sets potentially harmful precedents for future encroachments on personal liberty. In spite of protestations to the contrary, some of these expanded powers may be unconstitutional and would likely have been found so in a day and time when the foundation principles of the nation were better understood and a bold love of liberty was more widely held within America.

- The act greatly expands the legal use of so-called "black bag" searches—in that there are broad powers granted to police agencies to conduct secret searches without notifying the subject of the search until after the search has been conducted. This power appears to extend to all suspected criminal circumstances, not only to potential acts of terrorism or war.

- Roving wiretaps that allow investigators to tap multiple telephones used by a single "suspect" may now be carried out nationally on a single court order. Previously, such wiretap orders were generally only allowed within the jurisdiction of the judge issuing the order and were subject to constraints that reduced the potential that abuses would occur.

- The broad latitude granted for secret searches and national search warrants that hold extra jurisdictional force begin to look suspiciously like writs of assistance and may be unconstitutional because the Fourth Amendment requires warrants to be issued "upon probable cause . . . particularly describing the place to be searched, and the persons or things to be seized."

- The act also allows the Central Intelligence Agency (CIA) to access foreign intelligence information obtained by domestic grand juries, as well as other information obtained in investigations and by law enforcement agencies—effectively creating an environment in which the CIA could spy on American citizens—in violation of long-standing U.S. policy. This particular power should be of concern to all Americans in light of a presidential appointment of a military man to lead the CIA, particularly considering that individual previously held positions with the National Security Agency (NSA), and condoned warrantless wiretaps in that assignment. Placing military personnel at the head of all major United States intelligence agencies has potentially ominous overtones. Throughout the world, such conditions have ultimately led to tyranny within nations that have followed this formula.

- Overall, the USA PATRIOT Act limits and reduces judicial oversight in the gathering of evidence, diminishes the distinction between the gathering of foreign intelligence and domestic law enforcement, and allows many of these provisions to be applied, not just against agents of foreign governments or against terrorists (which are defined under a very broad definition that may someday be abused), but against citizens of the nation who may, under some construction of the law, be deemed a threat.

Many have heard Benjamin Franklin's well-known perspective: "They who can give up essential liberty to obtain a little temporary safety deserve neither liberty nor safety."[179] That perspective must be considered in striking the proper balance between safety and the individual liberties vouched safe in the nation's "enabling documents."

---

[179]. Smyth, *Benjamin Franklin*, 6:382.

MODERN-DAY OFFENSES (UNREMITTING BETRAYALS)

James Madison's warning in this matter also bears repeating. In 1788, he said, "Since the general civilization of mankind, I believe there are more instances of the abridgement of the freedom of the people by gradual and silent encroachment of those in power than by violent and sudden usurpations."[180]

In light of the fact that the USA PATRIOT Act is laden with clauses that are apt to be abused at some point by overzealous government, let us hope that wisdom will prevail and the USA PATRIOT Act will be reconsidered.

Conclusion

As has been previously mentioned in this lecture series:

In his day, Thomas Jefferson spoke of actions taken by those in power that were inconsistent with liberty and proper government, saying,

> Single acts of tyranny may be ascribed to the accidental opinion of a day; but a series of oppressions, begun at a distinguished period, and pursued unalterably through every change of ministers, too plainly prove a deliberate, systematical plan of reducing us to slavery.[181]

As noted at the beginning of this lecture, Jefferson enumerated many of the "offenses of the king" in the Declaration of Independence. The serious student may find it interesting to carefully review the offenses noted in the Declaration, and consider the existence of parallel offenses in modern America. Are wholesome laws being ignored? Are the rights of the people being invaded? Is the administration of justice being obstructed? Have multitudes of offices been erected and are swarms of officers harassing the people and eating out their substance due to onerous levels of regulation and taxation? Are citizens of the nation being subjected to jurisdictions foreign to our constitution through foreign entanglements, treaties, and agreements? Is the right to trial by jury at risk? Have individuals been transported overseas to facilitate interrogation and trial? Is the fundamental form of our government being altered in daily practice by those who hold office in this nation? Jefferson proposed that leaders whose character is marked by such flaws must be defined as tyrants unfit to be rulers of a free people. If such is the case, modern Americans have solutions which were not available to the Americans of the 1770s. Their only option was armed rebellion to throw off the yoke of tyranny. Today, we are privileged to have a national charter called the United States Constitution. Regardless of how the constitution has been ignored and subverted in recent decades, it still exists, and ALL who hold office are still required to take an oath to uphold it. In addition, Americans still retain the right to vote. We may still select our leaders, and we

---

[180.] Elliot, *Debates*, 3:87.

[181.] Bergh, *Thomas Jefferson*, 1:193.

may still insist that they honor their oath of office, or we may remove them from office. An informed and actively engaged electorate that understands and upholds sound principles may save this nation without resorting to the violence and bloodshed which originally purchased the freedom of this land. It is imperative that such an informed electorate be again raised up in this nation! As Jefferson said: "If a nation expects to be ignorant and free . . . it expects what never was and never will be."[182]

The review of unremitting betrayals by those who currently hold office is not complete in this lecture, but simply an introduction to the challenges the nation faces as the leadership ignores their oath of office to uphold the United States Constitution. Hopefully, the serious student will build upon the foundation we have herein established, carefully reviewing the words of the Founding Fathers and comparing their words and actions to the words and actions of those who currently hold power. The "original intent" of this nation's founders in regard to the proper role of government may be unequivocally documented. Those sound original principles are almost universally violated by those who govern today. It is a great tragedy that this generation cares so little that those who govern run roughshod unimpeded over our foundation of liberty. Suffice it to say, we are at risk of losing it all.

The Preamble to the U.S. Constitution promotes the idea that the people are the keepers of the Constitution, and therefore, an informed electorate is the key to keeping all of their representatives in line with the proper constitutional principle. The people have a responsibility to be "constitutionalists," and it is a tragedy when those who so many look to for help in this responsibility are sowing the seeds of misunderstanding that will ultimately result in the destruction of this marvelous God-ordained document.

May God help us turn the hearts of the nation back to the sound principles of proper government that the blessings if liberty may be preserved for ourselves and our posterity!

[182.] To Col. Charles Yancey, in Bergh, *Thomas Jefferson*, 14:384.

8.

OF MONEY AND ECONOMICS

RECOMMENDED RESOURCES FOR THE SERIOUS STUDENT:

Basic Economics, by Clarence B. Carson
The Creature from Jekyll Island, by G. Edward Griffin
Economics in One Lesson, by Henry Hazlitt

QUOTES, ARTICLES, AND ORIGINAL SOURCES

Money

> Congress shall have power . . . To coin Money, regulate the Value thereof, and of foreign Coin, and fix the Standard of Weights and Measures. (United States Constitution, article 1, section 8, clause 5)

> No State shall . . . coin money; emit Bills of Credit; make any Thing but gold and silver Coin a Tender in Payment of Debts. (United States Constitution, article 1, section 10, clause 1)

In simplest terms, money is a medium of exchange by which goods that are desired are obtained. Since the beginning of time, mankind has exchanged goods and services through various mediums of exchange. Long before the founders of this nation set about establishing the nation's monetary standard, thousands of years of mankind's experience had defined the requirements of a successful, stable money system. Barter systems initially prevailed (exchanging a cow for pigs). Challenges developed when one had a cow or a pig and wanted a few eggs for a meal. Multiple exchanges became necessary to come to an exchange that was fair to both parties. Facilitating easy exchanges necessitated finding an exchange medium (money) that was universally acceptable to all who may wish to exchange. Experience determined that money must have *intrinsic value* in order to be desirable for exchange. It must be *easily divisible* to ensure that exact amounts could be given upon exchange. It must be *durable* so it would not be lost through exposure to the elements or moth or corrosion. And it must be *relatively scarce*. Precious metals, particularly gold and silver, met all requirements: intrinsic value, easily divisible, durable, and relative scarcity.

To finance the Revolutionary War, both the national government and the states had resorted to printing paper money that was backed by the "full faith and credit" of the government, but was not fully redeemable with "real" money. The money was not tied to precious metal. The experience was a disaster. The economy collapsed. Unbacked paper does not meet the defined qualifications for money: it does not have intrinsic value, it is not durable, and it certainly is not scarce.

In recognition of their painful experience with paper money, the Founding Fathers of this nation sought to prevent future forays in this area and to establish the nation upon sound economic principles.

During the 1787 Constitutional Convention, they debated the issue of paper money. James Madison's *Journal of the Federal Convention* clearly indicates their "original intent" to preclude the nation from suffering under an unbacked paper money supply. Noting the experience in the early history of this nation and of nations in Europe, it was suggested that allowing the government to print unbacked paper money "would be as alarming as the mark of the Beast in Revelation." It was also noted that the entire proposed constitution would be a failure if the power to print money was allowed. The convention voted in favor of preventing the issue of unbacked paper money.[183] Later debates in the convention confirm the concerns held about paper money.[184]

Also, in Federalist no. 42 and 44, James Madison briefly touches upon the issue of paper money.

As the United States was established, the founders of the nation understood the importance of creating a soundly-based money system if the nation was to survive. Brevity necessitates that only a few statements by the nation's founders be noted as further evidence of their "original intent":

George Washington

[183.] See Madison, *Journal*, 2:541-3.
[184.] See Madison, *Journal*, 2:620.

OF MONEY AND ECONOMICS

George Washington wrote,

> I am well aware that appearances ought to be upheld, and that we should avoid as much as possible recognizing by any public act the depreciation of our currency; but I conceive this end would be answered, as far as might be necessary, by stipulating that all money payments should be made in gold and silver, being the common medium of commerce among nations.[185]

> Every other effort is in vain unless something can be done to restore [the currency's] credit . . . The liberties and safety of this country depend upon it; the way is plain; the means are in our power. But it is virtue alone that can effect it.[186]

> Experience has demonstrated the impracticality long to maintain a paper credit without funds for its redemption. The long depreciation of our currency was in the main a necessary effect of the want of those funds.[187]

> Uniformity in the currency [and in the] weights and measures of the United States is an object of great importance, and will, I am persuaded, be duly attended to.[188]

Thomas Jefferson also felt it critically important to keep the nation's monetary system on a sound footing of precious metal, saying,

> One of the great advantages of specie as a medium is that, being of universal value, it will keep itself at a general level . . . . [quoting Adam Smith, Jefferson notes] that "the commerce and industry of a country cannot be so secure when suspended on the Daedalian wings of paper money as [when] on the solid ground of gold and silver."[189]

> Specie is the most perfect medium, because it will preserve its own level; because, having intrinsic and universal value, it can never die in our hands; and it is the surest resource of reliance in time of war . . . . The trifling economy of paper as a cheaper medium, or its convenience for transmission, weighs nothing in opposition to the advantages of the precious metals . . . . [Paper money] is liable to be abused, has been, is, and forever will be abused, in every country in which it is permitted.[190]

[185.] To the President of Congress, in Fitzpatrick, *George Washington*, 11:217.
[186.] To Edmund Pendleton, in Fitzpatrick, *George Washington*, 17:52.
[187.] To John Laurens, in Fitzpatrick, *George Washington*, 21:106.
[188.] George Washington's first annual address, in Fitzpatrick, *George Washington*, 30:493.
[189.] To John W. Eppes, in Bergh, *Thomas Jefferson*, 13:412.
[190.] Ibid., 13:430. Jefferson's entire letter to Eppes is worthy of careful consideration, as it is an insightful review of this subject. For the entire letter, see Bergh, *Thomas Jefferson*, 13:404-432.

The word "specie" is not commonly used today, but was in common usage during the founding era of the United States. Noah Webster defined it thus: "Coin; copper, silver, or gold coined and used as a circulating medium of commerce."[191] So, specie is not just not paper money, it is also not the worthless base metal coin of today which masquerades as money. It is also of interest to note the meaning of the term Jefferson used to describe paper money: "Daedalian." The term harkens back to Daedalus, the mythical ancient Athenian who supposedly invented wings and his son Icarus who experienced disaster in his attempt to soar to great heights in flight. It would seem that Jefferson chose his imagery in a manner which conveyed his point eloquently—capturing the concept of paper money as a fragile mythical hope that will ultimately end in disaster!

Coinage Act

Through the joint efforts of George Washington and Thomas Jefferson, Congress stepped up to their constitutionally mandated responsibility to establish a sound monetary system for the United States. Congress passed the Coinage Act of 1792, which firmly established gold and silver as the medium of exchange for the United States. The Coinage Act of 1792 established the United States mint, defined coin denominations in terms of precious metal (gold and silver), and established the weights of those coins and the metal content of the coins. It also established the proportional value of pure gold to pure silver at fifteen to one. It is also of interest that the act emphasized the serious responsibility of keeping the United States monetary system pure, as it established the death penalty for mint officers who might be tempted to debase the United States system of coinage!

Unfortunately, the Coinage Act of 1965 (which created the base metal coins we have in circulation today that have no intrinsic value) and several other tragic actions by both the Congress and the executive branch have superseded and subverted the "self-evident" truths of a proper monetary system, and the United States is now adrift in a boundless sea in which the financial stability of the nation has been destroyed.

Inflation Caused by Government Fiscal Policy

Inflation is rampant because the national government now creates unbacked debt-based paper money at will to "fund" profligate and wastrel programs that are not allowed under the limits established within the United States Constitution. This dishonest and pernicious practice distorts the economy, erodes personal savings, and places future generations in bondage.

[191.] American Dictionary of the English Language [1828]

OF MONEY AND ECONOMICS

As mentioned in lecture 4 (American History Time Line), after World War I, in an effort to make required war reparations, Germany resorted to printing vast sums of unbacked paper money to make those payments. The result was a debauching of the German currency and economy. Just as the American monetary basis is defined in "dollars," the German monetary system was based upon their money unit called the German mark. The following is a table that exposes how this practice of printing unbacked paper money destroyed the purchasing power of the German mark.

Hyperinflation: Wiemar, Germany, January 1919 to November 1923
Number of German Marks Needed to Buy One Ounce of Gold or Silver

Date	Silver	Gold
Jan 1919	12	170
May 1919	17	267
Sept 1919	31	499
Jan 1920	84	1,340
May 1920	60	966
Sept 1920	75	1,201
Jan 1921	84	1,349
May 1921	80	1,288
Sept 1921	139	2,175
Jan 1922	249	3,976
May 1922	375	6,012
Sept 1922	1,899	30,381
Jan 1923	23,277	372,447
May 1923	44,397	710,355
June 5, 1923	80,953	1,295,256
July 3, 1923	207,239	3,315,831
Aug 7, 1923	4,273,875	68,382,000
Sept 4, 1923	16,839,937	269,439,000
Oct 2, 1923	414,484,000	6,631,749,000
Oct 9, 1923	1,554,309,000	24,868,950,000
Oct 16, 1923	5,310,567,000	84,969,072,000
Oct 23, 1923	7,253,460,000	1,160,552,882,000
Oct 30, 1923	8,419,200,000	1,347,070,000,000
Nov 5, 1923	54,375,000,000	8,700,000,000,000
Nov 13, 1923	108,750,000,000	17,400,000,000,000
Nov 30, 1923	543,750,000,000	87,000,000,000,000

This is an example of how hyperinflation can occur when governments adopt a policy of creating vast sums of unbacked paper money. While the United States has not yet experienced this level of inflation, the nation is on a path that is taking the nation's monetary system to the brink of similar economic chaos.

The solution lies in returning to the limited scope and bounds within which the national government was originally established, turning from a process that creates unbacked printing press paper "money" upon the whim of national leaders and reestablishing a recognition of real money based upon the wisdom of the ages and the founder's original intent.

NATIONAL DEBT

The Founding Fathers of the United States considered a national debt to be a great burden that was to be avoided and resolved with the greatest of diligence. They considered it to be a bane to the liberty of the nation and counseled most emphatically that the nation guard against it.

In his annual State of the Union reports to Congress, George Washington spoke often of the burden of national debt. Thomas Jefferson devoted a great deal of time in each of his annual State of the Union reports to reviews of the nation's efforts to retire the national debt. The efforts to accomplish that were largely based upon sale of federal lands to citizens of the United States (only). This accomplished at least two great goals: it placed within the power of the people the means to produce prosperity for themselves and the nation, and it removed the debt that burdened the nation. In this we may see an example of the "original intent" of the Founding Fathers.

It is interesting to note that the last time the nation was completely debt free was during the Andrew Jackson administration, and that was achieved through the sale of federally held land.

GEORGE WASHINGTON ON DEBT

Washington felt that the national debt should be paid without delay, saying,

> I entertain a strong hope that the state of the national finances is now sufficiently matured to enable you to enter upon a systematic and effectual arrangement for the regular redemption and discharge of the public debt, according to the right which has been reserved to the government. No measure can be more desirable, whether viewed with an eye to its intrinsic importance or to the general sentiment and wish of the nation.[192]

[192.] Fourth annual address to Congress, in Fitzpatrick, *George Washington*, 11:217.

OF MONEY AND ECONOMICS

> No pecuniary consideration is more urgent than the regular redemption and discharge of the public debt; on none can delay be more injurious, or an economy of time more valuable.[193]

> The time which has elapsed since the commencement of our fiscal measures has developed our pecuniary resources so as to open a way for a definitive plan for the redemption of the public debt. It is believed that the result is such as to encourage Congress to consummate this work without delay. Nothing can more promote the permanent welfare of the nation, and nothing would be more grateful to our constituents. Indeed, whatsoever is unfinished of our system of public credit cannot be benefitted by procrastination; and as far as may be practicable, we ought to place that credit on grounds which cannot be disturbed, and to prevent that progressive accumulation of debt which must ultimately endanger all governments.[194]

> It will afford me heartfelt satisfaction to concur in such further measures as will ascertain to our country the prospect of a speedy extinguishment of the debt. Posterity may have cause to regret if, from any motive, intervals of tranquility are left unimproved for accelerating this valuable end.[195]

Washington also advised that the nation avoid national debt when possible and quickly repay it when incurred:

> As a very important source of strength and security, cherish public credit. One method of preserving it is to use it as sparingly as possible, avoiding occasions of expense by cultivating peace, but remembering also that timely disbursements to prepare for danger frequently prevent much greater disbursements to repel it; avoiding likewise the accumulation of debt, not only by shunning occasions of expense, but by vigorous exertions in time of peace to discharge the debts which unavoidable wars may have occasioned, not ungenerously throwing upon posterity the burden which we ourselves ought to bear.[196]

THOMAS JEFFERSON ON DEBT

Thomas Jefferson was no less emphatic in his resolve to extinguish public debt, saying,

---

[193]. Fifth annual address to Congress, in Fitzpatrick, *George Washington*, 33:168.
[194]. Sixth annual address to Congress, in Fitzpatrick, *George Washington*, 34:36.
[195]. Eighth annual address to Congress, in Fitzpatrick, *George Washington*, 35:319.
[196]. Farewell Address, in Fitzpatrick, *George Washington*, 35:240.

> I . . . place economy among the first and most important of republican virtues, and public debt as the greatest of the dangers to be feared.[197]

> I am for . . . applying all the possible savings of the public revenue to the discharge of the national debt.[198]

> I consider the fortunes of our republic as depending, in an eminent degree, on the extinguishment of the public debt before we engage in any war; because, that done, we shall have revenue enough to improve our country in peace and defend it in war, without recurring either to new taxes or loans. But if the debt should once more be swelled to a formidable size, its entire discharge will be despaired of, and we shall be committed to the English career of debt, corruption, and rottenness, closing with revolution. The discharge of the debt, therefore, is vital to the destinies of our government.[199]

> The principle of spending money to be paid by posterity, under the name of funding, is but swindling futurity on a large scale.[200]

It is of interest to note that in his correspondence, Jefferson often referred to his abhorrence of national debt, and he held the view that if incurring a debt was found to be unavoidable, the nation must "never borrow a dollar without laying a tax in the same instant for paying the interest annually, and the principle within a given term."[201] He was also adamant that the policy must be to repay the debt within twenty years to avoid burdening posterity with the debts incurred by the current generation.[202] As already noted, this attitude reflects the worthy advice offered by George Washington in his Farewell Address. The policy of current national leaders is diametrically opposed to this sound advice. Indeed, the siren call of unremitting debt is often accompanied by the scurrilously spoken falsehood that we must incur debt "for the good of the children." It would seem that many things which are currently being done in the name of future generations are in reality being thrown ungenerously upon the backs of future generations by a selfish, self centered generation that is profligate and undisciplined, and unwilling to make hard decisions that require self denial for the true good of the children, indeed for the good of generations of children yet unborn!

[197.] Bergh, *Thomas Jefferson*, 15:47.
[198.] To Eldrige Gerry, in Bergh, *Thomas Jefferson*, 10:77.
[199.] To Albert Gailatin, in Bergh, *Thomas Jefferson*, 12:324.
[200.] Bergh, *Thomas Jefferson*, 15:23.
[201.] To John W. Eppes, in Bergh, *Thomas Jefferson*, 13:269.
[202.] Ibid., 13:270-3, 357-8.

THE SIXTEENTH AMENDMENT

Over the years, the nation has strayed far from these principles of sound money upon which the country was established! Early in the twentieth century, there was a dramatic shift from these concepts, and the nation has adopted policies that have created great risk to the liberties of the people. The year 1913 was a particularly bad year for the United States! In 1913, some major changes in the structure of the nation occurred. That year, the Sixteenth Amendment was ratified, creating the federal income tax. This concept allows the national government to directly tax individual Americans and take money from them without going through the state legislatures as they had previously been required to do.

THE SEVENTEENTH AMENDMENT

The Seventeenth Amendment was also ratified in 1913. This amendment changed the way United States senators come to office. Prior to this time, the senators were appointed by the individual state legislatures. By this original means, the states retained representation at the national level and, thereby, were part of the power-checking balances that were originally created to prevent the national government from straying into areas it was constitutionally denied power. The Seventeenth Amendment removed the states as political entities from the formula and assigned the election of the senators directly to the people of the states. Recall that the Founding Fathers of the United States were very concerned with accrual of power, dividing and subdividing it to ensure that it could not be gathered to the point that tyranny could be implemented. They also carefully divided the *sources* of power that each office looked to in order to obtain power. Originally, members of the House of Representatives were directly elected by the *people* of their states. The senators were selected by the *state legislators*. The president was elected by a special single-purpose legislature called the *electoral college* that was tasked with the responsibility to chose the president and then was dissolved. By this means, no one single power base could overwhelm the others and have inordinate power at the expense of the others. The Seventeenth Amendment upset this delicate balance of power, removing the states and placing additional power in the hands of the masses, which could possibly be persuaded by eloquent demagogues to violate the principles of limited government and individual rights.

Prior to (and since) the Seventeenth Amendment, those that sought election to the House of Representatives often went to their power base (the people) and promised to deliver tempting (often costly) programs to the people if they were elected. Once elected, they arrived in Washington DC eager to deliver upon those promises and thereby ensure their reelection in two years. Since virtually all of the members of the House made such promises to facilitate their election, the various members of Congress were eager to help one another enact these promises. Of course, a bill does not become a law until *both* houses of Congress (and the president) approve. Consequently, as with all bills, these expensive promise-fulfilling bills that were passed by the House of Representatives next went to the Senate, where the senators examined them. Since expenditures that exceeded the revenue brought into the national government by normal constitutional means (in general, import taxes) would require additional tax funds to support, the senators recognized that any additional extravagant financial requirements would result in them having to increase the tax assessment to the states based upon the populations of the states (see U.S. Constitution, article 1, section 9, clause 4). The senators also knew that the state legislatures would oppose having to raise taxes upon the people of their state to meet their national tax assessment, and they knew that their future reappointment to the United States Senate would be placed in jeopardy by taking such a position. So prior to the ratification of the Seventeenth Amendment, they would prevent passage of the bills submitted by the House that were beyond the financial means of the nation. By this careful "check and balance," the nation was, by and large, prevented from dramatically expanding the size and scope of the national government. With the passage of the Seventeenth Amendment, the *people (not the states)* became the power source of the senators, so the senators consequently adopted election tactics similar to the practices that had been successfully employed by the House of Representatives in their efforts to get elected. They began making promises, such as to deliver expensive "gifts," to their electorate, thereby ensuring their election. After their election, when they arrived in Washington DC, they too sought to deliver upon their promises, just as the House members always had. And since the Sixteenth Amendment created circumstances that no longer required them to go back to the state legislatures to acquire additional tax money (since they now had the power to simply raise taxes and collect them directly from the people), they simply collaborated with the House of Representatives and both houses of Congress fulfilled their election promises and ensured their continued ability to hold office. No one was left to provide a "check" on profligate spending.

THE FEDERAL RESERVE SYSTEM

But since they felt reluctant to raise taxes to the individual taxpayer too fast because it could ultimately place their reelection in jeopardy, they adopted a plan that would allow the nation to greatly expand its expenditures by *borrowing* the sums of money necessary to deliver their expanded programs. In order to do this, they turned to the newly created Federal Reserve System, which had also been created in 1913.

The Federal Reserve System is a privately held and managed banking consortium which is operated for the financial profit of the owners of the system. In 1913 Congress granted this private banking consortium a monopoly by which they could manage the nation's economy. It was granted the power to create unbacked paper money out of thin air and loan it with interest charges attached to the national government. This facilitates the predilection of Congress to profligately deficit spend to their heart's content, because their requests to the Fed for more loans are always honored. The Fed manipulates the money supply and sets policy by which the economy of the nation lives or dies. This practice effectively turned the national economy over to bankers who would centrally manage the nation's money supply and profit from their activities. This policy is in close alignment with one of the main points of Karl Marx's *The Communist Manifesto*, which outlined the means and processes by which Marx suggested nations would be subjugated to communism. The fifth point of Marx's manifesto states, "Centralization of credit in the hands of the State, by means of a national bank with

State capital and an exclusive monopoly." Astonishingly, since its creation in 1913, the Federal Reserve has never been audited by a competent independent organization that could perform a comprehensive review and make an honest, full, complete, and straightforward report of the findings of their audit to the American people. The Fed is autonomous and has virtual free rein, acting without oversight and above any real regulation. G. Edward Griffin's book, *The Creature from Jekyll Island,* provides a detailed and expansive review of the Federal Reserve System and its effect on the economy of the United States.

Many are astonished by the statement that the Federal Reserve creates money out of thin air and, at the request of the United States Congress, loans it with interest attached to the nation. Fortunately, we have the sworn testimony of one of the early Federal Reserve leaders to support the position.

Eccles on Creation of Money

In testimony before the Banking and Currency Committee of the House of Representatives in 1935, Marriner Eccles, then-chairman of the Federal Reserve Board itself, said, "In purchasing offerings of Government bonds, the banking system as a whole creates new money, or bank deposits. When the banks buy a billion dollars of government bonds as they are offered—and you have to consider the banking system as a whole as a unit—the banks credit the deposit account of the Treasury with a billion dollars. They debit their Government bond account a billion dollars; or they actually create, by a bookkeeping entry, a billion dollars."

And Federal Reserve Governor Marriner Eccles again testified before the House Committee on Banking and Currency on September 30, 1941. Congressman Wright Patman asked Eccles how the Fed got the money to purchase two billion dollars worth of government bonds in 1933. Eccles answered, "We created it." Patman asked, "Out of what?" Eccles replied, "Out of the right to issue credit money." Patman questioned, "And there is nothing behind it, is there, except our government's credit?" Eccles responded, "That is what our money system is. If there were no debts in our money system, there wouldn't be any money."

It is astounding to note that during the years that Alan Greenspan was the chair of the Federal Reserve System, over $7.5 trillion were created out of thin air, and it appears that those who hold power (both within the Federal Reserve System and in the national government) continue in their determination to accelerate the nation along this path of national financial suicide. With trillions of new dollars pursuing finite quantities of goods and services, prices are driven upward (inflation). We should not be surprised as the once-respected dollar plummets against oil and all other nation's monetary systems. Because of the continuation of this national fiscal policy, it now takes far more dollars to purchase any goods or services today—whether it is oil or food or any other necessity. In spite of efforts by government agencies and many economic pundits to obfuscate the facts, government deficit spending and falsely based government and Federal Reserve economic policy are truly the greatest cause and source of inflation.

It is tragic to note how the nation for many decades has strayed from the sound financial counsel of those who founded this great nation! The effect of these modifications upon the nation's financial well-being has been profound! Since these changes have been implemented in the nation, the national debt has blossomed astronomically, and the money created by this polluted system has caused the purchasing power of the United States dollar to plummet. The chart below captures the essence of the matter by equating the national debt to the burden upon each man, woman, and child in the United States:

United States National Debt Comparison

Year	National Debt	Population	Per Capita Debt
1800	$82,976,294.00	5,309,000	$15.63
1900	$2,136,961,091.00	75,995,000	$28.12
1913	The Sixteenth Amendment (income tax) ratified, Seventeenth Amendment (direct election of U.S. Senators) ratified, Federal Reserve established		
1980	$930,200,000,000.00	226,542,199	$4,106.08
2006	$9,000,000,000,000.00	298,000,000	$30,200.00

It should be noted that the nine-trillion-dollar debt spoken of is not a true reflection of future financial commitments (debts) that have been made by the national government. For example, because some debts are carried "off the books" in a form of accounting chicanery, commitments to pay future social security, promised medical care, and other so-called "entitlement" programs are not included in the admitted national debt. If these debts are included in the accounting, the national debt is many tens of trillions of dollars higher!

It is difficult for most people to fully comprehend the magnitude of such huge numbers. The table below is perhaps another way to look at the size of the problem. It looks at the deficit in terms of stacks of one-thousand-dollar bills and how tall the stack would be to represent the dollars mentioned.

Stacks of Crisp New One-Thousand-Dollar Bills

4" stack = $1,000,000 (million)

333.33' stack = $1,000,000,000 (billion)

63.13 miles = $1,000,000,000,000 (trillion)

568.17 miles = $9,000,000,000,000 (nine trillion)

Today's politicians have buried the nation in debt. They have done this by ignoring the constitutional limits of their power, acting as though they have power to tax and spend for any whim that strikes them. They tax trillions of hard-earned dollars each year from the citizens of this land only to spend hundreds of billions more each year than they collect. Sadly, most of the spending is not authorized by the United States Constitution.

The solution is a return to the constraints of power on the federal government that exist within the United States Constitution. James Madison stated that the powers of the national government were "few and well defined." Perhaps, when the people of the nation again understand that fact, the nation's leadership will be compelled to abide by their oath to uphold the Constitution of the United States.

9.

The Moral Imperative

Recommended Resources for the Serious Student:

Political Sermons of the American Founding Era, edited by Ellis Sandoz
The Spirit of Laws, by Montesquieu

Quotes, Articles, and Original Sources

Freedom and morality are inextricably interwoven. True freedom cannot long be maintained if a people becomes debauched. Liberty is not licentiousness! One of the greatest challenges that currently faces the United States is that of moral slippage. This challenge faces the nation from the very highest positions of leadership to the common citizen on the street. It is reflected in our actions, in our words, in our manner of dress, in what we call entertainment, music, and art, and a host of other manifestations. Moral character really does matter—individually, within families, in communities, and within the nation. In years gone by, the moral slippages were not nearly so public as they are in today's society.

Part of the problem is found in the "heroes" that are offered to the people of the nation. Many of the modern heroes that are offered to the youth of this day are spiritual derelicts. They seem to shuttle between rehabilitation and jail, with riotous parties interspersed. Such behavior and activity have become blasé in modern society and seem to barely elicit a raised eyebrow anymore. Some of the individuals who are most exposed in the press and media are perhaps among the worst offenders in daily practice. And marriage and childbearing often seem to be unrelated based upon the behavior of many highly publicized public figures. America is really better than what receives the most media frenzy. Certainly, America started off better than what is commonly accepted practice today!

Part of the problem too is found in leadership positions within the nation. Far too many people who hold elected office have allowed themselves to accept a lower standard of behavior for their personal behavior, and that behavior often becomes very public. Some of the more "common" citizens within the nation have consequently allowed themselves to embrace a similar standard based upon the poor example provided by the "leadership." Society suffers for it.

THE MORAL IMPERATIVE

The Founding Fathers of the United States had a far different perspective in this matter! They noted the importance of electing leaders with sound moral character and admonished the nation to choose their leaders wisely. As an example, Noah Webster said, "When a citizen gives his [vote] to a man of known immorality, he abuses his trust; . . . he betrays the interest of his country".[203] In light of this, it is astonishing today when the shocking private behavior of leaders is brushed off with comments to the effect that their private behavior has no reflection on their leadership ability and, consequently, should be irrelevant to their public honors.

Abigail Adams

Abigail Adams, wife of John Adams, and ardent patriot in her own right, recognized the worth of a high and godly standard in the cause of liberty, saying,

> A patriot without religion, in my estimation, is a great paradox as an honest man without the fear of God. Is it possible that he whom no moral obligations bind, can have any real good will towards men? Can he be a patriot who by an openly vicious conduct, is undermining the very bonds of society? . . . The Scriptures tell us righteousness exalteth a Nation.[204]

[203.] *Letters to a Young Gentleman Commencing his Education*, 19.
[204.] Excerpt from *Warren-Adams Letters*, vol. I, 1743-1777, Massachusetts Historical Society Collections, 72

For the good of the nation, it is wise to examine the moral character of those who put themselves forward as leaders and select our leaders based upon the highest standards!

And while many in society today believe that government has no role in the preservation of morals, the Founding Fathers of America had been steeped in a far different perspective! In Blackstone's *Commentaries on the Laws of England*, he recognizes the responsibility of society to preserve its virtue and morality and suggests that when a moral indiscretion becomes known publicly, it is the right of society to correct that activity:

> No matter how abandoned may be a man's principles, or how vicious his practice, provided he keeps his wickedness to himself, and does not violate public decency, he is out of the reach of human laws. But if he makes his vices public, then they become by his bad example, of pernicious effect to society, and it is the business of human laws to correct them.[205]

From this we are led to understand that when morality is involved, when activities become public knowledge that would offend normal morality, then public laws have a responsibility and a right to respond. Bringing back this moral standard to society will require a concerted effort in light of how far the nation has strayed from this baseline principle!

While it seems apparent that many today are collaborating to undermine the moral character of the United States, it has not always been that way. The intent of this lecture, indeed the intent of the entire lecture series, is to expose the student to the perspective that was widely held as the nation was founded. The religious and moral roots of America were well-known just a few generations ago. However, decades of concerted efforts by historical revisionists have greatly modified the general understanding of how thoroughly the founders of this nation were imbued with a religious and moral sense of decorum.

Prior to the American founding era, great thinkers had written much regarding this matter of how virtue, religious principle, and freedom are interwoven.

OF VIRTUE AND FREEDOM

Baron de Montesquieu, in his monumental work *The Spirit of Laws*,[206] discussed at great length the various forms of government that he observed.

In their formative years, virtually all of the American founders carefully studied the works of Montesquieu (see Montesquieu's biographical sketch in the appendix). As has been noted

---

[205.] Blackstone, *Commentaries*, 1:120

[206.] The first English edition was Thomas Nugent's translation (London: Nourse, 1750); references to *The Spirit of Laws* found herein are taken from this original translation, and notation reflects the original format of the text: book, chapter, paragraph—i.e., V, 14, (30) denotes book V, chapter 14, paragraph 30.

herein, he wrote upon a broad spectrum of government-related subjects. Interestingly, he focused many of his thoughts on virtue and freedom, and the founders had attentively studied Montesquieu's writings and had given careful consideration to the perspectives he brought forth. The following are examples of the wisdom of Montesquieu in regard to the subject of republics (which is the form of government that was originally created and intended for the United States—see lecture 2) and the necessity of virtue within a republic if it was to survive.

Virtue and Republics—Freedom Is Dependent upon Public and Private Virtue

It is interesting to note how closely Montesquieu tied the survival of a republic to public virtue. While he does link virtue to love of the republic, equality, and frugality,[207] he discusses at length the necessity of morals and sexual purity in order for the nation to survive.

> The love of our country is conducive to a purity of morals, and the latter is again conducive to the love of our country.[208]

> In what kind of government censors are necessary? My answer is, that they are necessary in a republic, where the principle of government is virtue.[209]

> When a people are virtuous, few punishments are necessary.[210]

Chapter 8 of Montesquieu's book 7 is titled "Of Public Continency." Noah Webster defined "continency" as pertaining to self-restraint and abstention from sexual activity.[211] In this chapter, Montesquieu links the moral tenor of a nation to its survival:

> So many are the imperfections that attend the loss of virtue in women, and so greatly are their souls degraded, when this principle guard is removed, that in a popular state public incontinency may be considered as the last of miseries, and as a certain forerunner of a change in the constitution.[212]

His reference to "a popular state" pertains to the form of government wherein the leaders are elected by the people through their popular vote. If his observation is correct, in

---

[207.] Montesquieu, *The Spirit of Laws*, see V, 2, (1); V, 3, (1, 2).
[208.] Montesquieu, *The Spirit of Laws*, V, 2 (2)
[209.] Montesquieu, *The Spirit of Laws*, V, 19, (14)
[210.] Montesquieu, *The Spirit of Laws*, VI, 11, chapter heading
[211.] *American Dictionary*
[212.] Montesquieu, *The Spirit of Laws*, VII, 8, (1)

nations such as the United States, the preservation of the nation depends upon the virtue of the people.

THE U.S. FOUNDERS ON THE NECESSITY OF VIRTUE

The concept of virtue and public morality was well understood and embraced by those who founded the United States. In 1787, Benjamin Franklin observed,

> Let me add that only a virtuous people are capable of freedom. As nations become corrupt and vicious, they have more need of masters.[213]

Franklin recognized that if a people refused to govern themselves and keep their behavior within proper bounds, others would come to govern them and, through compulsory means, enforce compliance.

In his first inaugural address, President George Washington linked the future success of the republic to moral imperatives, saying,

> The foundation of our national policy will be laid in the pure and immutable principles of private morality, and the preeminence of free government be exemplified by all the attributes which can win the affections of its citizens and command the respect of the world. I dwell on this prospect with every satisfaction which an ardent love for my country can inspire, since there is no truth more thoroughly established than that there exists in the economy and course of nature an indissoluble union between virtue and happiness; between duty and advantage; between the genuine maxims of an honest and magnanimous policy and the solid rewards of public prosperity and felicity; since we ought to be no less persuaded that the propitious smiles of Heaven can never be expected on a nation that disregards the eternal rules of order and right which Heaven itself has ordained; and since the preservation of the sacred fire of liberty and the destiny of the republican model of government are justly considered, perhaps, as deeply, as finally, staked on the experiment intrusted to the hands of the American people.[214]

That devotion to virtue continued throughout President Washington's administration, and in his timeless Farewell Address, as he bid a public farewell to the nation he had tirelessly served for forty-five years, George Washington reminded the nation of its importance and reflected upon his understanding of this marvelous principle with the following endorsement:

---

[213]. To the Abbes Chalut and Arnaud, 17 April 1787, in Smyth, *Benjamin Franklin*, 9:569.
[214]. Richardson, *Messages and Papers*, 1:44-5.

> Of all the dispositions and habits which lead to political prosperity, religion and morality are indispensable supports. In vain would that man claim the tribute of patriotism who should labor to subvert these great pillars of human happiness—these firmest props of the duties of men and citizens. The mere politician, equally with the pious man, ought to respect and to cherish them. A volume could not trace all their connections with private and public felicity. Let it simply be asked, Where is the security for property, for reputation, for life, if the sense of religious obligation desert the oaths which are the instruments of investigation in courts of justice? And let us with caution indulge the supposition that morality can be maintained without religion. Whatever may be conceded to the influence of refined education on minds of peculiar structure, reason and experience both forbid us to expect that national morality can prevail in exclusion of religious principle.
>
> It is substantially true that virtue or morality is a necessary spring of popular government. The rule indeed extends with more or less force to every species of free government. Who that is a sincere friend to it can look with indifference upon attempts to shake the foundation of the fabric?[215]

And John Adams, the nation's first vice president and second president, captured the concept most succinctly when he said, "Our Constitution was made only for a moral and religious people. It is wholly inadequate to the government of any other."[216]

The student will recall that the founders of this nation considered religion and morality so important that when they enacted the Northwest Ordinance of 1787 and reenacted it under the new constitution in 1789, they stipulated that all states that desired to join with them and become part of the United States should require that religion, morality, and knowledge be taught in their schools. Article 3 of the Northwest Ordinance states,

> Religion, morality, and knowledge, being necessary to good government and the happiness of mankind, schools and the means of education shall forever be encouraged.

As the new nation set forth under its banner of freedom, Samuel Adams, the Father of the American Revolution, observed,

> The sum of all is, if we would most truly enjoy the gift of Heaven, let us become a virtuous people; then shall we both deserve and enjoy it. While, on the other

---

[215] Richardson, *Messages and Papers*, 1:212.
[216] C. F. Adams, *John Adams*, 4:31.

hand, if we are universally vicious and debauched in our manners, though the form of our Constitution carries the face of the most exalted freedom, we shall in reality be the most abject slaves.[217]

And on another occasion, Samuel Adams observed,

> I thank God that I have lived to see my country independent and free. She may long enjoy her independence and freedom if she will. It depends on her virtue.[218]

And the privilege of worshiping and practicing one's religious was ensured at the constitutional level with the ratification of the First Amendment:

> Congress shall make no law respecting an establishment of religion, or prohibiting the free exercise thereof.

This amendment recognizes and protects the God-given, unalienable right to worship. It does not foster the current (official) practice of seeking to make the nation free from religion. It is interesting to note that the same Congress that passed this amendment also passed the previously mentioned Northwest Ordinance, which required all new states to ensure that religion and morality were encouraged and linked to the educational process!

During the initial decades of our national sovereignty under the United States Constitution, the importance of the general population of the nation retaining its virtue and its commitment to the fundamental principles of freedom were often mentioned by the nation's leadership as a reminder of each individual's duty in the conservation of the nation. In speaking of the preservation of liberty and proper government during his first inaugural address, James Monroe said,

> The Government has been in the hands of the people. To the people, therefore, and to the faithful and able depositories of their trust is the credit due. Had the people of the United States been educated in different principles, had they been less intelligent, less independent, or less virtuous, can it be believed that we should have maintained the same steady and consistent career or been blessed with the same success? While, then, the constituent body retains its present sound and healthful state everything will be safe. They will choose competent and faithful representatives for every department. It is only when the people become ignorant

---

[217.] William V. Wells, *The Life and Public Services of Samuel Adams: Being a Narrative of His Acts and Opinions, and of His Agency in Producing and Forwarding the American Revolution, with Extracts from His Correspondence, State Papers, and Political Essays* (Boston: Little, Brown, 1888), 1:22-3.

[218.] Wells, *Samuel Adams*, 3:175.

and corrupt, when they degenerate into a populace, that they are incapable of exercising the sovereignty. Usurpation is then an easy attainment, and an usurper soon found. The people themselves become the willing instruments of their own debasement and ruin.[219]

It is interesting that in voicing his concerns about an "open" immigration policy, Thomas Jefferson voiced his concerns that some would come to this nation who were not well founded in moral issues and thereby undermine the form of government that would allow full liberty. He suggested that the proper form of government that the United States enjoyed would be polluted by having "foreign/alien" influence injected into the election/legislative process through an immigration policy that had foreign concepts of government made popular and fostered within the United States as large numbers of people entered the United States that were not steeped in the principles upon which this nation was founded and that it could possibly ultimately destroy the constitutional republic that allowed liberty to prevail in the United States, saying,

> Every species of government has its specific principles. Ours perhaps are more peculiar than those of any other in the universe. It is a composition of the freest principles of the English constitution, with others derived from natural right and natural reason. To these nothing can be more opposed than the maxims of absolute monarchies. Yet from such we are to expect the greatest number of emigrants. They will bring with them the principles of the governments they leave, imbibed in their early youth; or, if able to throw them off, it will be in exchange for an unbounded licentiousness, passing, as is usual, from one extreme to another. It would be a miracle were they to stop precisely at the point of temperate liberty. These principles, with their language, they will transmit to their children. In proportion to their numbers, they will share with us the legislation. They will infuse into it their spirit, warp and bias its directions, and render it a heterogeneous, incoherent, distracted mass.[220]

It is beyond question that religion, morality, and their importance to the maintenance of proper government were well understood by those who founded this nation!

And virtue was not simply to be reflected in the public acts of the nation. Private virtue was enjoined also. The following is an excerpt from a letter Thomas Jefferson wrote from Paris, France, on August 19, 1785, to his nephew Peter Carr in Virginia regarding the importance of living a virtuous and moral life,

> Pursue the interests of your country, the interests of your friends, and your own interests also, with the purest integrity, the most chaste honor. The defect of

---

[219.] Richardson, *Messages and Papers*, 1:575-576.
[220.] Bergh, *Thomas Jefferson*, 2:120-121.

these virtues can never be made up by all the other acquirements of body and mind. Make these, then, your first object. Give up money, give up fame, give up science, give the earth itself and all it contains, rather than do an immoral act. And never suppose, that in any possible situation, or under any circumstances, it is best for you to do a dishonorable thing, however slightly so it may appear to you. Whenever you are to do a thing, though it can never be known but to yourself, ask yourself how you would act were all the world looking at you, and act accordingly. Encourage all your virtuous dispositions.[221]

Virtue in Early United States Noted

And this concept of virtue, religion, and morality was so ingrained in the soul of the United States that it was readily detected by observers who were willing to recognize it. As noted in lecture 1, Alexis de Tocqueville, in his *Democracy in America*, observed the universal importance of religion in the early days of the United States.[222]

Alexis de Tocqueville

[221.] Bergh, *Thomas Jefferson*, 5:82.
[222.] Tocqueville, *Democracy in America*, 1:309-313.

Such being the case, the United States of America has testimonies of two Frenchmen from two different centuries (Montesquieu early in the eighteenth century and Tocqueville early in the nineteenth century) who independently recognized a great truth that seems to be elusive to far too many modern Americans. That truth is that preserving liberty and the form of government we were bequeathed requires the nation to live within a moral imperative. Virtue really does matter if the nation is to survive.

THE IMPORTANCE OF RELIGION, MORALITY, AND VIRTUE TODAY

It is of interest that, in the early 1700s, as he wrote of the different forms of government, Montesquieu tried to capture in a *single* word the essence of each of the different forms of government he was studying. When he selected the word that he felt best fit a republic, which is the form of government that was established by our Founding Fathers, he chose the word "virtue."[223] Isn't that interesting—virtue. His perception is still true today. Virtue in the nation is one of the essential elements if we are to maintain the form of government the founders were inspired to establish for this nation and if we are to be strong and free.

The United States of America was established as a constitutional republic. Montesquieu and the founders of this nation understood that the moral character of the nation really matters if a republic is to survive. By recognizing that great fact and seeking to preserve the foundation principles upon which this nation was founded, we may preserve the blessings of liberty for ourselves and our posterity.

And we must never forget that each succeeding generation must have instilled in their hearts the moral character that is required to maintain the principles upon which this nation was founded. Jefferson warned us, "Virtue is not hereditary."[224] Virtue must be taught and expected.

This nation faces perilous times ahead. Perhaps more that any other time in the history of the nation, we face a moral crisis—in our leadership, in the general apathy of the people of the nation, in our nation's widespread acceptance of the godless philosophies of secular humanism, and in the pervasive perversions that are embraced without thought by such a broad spectrum of our population. Under the goading of godless leaders who hold little sacred and under the influence of a ubiquitous education system that teaches principles devoid of God, we have strayed far from the foundation principle of the nation. It would seem that the nation is forsaking God, and as a consequence, perhaps He is forsaking the nation.

What James Madison eloquently observed, could be said of our time:

> Is there no virtue among us? If there be not, we are in a wretched situation. No theoretical checks, no form of government, can render us secure. To suppose that

---

[223.] Montesquieu, *The Spirit of Laws*, V, 1, (2).

[224.] Ford, *Thomas Jefferson*, 10:227. See also Thomas Paine's *Common Sense*.

any form of government will secure liberty or happiness without any virtue in the people, is a chimerical idea.[225]

Chimerical is that which is merely imaginary, vain, fanciful, wildly or vainly conceived. It comes from the mythical monster called "chimera." The monster is described as having three heads: that of a lion, that of a goat, and that of a fire-breathing dragon. The foremost part of its body was said to be that of a lion, the middle portion a goat, and the hind portion that of a dragon. By describing and likening something to such wildly fanciful imagination, Madison reminds us of the impossibility of the nation surviving if it lacks virtue.

If this nation is to survive the challenges it faces, it must, first and foremost, return to that God who made it free. It must recognize His hand in all things and become obedient to His commandments. We must begin again to hold our national, state, and local leadership to a standard that reflects the godly principles upon which the nation was built.

The scope and magnitude of our nation's current moral turpitude cannot be underestimated, nor can the urgency of our return to God be overstated. During the Constitutional Convention of 1787, George Mason stated, "As nations cannot be rewarded or punished in the next world, they must be in this. By an inevitable chain of causes and effects, Providence punishes national sins by national calamities."[226]

Thomas Jefferson seemed to concur, saying,

> And can the liberties of a nation be thought secure when we have removed their only firm basis, a conviction in the minds of the people that these liberties of the gift of God? That they are not to be violated but with His wrath?[227]

We must pray that we, as a nation, have not passed the point of no return and we now face only the imminent justice of an offended God!

[225.] Elliot, *Debates*, 3:536-7.
[226.] Madison, *Journal*, vol. 2, Wednesday August 22, 1787
[227.] Jefferson's "Notes on Virginia," in Bergh, *Thomas Jefferson*, 2:227.

10.

THE RIGHT TO KEEP AND BEAR ARMS

RECOMMENDED RESOURCES FOR THE SERIOUS STUDENT:

Declaration of Independence
United States Constitution
View of the Constitution of the United States by St. George Tucker

QUOTES, ARTICLES, AND ORIGINAL SOURCES

Many today attempt to obfuscate the true purpose of the Second Amendment to the United States Constitution. They speak of it in euphemistic terms that skirt around the logic that brought this amendment into the Bill of Rights. Many today refuse to recognize that this is an individual God-given right that the founders considered one of their unalienable rights. It was not included as a nebulous collective right of the state. It has nothing to do with pleasurable pastimes many associate with shooting. It has everything to do with the preservation of life, liberty, property, and proper government. It has to do with preserving mankind's freedom from tyranny. The Second Amendment is the people's final defense of their God-given rights against criminals or tyrants, both foreign and domestic. That is the original intent of the Founding Fathers!

THE RIGHT TO KEEP AND BEAR ARMS

> The congress of the United States possesses no power to regulate, or interfere with the domestic concerns, or police of any state: it belongs not to them to establish any rules respecting the rights of property; nor will the constitution permit any prohibition of arms to the people; or of peaceable assemblies by them, for any purposes whatever, and in any number, whenever they may see occasion.[228]

[228.] Tucker, *View*, 253.

TO PRESERVE THE NATION

The United States Constitution Second Amendment states,

> A well regulated Militia, being necessary to the security of a free State, the right of the people to keep and bear Arms, shall not be infringed.

MODERN GUN CONTROL LAWS

In spite of these unequivocal declarations of "original intent," it is said that there are currently over twenty-five thousand gun control laws on the books throughout the United States. In spite of the best intentions of those enacting those laws, by and large, the effect has been to disarm innocent and law-abiding citizens while the criminal and violent elements of society have retained their firearms and are thus able to exercise their nefarious designs upon the largely disarmed populace with greater impunity.

While many of the multitudinous laws that have been enacted throughout the different political entities of the nation could be mentioned, at the national level, we will cite only a few as examples:

> *The 1934 National Firearms Act*—controlled fully automatic machine guns, short shotguns, and short rifles and established a two-hundred-dollar tax to sell or transfer those firearms

> *The 1938 National Firearms Act*—effected interstate and international sale of firearms

> A 1964 act that prohibited mailing concealable firearms (in part at least as a response to the shooting of Lee Harvey Oswald by Jack Ruby with a pistol on national television after the assassination of President John Fitzgerald Kennedy)

> *The 1968 Gun Control Act*—was passed in response to the assassinations of President John F. Kennedy, Martin Luther King, and Robert F. Kennedy. It is of interest to note that, according to material included in the official Lyndon B. Johnson Presidential Library, this act had virtually no possibility of being enacted by the United States Congress until (at the behest of President Johnson) it was fostered through an intensive lobbying effort on late-night television talk shows by a group of movie stars. These celebrities had played many roles on the silver screen as gun-toting "macho" men who knew much about firearms. They hit the talk show circuit playing off the public's perception of them in their imaginary screen roles, solemnly admonishing the American public that the nation needed the "protection" this act would provide and advising the viewers to contact their senators and congressmen to plead with them to vote for the act. Congress was flooded by requests from Americans who bought the ploy, and the act became law.

The 1993 Brady Handgun Act—instituted requirements for waiting periods for handgun purchases and background checks in response to the attempted assassination of President Ronald Reagan and others who were wounded.

Others could be mentioned, but these will suffice as federal-level enactments that the media often mentions.

As a result of a concerted effort by the mass media, leaders, and educators to foster gun control, the subject is currently an extremely controversial topic in the modern world. As a result of the emotionalism that has come to surround the topic, it is not surprising that the arguments surrounding the issue are a mass of confusion.

THE MILLER SUPREME COURT CASE

An example of the confusion in the arguments in this matter may be found in the 1939 *United States vs. Miller* supreme court case, which is often cited by "gun control" advocates as the basis for their position that more firearms control laws are not only needed, but fully in keeping with the intent of the Second Amendment. In brief, the following is a synopsis of the basis of the case:

> In search for other contraband, federal officers detained Jack Miller and Frank Layton.
>
> While they were not found in possession of the contraband the officers were searching for, Mr. Miller and Mr. Layton were discovered transporting a short barrel shotgun.
>
> Possession of this short-barreled shotgun was deemed by federal officers as a violation of the National Firearms Act of 1934, and the two were thus arrested and charged with that violation.
>
> Mr. Miller claimed that the law violated his Second Amendment rights.
>
> The case was reviewed at several levels of the court system, with varying outcomes.
>
> The United States Supreme Court agreed to review the case.
>
> Mr. Miller died in the interim.
>
> As the case came before the Supreme Court, neither Mr. Miller (because of his death) or Mr. Layton or their attorney appeared before the Supreme Court.
>
> The United States Justice Department presented their case against Miller.

No defense in the case was made.

The Supreme Court ruled in favor of the Justice Department, in essence saying,

> The purpose of the Second Amendment is to assure that civilians could respond to the defense of their country with weapons which are of the type currently used in military situations, and no evidence has been offered which would indicate that a sawed off shotgun could be used in a military situation, so the law against sawed off shotguns stands.

Military use of shotguns with barrel lengths of less than eighteen inches in World War I and other United States military actions was well-known at the time, but because no defense was presented, this information was not brought forth, so the conviction stood.

It is of extreme interest that the current argument against so-called "assault weapons" is that there is no possible reason civilians could have a need for them—utterly contradicting the rationale used in the *Miller* case. It is also of interest that in spite of almost universal efforts to demonize "assault weapons" and create an image that they are somehow inherently more "evil" than any other type of firearm, it has been observed by some pundits that almost anything (including baseball bats, knives, and rocks) can be an "assault weapon."

While, in recent years, gun control laws have not generally been overturned based upon the Second Amendment, it is interesting to note that in March of 2007, the District of Columbia Court of Appeals (a federal court) ruled that Washington DC's Firearms Control Act of 1976 was unconstitutional based upon the Second Amendment. It is certain that ruling will be appealed to the Supreme Court, and parties on both sides of the issue will watch the outcome of the appeal with interest![229]

[229.] On June 26, 2008, in a 5-4 decision, the United States Supreme Court ruled in the District of Columbia vs. Heller Case that the 1976 Washington DC ban on handguns was unconstitutional based upon the Second Amendment. The decision recognized and upheld the right to keep and bear arms as an individual right. However, in the body of the decision (and particularly in the final paragraph of the majority opinion statement) the court made a dramatic departure from the founder's original intent in the matter in that the decision grants to government entities the power to infringe upon the right to keep and bear arms as long as the government does not resort to blanket or absolute firearm bans. It would appear from this that the Supreme Court has opened the doors and authorized expansive and onerous restrictions which government entities at all levels will be free to impose upon owners of firearms. In fact, after the decision, Washington DC immediately implemented regulations which confirm that this approach will be the methodology by which restriction of the Second Amendment rights will be further infringed. The decision will likely result in a multitude of new laws which will further undermine the right to keep and bear arms, and erode the true purpose of the amendment. Perhaps it puts this great God-given right at a greater risk than it has ever faced since this nation was founded.

THE RIGHT TO KEEP AND BEAR ARMS

HISTORICAL PERSPECTIVE

In keeping with our commitment to review principles in accordance with the "original intent" of the American Founding Fathers, we must go back to a period long before the American founding era to obtain a basis of understanding of why the Second Amendment became part of the United States Constitution.

This great right to keep and bear arms was not a new concept that sprang into existence late in the eighteenth century at the whim of a few "gun fanatics" who happened to be founding a new nation. The concept of the right of defense, the necessity of retaining weapons necessary to that right, and the efforts of would-be tyrants to disarm the population they would subjugate is recorded in the earliest writings that currently exist.[230]

The God-given right (even the obligation) of preserving the ability of self-defense has been recognized by society throughout history. Many examples could be cited, but perhaps a few will suffice.

Alfred the Great

Alfred the Great began his reign in 872 in England. Under his righteous rule, *all* of his people were required to be armed with personal weapons and were subject to perform in the defense of the nation. This policy formulated and canonized the tradition of free men under English law.

This tradition was even carried forward under the Norman's declaration of the Assize of Arms of 1181. And the 1689 English Declaration of Rights noted and protected the right of Englishmen to keep and bear arms (remember, even after they had relocated to America, the colonists still considered themselves Englishmen).

[230.] For example, 1 Samuel 13:19-22.

Armed Colonists Going to Church

In light of this heritage, we should not be surprised that early in the colonization process, laws were passed that not only protected the right to be armed, but in many instances *required* it. Examples may be found in a 1623 Virginia law that required travelers to be armed, a 1631 law that required target practice on Sunday and churchgoers to bring their arms to Sunday services, a 1658 law requiring every household to have an operational firearm, and a 1673 law stipulating that the government would provide a firearm to householders who could not purchase one (the government was to be reimbursed for the firearm when the householder was able to do so). Massachusetts required all to be armed and, in 1644, stipulated a fine for anyone found not in compliance with this requirement.[231]

[231.] See documentation compiled in 1982 by the United States Senate Subcommittee on the Constitution, *The Right to Keep and Bear Arms* (Washington: U.S. Government Printing Office, 1982).

Cesare Beccaria

And of course, others wrote of the right of self-defense and efforts to disarm people—even non-Englishmen and non-Americans—because the right is universal and applies to all mankind because it is truly one of the unalienable God-given rights spoken of in the Declaration of Independence. For example, Cesare Beccaria, who was not a Founding Father of the United States, but who was contemporary with them wrote in 1764,

> The laws that forbid the carrying of arms . . . disarm those only who are neither inclined nor determined to commit crimes . . . Such laws make things worse for the assaulted and better for the assailants; they serve rather to encourage than to prevent homicides, for an unarmed man may be attacked with greater confidence than an armed man.[232]

In testimony of the truth of this statement, it is interesting to note that in America, those locations that have the most strict gun-ownership laws and that thereby deny the great bulk of the population from gun ownership become virtual "murder capitals" because the criminal element remains armed and may go about their wickedness with virtually no risk or opposition.

[232.] Quoted in Dr. Gary Kleck, *Point Blank: Guns and Violence in America* (New York: Aldine de Gruyter, 1991).

TO PRESERVE THE NATION

BLACKSTONE'S COMMENTS

And as often mentioned in this lecture series, prior to the unfolding of the American Revolution, Sir William Blackstone wrote a marvelous compilation of English law titled *Commentaries on the Laws of England*. Without exception, those we refer to as the Founding Fathers of this nation studied Blackstone's *Commentaries* prior to the Revolutionary War. Therein Blackstone notes the right of self-defense as one of mankind's unalienable rights:

> [Self-defense is] justly called the primary law of nature, so it is not, neither can it be in fact, taken away by the laws of society.[233]

In keeping with that wisdom, the Second Amendment was included in this nation's bill of rights to ensure the future protection of that God-given right.

Notwithstanding the pronouncements of presidents, congressmen, senators, governors, and the media, the Second Amendment has absolutely nothing to do with hunting, target shooting, plinking (that is, shooting at cans, etc.), collecting guns, or a "lifestyle." While these are often enjoyable and pleasant pastimes for those who participate in them, they are a minor side benefit to this great God-given inalienable right. The truth of the matter is that the Second Amendment has everything to do with the preservation and protection of life, liberty, and property. It is the last line of defense for the individual, the family, and the nation.

AMERICA'S REVOLUTIONARY WAR EXPERIENCE

As a result of the efforts of many to "demonize" firearms and to promote a false conception regarding the original purpose of the Second Amendment, there is an unprecedented effort underway today in our nation to disarm the people of this nation. In fact, to find anything anywhere near as premeditated and so determined on a nationwide basis, we must go back to before this nation became a nation—we have to go back to 1775 when the king tried to disarm the "upstart" colonists. Most Americans do not realize that the issue of disarming the citizens was the issue that precipitated the ride of Paul Revere and caused brave men to die at Lexington and Concord. On that fateful April day, the king's officers had dispatched his troops to confiscate the powder and lead (the ammunition) of the colonists. This British attempt to deny the colonists' right to keep and bear arms became a major driving force that rallied Americans throughout the colonies to armed resistance. This fundamental right—the importance of preserving the ability of every American to defend his liberties—became one of the principal arguments of our Founding Fathers for independence.

---

[233]. Blackstone, *Commentaries*, 3:4.

THE RIGHT TO KEEP AND BEAR ARMS

Because of their personal experience with tyranny and their understanding of the necessity of arms to prevent or overthrow tyranny, the Founding Fathers of this nation had a clear, correct, and unmistakable view of the subject. When we understand the position of the Founding Fathers on the individual right to keep and bear arms, we may better understand the reasons this God-given right was included in the Bill of Rights and why it is imperative that we preserve it today. In the interest of brevity, only a few statements of the founders must suffice.

COMMENTS OF AMERICA'S FOUNDING FATHERS

To facilitate the ratification of the Constitution and even before the Bill of Rights were drafted and ratified, James Madison wrote,

> [The Constitution preserves] the advantage of being armed which Americans possess over the people of almost every other nation . . . (where) the governments are afraid to trust the people with arms.[234]

Of course, the Bill of Rights were created in order to further recognize and protect unalienable God-given rights and to place additional emphasis on the fact that unless a power was specifically granted to the national government, the national government did *not* have the power in question.

And later, while in Congress, Madison supported the concept of an armed citizenry being necessary to preserve the freedom of the nation:

> The right of the people to keep and bear . . . arms shall not be infringed. A well regulated militia, composed of the body of the people, trained to arms, is the best and most natural defense of a free country.[235]

The intent that firearms be available universally was a common subject for comment during the American founding era:

> Whereas, to preserve liberty, it is essential that the whole body of the people always possess arms, and be taught alike, especially when young, how to use them.[236]

> The great object is, that every man be armed . . . Every one who is able may have a gun.[237]

[234.] Federalist no. 46
[235.] *Annals of Congress* 1789, 434.
[236.] Richard Henry Lee, *Pennsylvania Gazette*, February 20, 1788.
[237.] Patrick Henry in Elliot, *Debates*, 3:386.

TO PRESERVE THE NATION

As the new nation was being formed, Thomas Jefferson wrote in support of an armed citizenry,

> No free men shall ever be debarred the use of arms.[238]

Samuel Adams

And Samuel Adams, the Father of the American Revolution, felt it natural for free men to be armed, saying,

> The Constitution shall never be construed . . . to prevent the people of the United States who are peaceable citizens from keeping their own arms.[239]

Noah Webster saw an armed citizenry as essential to preserving liberty, asserting,

---

[238.] Ford, *Thomas Jefferson*, 2:27.
[239.] Samuel Adams, *Debates and Proceedings in the Convention of the Commonwealth of Massachusetts.* Edited by Pierce and Hale (Boston: 1850), 86-7.

> Before a standing army or a tyrannical government can rule, the people must be disarmed; as they are in almost every kingdom in Europe. The supreme power in America cannot enforce unjust laws by the sword; because the whole body of the people are armed, and constitute a force superior to any band of regular (or professional) troops that can be, on any pretense, raised in the United States.[240]

Many have observed that the Second Amendment was written to ensure that the other nine amendments and the Constitution were preserved in their entirety.

And it is of note that the currently vogue falsehood that the "militia" mentioned in the Second Amendment referred to the national guard (which was not even created until the twentieth century) may be debunked with many statements by this nation's founders. One statement that George Mason made in the debate at the ratification convention before the Virginia Assembly must suffice:

> I ask, sir, what is the militia? It is the whole people, except for a few public officials.[241]

ARMS REQUIRED FOR FREEDOM

Power to refuse or to counter abuse of power sometimes becomes necessary. In his review of the United States Constitution and the Bill of Rights, St. George Tucker, one of the preeminent constitutional scholars of America's founding era, touches upon the necessity of the people being armed to ensure the ability to ultimately enforce their rights if they are ever violated and of governments that use the flimsiest or most obtuse rationale as excuse for the disarming of the citizenry of the nation. Modern America suffers from this malady as a gullible, disinterested, and apathetic populace that falls for almost every contrived method to remove what Tucker terms the "true palladium [that which affords effectual defense, protection and safety] of liberty."

> This may be considered as the true palladium of liberty . . . The right of self defense is the first law of nature; in most governments it has been the study of rulers to confine this right within the narrowest limits possible. Wherever standing armies are kept up, and the right of the people to keep and bear arms is, under any color or pretext whatsoever, prohibited, liberty, if not already annihilated, is on the

---

[240.] Noah Webster, "An Examination of the Leading Principles of the Federal Constitution" (1787) in *Pamphlets on the Constitution of the United States*, edited by Paul Leicester Ford (Chicago, IL: 1888).

[241.] Elliot, *Debates*, vol. 3.

brink of destruction. In England, the people have been disarmed, generally, under the specious pretext of preserving the game; a never failing lure to bring over the landed aristocracy to support any measure, under the mask, though calculated for very different purposes. True it is, their bill of rights seems at first view to counteract this policy; but the right of bearing arms is confined to Protestants, and the words suitable to their condition and degree, have been interpreted to authorize the prohibition of keeping a gun or other engine for the destruction of game, to any farmer, or inferior tradesman, or other person not qualified to kill game. So that not one man in five hundred can keep a gun in his house without being subject to a penalty.[242]

While the intent of the founders in preserving the right to keep and bear arms was clearly understood in the American founding era, great efforts have been made today through many educational processes to create an intense, unwarranted fear of firearms in the hearts of the American populace. It is interesting to note that it was not many years ago that shooting was taught in public schools and many high schools had shooting ranges in the basement of the school. It is also of interest that school shootings were virtually unheard of in those days.

THOMAS JEFFERSON'S ADVICE

In light of the frenzied fear of firearms that is fostered throughout the nation today, most modern Americans are baffled by the advice that Thomas Jefferson wrote to his nephew Peter Carr in August 1785. At the time he wrote this letter, Jefferson was living in France and serving as the United States ambassador. He wrote his young nephew, Peter Carr, giving him advice regarding moral standards, educational pursuits, and life in general. In the letter, he wrote,

> Consider what hours you have free from the school and the exercises of the school. Give about two of them, every day, to exercise; for health must not be sacrificed to learning. A strong body makes the mind strong. As to the species of exercise, I advise the gun. While this gives a moderate exercise to the body, it gives boldness, enterprise, and independence to the mind. Games played with the ball, and others of that nature, are too violent for the body, and stamp no character on the mind. Let your gun, therefore, be the constant companion of your walks.[243]

[242.] Tucker, *View*, 238-9.
[243.] Bergh, *Thomas Jefferson*, 5:82-7.

THE RIGHT TO KEEP AND BEAR ARMS AS AN INDIVIDUAL RIGHT

In spite of all the evidence noted herein, there is still a vigorous debate in modern society regarding the "right to keep and bear arms" as an individual right. That fact encourages the following review to alert the student to arguments that are frequently brought forward by individuals and organizations who seek to undermine or destroy this individual God-given right.

Some today argue that the "right of the people" referred to in the Second Amendment was a collective right of the state (meaning, the government).

If such were the case, those who hold this opinion would render the reading of the Second Amendment as follows:

> A well regulated Militia, being necessary to the security of a free State, the right of the state to keep and bear Arms, shall not be infringed.

Of course, it would seem reasonable to assume that if that were the case, the same approach could apply to both the First and Fourth Amendments:

Recall that the First Amendment reads,

> Congress shall make no law respecting an establishment of religion, or prohibiting the free exercise thereof; or abridging the freedom of speech, or of the press; or the right of the people peaceably to assemble, and to petition the Government for a redress of grievances.

The new reading would thus be rendered:

> Congress shall make no law respecting an establishment of religion, or prohibiting the free exercise thereof; or abridging the freedom of speech, or of the press; or the right of the state peaceably to assemble, and to petition the Government for a redress of grievances.

The Fourth Amendment currently reads,

> The right of the People to be secure in their persons, houses, papers, and effects, against unreasonable searches and seizures, shall not be violated, and no Warrants shall issue, but upon probable cause, supported by Oath or affirmation, and particularity describing the place to be searched, and the persons or things to be seized.

It would become the following:

> The right of the state to be secure in their persons, houses, papers, and effects, against unreasonable searches and seizures, shall not be violated, and no Warrants

shall issue, but upon probable cause, supported by Oath or affirmation, and particularity describing the place to be searched, and the persons or things to be seized.

Of course, such an approach is readily seen as absurd. The rights recognized and protected in the First, Second, and Fourth Amendments are clearly individual rights, and the intention of the Bill of Rights was to recognize, protect, and preserve those rights.

Punctuation and the Second Amendment

And perhaps we should briefly mention the matter of commas included in the Second Amendment. This argument proposes that the placement of the three commas found in some published versions indicates some perverse interpretation that removes the "right to keep and bear arms" from the people and makes it a collective right of the state.

The rules of commas were not nearly so hard and fast in the founding era as they are today. After the United States Constitution was written and the Bill of Rights was incorporated into the document, Noah Webster was instrumental in "Americanizing" and standardizing spelling and punctuation rules for the new nation. Prior to that time, commas were often placed to denote a kind of "rhetorical pause" for emphasis, so they were salted generously into writings.

It is interesting to note that the amendment passed by Congress reads,

> A well regulated Militia, being necessary to the security of a free State, the right of the people to keep and bear Arms, shall not be infringed." (three commas)

The amendment that was distributed to the states (after being passed by the Congress) and ratified by the states reads,

> A well regulated Militia being necessary to the security of a free State, the right of the people to keep and bear Arms shall not be infringed. (one comma)

St. George Tucker uses this version with only one comma in his writings about the Constitution and the Bill of Rights.

Both versions are used in official U.S. government publications, and either form has been demonstrated to the satisfaction of historical experts in punctuation to not affect the intended meaning that the right to keep and bear arms was an individual right protected by the Second Amendment. Of course, in addition to the punctuation experts, we have the unequivocal record of the written and spoken testimonies of the founders of this nation regarding the true purposes of the Second Amendment.

THE STATE CONSTITUTIONS AND THE RIGHT TO KEEP AND BEAR ARMS

It is also be of interest to note that forty-four states have included in their constitutions a recognition of the right to keep and bear arms. Thirty-one of those states explicitly recognize the right as an individual right and often mention self-defense as a reason. Six states do not explicitly recognize the right to keep and bear arms in their constitutions.

CONCLUSION

The Second Amendment to the United States Constitution unequivocally protects the individual God-given right of all mankind to keep and bear arms to protect their lives, liberty, and property from tyrants and criminals, both foreign and domestic. It is a right that must not be infringed.

RECOMMENDED CONTEMPORARY READINGS:

Gary Kleck, *Point Blank: Guns and Violence in America* (New York: Aldine de Gruyter, 1991), 512 pages.

Roger D. McGrath, *Gunfighters, Highwaymen and Vigilantes: Violence on the Frontier* (CA: University of California Press, 1984 [hardback, 307 pages]; 1987 [paperback, 288 pages]).

John R. Lott Jr., *More Guns Less Crime* (CA: University of Chicago Press, 1998), 321 pages

11.

OF EDUCATION AND FREEDOM

RECOMMENDED RESOURCES FOR THE SERIOUS STUDENT:

McGuffey's Readers
An American Dictionary of the English Language, Noah Webster's 1828 Dictionary
The Humanist Manifestos (I, II, III)

QUOTES, ARTICLES, AND ORIGINAL SOURCES

Proper education, based upon correct principles, is essential in order to preserve liberty, proper government, and a sound society. False educational ideas ultimately subvert and destroy liberty, proper government, and society. This lecture is approached in a way that introduces the student to the educational philosophies that helped establish the foundation of a free, prosperous, happy, and respected America, an educational approach that developed noble character and built sound understanding of foundational principles, allowing the nation to have leaders *and* citizens who were good and wise and honest. In contrast to that, the student is then introduced to the shifting sands of modern educational philosophies that are undermining the character of the nation and removing the proven principles that have been demonstrated through the ages to bring forth worthy fruits. The new philosophies denigrate the names and character of the nation's founders and others who brought forth good works and seem to encourage the student to adopt belief systems foreign to the ennobling concepts that allowed this nation to blossom so marvelously. The new educational approach seems to be that all belief systems are of equal worth, *except* the one by which this nation was established, and that the foreign belief systems are to be promoted at the exclusion of the original American belief system.

The adverse effect of the new philosophies is seen in countless ways throughout the nation! Sound doctrines are set aside in favor of situational ethics. Honesty, integrity, morality, work ethic, family unity, and numerous other wonderful values are suffering as the fruits of the new philosophies are harvested. The principles of proper government and individual God-given rights are cast aside in favor of philosophies foreign to Americanist ideals. We note again Thomas Jefferson's concern that by importation of people who hold ideas foreign to the principles of liberty and proper government, the nation and our freedom will be destroyed as these unsound doctrines are made popular in the nation and become adopted by large segments of society:

> Every species of government has its specific principles. Ours perhaps are more peculiar than those of any other in the universe. It is a composition of the freest principles of the English constitution, with others derived from natural right and natural reason. To these nothing can be more opposed than the maxims of absolute monarchies. Yet from such we are to expect the greatest number of emigrants. They will bring with them the principles of the governments they leave, imbibed in their early youth; or, if able to throw them off, it will be in exchange for an unbounded licentiousness, passing, as is usual, from one extreme to another. It would be a miracle were they to stop precisely at the point of temperate liberty. These principles, with their language, they will transmit to their children. In proportion to their numbers, they will share with us the legislation. They will infuse into it their spirit, warp and bias its directions, and render it a heterogeneous, incoherent, distracted mass.[244]

Whether the false concepts are imported from foreign lands or they are home-grown and fostered by un-American Americans matters not—they are pernicious and destructive of the foundation of the nation. If enough Americans are deceived into adopting the subversive concepts and by their vote they implement them, it will be as destructive to the nation as if it had been captured by a foreign power and subdued by force! Education in and understanding of Americanist principles are essential to the preservation of the nation!

As we have pointed out elsewhere in this lecture series, much of the early educational experience in this nation was scripture-based. Students learned to read from the scriptures, and many of their earliest lessons were based upon the character-building examples found within the scriptures. As previously noted in lecture 1, *The New England Primer* was the primary book of instruction that was used from 1690 forward to teach students how to read and the basis from which it taught was the Holy Bible. Perhaps it is appropriate that the foundation of American education was originally built upon this approach. Anciently, the value and effect of education was well understood. Examples are found in the Holy Scriptures:

Proverbs 22:6
Train up a child in the way he should go: and when he is old, he will not depart from it.

Isaiah 5:13
Therefore my people are gone into captivity, because [they have] no knowledge: and their honourable men [are] famished.

---

[244]. Bergh, *Thomas Jefferson*, 2:220-1.

TO PRESERVE THE NATION

Hosea 4:6

My people are destroyed for lack of knowledge.

As this nation was established, educational efforts focused on the building of moral character. Noted below are examples from Washington's early life. Each concept has a wealth of character that is worthy of deep consideration.

The following are selections from George Washington's *Rules of Civility and Decent Behaviour in Company and Conversation,* **which are noted in the lecture:**

> 22nd Shew not yourself glad at the Misfortune of another though he were your enemy.
> 23rd When you see a Crime punished, you may be inwardly Pleased; but always shew Pity to the Suffering Offender.
> 49th Use no Reproachfull Language against any one neither Curse nor Revile.
> 50th Be not hasty to believe flying Reports to the Disparagement of any.
> 51st Wear not your Cloths, foul, unript or Dusty but See they be Brush'd once every day at least and take heed that you approach not to any uncleaness.
> 56th Associate yourself with Men of good Quality if you Esteem your own Reputation; for 'tis better to be alone than in bad Company.
> 108th When you Speak of God or His Attributes, let it be Seriously & with Reverence. Honour & Obey your Natural Parents altho they be Poor.
> 109th Let your Recreations be Manfull not Sinfull.
> 110th Labour to keep alive in your Breast the Little Spark of Celestial fire Called Conscience.

It seems that today it would be valuable to the nation were students to receive principles such as these as they received their early instruction!

As the nation was established, the importance of a morality-based educational system was well understood and promoted. The founders were absolutely convinced that such an educational system was essential to the survival of the nation. Their early legislative enactments reflected this position. As previously noted, article 3 of the 1787 Northwest Ordinance states,

> Religion, morality, and knowledge, being necessary to good government and the happiness of mankind, schools and the means of education shall forever be encouraged.

It is interesting to note that early in the Constitutional Convention of 1787, the concept of a national university was discussed. The importance of fostering proper education in the effort to preserve the nation was recognized by all. In fact, the first draft of a suggested new constitution that was offered near the end of May 1787 included the establishment of a national university. It is also of interest to note that the Constitution that was signed on September 17, 1787, contained no mention of power being granted to the national government to participate in the educational process in any way. Of course, the Tenth Amendment makes absolutely clear the stipulation that unless power was specifically granted to the national government, it *does not have that power.* We may reasonably infer from this that the national government was not to hold the reins of the American educational system.

In several of his letters, George Washington mused that a national university would be desirable, but he also was adamant in his position that all must adhere to the existing Constitution, saying,

> But the constitution which at any time exists till changed by an explicit and authentic act of the whole people is sacredly obligatory upon all.[245]

Consequently, since the power to direct education was not delegated within the Constitution to the national government, Washington did not press the matter.

Thomas Jefferson also made many comments regarding the importance of education in order that the people may be capable of self-government. Of course, it will be recalled that Thomas Jefferson was instrumental in the establishment of the University of Virginia, but he recognized that if the nation was to participate in the process of public education, a constitutional amendment would be necessary.[246] The following are a number of statements by Jefferson on the subject of education. The reference source, volume, and page of the statement are noted with the quotation:

> Say ... whether peace is best preserved by giving energy to the government, or information to the people. This last is the most certain and the most legitimate engine of government. Educate and inform the whole mass of the people. Enable them to see that it is their interest to preserve peace and order, and they will preserve them. And it requires no very high degree of education to convince them of this. They are the only sure reliance for the preservation of our liberty.[247]

> If a nation expects to be ignorant and free, in a state of civilization, it expects what never was and never will be.[248]

---

[245]. Farewell Address in Richardson, *Messages and Papers*, 1:205-16.
[246]. See Bergh, *Thomas Jefferson*, 13:354.
[247]. To James Madison, in Bergh, *Thomas Jefferson*, 6:392.
[248]. Bergh, *Thomas Jefferson*, 14:384.

It [should not] be proposed to take [the] ordinary branches [of education] out of the hands of private enterprise, which manages so much better all the concerns to which it is equal.[249]

[Correct principles] ought to be instilled into the minds of our youth on their first opening. The boys of the rising generation are to be the men of the next, and the sole guardians of the principles we deliver over to them.[250]

Education is the true corrective of abuses of constitutional power.[251]

Noah Webster, who is considered to be one of the nation's founders, was also considered one of the nation's principal educators, and his educational materials were strongly founded on a moral basis. In fact, it has been said that he taught millions to read, but none to sin. He wrote numerous texts and reading and spelling books. His *History of the United States* contained sound advice to students.

Noah Webster

The following are selections from Noah Webster's "Advice to the Young" in *History of the United States*, which are noted in the lecture. These selections are included to expose the reader to the noble principles that were openly taught in the schools during the formative years of this nation:

[249.] Bergh, *Thomas Jefferson*, 3:423.
[250.] Bergh, *Thomas Jefferson*, 12:360.
[251.] Ford, *Thomas Jefferson*, 10:161.

OF EDUCATION AND FREEDOM

"Honor thy Father and thy Mother. Children, obey your parents in all things."

"Parents are the natural guardians of their children. It is their duty to feed, clothe, protect and educate them; and for these purposes it is proper and necessary that parents should have authority to direct their actions."

"It is proper that parents should be entrusted with the instruction of children . . ."

" . . . children should obey their parents . . . their obedience should be prompt and cheerful."

" . . . it is a primary duty of children to 'Honor their father and mother.' . . . it forbids all rudeness and ill manners towards them."

"Among the first and foremost important truths which you are to learn, are those which relate to God and religion."

" . . . things around you cannot have made themselves . . . it must have had a creator, some being that had power to act or move, and to bring the stone into existence."

" . . . . the first animal of every kind must then have had a creator, distinct from the animal himself."

" . . . . with absolute certainly, that there must be a being who has been the creator . . ."

" . . . . the Being who could make such things must possess immense power, all together superior to the power of any being that you see on the earth . . . inquire who is this being . . ."

"We are compelled to believe that there is a Being of vast and unlimited power . . . the creator has not left mankind in ignorance on this subject. He has graciously revealed his character to man . . . the Bible."

"God is not only all-powerful, but all-wise: and his wisdom is displayed in the admirable structure of whatever he has made; . . . . God is a benevolent Being. 'God is love, . . . ' The earth contains inexhaustible stores for supplying the wants and desires of living creatures."

" . . . God is a holy Being; . . . he is perfectly free from any sinful attributes or dispositions . . . . God is your Supreme or Sovereign Ruler . . . God has then a complete right to direct all the actions of the beings he has made."

"Man is a being of a higher order; he is furnished with understanding or intellect . . . soul or spiritual part of man . . . a moral being . . . . God is your creator and rightful governor . . . what is his will concerning you; . . . God requires you to perform some duties, and fill some useful station among other beings."

In his textbook, Noah Webster introduced the term "Secret Combinations." It is a term coined to describe conspiratorial efforts to usurp power or destroy liberty, proper government, or pursue improper designs:

"By the laws of creation, and by our civil constitution, all men have equal rights to protection, to liberty, and to the free enjoyment of all the benefits and privileges of government. All secret attempts, by associations or otherwise to give one set of men or one party, advantages over another are mean, dishonorable and immoral. All secret combinations of men to gain for themselves or their party, advantages in preferments to office, are trespasses upon the rights of others."

" . . . nothing can be honorable which is morally wrong."

"God commands you to choose for rulers, just men who will rule in the fear of God. The preservation of a republican government depends on the faithful discharge of this duty; if the citizens neglect their duty and place unprincipled men in office, the government will soon be corrupted; laws will be made, not for the public good, so much as for selfish or local purposes; corrupt or incompetent men will be appointed to execute the laws; the public revenues will be squandered on unworthy men; and the rights of the citizens will be violated or disregarded."

"To young men I would recommend that their treatment of females should be always characterized by kindness, delicacy and respect . . ."

" . . . the chief temporal advantages of Christianity, the elevation of the female character. Let justice then be done to their merits; guard their purity; defend their honor; treat them with tenderness and respect."

"Q. Should not beasts as well as men be treated with mercy?

A. They ought indeed. It is wrong to give needless pain even to a beast . . . If a man treats his beast with cruelty, beware of trusting yourself in his power. He will probably make a severe master and a cruel husband."

OF EDUCATION AND FREEDOM

William Holms McGuffey

Another individual who should be noted as a wonderful educator during the early years of America is William Holmes McGuffey. As a young person, he hungered and thirsted after knowledge and understanding. Once he had prepared himself, he became a great educator. In 1836, he published the first edition of the *McGuffey Readers*. Together with later editions, more than 125 million *McGuffey Readers* have been published. They are a series of books that establish the basic foundation by first teaching the student to read, and then they go on to teach great concepts of character, wisdom, and service. Over the years, the *McGuffey Readers* established the basis of education for millions of Americans and taught them noble character traits in the process. They are still available today and are a wonderful tool that can help educate young Americans and their parents.

Unfortunately, concurrent with the publication of some of these great educational tools, Karl Marx published his scurrilous *The Communist Manifesto*. Since lecture 13 reviews *The Communist Manifesto* in some detail, the manifesto will not be considered at length at this time. Perhaps it will suffice to note that in *The Communist Manifesto*, Marx wrote that he intended to "destroy the most hallowed of relations" by modifying the educational system. And the last of the ten points of *The Communist Manifesto* states the communist intention to provide "free education for all children in public schools." The reader is admonished to consider and compare and contrast the purposes for education as proposed by the American Founding Fathers versus the educational purposes proposed by Marx. The American tradition taught liberty, justice, individual God-given rights, proper government, and, in general, ennobling concepts that lifted and blessed the lives of mankind. Marx, on the other hand, sought to capture the educational system in order to subjugate and implement tyranny over mankind. From this, it should be apparent to all that the *principles* in the education system determine whether or not the education is of value. Those who seek education today would be wise to be alert and consider the basis upon which their educational process is founded!

As a consequence of this new Marxist educational philosophy in America during the late 1800s, signs of changes in the education system of the United States began to emerge. Dr. A. A. Hodge of Princeton noted these emerging changes.

Dr. A. A. Hodge

Dr A. A. Hodge on America's Public Education System

> It is capable of exact demonstration that if every party in the State has the right of excluding from public schools whatever he does not believe to be true, then he that believes most must give way to him that believes least, and then he that believes least must give way to him that believes absolutely nothing, no matter in how small a minority the atheists or agnostics may be. It is self-evident that on this scheme, if it is consistently and persistently carried out in all parts of the country, the United

States system of national popular education will be the most efficient and widespread instrument for the propagation of atheism which the world has ever seen.[252]

John Dewey

And by the mid-1930s, a new educational philosophy was being promoted by John Dewey, who is considered by many to be the "Father of Modern American Education." Dewey coauthored the *Humanist Manifesto,* and its tenets have become the basis of the American educational system. It is interesting to note that the humanist "religion" has become, or is becoming, the de facto religion that is constantly taught in public schools throughout the United States; and it is fast becoming the official "religion" of all things public within the nation.

As of this writing, there are three iterations of the *Humanist Manifesto*. Each is designed to supplement and build upon the previous manifesto. *Humanist Manifesto I* was written in 1933. The second manifesto was written in 1973, and the third was written in 2003.

The reader is admonished to note the presence of the doctrines of the *Humanist Manifestos* in the public school curriculum, in public discourse, and in the media.

---

[252] A. A. Hodge, *Popular Lectures on Theological Themes* (Philadelphia: Presbyterian Board of Publications, 1887).

TO PRESERVE THE NATION

The following are excerpts from the *Humanist Manifestos* that are noted in the lecture:

Humanist Manifesto I **(1933)**

> "Religious humanists regard the universe as self-existing and not created."

Of course, this doctrine denies the existence of a Divine Creator.

> "Humanism believes that man is a part of nature and that he has emerged as a result of a continuous process."

This doctrine presupposes the evolutionary process, and that man is no higher creation than other animals which exist on the earth.

> "Humanism asserts that the nature of the universe depicted by modern science makes unacceptable any supernatural or cosmic guarantees of human values."

Apparently, Humanists believe there are no values that are unique to humanity, or of a higher nature.

> "Religious humanism considers the complete realization of human personality to be the end of man's life and seeks its development and fulfillment in the here and now."

Humanists would have us believe that the sum and substance of mankind's existence is tied to the here and now, and there is no hereafter, therefore no judgment or rewards for one's actions.

> "A socialized and cooperative economic order must be established to the end that the equitable distribution of the means of life be possible."

It is interesting that throughout their doctrine is a socialistic perspective of the forcible redistribution of mankind's wealth.

> "We consider the religious forms and ideas of our fathers no longer adequate."

It is interesting that this philosophy rejects the religious beliefs of our forefathers.

Humanist Manifesto II **(1973)**

> "As in 1933, humanists still believe that traditional theism, especially faith in the prayer-hearing God, assumed to love and care for persons, to hear and understand their prayers, and to be able to do something about them, is an

> unproved and outmoded faith . . . Reasonable minds look to other means for survival."

Note the efforts to destroy a belief in a prayer-hearing God who cares for and loves His children. Humanists would have us believe that God cannot hear prayers or do anything about them. They believe that those with rational minds will seek other answers. Karl Marx held a similar dogma, writing "religion . . . is the opium of the masses."[253]

> "Traditional moral codes and newer irrational cults both fail to meet the pressing needs of today and tomorrow."

An effort is made to differentiate the needs of mankind today from those of days gone by. After all, mankind is continuously evolving, and consequently, needs must also evolve. Of course, this perspective not only helps unseat God, but also helps unseat the concept that the foundation principles of this nation are timeless and based upon human nature, not the technology that is in use in society at any given time. Note that the moral code of days gone by is unseated by a new code. Is this the basis of the so-called "new morality?"

> "We find insufficient evidence for belief in the existence of a supernatural; it is either meaningless or irrelevant . . . we begin with humans not God, nature not deity."

In the judgment of humanists, it would appear that God does not exist, and humans are the sum and substance of all reason in the universe.

> "We can discover no divine purpose or providence for the human species . . . humans are responsible for what we are or will become. No deity will save us; we must save ourselves."

God will not save us. We must save ourselves. Mankind's reason is the sum and substance of all we may rely upon. Since there is no God, we must believe that mankind has no divinely established purpose.

> "Promises of immortal salvation or fear of eternal damnation are both illusory and harmful . . . There is no credible evidence that life survives the death of the body."

---

[253]. Marx, *Contribution to the Critique of Hegel's Philosophy of Right* [Feb. 1844]

Based upon everything that has gone before in this manifesto, logic would tell us that it is obviously there is no afterlife. It would seem that humanists would have us believe that when one dies, all ceases to exist for that individual.

> "Ethics is autonomous and situational."

Ethics stand alone, and are based upon the situation. This position would have us believe that there are no absolutes. Apparently, as long as an individual can justify a position in their mind (regardless of how convoluted the conclusion is), anything is ethical, and society bears sad daily testimony of how widely this is concept is accepted.

> "We strive for the good life, here and now."

Since the belief of the humanist is that the here and now is all there is, this is perfectly logical. Of course, this leads to a very hedonistic society that selfishly seeks only its own pleasure.

> "Reason and intelligence are the most effective instruments that humankind possesses. There is no substitute: neither faith nor passion suffices in itself."

It would seem that the reason and logic of mankind trumps all other thought processes.

> "In the area of sexuality, we believe that intolerant attitudes, often cultivated by orthodox religions and puritanical cultures, unduly repress sexual conduct. The right to birth control, abortion, and divorce should be recognized . . . neither do we wish to prohibit, by law or social sanction, sexual behavior between consenting adults. The many varieties of sexual exploration should not in themselves be considered 'evil . . . ' a civilized society should be a tolerant one . . . individuals should be permitted to express their sexual proclivities and pursue their life-styles as they desire . . . Moral education for children and adults is an important way of developing awareness and sexual maturity."

This position has led to a wide variety of sex education programs in the United States and throughout the world. It has also led to what is termed the "new morality," which in fact is simply the old immorality. Hedonistic lifestyles and seeking pleasures seem to be the sole reason for existence for many who have been raised on this doctrine. The moral tenor of the nation has slipped dramatically since the implementation of these concepts, the sacred nature of the God-ordained family is rarely considered, and the rights of the unborn child have been set aside.

> "The individual must experience a full range of civil liberties in all societies . . . also includes a recognition of an individual's right to die with dignity, euthanasia, and the right to suicide."

OF EDUCATION AND FREEDOM

Apparently, since in the view of the humanist mankind are simply another animal species coexisting with other animals on the earth, life is as cheap for humans as it is for any other animal species, perhaps even more so.

> "We must extend participatory democracy in its true sense to the economy, the school, the family, the workplace, and voluntary associations."

We have reviewed at length in this lecture series the dangers of democracy, the position of the American Founding Fathers on this subject and the views of those who would implement tyranny upon the world through democracy. It is interesting that the humanist perspective correlates with the views of Marx, Lenin, Mao, and others of their ilk, while contradicting this nation's founders!

> "The state should encourage maximum freedom for different moral, political, religious, and social values in society."

Apparently, humanists promote the concept that all "belief systems" are of equal value and are to be fostered within society.

> "society should provide means to satisfy their basic economic, health, and cultural needs, including, wherever resources make possible, a minimum guaranteed annual income."

Again, a Marxist perspective of forcible redistribution of wealth is promoted. It would require **taking** (by force of government) from someone who "has" and giving to someone who "has not" to guarantee these things.

> "We believe in the right to universal education."

This premise reflects the tenth point of Marx's *The Communist Manifesto*[254] and should be taken as a warning that the *wrong* kind of education can be destructive of the principles upon which this nation was established. All education is not of equal value, and education that destroys or unseats core values of proven worth is less than useless—even detrimental to the survival of priceless truth.

> "We deplore the division of humankind on nationalistic grounds . . . the best option is to transcend the limits of national sovereignty and to move toward the building of a world community . . . we look to the development of a system of

---

[254.] See lecture 13 herein.

> world law and a world order based upon transnational federal government . . . the building of world community."

Humanists would dissolve the United States of America, overthrow the charter that guarantees mankind's God-given rights, the United States Constitution, and establish a worldwide government based upon the godless, socialistic principles of humanism.

> "We believe in the peaceful adjudication of differences by international courts and by the development of the arts of negotiation and compromise."

The international courts systems are not founded upon the liberty-preserving principles upon which the United States Court system is based. They have proven themselves throughout history to be a source of tyranny, destroying individual God-given rights and following the precepts of democracy or some other form of totalitarian force. Americans will find themselves stripped of rights they have come to take for granted if they become subject to international court systems.

> "The world community must engage in cooperative planning concerning the use of rapidly depleting resources . . . Ecological damage, resource depletion, and excessive population growth must be checked by international concord . . . We must free our world from needless pollution and waste."

Herein we find the basis of the "environmental movement" that is sweeping the nation. It is based upon "scarcity" doctrine, the concept of diminishing resources and scare tactics that are intended to wrest control of the means of production and distribution from individuals and families and placing those resources under the power of government. Controlling the universal resources of all things in the environment will result in absolute control over mankind, for if "the environment" is controlled (since it is all encompassing), what is left to be independently managed by individuals and families for their sustenance? The historic perspective that was held by the generation that established this nation was one of a loving God who wisely provided abundant resources for all of His children. During the founding period of the United States, it was believed that by conforming to God's will and wisdom, mankind would prosper and thrive in God's gracious abundance. Knowing His will and abiding it became a central focus of the nation. The nation has shifted from this historic perspective of abundance wherein all are free to enjoy prosperity and open exchange to a perspective of scarcity that will ultimately result in the implementation of government control of the means of production and/or distribution—which is the very definition of socialism.

> "The problems of economic growth and development can no longer be resolved by one nation alone; they are worldwide in scope. It is the moral obligation of the developed nations to provide—through an international authority that safeguards human rights—massive technical, agricultural, medical, and economic assistance, including birth control techniques, to the developing portions of the globe. World poverty must cease. Hence extreme disproportions in wealth, income, and economic growth should be reduced on a worldwide basis."

Again, world government is fostered, with the overtones of a global socialist tyranny that will forcibly redistribute all of mankind's means and subjugate humanity to the whims of the ruling elite who will, presumably, know what is best for all of mankind. Abortion is euphemistically referred to in this passage as "birth control techniques."

Many today note the sad proliferation of filth and perversion that are so widely recognized throughout society. In many ways, from a moral perspective, society seems to be in a downward spiral. Perhaps this condition, at least in part, may be attributed to the almost universal promotion within society of the perspective of the *Humanist Manifestos*. Based upon this nearly universal promotion and the prohibition of "traditional" religion in "official government" settings, the tenets of humanism are becoming a sort of "official religion" for public consumption.

In 1962, without a single supportive precedent and in contradiction of over 170 years of historical convention, the U.S. Supreme Court banned God from our public schools. This action officially severed the connecting cord between the public schools and the source of divine intelligence, the Creator. That void has, increasingly, been filled with the godless philosophies of humanism, as noted herein.

The theories of Darwin are inextricably interwoven with the philosophies of humanism in a seamless web, and the two doctrines are taught as one. Darwinian evolutionary theory, in full concurrence with humanism, unabashedly states that mankind are simply highly developed animals ("Man is descended from a hairy quadruped, furnished with a tail and pointed ears, probably arboreal in its habits").[255] In light of this, society should not be surprised when people so indoctrinated seek to fulfill animalistic expressions to the detriment of society.

---

[255] See *Descent of Man* by Charles Darwin.

TO PRESERVE THE NATION

Charles Darwin

When, in accord with the *Humanist Manifestos*, our schools teach the anatomy and mechanics of reproduction, along with "alternative lifestyles" and "solutions" such as abortion to unplanned pregnancies but refuse to teach morality and the sacred nature of chastity and marital fidelity, can we not project the moral demise of our children and our nation?

When students can no longer discern the monumental differences between the ennobling principles of the United States Constitution and the debauched precepts of Karl Marx's *The Communist Manifesto*, it is not difficult to anticipate the erosion of respect for both God's laws and the proper principles of law upon which this nation was founded.

When values, attitudes, and beliefs taught in our public schools are the godless philosophies dear to the hearts of the secular humanist, is it difficult to project the destruction of our Godly heritage and beliefs?

America, indeed, has a Godly heritage that is no longer being taught in our public schools, and the nation, sadly, is beginning to reap the whirlwind.

While the founders of the United States noted the importance of a character building, morals-based education in which American principles of liberty could flourish, others have noted the counterpoint by which the foundation of the nation could be undermined and destroyed. It is interesting how the enemies of freedom outlined and documented their plans to destroy everything that made America great.

OF EDUCATION AND FREEDOM

On Using Education to Destroy America

William Foster

William Foster was the head of the Communist Party USA. In his book *Toward Soviet America,* he wrote,

> The schools, colleges and universities will be coordinated and grouped under the National Department of Education and its state and local branches. The studies will be revolutionized, being cleansed of religious, patriotic and other features of the bourgeois ideology. The students will be taught on the basis of Marxian dialectical materialism, internationalism and the general ethics of the new Socialist society. Present obsolete methods of teaching will be superseded by a scientific pedagogy.

Conclusions

1. The national government has no constitutional role to play in the educational effort. Turning education over to a globally administered philosophy would be even more dangerous!
2. Education is essential to freedom (literacy, the ability to carry out independent rational thought, understanding of "Americanist" principles of individual God-given rights and liberty, etc.)

3. Among the proper principles the founders of the United States considered necessary to a complete education was an understanding of religion and morality.
4. Education that debauches religion, morality, and the baseline principles of liberty upon which the American experiment is based will result in the destruction of the nation.

In Summary

While education is essential to a free and prosperous nation, no element or role in that process is granted to the national government.[256] That role and responsibility rightly belongs to the individual, the family, and local associations created and controlled by the people.

Recommended for Additional Review

New England Primer (1690)
Catechism on the US Constitution, by Arthur J. Stansbury (1828)
History of the United States, by Noah Webster (1832)
 -Advice to the Young
 -Speller
McGuffy's Readers
 -Original
 -Christian
The Communist Manifesto
Humanist Manifestos I, II, III
Tornado in a Junk Yard, by James Perloff
 -*The Case Against Darwin,* by James Perloff
George Washington's Rules of Civility and Decent Behavior
The Bullet Proof George Washington
America's Godly Heritage, by David Barton
 -Video
 -Transcript
Education and the Founding Fathers, by David Barton
 -Video
Up From Slavery, by Booker T. Washington
The Mainspring of Human Progress, by Henry Grady Weaver
The Law, by Frederick Bastiat

[256.] See Amendment 10.

12.

Washington's Farewell Address

Recommended Resources for the Serious Student:

George Washington's Farewell Address (see appendix)

Quotes, Articles, and Original Sources

A normal detailed comprehensive review of the Farewell Address takes six hours of lecture, students are required to write six papers on subjects discussed within the Farewell Address, and students must review and understand approximately five hundred vocabulary words that are taken from the Farewell Address and that are defined using Noah Webster's *An American Dictionary of the English Language.*[257]

The Farewell Address captures so succinctly the founder's perspective on so many current issues pertaining to the preservation of American liberty that many liberty-loving Americans wish for politicians to include a review of it in their daily routine. If all who hold office would perform each of the following activities each morning before reporting to their office, the probability of the nation retaining its proper government would improve dramatically:

1. Kneel before God and offer daily prayers
2. Participate in some form of daily scripture study
3. Read the entire U.S. Constitution
4. Read Washington's Farewell Address

This lecture and review is a "connect the dots" experience. The counsel contained in the Farewell Address is timeless. It is therefore important to liken the Farewell Address to today's current events and identify how applying Washington's timeless advice would

---

[257]. See appendix for "George Washington's Farewell Address Vocabulary Words."

have kept this nation on a path of peace, prosperity, respect, happiness, and tranquility, thereby "connecting the dots" from Washington's timeless advice to the needs of the nation today.

This lecture/chapter is not intended to be a comprehensive review of the Farewell Address, but to introduce some of the timeless principles of sound government that George Washington emphasized in his address and set the student on a personal journey of discovery that will motivate a vigorous effort to restore the nation's foundation.

Washington considers a broad spectrum of topics within his Farewell Address!

He speaks of his love of this country.
He requests God's blessings upon this nation.
He pleads for the unity of the nation.
He advises the nation to avoid an overgrown military.
He offers warnings against designing men involved in combinations and associations.
He enjoins strict obedience to the Constitution, strongly instructing against tampering with the Constitution.
He warns of the dangers of political parties and party spirit.
He reiterates that under the Constitution, government powers are distributed and divided to avoid dangerous consolidation (there is to be no encroachment between government departments).
He speaks of preserving the republic.
He notes that making changes to the constitutional form of government may *only* be done by amendment.
There is to be *no* usurpation of power by government officials.
He reminds the nation of the necessity of religion and morality in order to be free.
He speaks of preserving property and justice in courts.
He admits the necessity of knowledge if a nation is to be free.
He counsels the nation to make careful, wise, and limited use of public debt and credit.
He speaks briefly of the necessity of taxes and revenue to perform assigned tasks.
He gives detailed advice regarding foreign policy.
He pleads with the nation to avoid entangling alliances with foreign powers.
He notes great truths regarding foreign trade.
He offers dire warnings to avoid foreign influence in our government.
He stresses the importance of national neutrality in the affairs of nations.
He speaks favorably about good laws and free government—the ever-favorite object of his heart.

Washington's Farewell Address was published in 1796 as Washington neared the end of his second presidential term. He had determined that he would not seek a third term. Of course, the Constitution at that time did not have any term limits on the president.

WASHINGTON'S FAREWELL ADDRESS

Washington could have sought a third term, and no one would have thought anything of it. In fact, many people would have been pleased for Washington to serve until the end of his life. But Washington was no power-monger, and he did not think it necessary or proper for a president to continue to serve for an unlimited length of time.

It is interesting to note that even during his first term of office, Washington had strongly considered not serving a second term. In fact, he had prepared a draft of a sort of farewell address to be delivered at the end of his first term. But many close advisors whom he regarded highly requested that he continue for the second term due to several circumstances of national concern that existed as he closed out his first term.

During his second term, President Washington was able to resolve the issues that had been of such great concern during his first term and felt that there were no outstanding issues that required him to stay in office any longer. He looked forward with great anticipation to his well-earned and (in his view) long-overdue retirement.

George Washington

During May of 1796, George Washington drafted the farewell address that he would deliver in the fall. He delivered this draft to others (primarily Alexander Hamilton) to be examined and receive input and suggestions. By mid-September 1796, the final draft was completed and he was ready to sign and deliver it to the nation.

While Washington never personally delivered this Farewell Address in a speech, the message was published to the nation and read before the House of Representatives.

For about 150 years after this address was delivered, American students carefully studied the address, and American government was greatly enhanced by the knowledge that people had of the principles that Washington promoted within the address. In recent decades, the Farewell Address has not received much attention from students or leaders, and the nation has strayed from the principles found therein at an increasingly accelerating rate. The nation now has seemed to forget the principles and has largely abandoned the principles that served the nation so wonderfully for so long. A timely return to Washington's advice would restore much of great value to America.

The following are excerpts from Washington's Farewell Address which are discussed in the lecture, with brief commentary:

Washington begins the Farewell Address by pointing out that a new election is quickly approaching and that he would not be participating as a candidate in the election. He very directly declines to be considered among the number from whom the choice is to be made for the new president. He notes his love of the country and indicates that his decision to not run again should not in any way be considered a diminishment of his love for the country, saying,

> I am influenced by no diminution of zeal for your future interest, no deficiency of grateful respect for your past kindness, but am supported by a full conviction that the step is compatible with both.

He speaks of the fact that he has been twice called to the office and it has been a sacrifice for him to serve in that office, but his service has been in deference to the wishes of the country. He had hoped to be able to step out of the office earlier, but because of the aforementioned challenges that faced the nation at the end of his first term, he chose to stay on for the good of the country.

He admits that his choice to leave office now comes at a time that is both good for him and for the nation. His love for the country does not preclude him from taking this step at this time.

> Choice and prudence invite me to quit the political scene, patriotism does not forbid it.

Washington mentions his perceived inadequacies that he felt were so apparent as he administered the office, always seeming to recognize his frailties and weaknesses. He speaks of his debt of gratitude for the blessings and honors that his country has bestowed upon him. He was honored to serve his country.

He touches briefly upon a spirit of criticism that had seemed to pervade much of the country during his second administration. He makes a point of thanking the nation for their continued support throughout his second administration, in spite of the criticisms that some had whispered. He then implores heaven for continued support, speaking of

> [his] unceasing vows that Heaven may continue to you the choicest tokens of its beneficence; that your union and brotherly affection may be perpetual; that the free Constitution which is the work of your hands may be sacredly maintained.

WASHINGTON'S FAREWELL ADDRESS

Always conscious of the hand of God that played such a role in the establishment and preservation of the United States, he pleads with God that His blessings will continue to be poured out upon the American nation and they will be sustained by His hand.

After making this point, he says, "Here, perhaps, I ought to stop." But then he thinks better of it and, fortunately for future generations of freedom-loving Americans, continues with some advice that is timeless for America, saying,

> But a solicitude for your welfare which can not end but with my life, and the apprehension of danger natural to that solicitude, urge me on an occasion like the present to offer to your solemn contemplation and to recommend to your frequent review some sentiments.

It is interesting to note that he recommends frequent review of his advice. The hope has already been mentioned that American leadership will again take his advice to heart!

He couches his advice in an interesting way. He notes that he has no ulterior motives. He will not be seeking future office or emolument. He has nothing to gain with this timely advice, offering his counsel as

> the disinterested warnings of a parting friend, who can possibly have no personal motive to bias his counsel.

He speaks of how deeply the feeling of liberty is bestowed upon Americans, saying,

> Interwoven as is the love of liberty with every ligament of your hearts.

Washington then spends quite an amount of time expressing his great desire that the nation be unified and become *one nation*. He speaks of the nation's unity being the main pillar of the real independence of the nation. He ties the nation's unity to tranquility at home and peace abroad and prosperity here at home. Unity is critically important to the nation and to its liberty. Today, the nation seems to be so foolishly dividing and subdividing its unity to the point that the nation is at great risk.

He warns the nation against those that will be covertly and insidiously attempting to undermine the nation's unity, saying,

> Indignantly frowning upon the first dawning of every attempt to alienate any portion of our country from the rest or to enfeeble the sacred ties which now link together the various parts.

He then speaks of the only name by which the people of this nation should be known: *American*!

> Citizens by birth or choice of a common country, that country has a right to concentrate your affections. The name of AMERICAN, which belongs to you in your national capacity, must always exalt the just pride of patriotism more than any appellation derived from local discriminations. With slight shades of difference, you have the same religion, manners, habits, and political principles. You have in a common cause fought and triumphed together. The independence and liberty you possess are the work of joint councils and joint efforts, of common dangers, sufferings, and successes.

In generations past, those that came to America came to become Americans in every way. They wanted to embrace this nation wholeheartedly! They wanted to embrace the principles the nation was founded upon. They wanted all of the opportunities that came with being in the land of the free and the home of the brave. Tragically, all too often today, there seems to be a growing effort to divide the nation and focus on those things that make us different.

In Washington's day, there were regional antipathies that were based upon geographic location. He pointed out the logical synergism between the different parts of the nation and how each part was benefited by the natural strength of the other parts. Together, they created a nation of great capability and complementary strength. Together they could easily resist the efforts of foreign powers to overcome the nation.

Washington then speaks at length in warning the nation against foreign alignments that would undermine the unity of the nation, saying that if the nation becomes strong and unified, it will not need foreign powers to be involved in anything American. The nation can stand on its own two feet, without any foreign influence.

He then warns against a military force that would grow too large for the good of the nation:

> Avoid the necessity of those overgrown military establishments which, under any form of government, are inauspicious to liberty, and which are to be regarded as particularly hostile to republican liberty.

As a patriot, he seeks the continued unity of the nation and admonishes the nation to "distrust the patriotism of those who in any quarter may endeavor to weaken its bands."

The unity of the nation is necessary to preserve the concepts put forth in the United States Constitution. Segments of the nation seeking special consideration at the expense of other segments tends to not only fragment the nation and breed distrust but also to create an environment that diverts the nation from the path of limited, proper government.

> A government for the whole is indispensable.

It seems from this that the nation should be warned against so-called "special interests." Special interest groups often seek some measure of largess (gifts or dispensations from the government) at the expense of others within the nation. They seek to pull the levers of the government on their behalf, and such action generally has some cost associated with it that must be borne by some other element of society. He warns the nation that these kinds of "alliances" ultimately work against the unity of the entire nation and, therefore, weaken the country:

> No alliances, however strict, between the parts can be an adequate substitute.

Unity of the whole nation is the desirable condition and alignments that pit the interests of one group against another are not a good substitute for the nation being united as one. Special interests are ultimately divisive for the nation and will pull the nation to a lower level of national achievement.

Washington then goes on to endorse the United States government as formed under the Constitution, praising the process by which it was brought about, noting how it is vastly superior to the old constitution, the Articles of Confederation, and noting the wisdom in having a legal method to modify it if necessary, but admonishing the nation to be obedient to the form of government created by the Constitution and advising that the document be held sacred, only changing it by the legal process, saying,

> This Government, the offspring of our own choice, uninfluenced and unawed, adopted upon full investigation and mature deliberation, completely free in its principles, in the distribution of its powers, uniting security with energy, and containing within itself a provision for its own amendment, has a just claim to your confidence and your support. Respect for its authority, compliance with its laws, acquiescence in its measures, are duties enjoined by the fundamental maxims of true liberty. The basis of our political systems is the right of the people to make and to alter their constitutions of government. But the constitution which at any time exists till changed by an explicit and authentic act of the whole people is sacredly obligatory upon all. The very idea of the power and the right of the people to establish government presupposes the duty of every individual to obey the established government.

The Declaration of Independence notes the right of the people to alter or abolish their governments, but Washington emphasizes that *all* are obligated to be bound to uphold the Constitution until the document is changed by an authentic act of the whole people. That process of change is defined within article 5 of the Constitution.

Washington goes on to warn against groups or individuals who may seek to fulfill their agenda by skirting around the constitutionally mandated safeguards, saying,

> All obstructions to the execution of the laws, all combinations and associations, under whatever plausible character, with the real design to direct, control, counteract, or awe the regular deliberation and action of the constituted authorities, are destructive of this fundamental principle and of fatal tendency.

He then introduces his concerns about factions that will rise up and influence the people of America to follow a path that will be destructive to the nation. Shortly, he will review his concerns about political parties, but at this point, he mentions other groups that will seek their own agendas at the expense of the nation. He speaks of how actions may appear popular, and even beneficial, but if they are beyond the established scope of proper government, evil men will ultimately use these unauthorized actions to destroy the good which now exists:

> However combinations or associations of the above description may now and then answer popular ends, they are likely in the course of time and things to become potent engines by which cunning, ambitious, and unprincipled men will be enabled to subvert the power of the people, and to usurp for themselves the reins of government, destroying afterwards the very engines which have lifted them to unjust dominion.

He goes on to warn in the strongest terms that the nation avoid innovative changes that may destroy the proper government the people then enjoyed.

> Toward the preservation of your Government and the permanency of your present happy state, it is requisite not only that you steadily discountenance irregular oppositions to its acknowledged authority, but also that you resist with care the spirit of innovation upon its principles, however specious the pretexts. One method of assault may be to effect in the forms of the Constitution alterations which will impair the energy of the system, and thus to undermine what can not be directly overthrown.

His advice is: do not innovate beyond the bounds established by the Constitution! Live within the bounds!

> Liberty itself will find in such a government, with powers properly distributed and adjusted, its surest guardian.

Do not concentrate power or tamper with the separation of powers. Do not innovate upon the separation of powers or checks and balances found within the Constitution. These limits were placed there to ensure the protection of liberty.

He then introduces his concerns about "the danger of parties in the State," meaning political parties. He is very concerned that parties will ultimately destroy the principles the nation was founded upon and overthrow the liberty of the people.

> I have already intimated to you the danger of parties in the State, with particular reference to the founding of them on geographical discriminations. Let me now take a more comprehensive view, and warn you in the most solemn manner against the baneful effects of the spirit of party generally.

Political parties were viewed by Washington and many of the other Founding Fathers with great concern. They felt that if political parties gained prominence within the nation, party spirit would begin to take precedence over the foundation principles of the nation, and the liberty of the people would be put at risk. Their view was that political parties would ultimately bring tyranny to the nation.

> The alternate domination of one faction over another, sharpened by the spirit of revenge natural to party dissension, which in different ages and countries has perpetrated the most horrid enormities, is itself a frightful despotism. But this leads at length to a more formal and permanent despotism. The disorders and miseries which result gradually incline the minds of men to seek security and repose in the absolute power of an individual, and sooner or later the chief of some prevailing faction, more able or more fortunate than his competitors, turns this disposition to the purposes of his own elevation on the ruins of public liberty . . . .

> . . . the common and continual mischiefs of the spirit of party are sufficient to make it the interest and duty of a wise people to discourage and restrain it.

> It serves always to distract the public councils and enfeeble the public administration. It agitates the community with ill-founded jealousies and false alarms; kindles the animosity of one part against another; foments occasionally riot and insurrection. It opens the door to foreign influence and corruption, which find a facilitated access to the government itself through the channels of party passion. Thus the policy and the will of one country are subjected to the policy and will of another.

Washington is careful to note that in the type of government that was created by the United States Constitution (where the elective process is used to choose representatives), political parties are particularly dangerous and should be avoided.

> In those of the popular character, in governments purely elective, it is a spirit not to be encouraged.

Under political parties, there is a constant tendency to agitate and inflame the passions of the populace.

> There being constant danger of excess, the effort ought to be by force of public opinion to mitigate and assuage it. A fire not to be quenched, it demands a uniform vigilance to prevent its bursting into a flame, lest, instead of warming, it should consume.

He then admonishes those who hold office to keep their actions within the spheres defined within the Constitution and avoid encroachment.

> It is important, likewise, that the habits of thinking in a free country should inspire caution in those intrusted with its administration to confine themselves within their respective constitutional spheres, avoiding in the exercise of the powers of one department to encroach upon another. The spirit of encroachment tends to consolidate the powers of all the departments in one, and thus to create, whatever the form of government, a real despotism.

He speaks of the love of power that afflicts so many mortals and the proneness of humans to seek, obtain, and then begin to abuse power. This tendency led the Founding Fathers of the nation to divide and subdivide power to ensure that it would not accrue and ultimately result in tyranny. Washington suggests that if the design within the Constitution proved inadequate, or needed modification, that the nation should change it by the defined amendment process and not allow the modification by any other means.

> If in the opinion of the people the distribution or modification of the constitutional powers be in any particular wrong, let it be corrected by an amendment in the way which the Constitution designates. But let there be no change by usurpation; for though this in one instance may be the instrument of good, it is the customary weapon by which free governments are destroyed.

At this point in his Farewell Address, Washington begins speaking of other principles that are necessary to the preservation of liberty and proper government. He notes that religion and morality are essential to maintain the freedom that has been bequeathed to the people of the nation.

> Of all the dispositions and habits which lead to political prosperity, religion and morality are indispensable supports.

Washington reminds the nation that in order for property, reputation, and life to be kept secure, religion is essential. He speaks of how the oaths that are taken in court, and the ability to trust those oaths, are tied to religious belief.

> Reason and experience both forbid us to expect that national morality can prevail in exclusion of religious principle.

> It is substantially true that virtue or morality is a necessary spring of popular government.

Religion and morality are necessary if the form of government established for the United States is to be preserved.

Washington then notes the great importance of knowledge and the necessity of an educated electorate that understands the Americanist principles of proper government if the nation is to be able to maintain its liberty.

> Promote, then, as an object of primary importance, institutions for the general diffusion of knowledge.

Washington then moves on to review public credit (debt). He advises using it sparingly. Cultivate peace because war brings debt. Protect the nation by keeping it strong enough to deter acts of aggression against America by other opportunistic nations so the United States will not be drawn into war because it is attacked. He admonishes the nation to not accumulate debt and hopes to avoid burdening posterity with national debts.

> As a very important source of strength and security, cherish public credit. One method of preserving it is to use it as sparingly as possible, avoiding occasions of expense by cultivating peace, but remembering also that timely disbursements to prepare for danger frequently prevent much greater disbursements to repel it; avoiding likewise the accumulation of debt, not only by shunning occasions of expense, but by vigorous exertions in time of peace to discharge the debts which unavoidable wars have occasioned, not ungenerously throwing upon posterity the burthen which we ourselves ought to bear. The execution of these maxims belongs to your representatives; but it is necessary that public opinion should cooperate.

At this point, Washington begins his review of foreign policy and entangling alliances with foreign powers. As with everything in the Farewell Address, modern American leadership needs to carefully review the sound, timeless advice Washington offers to America!

> Observe good faith and justice toward all nations. Cultivate peace and harmony with all. Religion and morality enjoin this conduct.

He infers that if the nation does this, God will allow the nation to enjoy peace and happiness:

> Can it be that Providence has not connected the permanent felicity of a nation with its virtue?

The nation is not to become a slave to its foreign alignments. It is to preserve its national independence and not align for or against other nations on a permanent basis.

TO PRESERVE THE NATION

> Nothing is more essential than that permanent, inveterate antipathies against particular nations and passionate attachments for others should be excluded . . .
>
> . . . just and amicable feelings toward all should be cultivated. The nation which indulges toward another an habitual hatred or an habitual fondness is in some degree a slave. It is a slave to its animosity or to its affection, either of which is sufficient to lead it astray from its duty and its interest . . . .
>
> Antipathy in one nation against another disposes each more readily to offer insult and injury, to lay hold of slight causes of umbrage, and to be haughty and intractable when accidental or trifling occasions of dispute occur.
>
> Hence frequent collisions, obstinate, envenomed, and bloody contests. The nation prompted by ill will and resentment sometimes impels to war the government . . .
>
> . . . likewise, a passionate attachment of one nation for another produces a variety of evils. Sympathy for the favorite nation, facilitating the illusion of an imaginary common interest in cases where no real common interest exists . . .

The reader is admonished to consider how this nation's current alignment with the United Nations or other United Nations-sanctioned organizations such as the North Atlantic Treaty Organization (NATO) or Southeast Asian Treaty Organization (SEATO) have drawn the United States into wars that were not, by any stretch of the imagination, American wars (of course, since World War II the wars the United States has entered into were not entered into by the constitutionally mandated method defined in the United States Constitution, article 1, section 8, clause 11).

> Infusing into one the enmities of the other, betrays the former into a participation in the quarrels and wars of the latter without adequate inducement or justification. It leads also to concessions to the favorite nation of privileges denied to others, which is apt doubly to injure the nation making the concessions by unnecessarily parting with what ought to have been retained, and by exciting jealousy, ill will, and a disposition to retaliate.

Washington observes that falsely based international alignments often result in U.S. citizens forgetting where their true loyalties should lie and leads them to betray the best interests of their nation and fellow citizens. This betrayal is often carried out in such a manner as to bring false criticism upon citizens who have a more appropriate view of foreign affairs—even causing true patriots to be heavily criticized and even persecuted by less enlightened individuals or organizations who have been duped into false sympathies and loyalties.

It gives to ambitious, corrupted, or deluded citizens (who devote themselves to the favorite nation) facility to betray or sacrifice the interests of their own country without odium, sometimes even with popularity, . . .

. . . such attachments are particularly alarming to the truly enlightened and independent patriot. How many opportunities do they afford to tamper with domestic factions, to practice the arts of seduction, to mislead public opinion, to influence or awe the public councils! Such an attachment of a small or weak toward a great and powerful nation dooms the former to be the satellite of the latter.

Against the insidious wiles of foreign influence (I conjure you to believe me, fellow-citizens) the jealousy of a free people ought to be constantly awake, since history and experience prove that foreign influence is one of the most baneful foes of republican government . . . Excessive partiality for one foreign nation and excessive dislike of another cause those whom they actuate to see danger only on one side, and serve to veil and even second the arts of influence on the other.

Real patriots who may resist the intrigues of the favorite are liable to become suspected and odious, while its tools and dupes usurp the applause and confidence of the people to surrender their interests.

The great rule of conduct for us in regard to foreign nations is, in extending our commercial relations to have with them as little political connection as possible.

Europe has a set of primary interests which to us have none or a very remote relation. Hence she must be engaged in frequent controversies, the causes of which are essentially foreign to our concerns. Hence, therefore, it must be unwise in us to implicate ourselves by artificial ties in the ordinary vicissitudes of her politics or the ordinary combinations and collisions of her friendships or enmities.

Why forego the advantages of so peculiar a situation? Why quit our own to stand upon foreign ground? Why, by interweaving our destiny with that of any part of Europe, entangle our peace and prosperity in the toils of European ambition, rivalship, interest, humor, or caprice?

It is our true policy to steer clear of permanent alliances with any portion of the foreign world . . .

TO PRESERVE THE NATION

> 'Tis folly in one nation to look for disinterested favors from another; that it must pay with a portion of its independence for whatever it may accept under that character . . .

At this point in the Farewell Address, George Washington begins to recap some of the advice he so lovingly offered to the nation he literally gave his life for—forty-five years of selfless service! He says he offers his counsel as "an old and affectionate friend." But he was far more than that! He was truly the indispensable man! He was the man the nation leaned upon so heavily! Certainly, there were times when some in the nation found fault with him, but by and large, the nation held him in the highest regard. They knew he could be trusted implicitly with power. He would be no tyrant—ever! They knew he would make whatever sacrifice was necessary to bring liberty to the nation. Modern "revisionist" historians have tried to denigrate his name and his character, but those who truly come to know this man, George Washington, will discover that he was one of the noblest men who has walked this earth.

As he brings this marvelous message to a close, he asks the nation to be wise and vigilant in order to "prevent our nation from running the course which has hitherto marked the destiny of nations."

In George Washington's view, America was destined to be different from other run-of-the-mill nations. America has things no other nations have been blessed with. Not only does the nation have liberty, recognizing liberty and rights as a gift from God, but the nation also has a government that was not only designed to recognize those God-given rights and liberties but also to protect them! Washington felt that the people of this nation would become the freest people on the earth, and therefore, we were to act in such a manner as to prevent the nation from being relegated into the dustbin as other nations have allowed to happen to themselves.

He again reiterates his advice against political parties, not allowing political parties to derail the great principles upon which this nation was founded, saying, "moderate the fury of party spirit."

He pleads with the people of the nation to not let foreign powers influence the character and direction of our government.

> [He] warn[s] against the mischiefs of foreign intrigue.

Washington foresees the time in which the leaders of the land will feign to be true patriots but will truly be wolves in sheep's clothing, deceiving the people of the nation as they undermine the foundation of the nation.

> [He admonishes us to] guard against the impostures of pretended patriotism.

He again reiterates the imperative necessity that the United States preserve its independent sovereignty in the affairs of nations and maintains scrupulous neutrality so we will not be drawn into the unremitting conflicts that plague the nations of the world.

WASHINGTON'S FAREWELL ADDRESS

> The duty of holding a neutral conduct may be inferred, without anything more, from the obligation which justice and humanity impose on every nation, in cases in which it is free to act, to maintain inviolate the relations of peace and amity toward other nations.

We will have peace and friendship with other nations if America follows this course. And it will allow America to progress in its own right, following the course it chooses to follow.

> [He advises to] gain time to our country to settle and mature its yet recent institutions, and to progress without interruption to that degree of strength and consistency which is necessary to give it, humanly speaking, the command of its own fortunes.

In the last couple of paragraphs, he asks God to correct any errors he may have committed while he led the country. While he did not intentionally do wrong, he admits that errors are likely and hopes God will deflect any problems that may result.

> Though in reviewing the incidents of my Administration I am unconscious of intentional error, I am nevertheless too sensible of my defects not to think it probable that I may have committed many errors. Whatever they may be, I fervently beseech the Almighty to avert or mitigate the evils to which they may tend....

> I shall also carry with me the hope that my country will never cease to view them with indulgence, and that, after forty-five years of my life dedicated to its service with an upright zeal, the faults of incompetent abilities will be consigned to oblivion, as myself must soon be to the mansions of rest....

> Relying on its kindness in this as in other things, and actuated by that fervent love toward it which is so natural to a man who views in it the native soil of himself and his progenitors for several generations, I anticipate with pleasing expectation that retreat in which I promise myself to realize without alloy the sweet enjoyment of partaking in the midst of my fellow-citizens the benign influence of good laws under a free government—the ever-favorite object of my heart, and the happy reward, as I trust, of our mutual cares, labors, and dangers.

With that, George Washington bids farewell to the nation he served so faithfully for forty-five years. He stood with the nation as it went through all of the trials and vicissitudes it faced as it stepped forward and became a free and independent nation among nations. Washington had power thrust upon him continually during that period, but he constantly deflected power away from himself, only exercising it in a manner that allowed liberty to take root in this land.

TO PRESERVE THE NATION

He set a standard for the presidency. There were no presidents prior to him, so there were no precedents to bind his actions. As president, he probably could have done anything he chose to do because the people trusted him so implicitly that they would not have questioned his actions, but he restrained himself within the bounds of the Constitution he helped create—binding himself down with the chains of the Constitution, as Jefferson phrased it.

There was a quiet dignity about George Washington that gave assurance to all that the nation was in good hands—especially since he loved the country as deeply as he did.

(Review Washington's Farewell Address, consider the above-noted topics, and apply the advice given in the Farewell Address to modern circumstances—see appendix for complete text of Washington's Farewell Address and George Washington's Farewell Address vocabulary words.)

13.

THE COMMUNIST MANIFESTO

RECOMMENDED RESOURCES FOR THE SERIOUS STUDENT:

The Communist Manifesto (see appendix)

QUOTES, ARTICLES, AND ORIGINAL SOURCES

Many today suggest that "communism is dead." Those who believe that statement are either delusional, ill-informed, deceived or they are deceivers. While more than a billion human beings throughout the world still suffer under the tyranny that is openly touted as "communism," hundreds of millions of other humans still chafe under regimes that may call themselves by some other name, but in reality, they are simply communism masquerading as something else. It is said that a rose by any other name is still a rose, and it may likewise be said that communism by any other name is still communism. Regardless of the appellation, if the principles are communist principles, communism is alive and continues as a threat to humanity.

Many so-called "former" communists in the Eastern Bloc countries, such as the former Soviet Union, continue to suspiciously act like communists (in spite of their protestations to the contrary). Because this "scarlet beast" is not dead and continues to threaten all of humanity, it is important to understand the philosophies and purposes of this movement. The communist philosophy is diametrically opposed to the philosophies upon which the United States of America was originally founded and is opposed to the liberties, proper government, and God-given unalienable rights protected under the United States Constitution!

If Americans truly come to understand the tenets of communism and become awakened to the threats these tenets pose to all they cherish, they will become alert and actively engaged to make certain that these tenets that have crept into the American form of government are expunged from the practices of the nation. And they will do all in their power to make certain that they do not gain further inroads into the nation. Unfortunately, ignorance, apathy, and other motivations have led many modern Americans to accept a great number of the philosophies promoted by Marx. Most Americans would be appalled and offended if confronted with the evidence that some of their pet programs are Marxist in their origins, but tragically, in many instances, they would still support their implementation.

This lecture is offered to help expose the unvarnished threats of Marxism and assist Americans in their ability to recognize communism and effectively defeat the efforts of its adherents to promote it within the United States. By studying their strategies and tactics, effective plans may be fostered to defeat this pernicious doctrine.

We begin our review of this topic with a brief overview of the man most closely associated with this doctrine of communism—Karl Marx.

Karl Marx and the Manifesto

Karl Marx

Karl Heinrich Marx was born in a Prussian town that is now in the Rhineland of Germany on May 5, 1818. He was of Jewish ancestry, but his father had left the faith and no longer practiced it.

He was not born into poverty as many would have us believe, but into a solidly middle-class family. He lived a very comfortable life while in his father's home. In his youth, he never was even superficially exposed to the deep poverty and hardship or squalid working conditions of the working class that he played upon as he later brought forth his diabolical political philosophies.

In his later life, his pretended empathy for the working man was all a pretense to promote the philosophy he fostered. Even in his youth, his father held some concern for the cold and uncaring attitude he exhibited. He often seemed detached from the needs of humanity.

His father was a lawyer who sent him to the finest schools, considering him to possess a "gifted" mind.

Karl Marx's father would be considered an "indulgent" father, supplying Marx with a generous allowance through school, and even when Marx was married and had children.

When Marx was a young student, he was a top student and avid reader. Because of this ability, his grades, and his interest in higher education, he was accepted into university studies.

He initially attended the University of Bonn, but quickly became a lazy student, spending far more time in taverns drinking with his friends than studying.

He continually demanded money from his father, lying to him about his diligent studies and scholastic achievements, but rarely attended class, and he used the money his father sent to him to buy alcohol for himself and his newfound drinking friends.

His attendance and activities prompted the school authorities to begin the process to expel him for what was termed "nocturnal drunkenness and riot."

In light of the pending expulsion, he left the University of Bonn and enrolled in the University of Berlin.

The migration to a new university did not change his habits. He continued to spend most of his time drinking in local taverns with his so-called "intellectual" friends.

They intellectualized and debated about many different ideas and philosophies, sharing radical ideas about abolishing Christianity and marriage, how despicable the profit motive was in business, abolishing private property, etc.

During this time, Marx was noticed by some revolutionaries at the university, and they took an interest in him, seeing in him someone who could be valuable to their cause.

They convinced him that he needed a diploma to give him credibility, so they convinced him to send a "doctoral thesis" to the University of Jena and ask for a degree.

Today the University of Jena could be likened to a "diploma mill," an institution willing to award diplomas basically for the asking. Thus, Karl Marx became "Dr. Marx," which, in that era, meant that he had completed basic university studies.

With his newfound credibility and diploma, Marx was ready to move in new circles of influential revolutionary socialists. It should be pointed out that communism is socialism. Both names simply identify different shades, degrees, and flavors of the same poison. Communism is simply a violent, revolutionary form of socialism.

He obtained what turned out to be the only "real" job he ever held as an adult when he landed a job with a radical leftist newspaper in Cologne, Germany. The newspaper was closed by the government within only a few months because it advocated subversive and incendiary activities against the established government.

Frederick Engels

Around this time, Marx met Friedrich Engels, a socialist with money who would financially support him for the rest of his life as he promoted violent revolutionary socialism.

Within a few more months, Marx's advocacy of violent revolution resulted in his expulsion from Germany and France.

For a time, he and his wife lived in Brussels, Belgium, which was at the time a sort of center where socialists and communists from all over Europe gathered.

During this time, an effort was underway to unite all the different factions of this socialistic doctrine under one movement.

Deceptively noble sounding names were adopted during this unifying effort, including the title Federation of the Just and the League of Just Men.

In 1847, the name was changed to the Communist League, and it was determined that the movement needed a manifesto to further its purposes.

After some intrigue within the movement (a prominent socialist named Moses Hess had been previously selected to write the manifesto, but he was undermined by Engels and Marx, so the assignment was withdrawn from Hess); Marx and Engels were selected to write the manifesto.

They were instructed to have the manifesto ready by January 1848 because the communists had planned numerous uprisings, revolutions, and insurrections throughout Europe that spring and summer, and they needed some unifying document to bring all these activities together. These uprisings were in reality coordinated attacks on society that had been prepared for many months. They were not spontaneous responses to the concepts promoted within *The Communist Manifesto,* but the plan was to make it appear that the manifesto was the catalyst that "awakened" within the hearts of the Europeans a movement that spawned the efforts to overthrow their "oppressors." In reality, the violence was fomented by dedicated revolutionaries who organized and manipulated the destructive acts.

THE COMMUNIST MANIFESTO

The manifesto was completed and went to print in February 1848—just in time for the "spontaneous" uprisings.

The revolutions of the spring and summer of 1848 throughout Europe all came to nothing and quickly evaporated into thin air.

Not coincidentally, the so-called "new" movement was simply a rehash of the doctrines put forth by Adam Weishaupt and his "Order of the Illuminati," which he had formally organized on May 1, 1776. Communism is simply a continuation of the false philosophies of the Illuminati. Their doctrines are inextricably interwoven, as we shall see.

The doctrine of Weishaupt's Illuminati abhorred Christianity, sought the overthrow of the then-existing governments, sought to abolish laws protecting private property and inheritance, sought to destroy marriage and morality, and sought to remove the education of children from their parents.

In 1789, a few years after its inception, Weishaupt's Illuminati doctrine led to the bloodbath we call the French Revolution (which we shall review in lecture 14).

Since the "new" communist movement was simply a continuation and rewording of the philosophies of the Illuminati, we should not be surprised that the basic doctrine this new communist manifesto was to foster included a restatement of Illuminati philosophy:

1. Seeking the destruction of Christianity
2. Abolishing private property
3. Eliminating the family as a social unit
4. Abolishing all existing governments (the Illuminati had opposed the monarchies of Europe, but communism had retooled their focus to overthrow the growing middle class and business owners—a more ubiquitous and universal target to hate because by the time of *The Communist Manifesto*, monarchies were on the wane in Europe)
5. Establishing a new dictatorship of the proletariat (the working class)

These are but some among other similar doctrines that we shall point out as we open the manifesto and review it.

The outcome of Marx's writing assignment was called *The Communist Manifesto*. In many ways, it was really like a modern-day party "platform." Marx was paid to write it, but his name was not on the document until a couple of dozen years later.

Marx wrote other works, including *Das Kapital*, a large and obtuse book that was intended to justify violent revolution and to support the concept of a socialist economy. Like *The Communist Manifesto*, it is written in a stultified and clumsy style so typical of Marx's absurd written meanderings. Today, it is generally read only by the most devout of Marx's adherents who seem ready to cling to even his most muddled precepts.

A simple definition of socialism is "government ownership and/or control of the means of production and distribution." Thus, anything involved in production or distribution becomes a government target. And government does not necessarily need to "own" these means. Often, it is sufficient to control these means by regulation or directive. This means the control of wealth and the creation of prosperity. Land is probably the ultimate source of production, so it becomes a primary target of those who seek the economic control involved in a socialistic society.

A modern Webster dictionary defines socialism as

> A political and economic theory of social organization based on collective or governmental ownership and democratic management of the essential means for the production and distribution of goods; also, a policy or practice based on this theory.[258]

George Bernard Shaw

George Bernard Shaw, the noted English Fabian socialist, said,

> Socialism, reduced to its simplest legal and practical expression, means the complete discarding of the institution of private property by transforming it into public property and the division of the resultant income equally and indiscriminately among the entire population.[259]

[258.] *Webster's New International Dictionary*, 2nd ed., unabridged, 1951.
[259.] *Encyclopedia Britannica*, 1946 ed., 20:895.

For all the distinctions that different modern-day philosophers try to draw today between the different flavors of socialism, *The Communist Manifesto* drafted by Karl Marx and Friedrich Engels for the Communist League in 1848 is generally regarded as the starting point of modern socialism.[260]

The personal life of Marx was as undesirable as are his philosophies.

While he was not born in poverty, his wife and children lived an impoverished life in spite of some substantial inheritances and the ongoing lifelong financial support of Friedrich Engels.

Marx squandered his money, and often his family suffered terribly for it.

Karl and Jenny Marx had six children, and the family had a miserable life. One child died at birth. A daughter and son starved to death. Two daughters committed suicide.

Marx died alone and unmourned in March of 1883, at the age of sixty-five, a wretched man, associated with a wretched doctrine.

The modern followers of the doctrines he put forth almost seem to worship him, but his life truly was a manifestation of the dregs of false philosophies.

As we review *The Communist Manifesto,* remember that it is driven by a doctrine of class conflict. You will hear and read terms like "bourgeoisie" and "proletariat."

The bourgeoisie is supposedly the oppressors, made up of middle-class property owners. Historically, the bourgeoisie are the doctors and lawyers and the owners of businesses.

The proletariat is supposedly the oppressed wage-labor working class.

The following are excerpts from *The Communist Manifesto* that are noted in the lecture, with brief commentary between Marx's statements.

Preface by Friedrich Engels

> "The 'Manifesto' was published in the platform of the Communist League, a working men's association, first exclusively German, later on international, and, under the political conditions of the Continent before 1848, unavoidably a secret society."

Communism, like the Illuminati from which it sprang, is admitted by Engels to be a "secret society" by nature.

> "[The Communist Manifesto] is destined to do for history what Darwin's theory has done for biology."

Just as Darwin's theories seek to eliminate the recognition of the hand of God from the creation process of life, so communism seeks to cast God from society.

[260.] *Encyclopedia Britannica,* 1946 ed., 20:890.

TO PRESERVE THE NATION

THE COMMUNIST MANIFESTO

> "A spectre is haunting Europe—the spectre of communism."

A spectre is a ghastly, haunting apparition that menaces; it is of a fearful or horrible nature—perhaps this is the truest statement in Marx's writings.

> "The bourgeoisie has torn away from the family its sentimental veil, and has reduced the family relation into a mere money relation."

Marx seemed to lack the natural affection of family association, and consequently, this assumption of reducing the family to an economic definition would seem typical of Marx's aberrations.

> "The bourgeoisie forged the weapons that bring death to itself; it has also called into existence the men who are to wield those weapons—the modern working class—the proletarians."

All of Marx's efforts seem to breed conflict and violence. His imagery is one of hate and destruction.

> "Of all the classes that stand face to face with the bourgeoisie today, the proletariat alone is a genuinely revolutionary class. The other classes decay and finally disappear in the face of Modern Industry; the proletariat is its special and essential product."

Marx sought to unite workers into a violent revolutionary force that would destroy civilization and all it entails—family, religion, peace, property, freedom, etc.

> "Law, morality, religion, are to him so many bourgeois prejudices, behind which lurk in ambush just as many bourgeois interests."

Nothing he presents validates this position—it is simply based upon his perverse philosophies. This philosophy is intended to bring about the complete destruction of all that has bound society together, and a rejection of all that society has held sacred.

> "Their mission is to destroy all previous securities for, and insurances of, individual property."

Marx makes repeated references to the movement's desire to destroy anything held by individuals—property, rights, family relations, etc. Under communism, all is to be held by the "collective."

> "Society can no longer live under this bourgeoisie, in other words, its existence is no longer compatible with society."

Through his fomented class conflict, Marx sought to destroy the property holders, the middle class.

> "What the bourgeoisie therefore produces, above all, are its own grave-diggers. Its fall and the victory of the proletariat are equally inevitable."

Again, the imagery of death and destruction, which permeates the writings of Marx.

> "The immediate aim of the Communists is the same as that of all other proletarian parties: Formation of the proletariat into a class, overthrow of the bourgeois supremacy, conquest of political power by the proletariat."

Violence is the center-piece of his quest of conquest and the overthrow of society.

> "In this sense, the theory of the Communists may be summed up in the single sentence: Abolition of private property."

So communists seek the abolition of private property. In contrast, the Founding Fathers of America's liberty considered private property essential to the preservation of freedom:

ALEXANDER HAMILTON ON PROPERTY

> "In the general course of human nature a power over a man's subsistence amounts to a power over his will."[261]

JOHN ADAMS ON PROPERTY

> "Property is surely a right of mankind as real as liberty . . . . The moment the idea is admitted into society that property is not as sacred as the laws of God, and that there is not a force of law and public justice to protect it, anarchy and tyranny commence."[262]

JOHN LOCKE ON PROPERTY

> "Nobody can transfer to another more power than he has in himself, and nobody has an absolute arbitrary power over himself, or over another, to destroy his own life, or take away the life or property of another."[263]

---

[261]. Federalist no. 79
[262]. C. F. Adams, *John Adams*, 6:9, 280.
[263]. Locke, *Two Treatises of Civil Government*

FREDERIC BASTIAT ON PROPERTY CONFISCATION BY LAW

Frederic Bastiat

"When a portion of wealth is transferred from the person who owns it—without his consent and without compensation, and whether by force or fraud—to anyone who does not own it, then I say that property is violated; that an act of plunder is committed . . . When the law itself commits this act that it is supposed to suppress, I say that plunder is still committed, and I add that from the point of view of society and welfare, this aggression against rights is even worse."[264]

FREDERIC BASTIAT ON SOCIALISM

"Socialists look upon people as raw material to be formed into social combinations. But it is upon the law that socialism itself relies. Socialists desire to practice legal plunder, not illegal plunder. Socialists, like all other monopolists, desire to make the law their own weapon. And when once the law is on the side of socialism, how can it be used against socialism? For when plunder is abetted by the law, it does not fear your courts, your gendarmes, and your prisons. Rather, it may call upon them for help.

But how is this legal plunder to be identified? Quite simply. SEE IF THE LAW TAKES FROM SOME PERSONS WHAT BELONGS TO THEM, AND GIVES IT TO OTHER PERSONS TO WHOM IT DOES NOT BELONG. SEE IF THE LAW BENEFITS ONE CITIZEN AT THE EXPENSE OF ANOTHER BY DOING WHAT THE CITIZEN HIMSELF CANNOT DO WITHOUT COMMITTING A CRIME."[265]

---

[264]. Bastiat, *Law*, 1850.
[265]. Bastiat, *Law*, 1850.

The Communist Manifesto (Continued)

> "You are horrified at our intending to do away with private property... You reproach us, therefore, with intending to do away with a form of property, the necessary condition for whose existence is the non-existence of any property for the immense majority of society."

Again, the commitment of communists is to overthrow private property.

> "In one word, you reproach us with intending to do away with your property. Precisely so; that is just what we intend."

Seeking the destruction of the right to hold property, again repeated!

> "It has been objected that upon the abolition of private property, all work will cease, and universal laziness will overtake us."

It is interesting that as the Pilgrims established their colony in America in 1620, their economic system was based upon a socialistic philosophy of communal property. It was a form of nonviolent communism. What they found was that they would starve to death under the concept, proving by their experience that work ceased and laziness ensued. Only when they set up private ownership were the Pilgrims able to begin to prosper. It was essential to their very survival. And of course, the repeated failure of successive communist "five-year economic plans" in the former Soviet Union and the near-starvation conditions that continually exist under communism are testimony of the *fact* that communism does not result in effective, productive efforts by those who suffer under its yoke.

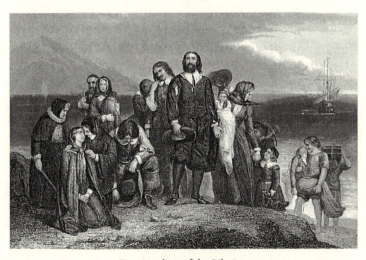

First Landing of the Pilgrims

"Abolition of the family! . . . this infamous proposal of the Communists."

Here Marx admits that the family unit is to be abolished.

"We destroy the most hallowed of relations, when we replace home education by social."

A new educational process would be established by which the children would be indoctrinated in the new revolutionary philosophies.

"But you Communists would introduce community of women, screams the bourgeoisie."

Marriage would be outlawed, and communal living would debase women, destroying the sacred relationship of husband, wife, and children.

As an example of how literally the adherents of Marx's philosophy would carry this out, the following report is noted:

1919 SOVIET OF SARALOF DECREE

"Beginning with March 1, 1919, the right to possess women between the ages of 17 and 32 is abolished . . . this decree, however, not being applicable to women who have five children . . . By virtue of the present decree no woman can any longer be considered as private property and all women become the property of the nation . . . The distribution and maintenance of nationalized women, in conformity with the decision of responsible organizations, are the prerogative of the group of Saralof anarchists . . . All women thus put at the disposition of the nation must, within three days after the publication of the present decree, present themselves in person at the address indicated and provide all necessary information . . . *Any man who wishes to make use of a nationalized woman must hold a certificate* issued by the administrative Council or a professional union, or by the Soviet of workers, soldiers or peasants, attesting that he belongs to the working class . . . Every worker is required to turn in 2% of his salary to the fund . . . Male citizens not belonging to the working class may enjoy the same rights provided they pay a sum equivalent to 250 French francs, which will be turned over to the public fund . . . Any women who by virtue of the present decree will be declared national property will receive from the public fund a salary equivalent to 575 French francs a month . . . . Any pregnant woman will be dispensed of her duties for four month before and three months after the birth of the child . . . One month after birth, children will be placed in an institution entrusted with their care and education. They will remain there to complete their instruction and education at the expense of the national fund until they reach the age of seventeen . . . All those who refuse to recognize the present decree and to cooperate with the authorities shall be declared enemies of the people, anti-anarchists, and shall suffer the consequences."[266]

THE COMMUNIST MANIFESTO (CONTINUED)

> "Communism abolishes eternal truths, it abolishes all religion, and all morality, instead of constituting them on a new basis; it therefore acts in contradiction to all past historical experience."

The communists seek to abolish and destroy all religion, morality, and belief in God.

> "The communist revolution is the most radical rupture with traditional property relations."

Again, property rights are to be destroyed.

> "We have seen above that the first step in the revolution by the working class is to raise the proletariat to the position of ruling class to win the battle of democracy."

As previously noted in lecture 2, in exact opposition to America's founders, Marx and his inheritors seek first to implement democracy, then to take the subsequent steps of full-blown communism.

> "[Communism, implemented, will] centralize all instruments of production in the hands of the state."

By definition, socialism controls the means of production or distribution, seizing them from the individual, and gathering them to be controlled by the state.

> "This cannot be effected except by means of despotic inroads on the rights of property."

How many times does he have to remind us that the right to private property will be destroyed?

The Communist Manifesto outlines a ten-point process by which this despotism will be imposed upon the nations of the world. Americans would be wise to carefully

---

[266.] Quoted by Gabriel M. Roschini in his article, "CONTRADICTIONS CONCERNING THE STATUS OF WOMEN IN SOVIET RUSSIA," which appears in "THE PHILOSOPHY OF COMMUNISM," by Giorgio La Pira and others, Fordham University Press, New York, 1952, pp. 97-98.

examine these points and honestly evaluate the degree to which they are being adopted in this nation.

Ten Points of The Communist Manifesto

1. Abolition of property in land and application of all rents of land to public purposes.
2. A heavy progressive or graduated income tax.
3. Abolition of all rights of inheritance.
4. Confiscation of the property of all emigrants and rebels.
5. Centralization of credit in the hands of the state, by means of a national bank with state capital and an exclusive monopoly.
6. Centralization of the means of communication and transport in the hands of the state.
7. Extension of factories and instruments of production owned by the state, the bringing into cultivation of wastelands, and the improvement of the soil generally in accordance with a common plan.
8. Equal liability of all to work. Establishment of industrial armies, especially for agriculture.
9. Combination of agriculture with manufacturing industries, gradual abolition of all the distinction between town and country by a more equable distribution of the populace over the country.
10. Free education for all children in public schools. Abolition of children's factory labor in its present form. Combination of education with industrial production.

Closing Words of The Communist Manifesto

"The Communists disdain to conceal their views and aims. They openly declare that their ends can be attained only by the forcible overthrow of all existing social conditions. Let the ruling classes tremble at a Communist revolution. The proletarians have nothing to lose but their chains. They have a world to win.

"Working men of all countries, unite!"

The Communist Manifesto is a dreary formula by which all that is cherished by mankind is to be overthrown and destroyed. It is based upon compulsion and fear and seeks the violent destruction of liberty.

(Review The Communist Manifesto—*see appendix for complete text of* The Communist Manifesto*)*

14.

ALL REVOLUTIONS ARE NOT CREATED EQUAL (THE AMERICAN REVOLUTION VS. SUBSEQUENT REVOLUTIONS)

RECOMMENDED RESOURCES FOR THE SERIOUS STUDENT:

* *Further Reflections on the Revolution in France*, Edmund Burke
* *The French Revolution*, Nesta Webster
* *Proofs of a Conspiracy* (1798), John Robinson
* *Memoirs Illustrating the History of Jacobinism* (1798), A. Barruel
* *Philip Dru: Administrator* (1912), Edward Mandell House

QUOTES, ARTICLES, AND ORIGINAL SOURCES

Initially, this lecture was planned to present only material that compared and contrasted the American Revolution and the French Revolution, which occurred only a few short years apart. Further consideration led to the thought that virtually all revolutions (at least since the American Revolution) shared more in common with the French Revolution than with the American Revolution; therefore, it is fitting to compare and contrast those revolutions with each other and the American Revolution.

Enough time and space has been spent in this lecture series extolling the virtues of the Americanist principles that came forth in the founding era of this nation to ensure that it is not necessary to review in depth the fundamental principles that motivated the American Revolution and the Constitution, which was framed within a few short years, as well as the magnificent Bill of Rights.

A cursory review will perhaps be tolerated, but nothing too strenuous. One need only consider and remember previous lectures, including the following:

> The purposes for which the new settlers came to America

TO PRESERVE THE NATION

The spiritual foundation and tone of the nation's "enabling documents," its original education system, and the recognition of God's hand by those who were present during the great events of the founding

One need only quickly review the monumental words of the Declaration of Independence to know of the fundamental belief in God as our creator, the fact that our rights are gifts from God, and that the role of proper government is to preserve those God-given rights.

One need only consider the writings of the Founding Fathers as they expressed their observation of the hand of God in the preservation of their efforts to gain their liberty and in the actual success they enjoyed in the creation of the new United States Constitution.

In short, we have a record of what those who founded the United States said *and* did by which we may judge their motivation and actions.

Men like George Washington, Benjamin Franklin, Thomas Jefferson, John Adams, John Hancock, Samuel Adams, James Madison, and others are rightly considered to be heroes in the great cause of liberty.

In spite of strained efforts by modern historical "revisionists" to draw parallels and similarities between the modern "revolutionaries" and the men of the American founding era, we will discover that the American founders have virtually nothing in common with the revolutionaries we will consider in this lecture as we compare and contrast the various revolutions.

In his Farewell Address, which we have reviewed, George Washington spoke of Americans: "With slight shades of difference, you have the same religion, manners, habits, and political principles."

So it was at the beginning of the revolution against England. The people of the American continent shared with their counterparts in the British Isles "with slight shades of difference, the same religion, manners, habits, and political principles."

In general, the Americans and peoples of the British Isles were people who embraced honesty, integrity, justice, fairness, indeed, all of the honorable traits we admire.

They shared a common heritage of a love of liberty.

They largely emulated each other in attempts to culture and refinement.

They loved education and largely studied the same sources of learning.

Certainly there were differences that had developed as a result of their settings and circumstances, but they considered themselves brothers in every way.

The move to independence by the Americans was not motivated by a rejection of that which was good among the "Mother Country," it was not motivated by hatred of all things British, but was a move motivated by a rejection of oppressive government.

ALL REVOLUTIONS ARE NOT CREATED EQUAL
(THE AMERICAN REVOLUTION VS. SUBSEQUENT REVOLUTIONS)

The idea that a king could arbitrarily and unilaterally overrule and destroy the God-given rights of the people was what the fledgling American nation rebelled against.

The causes of the rebellion were clearly defined and spelled out for the entire world to understand as the American people set forth their Declaration of Independence.

Those we call the founders were honest, forthright, and upright in the declaration of their intentions, and they demonstrated by their action thereafter their integrity.

And while there were substantial numbers of people within the United States, called Tories, who did not support independence from Great Britain and even many who went so far as to fight on the side of the British during the Revolutionary War, there were not official acts of revenge carried out against these people by the U.S. government after the Revolutionary War ended.

Although there were instances of individuals acting vengefully, and some of the Tories had their land and property lost or damaged during war, there were no laws passed after the war that would confiscate the property of Tories, nor were there firing squads or hangings carried out by the government.

Quite to the contrary, after the war with England ended, many honorable Americans continued to repay personal debts owed to the British.

Indeed, this desire to be honorable in their dealings with their fellow man ran so deep in the American mind that the authors of the United States Constitution wrote into article 6 of the Constitution that "All Debts contracted and Engagements entered into, before the Adoption of this Constitution, shall be as valid against the United States under this Constitution, as under the Confederation" (speaking of the former constitution, the Articles of Confederation).

These people were God-fearing and honorable to the core!

Of course, we have reviewed at length the efforts to which the founders went to create a government that had limited, specific, enumerated powers and that were held in check by checks and balances so that the government did not hold the power to abuse the God-given rights of the people.

Then they went even further to put forth a bill of rights to further constrain the national government and prevent abuses.

They also demonstrated their desire for liberty by peacefully passing power from one administration to the next through the constitutionally defined processes.

This phenomenon shall be examined further in the next lecture as we discuss how George Washington constantly deflected power when it was thrust upon him.

Thus, in brief, is a synopsis of the motives of the American Revolution and the subsequent establishment of their national government.

Now let us lay the foundation of the motivations of the revolutions that have followed the American Revolution and in which so many strain to find parallels and similarities to the American Revolution.

To do so, one must recall the Order of the Illuminati, which was officially established in Europe by Adam Weishaupt on May 1, 1776, just as the American Revolution was getting underway. The Illuminati was a secret society, just as communism was as it began to fester in Europe in the mid-1800s.

As previous reviewed, the following are some of the principles of the Illuminati.

The doctrine of Weishaupt's Illuminati

—abhorred Christianity,
—sought the overthrow of the then-existing governments,
—sought to abolish laws protecting private property and inheritance,
—sought to destroy marriage and morality, and
—sought to remove the education of children from their parents.

During the era of the Illuminati, the then-existing governments of Europe were mostly monarchies, so the Illuminati focused its revolutionary efforts against the monarchies of the day.

The philosophies and doctrines of the Illuminati ultimately led, in 1789, to the bloodbath we call the French Revolution.

Subsequent convulsions and rebellions have been simply recurrences of warmed-over servings of Illuminati drivel.

In fact, France has been internally convulsed three times by this doctrine: (1) in 1789 in the French Revolution, (2) in 1848 as a result of the concerted efforts of the secret society Karl Marx collaborated with in the bringing forth of *The Communist Manifesto* (which, you will recall from lecture 13 was simply a rehash of Weishaupt's new order), and (3) in 1871 in the aftermath of the Franco-Prussian War.

Marx's scurrilous *The Communist Manifesto* was the platform upon which the Russian tyranny was built in 1917, as it was later in the establishment of Red China, the Korean tyranny, the fall of Vietnam to communism (and much of Southeast Asia, including Cambodia, Laos, and other nations), and the fall of Cuba to communism; and of course the list of nations threatened by this virulent violent form of tyranny continues to grow.

Each tragic revolution will not be reviewed in detail in this lecture, but the student may be assured that the formula is well established and is replicated over and over as these false revolutionary philosophies capture nation after nation.

A review of some of the specifics in the various nations may, in general, be applied to all of the nations who have fallen victim to this diabolical scourge.

Let us begin with the French Revolution. It began in earnest in 1789, although it had been fomenting for some time.

ALL REVOLUTIONS ARE NOT CREATED EQUAL
(THE AMERICAN REVOLUTION VS. SUBSEQUENT REVOLUTIONS)

Charles Dickens

Charles Dickens begins his classic novel *A Tale of Two Cities*, which is an account of the events surrounding the French Revolution, with the words "It was the best of times, it was the worst of times." Thus he begins his tale of the French Revolution.

At first, some of the brightest American minds assumed that the similarities between the American Revolution and the French Revolution were complete.

Thomas Jefferson, for example, perhaps by his love for all things French and perhaps because of his love of liberty that he assumed all mankind shared, was initially an ardent supporter of the French Revolution, assuming it to be the precursor to another glorious victory for the cause of liberty.

Edmund Burke was an English statesman who lived during the American founding era and who often spoke in England in defense of the American Revolutionary movement. In 1790 he wrote his *Reflections on the Revolution in France*. In that lengthy treatise, he soundly criticized the French Revolution. When Thomas Jefferson read Burke's perspective on the French Revolution, he angrily denounced Burke's observations.

TO PRESERVE THE NATION

Edmund Burke

The outcome of the events surrounding the French bloodbath confirmed Burke's observations, which proved more accurate than Jefferson's assumptions and hopes. Burke went so far as to accurately state that the French Revolution would end in disaster and that it was "the enemy of liberty."

Jefferson's assumptions, and his hopes for the French Revolution, were soon dashed in a bloodbath of debauchery and licentiousness, which created a greater tyranny than anyone has a right to fully unfold.

As previously noted herein, all revolutions are not created equal!

Rare have been the revolutions that resulted in as perfect a liberty as resulted in the aftermath of the American Revolution of 1776.

A review of the French Revolution would be incomplete without mentioning a couple of the characters whose names are inextricably interwoven with the French Revolution.

ALL REVOLUTIONS ARE NOT CREATED EQUAL
(THE AMERICAN REVOLUTION VS. SUBSEQUENT REVOLUTIONS)

Rousseau

Jean-Jacques Rousseau must be considered to be a sort of "godfather" to the French Revolution. He was a philosopher who lived 1712-1778. He was born in Switzerland, but moved to Paris, France in 1742.

While he wrote extensively, perhaps his most influential work was his 1762 writing called *The Social Contract*.

His personal life was something of a disaster. He fathered several children and abandoned them with the excuse that he would have been a poor father (which his actions demonstrated him to be).

Rousseau was one of the first writers to seriously attack the institution of private property and, therefore, is considered a kind of harbinger of modern socialism and communism.

In his perspective, the government is charged with implementing and enforcing the general will of the people. He opposed the ideas of representative government and felt that the people should make the laws directly—democratically (remember our discussions of democracy and how the Founding Fathers opposed it and how Marx, Lenin, Chairman Mao, and others fostered it and continue to foster it today).

He also fostered the concept of a kind of "civil religion" wherein the bureaucracy of government became a sort of "god" to the people as it dispensed rights and largess.

In addition, unfortunately, Rousseau's ideas about education have profoundly influenced modern educational theory (this in spite of the fact he abandoned his own children and failed to measure up to his duty in their education).

Tragically, Rousseau's philosophies also profoundly influenced the French Revolution.

Robespierre

Robespierre is another of the rogues of the French Revolution you must meet.

He was a member of the Illuminati and sought the implementation of their society-destroying plans.

He sought to use force to bring about a society in which all members of society are equal (except, of course, the elite revolutionaries in the "inner circle" of power).

Every aspect of human life, every relationship, was to be regulated by the government.

As the revolution progressed, when Robespierre was at the height of his power, he acted as a god as he presided over the deaths of hundreds of thousands of French citizens (men, women, and children) as he carried out a plan to decimate the French population.

The plan was to eliminate religion and to eliminate literally millions of people because, said the revolutionaries, there are not enough resources—food, jobs, etc.—for all the people,

ALL REVOLUTIONS ARE NOT CREATED EQUAL
(THE AMERICAN REVOLUTION VS. SUBSEQUENT REVOLUTIONS)

so they decided to thin the ranks to meet their perception of what (in the modern vernacular) was "sustainable."

Ultimately, Robespierre met his end on the guillotine as the rogues at the top of the conspiracy eliminated him as one of the competitors to their power.

Guillotine

The guillotine is seen by many as the symbol of the French Revolution. Most think that only a relatively few of the aristocracy were put to death by this device, but this conception is an error.

Each day, for extended periods, carts full of men, women, and children were brought to the guillotines. In Paris, it is said that one executioner was able to guillotine twelve people every thirteen minutes. Other executioners were trained in his technique to facilitate more efficiently the elimination of the millions they wanted to murder.

Ultimately, the guillotine was viewed as too slow, so they began tying groups of people together and blowing them up.

Hundreds of children were rounded up in groups and brutally slaughtered with clubs, sabers, and guns.

Large-scale, wholesale mass drownings were instituted, beginning with priests, and expanded to great numbers of women and children.

Artificial famine was created by the revolutionaries to further their purposes.

Before the bloodbath was stopped, over one million French men, women, and children were murdered. Most of them were of the so-called "common" class, not aristocrats.

TO PRESERVE THE NATION

During the French Revolution, anything associated with religion was denigrated and destroyed. Atheism became the national religion. Faith was attacked from every possible direction, and the revolutionaries sought to eliminate morality.

Boys were to belong to their parents only until age five, and then they became the property of the state, to be raised and educated (shall we say indoctrinated) by the state to the standard of the revolutionaries.

Napoleon Bonaparte

One power-monger after another seized the reins of government with no improvement for the nation. As the people sickened of the bloodbath of debauchery brought on by the French Revolution, they sought someone who would rescue them from their plight. Napoleon Bonaparte was waiting in the wings. He promised them order, but in return the people must give him absolute power. The people agreed, and Napoleon reestablished another despotism.

In his Farewell Address, George Washington warned of such conditions, saying,

> The alternate domination of one faction over another, sharpened by the spirit of revenge natural to party dissension, which in different ages and countries has perpetrated the most horrid enormities, is itself a frightful despotism. But this leads at length to a more formal and permanent despotism. The disorders and miseries which result gradually incline the minds of men to seek security and repose in the absolute power of an individual, and sooner or later the chief of some prevailing

ALL REVOLUTIONS ARE NOT CREATED EQUAL
(THE AMERICAN REVOLUTION VS. SUBSEQUENT REVOLUTIONS)

faction, more able or more fortunate than his competitors, turns this disposition to the purposes of his own elevation on the ruins of public liberty.

This great truth is repeated over and over as nation after nation falls prey to false philosophies of government.

In France, the people endured eighty years of revolution, anarchy, despotism, dictatorship, and more revolution, never able to capture the beautiful balance of proper government that was established as the United States was founded.

Moving forward in history, recall the brief discussion during the lecture on Karl Marx and his manifesto of the revolutions that were fomented and planned well in advance by conspirators to coincide with the release of *The Communist Manifesto* in 1848.

In 1848, revolutions were created in France, Vienna, Berlin, Venice, London, Spain, Naples, and other places. There were sixty-four revolutionary outbreaks in Russia in the course of the year. All failed miserably, but not without creating much death and destruction and human misery.

The Franco-Prussian War gave the communist revolutionaries their next opportunity for power in France. As the Prussians entered Paris, France, in March 1871, the next major French revolutionary upheaval occurred.

At this time many of the debaucheries of the 1789 revolution returned. Churches were again desecrated, marriage was touted as slavery. France was ruled by the "commune," and when they realized they could not hold their power, they set out to burn Paris, destroying countless priceless treasures of art and culture. There were instances of mass executions of hostages. No less than thirty thousand men, women, and children died in the streets of Paris as the communist movement convulsed (again) to its ignominious end.

The next convulsion of note is the Russian Revolution.

No attempt will be made to examine the minute details of the Russian Revolution. We will not take the time to detail the agony of the communist revolution in Russia in 1917.

Suffice it to note, a small minority of dedicated revolutionaries took full advantage of some terribly difficult circumstances and seized power.

Prior to the revolution, Russia had lost millions of its best men in the brutal battlefields of the ongoing World War I.

Russia was suffering from terrible food shortages—at least partially caused by the sabotage of the communist revolutionaries.

Circumstances were such that there was much turmoil, and people were yearning for relief. The revolutionaries seized the opportunity and seized the power.

The record indicates that the revolutionaries were well funded, and the great majority of their funds were provided by Americans and Germans.

Of course, the Germans wanted a revolution in Russia because Russia was at war with Germany, and a successful revolution in Russia would remove Russia from World War I, thus freeing German troops from the Eastern Front and allowing them to be

TO PRESERVE THE NATION

transferred to the Western Front in France to reinforce the German troops who were fighting there.

While they were not present in Russia as the revolution began, several communist revolutionaries were to come to the center of the conflict and play key roles in the outcome.

Lenin

Stalin

As the revolution began, Lenin was in Switzerland. He had been exiled there for his efforts to overthrow the Russian czar in 1905.

Stalin was in a Siberian prison due to his previous subversive activities.

Leon Trotsky

ALL REVOLUTIONS ARE NOT CREATED EQUAL
(THE AMERICAN REVOLUTION VS. SUBSEQUENT REVOLUTIONS)

Trotsky was in the United States working in New York as a reporter.

With the overthrow of the czar and the establishment of a "provisional government," the Germans offered Lenin secret passage by rail into Russia.

Stalin was pardoned by the provisional government and was set free so he could return to Moscow.

Trotsky and about 275 revolutionaries set sail from New York, bound for Europe and onward to Moscow, in March 1917.

In the ensuing power struggle, Lenin and his crowd of Bolsheviks seized the reins of government and began their reign of terror.

They sought to fully implement the provisions of *The Communist Manifesto*, including,

1. The destruction of Christianity
2. The abolishment of private property
3. The elimination of the family as a social unit
4. The abolishment of the existing government
5. The establishment of a new dictatorship of the proletariat (the working class)

They did this through a reign of blood and horror.

Under Lenin, and later under Stalin, secret police had power to investigate, arrest, interrogate, torture, prosecute, hold secret trials, imprison, and execute. There was no limit on their power. No one was safe from their brutal methods. Loved ones simply disappeared. Fear was their tool. Families and communities were torn asunder by their methods.

At one point, Stalin bragged that he had murdered over ten million kulaks (landed peasants that refused to turn their farms over to Stalin, who wanted to turn them into collectivist farms). The kulaks were starved out, and they and their villages were destroyed by massive artillery attacks. Huge gulag prison systems were established to remove potential dissidents from society. Slave labor abounded. No one really knows how many people were killed as this tyranny descended upon this nation, but all estimates place the numbers as many tens of millions.

Chairman Mao

Fidel Castro

TO PRESERVE THE NATION

After World War II, through violent revolutionary activity, Chairman Mao subjugated hundreds of millions of Chinese in Mainland China and, subsequently, using coercive methods similar to the ones used by Lenin and Stalin, slaughtered tens of millions of the Chinese people.

The power bases established in Russia and China were used as instruments to foment revolutions all across the world.

A full review of all the turmoil and destruction of human life, liberty, and property that occurred (and continues to occur) under these revolutions is not possible, but briefly we mention the enslavement of the following countries: North Korea, North Vietnam, Cuba, the Congo, South Vietnam, Laos, Cambodia, and many lands where the struggles are ongoing, whose struggles are tied to the philosophies we have been reviewing herein. It is interesting to note that in many modern instances, the revolutionary forces are using deception to gain popular support and come into power through the power of the vote.

While he used violent revolutionary means to seize power, prior to his establishment of communist China, Chairman Mao was purported to be what the U.S. State Department called an "agrarian reformer." They wanted the people of the United States to believe that he was simply interested in the way the farmland in China was used. That in spite of Mao's long and well-documented track record as a communist revolutionary!

Cuba's Castro was touted as a modern George Washington of Cuba. Castro went so far as to assure his adoring supporters he was not a communist. Of course, after he seized power, he admitted that not only was he a communist, he had always been one. And it would be hard to imagine someone who could be farther removed from the character traits of George Washington!

In every instance of these seizures of power, the revolutionaries implemented terrorist actions reminiscent of the French Revolution of the late 1700s and have sought to carry out the theories that are central to the philosophies of the Illuminati and Marx:

1. The destruction of Christianity
2. The abolishment of private property
3. The elimination of the family as a social unit
4. The abolishment of the existing government
5. The establishment of a new dictatorship of the proletariat (the working class)

The brutality of the communist tactics are reflected in the example which was given in the introductory lecture wherein mention is made of a family in the former South Vietnam who, after the communists seized power there, felt that a family member who

ALL REVOLUTIONS ARE NOT CREATED EQUAL
(THE AMERICAN REVOLUTION VS. SUBSEQUENT REVOLUTIONS)

had died in the city of Hue during the 1968 Tet Offensive was to be envied due to the repressions the surviving family members were forced to endure under the new communist regime.

Pol Pot

And the extreme brutality of Pol Pot and his communist Khmer Rouge after they seized Cambodia is legend. Their methods of execution, starvation, forced labor, torture, and forced relocation of populations were exceptionally aggressive. Pol Pot and his criminal band murdered millions of their fellow countrymen, killing fully one-third of the nation's population during their reign of terror.

The French Revolution of the eighteenth century, subsequent European revolutions of the mid-1800s, Lenin's Russian Revolution, Chairman Mao's Chinese Revolution, Castro's Cuban Revolution, Ho Chi Minh's Vietnamese Revolution, Pol Pot's Cambodian Revolution, and a host of other twentieth-century revolutions have all resulted in a riot of carnage and destruction that crushed the human spirit and wrapped the people captured by the revolutions in darkness and despair.

Ho Chi Minh

To sum up the message of this lecture: indeed, all revolutions are not created equal!

The leaders of the American Revolution rebelled against a form of government that was unrestrained in the power it could wield and that could destroy or subvert the God-given rights of mankind.

Virtually all revolutionaries since that time have sought to seize all power in order to destroy all that is good and decent in society—all religious values, and individual God-given liberties.

The American Revolutionaries upheld that which ennobles the human spirit.

The subsequent revolutionaries brought tyranny and based their efforts on murder, deception, and force.

The American revolutionaries based their foundation upon timeless principles that are intended to counter and diffuse the natural tendency of mankind to seek, obtain, and then abuse power. They sought to keep the government as a servant to the people, not a master of the people. They viewed government as the protector of rights, not the dispenser of rights. Under the American system, government power is limited to a specific role and is prevented from usurping additional power.

The other revolutionaries we have been studying in this lecture sought for power. They sought (and even today continue to seek) to consolidate power, even unlimited power, to exercise it without restraint or bounds. These subsequent revolutionaries have been able to gain power over the people by use of force and trickery.

Principles of proper government have been universally ignored or subverted in revolutions subsequent to the American Revolution. Generally, when this has occurred,

**ALL REVOLUTIONS ARE NOT CREATED EQUAL
(THE AMERICAN REVOLUTION VS. SUBSEQUENT REVOLUTIONS)**

the people were searching for a master who would treat them with benevolence and kindness. The people were always vainly seeking a man, or men, who would give them liberty and freedom, while protecting them from themselves. What the people get with such an approach is cycle after cycle of revolution, violence, destruction, dictatorship, and tyranny.

If a people do not understand the timeless principles of liberty and proper, limited government, they are doomed to endlessly repeat this destructive cycle.

The key is to understand and apply the *principles* that will allow liberty to flourish. Those principles are inextricably tied to limiting government powers to specific essential duties and no more. The government must recognize that its purpose and duty is to safeguard the sacred individual God-given rights of its citizens.

Tragically, while America is unique in its origins, in its form of government, and its ability to preserve individual God-given liberties, America is turning away from its sound foundation and embracing false philosophies that have proven to destroy liberty and virtually all that is good in society.

If America is to preserve its greatness, it must turn from the failed philosophies of government power and vigorously seek the restoration of the foundation principles that made this nation the greatest, freest, most prosperous, most respected, and happiest nation on earth.

This nation faces perilous times ahead.

Perhaps more that any other time, the nation faces a moral crisis—in leadership, in the general apathy of the people of the nation, in the nation's widespread acceptance of the godless philosophies of secular humanism, and in the pervasive perversions that are embraced without thought by such a broad spectrum of the national population.

Under the goading of leaders that hold little sacred, and under the influence of a ubiquitous education system that teaches principles devoid of God and only rarely teaches a sound understanding of the foundation principles of this nation, the nation has strayed far from those foundation principles.

Unfortunately, it would seem that the nation is forsaking God and the foundation principles, and as a consequence, perhaps, He is forsaking the nation, and the national foundation is crumbling.

If this nation is to survive the challenges it faces, it must, first and foremost, return to that God who made it free. It must recognize His hand in all things and become obedient to His commandments.

The people of the nation must begin again to hold national, state, and local leadership to a standard that reflects the godly principles upon which the nation was built.

The scope and magnitude of the nation's current moral turpitude cannot be underestimated, nor can the urgency of our return to God and the principles of limited government that operates within the bounds that were originally established be overstated.

As has been elsewhere noted herein, during the Constitutional Convention of 1787, George Mason stated,

TO PRESERVE THE NATION

George Mason

> As nations cannot be rewarded or punished in the next world, they must be in this. By an inevitable chain of causes and effects, Providence punishes national sins by national calamities.[267]

Caring citizens must pray that the nation has not passed the point of no return and now faces only the imminent justice of an offended God!

Perhaps, with the understanding that may be gained of this nation's origins and with a clear view of the false philosophies that have led to tyranny, Americans will be wise enough to return to our foundation of liberty and restore and preserve those blessings of liberty for ourselves *and* our posterity!

We have been reminded before: "Let me add that only a virtuous people are capable of freedom. As nations become corrupt and vicious, they have more need of masters."[268] "Our Constitution was designed only for a moral and religious people. It is wholly inadequate

---

[267.] Madison, *Journal*, vol. 2, Wednesday August 22, 1787.
[268.] To the Abbes Chalut and Arnaud, 17 April 1787, in Smyth, *Benjamin Franklin*, 9:569.

ALL REVOLUTIONS ARE NOT CREATED EQUAL
(THE AMERICAN REVOLUTION VS. SUBSEQUENT REVOLUTIONS)

for the government of any other."[269] Let us be a moral and religious people and live by the marvelous principles that were brought forth as this nation was founded under the inspiration of God and not be deceived into support of the false revolutionary forces that are so highly organized and so cleverly disguised throughout the world today. Let us preserve the nation we were bequeathed!

[269.] C. F. Adams, *John Adams*, 4:31.

15.

GEORGE WASHINGTON: "THE ELEGANT EXERCISE OF POWER"—A STUDY IN THE RARE, PURE EXERCISE OF MORTAL AUTHORITY

RECOMMENDED RESOURCES FOR THE SERIOUS STUDENT:

George Washington: A Collection, edited by W. B. Allen

QUOTES, ARTICLES, AND ORIGINAL SOURCES

Rare indeed is a mortal who can hold great power and not begin to abuse it. Such a man was George Washington. He spent his adult life having power thrust upon him by a nation that desperately needed his magnificent leadership, but in every case he faced, he only accepted the proffered power long enough to fulfill his duty, and then he would divest himself of the power as quickly as he could. All Americans seemed to know that Washington could be trusted with power and that he would never become a tyrant in any degree. He proved throughout his life that their trust in him was well founded!

It is human nature to seek power and then abuse it. Because the founders of this nation were great observers of human nature and recognized characteristics in the human character that tended toward tyranny, they wrote the United States Constitution to address those foibles. The Constitution was written to prevent the abuse of power. The authors sought to prevent general human tendencies from destroying the nation. Because of this, the Constitution is a timeless instrument of liberty. If it is strictly applied, it will prevent tyranny, regardless of technological advances in society. Technology changes, but human nature is constant.

This lecture will initially cite a few examples of how power tends to corrupt most men, and then we will review the life of George Washington, relying primarily upon his own pen to capture his attitude and perspective on power. We will review extensive quotations he wrote on the subject.

THE CORRUPTING INFLUENCE OF POWER

In his dire review of modern totalitarian governments, George Orwell captured the essence of oppressive government, noting:

GEORGE WASHINGTON: "THE ELEGANT EXERCISE OF POWER"
—A STUDY IN THE RARE, PURE EXERCISE OF MORTAL AUTHORITY

We know that no one ever seizes power with the intention of relinquishing it. Power is not a means; it is an end. One does not establish a dictatorship in order to safeguard a revolution; one makes the revolution in order to establish the dictatorship. The object of persecution is persecution. The object of torture is torture. The object of power is power. [270]

The desire to obtain—and then, ultimately, to abuse power—has been almost universally recognized by thinking men throughout the ages. The great statesman Lord Acton observed that "power corrupts, and absolute power corrupts absolutely."[271] Daniel Defoe noted, "All men would be tyrants if they could."[272]

Indeed, modern megalomaniacs have unequivocally demonstrated both in word and deed the truth of these statements! Two examples from the twentieth century must suffice.

During the 1930s and '40s, much of the world was engulfed in a conflagration that had its origins in a sweeping power grab by wicked tyrants. The National Socialist German Workers Party (Nazis) was a major sponsor of the effort to violently gain control of power over broad segments of humanity. The Nazis regime upheld a concept they called the "leader principle" (*führerprinzip*). In contrast with the foundation principles of the United States Constitution in which the power of government and individuals (regardless of their position within government) is limited to specific bounds, Nazi doctrine placed no limits upon the power that may be seized, held, and exercised by their "leader" (*führer*). In a section defining the *führerprinzip*, the organization book of the National Socialist German Workers Party states that the power of the chief executive "is not limited by checks and controls, by special autonomous bodies or individual rights, but it is free and independent, all-inclusive and unlimited . . . . He is responsible only to his conscience and the people."[273]

The revolutionary communist doctrine of Karl Marx was also at the center of the violent usurpation of power that engulfed much of the twentieth century, including the period in which the competing doctrine of the Nazis operated, and continuing even today. The revolutionary Soviet dictator Vladimir Lenin summarized his version of the power-mongering leader as follows: "The scientific concept of dictatorship is nothing else than this—power without limit, resting directly on force, restrained by no laws, absolutely unrestricted by rules."[274]

[270.] Statement by O'Brien, torture specialist in George Orwell's novel *1984*

[271.] Letter to Mandell Creighton, April 5, 1887, in Himmelfarb, Acton, 335-36.

[272.] Daniel Defoe, *The Kentish Petition*, addenda, 11 (1701).

[273.] From the Organization Book of the German National Socialist Party (1940).

[274.] V. I. Lenin, "A Contribution to the History of the Question of Dictatorship" (20 October 1920), in *Lenin's Collected Works*, 4th English ed. (Moscow, Russia: Progress Publishers, 1965), 31:340-361.

The Nazi and Soviet philosophies (both completely socialist, but "blood brother" tyrannies competing along with the other less overtly violent though equally poisonous socialist movements for the preeminent worldwide power position) are the antithesis of the form of government established under the United States Constitution in 1787. Individual God-given rights, personal liberty, and limited governmental power were at the core of the philosophy that led the Founding Fathers of the United States to bring forth the national charter that they authored. Those who founded the nation were painfully aware of mankind's natural tendency to garner then abuse power. They sought to forestall that tendency by safeguards they built into the form of government they created.

But it took individuals endowed with exceptionally remarkable characteristics to frame such a government. They held power, they recognized the inherent dangers of power, they had experienced firsthand the pain of tyranny, they loved liberty, they saw God as the source of their liberty and all other blessings, they wanted the blessings of liberty not only for themselves but also for their posterity, and they were willing to let go of power so liberty could endure.

Rare indeed is the mortal individual who obtains power and then eschews it when it is apparent that it may be held and expanded at will. George Washington was such a rare man. During his lifetime, he was constantly offered power. He resisted its allures, accepting it only when he felt duty-bound to fulfill his responsibility to his fellow countrymen, and then, when the duty was fulfilled, he would quickly divest himself of the power so he could return to his role as a "common" man. In spite of his best efforts to live his life unfettered by the accouterments of power and publicity, he was called upon incessantly during his forty-five-year labor of love for his country to shoulder power and exert a leadership role that would have corrupted lesser men. In many ways, he was a duty-bound servant that selflessly labored on behalf of the cause of liberty for his fellow man.

THE INCORRUPTIBLE WASHINGTON

While it would appear that lesser men can never obtain enough power to satisfy their insatiable lust for power, throughout his life Washington continually declined offers to hold power—even power that would have seemed to be almost unlimited within in his realm. On several occasions, when Washington was offered opportunities to become "king" of America, he adamantly declined, sorrowing that anyone would think him so crass as to be amenable to such an offer. When he held the supreme command of the only viable military force on the continent and when the officers and troops expressed their desire that he lead them in a coup to overthrow the established government of the nation, he vehemently declined, pleading with them to have patience and assuring them that peaceful solutions could be found for their complaints. At the close of the Revolutionary War, at what would appear (at the time) to be at his zenith in power and popularity, he resigned his command and commission before Congress and eagerly assumed that he would return to "private" life as a common citizen. When others pled with him to participate in the Constitutional Convention of 1787 (because they knew that the plan to restructure the government was

GEORGE WASHINGTON: "THE ELEGANT EXERCISE OF POWER" — A STUDY IN THE RARE, PURE EXERCISE OF MORTAL AUTHORITY

doomed to fail before the people if Washington's hand was not in the matter), he hesitated because he felt himself unfit. When he finally agreed to participate in the convention, he was compelled only by duty and only accepted the role as president of the convention to facilitate the orderly fulfillment of the business the convention had been convened to achieve. After fulfilling his duty before the convention, he again retired to private life, content to pursue his love of agriculture. When duty called again, being unanimously elected by the electoral college, he reluctantly served two arduous terms as the nation's first president, establishing a model for the office he dignified. Having completed two terms of office, again at a zenith of power, and fully able, if he desired, to retain the power of that office for life, he again graciously retired, offering loving advice to the nation he had so tirelessly served for his entire life. Even at that point, when he considered his final retirement, he was constantly called upon to provide desperately needed leadership to the foundling nation—even again submitting to the call of his countrymen and assuming the role of the nation's commander in chief when war threatened and quickly removing himself from the bonds of power as soon as the threat was resolved. Even in death, he resolved to be buried without pomp and ceremony, preferring to be quietly interred as a private citizen upon the land he loved so fervently.

Indeed, it may be said that Washington wasted and wore out his life in the service of his fellow countrymen, loving and serving them to the end of his days. Power did not corrupt him, and he proved time and time again that he had no desire to be a tyrant of any shade. He provided a marvelous example of a mortal man unmoved by power and completely trustworthy of its burdens.

It has been said that Washington was "first in war, first in peace, and first in the hearts of his countrymen."[275] He was all of that and more. He was the "indispensable man" in all of the magnificent events that unfolded in his lifetime—from his heroic efforts to save General Braddock's troops from slaughter during the French and Indian War, to his irreplaceable ministrations as the commander in chief of the Continental Armies during the Revolutionary War, to his steady hand as the president of the Constitutional Convention of 1787, to his foundation-establishing tenure as the first president of the United States.

Decades after Washington's death, Abraham Lincoln stated, "To add brightness to the sun or glory to the name of Washington is . . . impossible. Let none attempt it. In solemn awe pronounce the name and in its naked deathless splendor, leave it shining on."[276]

---

[275]. General Henry Lee ("Lighthorse" Harry Lee), eulogy in memory of George Washington, 26 December 1799, Philadelphia; also, resolution prepared by General Lee and presented to the House of Representatives by John Marshall.

[276]. Abraham Lincoln, Temperance address (delivered before the Springfield Washington Temperance Society, 22 February 1842), in Roy P. Basler, ed., *The Collected Works of Abraham Lincoln* (New Brunswick, NJ, 1953), 1:279.

TO PRESERVE THE NATION

Abraham Lincoln

By all contemporary accounts, George Washington was the preeminent personage whose leadership made possible the founding of the United States of America, and yet his writings and actions speak of a man who sought not for power or for the honor of the world, but only for the freedom and welfare of his country.

While volumes have been written regarding the monumental character and multifaceted accomplishments of this "indispensable" man, George Washington, the focus of this review is to support a brief examination of Washington's deflection of power from himself. The primary source of this sketch will be Washington's own writings, as compiled in W. B. Allen's *George Washington: A Collection* (Indianapolis: Liberty Fund). Allen relied almost entirely upon John C. Fitzpatrick's classic compiled writings of George Washington (*The Writings of George Washington from the Original Manuscript Sources, 1745-1799*, which was prepared under the direction of the George Washington Bicentennial Commission) to assemble his collection. While many dozens of examples of Washington's attitude toward power, and his reluctance to obtain and retain it, could be cited from his own words as compiled in this collection by W. B. Allen, brevity will allow only a few key samples to be included in this sketch. In general, quotations incorporated into this review will note the Allen reference thus: George Washington, Allen Collection, page number/s. Other sources, including those that mirror the Allen references are noted in more complete detail.

GEORGE WASHINGTON: "THE ELEGANT EXERCISE OF POWER" — A STUDY IN THE RARE, PURE EXERCISE OF MORTAL AUTHORITY

THE SELF-EFFACING WASHINGTON

In a July 4, 1774, letter to his neighbor, Bryan Fairfax, Washington notes that he felt that "the country never stood more in need of men of abilities and liberal sentiments than now"[277] In that letter, he mentions that in public matters, he has adopted a "maxim not to propose myself, and solicit for a second."[278] Washington lived his entire life by this credo.

In virtually every instance that he was asked to perform some service to his country, Washington remonstrated that he doubted his ability to perform the labor satisfactorily. This practice almost certainly contributed to the perception that many modern historians hold that Washington was not the intellectual, capable giant among men that he was. The following are a few examples of this tendency toward self-depredation that Washington exhibited:

In spite of his preeminent qualifications as the most able and suitable American for the assignment of commander in chief of the Continental Army, in June 1775, as he was nominated by the Continental Congress and appointed to that commission, Washington characteristically downplayed his qualifications and abilities. In addition, as became his habit as he served his nation, he declined a salary in the assignment:

> MR. PRESIDENT: Though I am truly sensible of the high honor done me, in this appointment, yet I feel great distress, from a consciousness that my abilities and military experience may not be equal to the extensive and important trust. However, as the Congress desire it, I will enter upon the momentous duty, and exert every power I possess in their service, and for the support of the glorious cause, I beg they will accept my most cordial thanks for this distinguished testimony of their approbation.
>
> But, lest some unlucky event should happen, unfavorable to my reputation, I beg it may be remembered by every gentleman in the room, that I, this day, declare with the utmost sincerity, I do not think myself equal to the command I am honored with.
>
> As to pay, Sir, I beg leave to assure the Congress, that, as no pecuniary consideration could have tempted me to accept this arduous employment, at the expense of my domestic ease and happiness, I do not wish to make any profit from it. I will

---

[277.] George Washington, Allen Collection, 33.
[278.] George Washington, Allen Collection, 33.

keep an exact account of my expenses. Those, I doubt not, they will discharge, and that is all I desire.[279]

Washington Takes Command of American Forces

His words were no affectation adopted for public consumption. In his most private communications, he was consistent with his private remonstrances. The following is his correspondence with his wife, Martha, shortly after his appointment as commander in chief:

> MY DEAREST: I am now set down to write to you on a subject, which fills me with inexpressible concern, and this concern is greatly aggravated and increased, when I reflect upon the uneasiness I know it will give you. It has been determined in Congress, that the whole army raised for the defense of the American cause shall be put under my care, and that it is necessary for me to proceed immediately to Boston to take upon me the command of it.
>
> You may believe me, my dear Patsy, when I assure you, in the most solemn manner, that, so far from seeking this appointment, I have used every endeavor in my power to avoid it, not only from my unwillingness to part with you and the family, but from a consciousness of its being a trust too great for my capacity, and that I should enjoy more real happiness in one month with you at home, than I have the most distant prospect of finding abroad, if my stay were to be seven

---

[279.] George Washington, Allen Collection, 40; also, "Washington Appointed Commander in Chief," *America* 3, 125-6.

GEORGE WASHINGTON: "THE ELEGANT EXERCISE OF POWER" — A STUDY IN THE RARE, PURE EXERCISE OF MORTAL AUTHORITY

times seven years. But as it has been a kind of destiny, that has thrown me upon this service, I shall hope that my undertaking it is designed to answer some good purpose. You might, and I suppose did perceive, from the tenor of my letters, that I was apprehensive I could not avoid this appointment, as I did not pretend to intimate when I should return. That was the case. It was utterly out of my power to refuse this appointment, without exposing my character to such censures, as would have reflected dishonor upon myself, and given pain to my friends. This, I am sure, could not, and ought not, to be pleasing to you, and must have lessened me considerably in my own esteem. I shall rely, therefore, confidently on that Providence, which has heretofore preserved and been bountiful to me, not doubting but that I shall return safe to you in the fall. I shall feel no pain from the toil or the danger of the campaign; my unhappiness will flow from the uneasiness I know you will feel from being left alone. I therefore beg, that you will summon your whole fortitude, and pass your time as agreeably as possible. Nothing will give me so much sincere satisfaction as to hear this, and to hear it from your own pen. My earnest and ardent desire is, that you would pursue any plan that is most likely to produce content, and a tolerable degree of tranquillity; as it must add greatly to my uneasy feelings to hear, that you are dissatisfied or complaining at what I really could not avoid.

As life is always uncertain, and common prudence dictates to every man the necessity of settling his temporal concerns, while it is in his power, and while the mind is calm and undisturbed, I have, since I came to this place (for I had not time to do it before I left home) got Colonel Pendleton to draft a will for me, by the directions I gave him, which will I now enclose. The provision made for you in case of my death will, I hope, be agreeable.

I shall add nothing more, as I have several letters to write, but to desire that you will remember me to your friends, and to assure you that I am, with the most unfeigned regard, my dear Patsy, your affectionate, &c.[280]

It is said that after General Washington's death, Martha Washington shut herself up in her room at Mount Vernon and spent her time sitting before the window that looked out on his tomb. Shortly before her death, Martha Washington destroyed all of the personal letters from her husband that she had in her possession.[281] Consequently, the above-noted correspondence offers a rare and interesting insight into the regard they held for each other.

[280.] George Washington, Allen Collection, 40-2; also, "Farewell to Mrs. Washington," *America* 3, 127-129.

[281.] "Farewell to Mrs. Washington," *America* 3, 127.

TO PRESERVE THE NATION

EFFORTS TO MAKE WASHINGTON KING

As a result of his undying devotion to serve his country and obtain liberty on behalf of the nation, numerous efforts were made to ensure his role as the leader of the nation. As the Revolutionary War wound down, one of the most overt attempts to induce Washington to accept the role of king was made by Colonel Lewis Nicola, an officer who served under Washington. In a letter to Washington on May 22, 1782, Nicola broached the subject to Washington. Washington immediately rebuked the thought, and Nicola was so ashamed to have put Washington in the position he had that he wrote three apologies to Washington in the days that followed. Excerpts from Washington's letter of rebuke follows and leave no doubt of Washington's despair at even the inference that he would entertain such a thought:

> No occurrence in the course of the war has given me more painful sensations than your information of there being such ideas existing in the army as you have expressed, and I must view with abhorrence and reprehend with severity.... I am much at a loss to conceive what part of my conduct could have given encouragement to an address which to me seems big with the greatest mischiefs that can befall my Country. If I am not deceived in the knowledge of myself, you could not have found a person to whom your schemes are more disagreeable... Let me conjure you, then, if you have any regard for your country, concern for yourself or posterity, or respect for me, to banish these thoughts from your mind, and never communicate, as from yourself or any one else, a sentiment of the like nature.[282]

Lesser men would have found a measure of flattery in such an idea as the offer of a kingship, but Washington found it not only abhorrent, but deeply saddening that anyone could conceive of him seeking such a position—indeed nothing in the course of the war hurt him so deeply.

AVERTING MUTINY AT NEWBURGH

Colonel Nicola's desire to have Washington installed as king was motivated by the congress's inability or unwillingness to address numerous grievances under which the Continental Army had labored for the many years of the war—no pay, poor or insufficient food, lack of necessary supplies, and a general perception that the difficult exigencies under which the army labored were not appreciated by the congress or the nation. Washington wrestled constantly with congress in an effort to receive redress for the soldiers and had

---

[282]. George Washington, Allen Collection, 203-4; also, George Bancroft, *History of the United States*, 5:558.

GEORGE WASHINGTON: "THE ELEGANT EXERCISE OF POWER"
—A STUDY IN THE RARE, PURE EXERCISE OF MORTAL AUTHORITY

small measures of success and numerous promises of relief. However, in the face of extended delays and many disappointments, the patience of the officers and soldiers wore thin, and rumblings of a planned coup stirred through the ranks. Some hoped that Washington would join the effort and be placed at the head of the nation. Washington personally attended a meeting of officers that were inclined to believe that the time had come to take matters into their own hands and relieve congress of their positions. The meeting had been called by an anonymous letter of invitation. Washington addressed the group, imploring them to withdraw from the brink they approached, and give the nation a chance to embrace the liberty they had fought so long and hard to achieve. The following is the text of his remarks on that momentous occasion:

Gentlemen,

By an anonymous summons, an attempt has been made to convene you together? how inconsistent with the rules of propriety!—how unmilitary!—and how subversive of all order and discipline, let the good sense of the army decide.

In the moment of this summons, another anonymous production was sent into circulation; addressed more to the feelings of passions, than to the reason & judgment of the army.—The author of the piece, is entitled to much credit for the goodness of his pen:—and I could wish he had as much credit for the rectitude of his heart—for, as men we see thro' different optics, and are induced by the reflecting faculties of the mind, to use different means to attain the same end:—the author of the address, should have had more charity, than to mark for suspicion, the man who should recommend moderation and longer forbearance—or, in others words, who should not think as he thinks, and act as he advises.—But he had another plan in view, in which candor and liberality of sentiment, regard to justice, and love of country, have no part, and he was right, to insinuate the darkest suspicion, to effect the blackest designs.

That the address is drawn with great art, and is designed to answer the most insidious purposes.—That it is calculated to impress the mind, with an idea of premeditated injustice in the sovereign power of the United States, and rouse all those resentments which must unavoidably flow from such a belief.—That the secret mover of this scheme (whoever he may be) intended to take advantage of the passions, while they were warmed by the recollection of mind which is so necessary to give dignity & stability to measures, is rendered too obvious, by the mode of conducting the business to need other proof than a reference to the proceeding.

Thus much, gentlemen, I have thought it incumbent on me to observe to you, to shew upon what principles I opposed the irregular and hasty meeting which was proposed to have been held on Tuesday last:—and not because I wanted a disposition to give you every opportunity, consistent with your own honor, and the dignity of the army, to make known your grievances.—If my conduct heretofore, has not evinced to you, that I have been a faithful friend to the army, my declaration of it at this time would be equally unavailing & improper.—But as I was among the first who embarked in the cause of our common country—As I have never left your side one moment, but when called from you, on public duty—As I have been the constant companion & witness of your distresses, and not among the last to feel, & acknowledge your merits—As I have ever considered my own military reputation as inseperably connected with that of the army—As my Heart has ever expanded with joy, when I have heard its praises—and my indignation has arisen, when the mouth of detraction has been opened against it—it can scarcely be supposed, at this late stage of the war, that I am indifferent to its interests.

But—how are they to be promoted? The way is plain, says the anonymous addresser—If war continues, remove into the unsettled country—there establish yourselves, and leave an ungrateful country to defend itself—But who are they to defend?—Our wives, our children, our farms, and other property which we leave behind us.—or—in this state of hostile separation, are we to take the two first (the latter cannot be removed)—to perish in a wilderness, with hunger cold & nakedness?—If peace takes place, never sheath your sword says he until you have obtained full and ample justice—This dreadful alternative, of either deserting our country in the extremest hour of her distress, or turning our arms against it, (which is the apparent object, unless Congress can be compelled into instant compliance) has something so shocking in it, that humanity revolts at the idea.

My God! What can this writer have in view, by recommending such measures?? Can he be a friend to the army?—Can he be a friend to this country?—Rather is he not an insidious foe?—Some emissary, perhaps, from New York, plotting the ruin of both, by sowing the seeds of discord & separation between the civil & military powers of the continent?—And what compliment does he pay to our understandings, when he recommends measures in either alternative, impracticable in their nature?

But here, gentlemen, I will drop the curtain;—and because it would be as imprudent in me to assign my reasons for this opinion, as it would be insulting to your conception, to suppose you stood in need of them.—A moment's reflection will convince every dispassionate mind of the physical impossibility of carrying either proposal into execution.

There might, gentlemen, be an impropriety in my taking notice, in this address to you, of an anonymous production—but the manner in which that performance has been introduced to the army—the effect it was intended to have, together with

GEORGE WASHINGTON: "THE ELEGANT EXERCISE OF POWER" — A STUDY IN THE RARE, PURE EXERCISE OF MORTAL AUTHORITY

some other circumstances, will amply justify my observations on the tendency of that writing.—With respect to the advice given by the author—to suspect the man, who shall recommend moderate measures and longer forbearance—I spurn it—as every man, who regards that liberty, & reveres that justice for which we contend, undoubtedly must—for if men are to be precluded from offering their sentiments on a matter, which may involve the most serious and alarming consequences, that can invite the consideration of Mankind; reason is of no use to us—the freedom of speech may be taken away—and, dumb & silent we may be led, like sheep, to the slaughter.

I cannot, in justice to my own belief, & what I have great reason to conceive is the intention of Congress, conclude this address, without giving it as my decided opinion; that that honourable body, entertain exalted sentiments of the services of the army;—and, from a full conviction of its merits & sufferings, will do it complete justice:—That their endeavors, to discover & establish funds for this purpose, have been unwearied, and will not cease, till they have succeeded, I have succeeded, I have not a doubt. But, like all other large bodies, where there is a variety of different interests to reconcile, their deliberations are slow? Why then should we distrust them?—and, in consequence of that distrust, adopt measures, which may cast a shade over that glory which, has been so justly acquired; and tarnish the reputation of an army which is celebrated thro' all Europe, for its fortitude and patriotism?—and for what is this done?—to bring the object we seek for nearer?—No!—most certainly, in my opinion, it will cast it at a greater distance.—

For myself (and I take no merit in giving the assurance, being induced to it from principles of gratitude, veracity & Justice)—a grateful sense of the confidence you have ever placed in me—a recollection of the cheerful assistance, & prompt obedience I have experienced from you, under every vicissitude of fortune,—and the sincere I feel for an army I have so long had the honor to command, will oblige me to declare, in this public & solemn manner, that, in the attainment of complete justice for all your toils & dangers, and in the gratification of every wish, so far as may be done consistently with the great duty I owe my country, and those powers we are bound to respect, you may freely command my services to the utmost of my abilities.

While I give you these assurances, and pledge my self in the most unequivocal manner, to exert whatever ability I am possessed of, in your favor—let me entreat you, gentlemen, on your part, not to take any measures, which, viewed in the calm light of reason, will lessen the dignity, & sully the glory you have hitherto maintained—let me request you to rely on the plighted faith of your country, and place a full confidence in the purity of the intentions of Congress; that, previous to your dissolution as an Army they will cause all your accounts to be fairly liquidated, as directed in their resolutions, which were published to you two days ago—and that they will adopt the most effectual measures in their power, to render ample justice to you, for your faithful and meritorious Services.—And let me conjure you, in the name of our common country—as you value your own sacred honor—as you respect the rights of humanity; as you regard the military & national character of America, to express your utmost horror & detestation of the man who wishes, under any specious pretenses, to overturn the liberties of our country, & who wickedly attempts to open the flood gates of civil discord, & deluge our rising empire in blood.

By thus determining—& thus acting, you will pursue the plain & direct road to the attainment of your wishes.—You will defeat the insidious designs of our enemies, who are compelled to resort from open force to secret artifice.—You will give one more distinguished proof of unexampled patriotism & patient virtue, rising superior to the pressure of the most complicated sufferings;—And you will, by the dignity of your conduct, afford occasion for posterity to say, when speaking of the glorious example you have exhibited to mankind, had this day been wanting, the world has never seen the last stage of perfection to which human nature is capable of attaining.[283]

Washington's disdain of the opportunity to seize power and perhaps build for himself a kingdom, his passion for the cause of liberty he had been so devoted to, his love of the nation, his brilliant intellect, and his incisive logic are all exposed in this address. It was on this occasion that, as Washington sought to read to the officers a letter from a Virginia congressman that promised relief, that he removed his reading "spectacles" from his coat pocket and, begging their indulgence, stated, "I have grown gray in your service, and now find myself growing blind."[284] While all hearts were softened, he went on reading the letter and then withdrew, leaving the meeting to its deliberations. The mutiny was averted by the simple love and character of Washington, and the nation was given the opportunity to continue in its journey to achieve liberty.

Later, Thomas Jefferson was to write of the potentially mutinous events at the close of the Revolution and George Washington's influence in preventing a tragic outcome:

> The moderation and virtue of a single character have probably prevented this Revolution from being closed, as most others have been, by a subversion of that liberty it was intended to establish.[285]

---

[283]. George Washington, Allen Collection, 217-21. Also, David Ramsay, *The Life of George Washington* (New York, 1807); and Fitzpatrick, George Washington, 26:226.

[284]. John Fiske, "Facing Bankruptcy and Mutiny," *America* 4, 35.

[285]. Letter, 16 April 1784, quoted in Bergh, *Thomas Jefferson*, 4:219.

**GEORGE WASHINGTON: "THE ELEGANT EXERCISE OF POWER"
—A STUDY IN THE RARE, PURE EXERCISE OF MORTAL AUTHORITY**

Washington Resigns as Continental Commander in Chief

History is filled with examples of military leaders who, at the close of the conflict they had been called to resolve, found themselves in control of the means of consolidating power within their own personal grasp. Succumbing to the siren call and allure of power, they thereby became the subduing tyrant over those they had been entrusted and commissioned to protect and defend. At the close of the Revolutionary War, Washington found himself not only in the position as the man who controlled the only organized armed force in the nation, but also as the man most adored and looked upon by the nation as their natural leader. Lesser men would have taken advantage of the opportunity and grasped for amalgamated personal power that could be solidified into an ongoing power base. Washington's actions as the war was brought to a close speak volumes of the character of the man and his disdain for "power-mongering." It would appear that he could not divest himself of the burden of power quickly enough! After the peace treaty between the United States and Britain had been signed, Washington waited until the British troops had been withdrawn from New York at the end of November 1783; then he bade farewell to his officers on December 4 and rode on to Annapolis to report to Congress and resign his commission.

Washington Resigns His Commission

His report and resignation was characteristically brief and to the point. In addition, it was self-effacing and humbly recognized the hand of God in the success of the revolution. He invoked the protection of the Almighty God upon the nation and then left, assuming he had put public life and all associated power behind him forever:

> Mr. President, The great events on which my resignation depended having at length taken place, I have now the honor of offering my sincere congratulations to Congress, and of presenting myself before them to surrender into their hands

the trust committed to me, and to claim the indulgence of retiring from the service of my country.

Happy in the confirmation of our independence and sovereignty, and pleased with the opportunity afforded the United States, of becoming a respectable nation, I resign with satisfaction the appointment I accepted with diffidence—a diffidence in my abilities to accomplish so arduous a task; which however was superseded by a confidence in the rectitude of our cause, the support of the supreme power of the Union, and the patronage of Heaven.

The successful termination of the war has verified the most sanguine expectations; and my gratitude for the interposition of providence, and the assistance I have received from my countrymen, increases with every review of the momentous contest.

While I repeat my obligations to the army in general, I should do injustice to my own feelings not to acknowledge, in this place, the peculiar services and distinguished merits of the gentlemen who have been attached to my person during the war. It was impossible the choice of confidential officers to compose my family should have been more fortunate. Permit me, sir, to recommend in particular, those who have continued in the service to the present moment, as worthy of the favorable notice and patronage of Congress.

I consider it as an indispensable duty to close this last act of my official life by commending the interests of our dearest country to the protection of Almighty God, and those who have the superintendence of them to His holy keeping.

Having now finished the work assigned me, I retire from the great theater of action, and bidding an affectionate farewell to this August body, under whose orders I have so long acted, I here offer my commission, and take my leave of all the employments of public life.[286]

THE CONSTITUTIONAL CONVENTION OF 1787

But Washington's desire for quietude and private life was not to be. His advice and counsel was constantly sought even in his self-imposed retirement. And as the nation teetered on the brink of dissolution under the faulty first constitution, the Articles of

---

[286.] George Washington, Allen Collection, 272-3; also, William Gordon, "Washington Resigns His Commission," *America* 3, 311-12.

GEORGE WASHINGTON: "THE ELEGANT EXERCISE OF POWER" — A STUDY IN THE RARE, PURE EXERCISE OF MORTAL AUTHORITY

Confederation, noble patriots sought to bring about a constitutional convention to correct the defects of the Articles. Washington was recognized by all who cared about the nation as the one essential delegate that must participate in the convention if the proposed convention was to have a prayer of a chance. Consequently, as plans were made to call a convention together in Philadelphia in 1787, George Washington received much pressure to participate. His home state of Virginia named him as a delegate to represent them, and other prominent and influential individuals whom Washington respected made numerous and gracious requests that he involve himself, but Washington not only hesitated, he seemed to genuinely wish that others who are more qualified (in his mind) be called to the task. He seemed to be unaware of how essential his participation was to a nation that was struggling to find its way.

Washington made numerous attempts to decline the position of delegate to the convention:

In a November 18, 1786, letter to James Madison, he mentions that he is honored with the request to participate, but cites his inability for a number of reasons.[287]

In response to another request from James Madison imploring his participation, he again attempts (December 16, 1786) to graciously extricate himself with numerous logical explanations.[288]

Edmund Randolph

---

[287] George Washington, Allen Collection, 343.
[288] George Washington, Allen Collection, 344-6.

In response (December 21, 1786) to notification from Virginia governor Edmund Randolph that the Virginia General Assembly had appointed him as a delegate to the convention, he expressed that while he felt greatly honored, he was not able to accept and suggested that another be named in his stead.[289]

As he struggled with the pressure he was receiving to go to the convention, he wrote a letter to David Humphreys (December 26, 1786) asking for his advice in the matter, but stating, "I have no inclination to go."[290]

On February 3, 1787, Washington informed Henry Knox of the efforts that were being made to influence him to attend the convention but that he had refused and that "it is not, at this time, my purpose to attend."[291]

In a March 10, 1787, letter to the secretary of foreign affairs, in which he considers the proposed task of the soon-to-be-convened convention, he mentions, "My name is in the delegation to this convention; but it was put there contrary to my desires, and remains contrary to my request."[292]

But finally, after much soul-searching, and full of a sense of duty to his country, Washington finally assents to attend the convention in a letter to Governor Edmund Randolph (March 28, 1787):

> It was the decided intention of the letter I had the honor of writing to your excellency the 21st. of December last, to inform you, that it would not be convenient for me to attend the Convention proposed to be holden in Philadelphia in May next; and I had entertained hopes that another had been, or soon would be, appointed in my place; inasmuch as it is not only inconvenient for me to leave home, but because there will be, I apprehend, too much cause to charge my conduct with inconsistency, in again appearing on a public theater after a public declaration to the contrary; and because it will, I fear, have a tendency to sweep me back into the tide of public affairs, when retirement and ease is so essentially necessary for, and is so much desired by me.
>
> However, as my friends, with a degree of solicitude which is unusual, seem to wish for my attendance on this occasion, I have come to a resolution to go, if my health will permit . . . .
>
> I hope your excellency will be found among the attending delegates. I should be glad to be informed who the others are . . . [293]

---

289. George Washington, Allen Collection, 347.
290. George Washington, Allen Collection, 352-3.
291. George Washington, Allen Collection, 354.
292. George Washington, Allen Collection, 358.
293. George Washington, Allen Collection, 359-60.

**GEORGE WASHINGTON: "THE ELEGANT EXERCISE OF POWER"
— A STUDY IN THE RARE, PURE EXERCISE OF MORTAL AUTHORITY**

So it was with great reluctance that Washington "recanted" his retirement and returned to public involvement. His words reflect a man who felt an obligation to abide in his previous public pronouncement of retirement, but felt a greater obligation to serve when called. He also inferred a regretful premonition that this action would draw him more fully back into full public service.

The convention was convened, and Washington was elected unanimously (as was ever the case) to act as president of the convention. And it would seem that those who sat in the convention fully understood that, as they wrote the duties of the president into the new constitution, they were writing the job description for the man who presided over their efforts to compose the charter under which liberty was to be preserved and under which the nation was to operate.

THE PRESIDENCY

After a grueling ratification process that resulted in the ratification of the new constitution, the new government of the United States was constituted under the new charter. Electors were selected as required under article 2, section 1 of the Constitution. The electors cast their votes, and Washington was unanimously elected as the first president of the United States. Duty called, and in spite of his reluctance to assume public office, Washington again answered the call of his countrymen.

George Washington Inauguration

His first inaugural address captures so much of the essence of the man and his moral character and his great hopes and yearnings for the nation he loved so dearly. He speaks eloquently of his love of the nation, of his concerns that he is inadequate to the responsibility that has been delegated to him, of the call to duty that motivated his acceptance of the responsibility, of his recognition of the hand of God in every aspect of the nation's struggles and successes, of his gratitude, of the importance of morality and virtue if the nation is to be all it is ordained to be, of the necessity of the nation's obedience to God's rules of order and right if liberty and the republican form of government is to be preserved, of his hopes that the people only modify the form of government after the most careful consideration and only through the process established within the Constitution, and of him again declining any salary for his service in the office that he was honored to hold. He closed with a petition to the divine and sought to turn the people to that source, rather than aggrandize himself as he assumed the highest office of the land:

Fellow-Citizens of the Senate and of the House of Representatives:

Among the vicissitudes incident to life no event could have filled me with greater anxieties than that of which the notification was transmitted by your order, and received on the 14th day of the present month. On the one hand, I was summoned by my country, whose voice I can never hear but with veneration and love, from a retreat which I had chosen with the fondest predilection, and, in my flattering hopes, with an immutable decision, as the asylum of my declining years—a retreat which was rendered every day more necessary as well as more dear to me by the addition of habit to inclination, and of frequent interruptions in my health to the gradual waste committed on it by time. On the other hand, the magnitude and difficulty of the trust to which the voice of my country called me, being sufficient to awaken in the wisest and most experienced of her citizens a distrustful scrutiny into his qualifications, could not but overwhelm with despondence one who (inheriting inferior endowments from nature and unpracticed in the duties of civil administration) ought to be peculiarly conscious of his own deficiencies. In this conflict of emotions all I dare aver is that it has been my faithful study to collect my duty from a just appreciation of every circumstance by which it might be affected. All I dare hope is that if, in executing this task, I have been too much swayed by a grateful remembrance of former instances, or by an affectionate sensibility to this transcendent proof of the confidence of my fellow-citizens, and have thence too little consulted my incapacity as well as disinclination for the weighty and untried cares before me, my error will be palliated by the motives which mislead me, and its consequences be judged by my country with some share of the partiality in which they originated.

Such being the impressions under which I have, in obedience to the public summons, repaired to the present station, it would be peculiarly improper to omit in this first official act my fervent supplications to that Almighty Being who rules over the universe, who presides in the councils of nations, and whose providential aids can supply every human defect, that His benediction may consecrate to the

GEORGE WASHINGTON: "THE ELEGANT EXERCISE OF POWER" — A STUDY IN THE RARE, PURE EXERCISE OF MORTAL AUTHORITY

liberties and happiness of the people of the United States a Government instituted by themselves for these essential purposes, and may enable every instrument employed in its administration to execute with success the functions allotted to his charge. In tendering this homage to the Great Author of every public and private good, I assure myself that it expresses your sentiments not less than my own, nor those of my fellow-citizens at large less than either. No people can be bound to acknowledge and adore the Invisible Hand which conducts the affairs of men more than those of the United States. Every step by which they have advanced to the character of an independent nation seems to have been distinguished by some token of providential agency; and in the important revolution just accomplished in the system of their united government the tranquil deliberations and voluntary consent of so many distinct communities from which the event has resulted can not be compared with the means by which most governments have been established without some return of pious gratitude, along with an humble anticipation of the future blessings which the past seem to presage. These reflections, arising out of the present crisis, have forced themselves too strongly on my mind to be suppressed. You will join with me, I trust, in thinking that there are none under the influence of which the proceedings of a new and free government can more auspiciously commence.

By the article establishing the executive department it is made the duty of the President "to recommend to your consideration such measures as he shall judge necessary and expedient." The circumstances under which I now meet you will acquit me from entering into that subject further than to refer to the great constitutional charter under which you are assembled, and which, in defining your powers, designates the objects to which your attention is to be given. It will be more consistent with those circumstances, and far more congenial with the feelings which actuate me, to substitute, in place of a recommendation of particular measures, the tribute that is due to the talents, the rectitude, and the patriotism which adorn the characters selected to devise and adopt them. In these honorable qualifications I behold the surest pledges that as on one side no local prejudices or attachments, no separate views nor party animosities, will misdirect the comprehensive and equal eye which ought to watch over this great assemblage of communities and interests, so, on another, that the foundation of our national policy will be laid in the pure and immutable principles of private morality, and the preeminence of free government be exemplified by all the attributes which can win the affections of its citizens and command the respect of the world. I dwell on this prospect with every satisfaction which an ardent love for my country can inspire, since there is no truth more thoroughly established than that there exists in the economy and course of nature an indissoluble union between virtue and happiness; between duty and advantage; between the genuine maxims of an honest and magnanimous policy and the solid rewards of public prosperity and felicity; since we ought to be no less persuaded that the propitious smiles of Heaven can never be expected on a nation that disregards the eternal rules of order and right which Heaven itself has ordained; and since the preservation of the sacred fire of liberty and the destiny of the republican model of government are justly considered, perhaps, as deeply, as finally, staked on the experiment entrusted to the hands of the American people.

Besides the ordinary objects submitted to your care, it will remain with your judgment to decide how far an exercise of the occasional power delegated by the fifth article of the Constitution is rendered expedient at the present juncture by the nature of objections which have been urged against the system, or by the degree of inquietude which has given birth to them. Instead of undertaking particular recommendations on this subject, in which I could be guided by no lights derived from official opportunities, I shall again give way to my entire confidence in your discernment and pursuit of the public good; for I assure myself that whilst you carefully avoid every alteration which might endanger the benefits of an united and effective government, or which ought to await the future lessons of experience, a reverence for the characteristic rights of freemen and a regard for the public harmony will sufficiently influence your deliberations on the question how far the former can be impregnably fortified or the latter be safely and advantageously promoted.

To the foregoing observations I have one to add, which will be most properly addressed to the House of Representatives. It concerns myself, and will therefore be as brief as possible. When I was first honored with a call into the service of my country, then on the eve of an arduous struggle for its liberties, the light in which I contemplated my duty required that I should renounce every pecuniary compensation. From this resolution I have in no instance departed; and being still under the impressions which produced it, I must decline as inapplicable to myself any share in the personal emoluments which may be indispensably included in a permanent provision for the executive department, and must accordingly pray that the pecuniary estimates for the station in which I am placed may during my continuance in it be limited to such actual expenditures as the public good may be thought to require.

Having thus imparted to you my sentiments as they have been awakened by the occasion which brings us together, I shall take my present leave; but not without resorting once more to the benign Parent of the Human Race in humble supplication that, since He has been pleased to favor the American people with opportunities for deliberating in perfect tranquillity, and dispositions for deciding with unparalleled unanimity on a form of government for the security of their union and the advancement of their happiness, so His divine blessing may be equally conspicuous in the enlarged views, the temperate consultations, and the wise measures on which the success of this Government must depend.[294]

EXAMPLES OF WASHINGTON'S WISHES TO DIVEST HIMSELF OF POWER

Based upon Washington's personal correspondence, his interest in withdrawing from the trappings of personal power and from the light of public life was genuine and real. Allen's collection of Washington's documents incorporates sufficiently numerous references to this wish, through Washington's own pen, to make the position unassailable. Other more expansive collections of Washington's writings make the position even surer. The position was stated and restated throughout his life, beginning early in his experience, even before the close of the French and Indian War and continuing through his presidential administrations and beyond. A few examples must suffice.

From a August 15, 1786, letter to John Jay:

> Retired as I am from the world, I frankly acknowledge I cannot feel myself an unconcerned spectator. Yet having happily assisted in bringing the ship into port & having been fairly discharged; it is not my business to embark again on the sea of troubles.[295]

In a April 25, 1788, letter to John Armstrong, Washington recalls that he was called out of retirement to fulfill his duty to the nation as the Constitution was created, but hopes he may quietly return to his private life:

> I well remember the observation you made in your letter to me of last year, "that my domestic retirement must suffer an interruption." This took place, notwithstanding it was utterly repugnant to my feelings, my interests, and my wishes; I sacrificed every private consideration and personal enjoyment to the earnest and pressing solicitations of those who saw and knew the alarming situation of our public concerns, and had no other end in view but to promote the interests of their Country; and conceiving, that under those circumstances, and at so critical a moment, and absolute refusal to act, might, on my part, be construed as a total dereliction of my Country, if imputed to no worse motives. Altho' you say the same motives induce you to think that another tour of duty of this kind will fall my lot, I cannot but hope that you will be disappointed, for I am so wedded to a state of retirement and find occupations

---

[294.] George Washington, Allen Collection, 460-3; George Washington's first inaugural address.
[295.] George Washington, Allen Collection, 334.

of a rural life so congenial; with my feelings, that to be drawn into public at my advanced age, could be a sacrifice that would admit of no compensation.[296]

In a April 28, 1788, letter to Marquis De Lafayette, Washington disavowed any interest in becoming president of the United States, saying,

> My decided predilection, is, that, (at my time of life and under my circumstances) the increasing infirmities of nature and the growing love of retirement do not permit me to entertain a wish beyond that of living and dying an honest man on my own farm. Let those follow the pursuits of ambition and fame, who have a keener relish for them, or who may have more years, in store, for the enjoyment.[297]

When faced with the possibility (probability) of being selected as the first president of the United States, Washington demurred to Alexander Hamilton in an August 28, 1788, letter,

> For you know me well enough, my good Sir, to be persuaded, that I am not guilty of affectation, when I tell you, that it is my great and sole desire to live and die, in peace and retirement on my own farm.[298]

In a May 10, 1789, letter to the United Baptist Churches in Virginia, Washington recalled the God-given victory of the Revolutionary War and of his only desire at the close of that conflict to step away from office and that only his sense of duty compelled him to return to public life:

> After we had by the smiles of Heaven on our exertions, obtained the object for which we contended, I retired at the conclusion of the war, with an idea that my country would have no farther occasion for my services, and with the intention of never entering again into public life. But when the exigency of my country seemed to require me once more to engage in public affairs, an honest conviction of duty superseded my former resolution, and became my apology for deviating from the happy plan which I had adopted.[299]

On January 9, 1790, Washington wrote to Catherine Macaulay Graham,

---

[296]. George Washington, Allen Collection, 386-7.
[297]. George Washington, Allen Collection, 392-3.
[298]. George Washington, Allen Collection, 417.
[299]. George Washington, Allen Collection, 532.

> Nothing short of an absolute conviction of duty could ever have brought me upon the scenes of public life again.[300]

On June 15, 1790, Washington wrote to David Stuart of his disdain of the accouterments of office, saying,

> Pride and dignity of office, which God knows has no charm for me? For I can truly say I had rather be at Mount Vernon with a friend or two about me, than to be attended at the Seat of Government by the Officers of State and the Representatives of every Power in Europe.[301]

During his first term as president of the United States, Washington often entertained thoughts of leaving the office at the soonest possible opportunity, as noted in this May 20, 1792, letter to James Madison:

> Without being able to dispose my mind to a longer continuation in the Office I have now the honor to hold. I therefore still look forward to the fulfillment of my fondest and most ardent wishes to spend the remainder of my days (which I cannot expect will be many) in ease and tranquility.[302]

WASHINGTON'S FAREWELL

At the time he determined to make his final farewell to pubic office and service, Washington wished to transmit a few parting words of advise and wisdom to the nation he had loved and served so unequivocally for his entire lifetime. His Farewell Address was published on September 19, 1796. In it, he begins by definitively stating that he was stepping away from the office that he had held and that he would not be willing to be considered again for the assignment. He mentions his ongoing yearning for his long-delayed retirement and his wish that he could have left the office behind at an earlier date, saying,

> The acceptance of and continuance hitherto in the office to which your suffrages have twice called me have been a uniform sacrifice of inclination to the opinion of duty and to a deference for what appeared to be your desire. I constantly hoped that it would have been much earlier in my power, consistently with motives which I was not at liberty to disregard, to return to that retirement from which I had been reluctantly drawn. The strength of my inclination to do this previous to the last election had even led to

---

[300]. George Washington, Allen Collection, 537.
[301]. George Washington, Allen Collection, 544.
[302]. George Washington, Allen Collection, 567.

the preparation of an address to declare it to you; but mature reflection on the then perplexed and critical posture of our affairs with foreign nations and the unanimous advice of persons entitled to my confidence impelled me to abandon the idea. I rejoice that the state of your concerns, external as well as internal, no longer renders the pursuit of inclination incompatible with the sentiment of duty or propriety, and am persuaded, whatever partiality may be retained for my services, that in the present circumstances of our country you will not disapprove my determination to retire.

The impressions with which I first undertook the arduous trust were explained on the proper occasion. In the discharge of this trust I will only say that I have, with good intentions, contributed toward the organization and administration of the Government the best exertions of which a very fallible judgment was capable, Not unconscious in the outset of the inferiority of my qualifications, experience in my own eyes, perhaps still more in the eyes of others, has strengthened the motives to diffidence of myself; and every day the increasing weight of years admonishes me more and more that the shade of retirement is as necessary to me as it will be welcome. Satisfied that if any circumstances have given peculiar value to my services they were temporary, I have the consolation to believe that, while choice and prudence invite me to quit the political scene, patriotism does not forbid it.[303]

He then went on to offer sound advice that, had it been unconditionally and unswervingly followed by the nation, the sound foundation upon which this nation was established would not be so badly eroded and warped as it is in the twenty-first century. The purpose of this review is not to review and expand upon the timeless monumental and magnificent wisdom of Washington's Farewell Address in its entirety, but to only touch upon the counsel he gave therein regarding power, its appropriate use, and likely abuses that must be guarded against.

In the body of his farewell, he eloquently and explicitly warned the nation against many of the efforts that certainly would be made (and which certainly have been and are being made) to usurp power within the nation. He warned of the power of parties within the nation's political structure, saying,

However combinations or associations of the above description may now and then answer popular ends, they are likely in the course of time and things to become potent engines by which cunning, ambitious, and unprincipled men will be enabled to subvert the power of the people, and to usurp for themselves the reins of government, destroying, afterwards the very engines which have lifted them to unjust dominion.[304]

[303.] George Washington, Allen Collection, 513; also, Richardson, *Messages and Papers*, 1:205-6.
[304.] George Washington, Allen Collection, 518-19; also, Richardson, *Messages and Papers*, 1:210.

GEORGE WASHINGTON: "THE ELEGANT EXERCISE OF POWER" — A STUDY IN THE RARE, PURE EXERCISE OF MORTAL AUTHORITY

Adding additional warning against party faction, saying it will ultimately lead to accrual of unbounded power—usually gathered into the hands of an individual tyrant, he stated,

> The alternate domination of one faction over another, sharpened by the spirit of revenge natural to party dissension, which in different ages and countries has perpetrated the most horrid enormities, is itself a frightful despotism. But this leads at length to a more formal and permanent despotism. The disorders and miseries which result gradually incline the minds of men to seek security and repose in the absolute power of an individual, and sooner or later the chief of some prevailing faction, more able or more fortunate than his competitors, turns this disposition to the purposes of his own elevation on the ruins of public liberty.[305]

He warned of the influence of foreign power and its efforts to derail the sound government that had been established for the nation. He warned of enemies who seek power within government "covertly and insidiously."[306] He warned of "designing men"[307] who subvert the nation to advance their position. In general, it may be stated that he warned the nation to be vigilant and jealously guard against arrogations of power that would lead to the loss of the nation's liberty.

Washington was painfully aware of the dangers of power and mankind's tendency to seek and then begin to abuse power, and he warned the nation to keep the power of government within the proper bounds that had been established as the nation was brought into being. Substantial portions of his Farewell Address are devoted to counsel. He explicitly warned against allowing those who hold power to stray beyond the bounds set by the charter of the nation, the United States Constitution, saying,

> It is important, likewise, that the habits of thinking in a free country should inspire caution in those intrusted with its administration to confine themselves within their respective constitutional spheres, avoiding in the exercise of the powers of one department to encroach upon another. The spirit of encroachment tends to consolidate the powers of all the departments in one, and thus to create, whatever the form of government, a real despotism. A just estimate of that love of power and proneness to abuse it which predominates in the human heart is sufficient to satisfy us of the truth of this position. The necessity of reciprocal checks in the exercise of political power, by dividing and distributing it into different depositories, and constituting each the guardian of the public weal against invasions by the others, has been evinced by experiments ancient and modern, some of them in our country and under our own eyes. To preserve them must be as necessary as

---

[305] George Washington, Allen Collection, 520; also, Richardson, *Messages and Papers*, 1:211.
[306] George Washington, Allen Collection, 515; also, Richardson, *Messages and Papers*, 1:207.
[307] George Washington, Allen Collection, 517; also, Richardson, *Messages and Papers*, 1:208-9.

to institute them. If in the opinion of the people the distribution or modification of the constitutional powers be in any particular wrong, let it be corrected by an amendment in the way which the Constitution designates. But let there be no change by usurpation; for though this in one instance may be the instrument of good, it is the customary weapon by which free governments are destroyed. The precedent must always greatly overbalance in permanent evil any partial or transient benefit which the use can at any time yield.[308]

In light of this knowledge, it is interesting to note Washington's devotion to constitutional limits of power within which he sought to live while he held the office and did not have the constraint of prior precedent to hold him back from licentious use of the power that could have been gathered to the executive office. In a letter to Alexander Hamilton dated May 15, 1796, Washington expressed that his wish was to make certain that he was understood as never seeking to expand the power of the president beyond what was defined in the United States Constitution:

I could have *no* view in extending the Powers of the Executive beyond the limits prescribed by the Constitution.[309]

And he followed that dictum in daily application to the challenges that faced him as the president. As he faced a difficult situation with the French, Washington corresponded with Alexander Hamilton on June 26, 1796, and expressed to him his desire to respond appropriately within the constraints of the Constitution:

Let me ask therefore. Do you suppose that the Executive, in the recess of the Senate, has power in such a case as the one before us, especially if the measure should not be *avowed* by authority, to send a special character to Paris, as Envoy Extraordinary, to give, and receive explanations? . . . If then an Envoy cannot be sent to Paris without the agency of the Senate, will the information you have received, admitting it should be realized, be sufficient ground for convening that body?

These are serious things; they may be productive of serious consequences; and therefore require very serious and cool deliberation.[310]

Even after leaving public office, and the power and glory associated (by some) with it, George Washington, ever the private man, included in his last will and testament a clause that he not be rendered great and public oblations upon his burial, stating,

---

[308]. George Washington, Allen Collection, 521-2; also, Richardson, *Messages and Papers*, 1:211-12.
[309]. George Washington, Allen Collection, 34; emphasis in the original.
[310]. George Washington, Allen Collection, 638.

**GEORGE WASHINGTON: "THE ELEGANT EXERCISE OF POWER"
— A STUDY IN THE RARE, PURE EXERCISE OF MORTAL AUTHORITY**

And it is my express desire that my Corpse may be Interred in a private manner, without parade, or funeral Oration.[311]

CONCLUSION

And so we end where we began.

Rare indeed is the mortal individual who obtains power and then eschews it when it is apparent that it may be held and expanded at will. George Washington was such a rare man. During his lifetime, he was constantly offered power. He resisted its allures, accepting it only when he felt duty-bound to fulfill his responsibility to his fellow countrymen, and then, when the duty was fulfilled, he would quickly divest himself of the power so he could return to his role as a "common" man. In spite of his best efforts to live his life unfettered by the accouterments of power and publicity, he was called upon incessantly during his forty-five-year labor of love for his country to shoulder power and exert a leadership role that would have corrupted lesser men. In many ways, he was a duty-bound servant that selflessly labored on behalf of the cause of liberty for his fellow man.

Washington was, indeed, "first in war, first in peace, and first in the hearts of his countrymen."[312] He was all of that and more. He was the "indispensable man" in all of the magnificent events that unfolded in his lifetime. And he proved himself worthy of the undying love of his countrymen, as well as their trust that he would never become their tyrant. Power held no allure for him. He loved liberty, and he lived his life to obtain it for himself and his countrymen, as well as all posterity. Washington lived a life that bears testimony that liberty was and is a God-given gift that is meant for all mankind. He lived a life that bears testimony that (however rare) it is possible for mere mortals to elegantly and righteously exercise power—eschewing unrighteous dominion over their fellow man. Would to God that such men as George Washington may once again be brought forth to lead a nation that so desperately needs such a leader!

[311.] George Washington, Allen Collection, 679.

[312.] General Henry Lee ("Lighthorse" Harry Lee), eulogy in memory of George Washington, 26 December 1799, Philadelphia; also, resolution prepared by General Lee and presented to the House of Representatives by John Marshall.

16.

Our Sacred Honor: Our Modern Duty to Preserve Our Liberties

Recommended Resources for the Serious Student:

* Lives of the Signers of the Declaration of Independence, a reprint of an 1848 original, published by WallBuilders Press.
* Wives of the Signers, The Women behind the Declaration of Independence. Excerpted from The Pioneer Mothers of America, originally published in 1912. Reprinted by WallBuilders Press.

It would seem that all who have the ability to think must be aware that modern America faces challenging times!

In recent years, the world has become heavily exposed to Christian author J. R. R. Tolkien's monumental epic book *The Lord of the Rings* about challenges and the lust for power and its effects upon character. Those who are familiar with the book and movies will admit that the times depicted were extremely challenging!

At one point, while lamenting their difficult circumstances, Frodo said,

> "I wish it need not have happened in my time!"

> "So do I," said Gandalf, "and so do all who live to see such times. But that is not for them to decide. All we have to decide is what to do with the time that is given us."[313]

The citizens of this nation have a heritage of faith-filled courageous forebears. We are the blessed beneficiaries of forebears who braved the great deep in little wooden ships and came to a forbidding wilderness to obtain the freedom they sought.

---

[313]. J. R. R. Tolkien, *Lord of the Rings: The Fellowship of the Rings* (Harper Collins Publishers, 1994), 50.

OUR SACRED HONOR: OUR MODERN DUTY TO PRESERVE OUR LIBERTIES

Many have ancestors who crossed the great plains of America and settled the barren valleys of the West on a similar quest. These brave souls proved their mettle in the face of unbelievable challenges.

What are modern Americans made of today? Are we of similar mettle and strength?

While many today would prefer to wrap themselves in a security blanket and safety net, others find challenges to be invigorating and relish the opportunity to demonstrate their strength, dedication, devotion, and growth.

Such individuals seem to be sustained by an inner fire that kindles other fires. Such individuals light the way and provide the vision that others may gain the faith to step forward and stretch their souls to reach higher heights than they imagined possible.

Such are those who have led the cause of liberty throughout history. Often, their efforts are based solely in faith, for there are no other apparent reasons to believe they will succeed; but as these intrepid souls continue forward in faith, they come to a more sure knowledge that God is with this great cause of liberty and that He will sustain them. Faith then grows beyond faith to assurance.

And there are almost countless examples that may be cited in life that confirm that we need challenges in order to grow and increase in strength and goodness.

And in times of great challenge or opportunity, there always must be a vanguard to go before and set the path and mark the way. Those in the vanguard are the hardy ones who clear the sage brush and prepare the fields so that crops may be planted and the harvest prepared for those that will follow.

Often, the vanguard faces extraordinary challenges and much discouragement. But that has always been the way, and those today who seek a restoration of liberty and proper government should not expect their lot to be different.

It would be foolish to expect that so celestial an article as freedom would not be challenged by world class opposition, as exemplified in the previous lecture about revolutions that produced tyranny and oppression. But rather than cause liberty-loving Americans to capitulate and retreat in fear and doubt, noting the magnitude and strength of the challenges should cause one's resolve to quicken and courageous determination to obtain victory to increase. And history has demonstrated the assurance that sacrifices in the cause of liberty are sanctifying.

And it would be exceptionally presumptuous on the part of those who cherish liberty to assume that they will merit the same reward as those who offered their all in sacrifice for this great and noble cause of liberty unless they, in like manner, are willing to offer the sacrifices necessary to preserve it.

Consider the regard felt for those that went before and set the path and marked the way in the cause of liberty and proper government. Indeed, it is more than regard the nation feels for them—it is the deepest reverence and respect. Those who went before are owed a debt that can only be approached by preserving that which they sacrificed so much to obtain. Perhaps a brief review will help provide understanding:

Early in his professional life, John Adams wrote to his wife explaining what he felt he must do to prepare himself for leadership in the "divine science" of politics. He wrote,

> The science of government is my duty to study, more than all other sciences; the arts of legislation and administration and negotiation ought to take place of, indeed

to exclude, in a manner, all other arts. I must study politics and war, that my sons may have liberty to study mathematics and philosophy. My sons ought to study mathematics and philosophy, geography, natural history and naval architecture, navigation, commerce, and agriculture, in order to give their children a right to study painting, poetry, music, architecture, statuary, tapestry, and porcelain.[314]

Today, each must consider their duty in this matter. Most Americans have ignored our responsibility in the science of government to the point that proper government, in practice, has become almost extinct in modern times. It is a matter that bears careful consideration today!

A brief backward glance reveals what it took to bring forth the liberty that generations of Americans have taken for granted:

In the years that preceded the Revolutionary War, a long train of abuses and usurpations by the British Crown against the colonists led to discontent. The citizens began to feel the heavy hand of tyranny and onerous taxation, the representative governments of the people had been ignored or abolished and replaced by officials of the crown, an effort was underway to disarm them, and justice was no longer available in the courts. In spite of pleadings and efforts at peaceful negotiation, nothing was done to lighten their burdens.

By 1775 the pressure had reached boiling point. The tension between the British and the colonists exploded into battle in April 1775 when British soldiers marched on Lexington and Concord, Massachusetts, in an attempt to confiscate the rebel's cache of weapons and to capture Samuel Adams and John Hancock, the men held largely responsible for the growing tide of dissent in the colonies.

Battle of Lexington

[314.] Quoted in Adrienne Koch, ed., *The American Enlightenment* (New York: George Braziller, 1965), 188.

OUR SACRED HONOR: OUR MODERN DUTY TO PRESERVE OUR LIBERTIES

The residents of Concord were forewarned and faced the British at Concord Bridge. The elite British soldiers were forced to make a hasty retreat back to Boston. All along their fifteen-mile march back, they were harassed by the patriots firing from behind trees, rocks, and fences. And they failed to capture John Hancock and Samuel Adams or confiscate their cache of guns and ammunition.

These early patriots were not conscripts who were compelled to arms by a draft board; they were volunteers who loved freedom; they were common folk like you and me today—farmers, craftsmen, laborers, husbands, fathers, and sons. But their courage set them apart as anything but common as they stood shoulder to shoulder on the principle of freedom, and as the shot that was heard around the world was fired, the revolution was begun.

But even as battle lines were drawn, many held back and shrank from the conflict. The following are the stirring pleas of the man who gave the nation the mighty battle cry—"give me liberty, or give me death!"—Patrick Henry:

> They tell us that we are weak; unable to cope with so formidable an adversary. But when, sir, shall we be stronger? Will it be the next week, or the next year? Will it be when we are totally disarmed, and when a British guard shall be stationed in every house? Shall we gather strength by irresolution and inaction? Shall we acquire the means of effectual resistance by lying supinely on our backs, and hugging the delusive phantom of hope, until our enemies shall have bound us hand and foot? Sir, we are not weak, if we make proper use of the means which the God of Nature hath place in our power.
>
> Three millions of people, armed in the holy cause of liberty, and in such a country as that which we possess, are invincible by any force which our enemy can send against us. Besides, sir, we shall not fight our battles alone. There is a just God who presides over the destinies of nations; and who will raise up friends to fight our battles for us. The battle, sir, is not to the strong alone; it is to the vigilant, the active, the brave. Besides, sir, we have no election. If we were base enough to desire it, it is now too late to retire from the contest. There is no retreat but in submission and slavery! Our chains are forged. Their clanking may be heard on the Plains of Boston! The war is inevitable—and, let it come! I repeat it, sir, let it come!
>
> It is in vain, sir, to extenuate the matter. Gentlemen may cry peace, peace—but there is no peace. The war is actually begun. The next gale that sweeps from the North will bring to our ears the clash of resounding arms! Our brethren are already in the field! Why stand we here idle? What is it that gentlemen wish? What would they have? Is life so dear, or peace so sweet, as to be purchased at the price of chains and slavery? Forbid it, Almighty God! I know not what course others may take; but as for me, give me liberty, or give me death![315]

[315.] William Wirt, Patrick Henry's call to arms, *Great Epochs in American History*, 3:108; Patrick Henry, "Give Me Liberty or Give Me Death," *America*, vol. 3, 117-18.

And so it was that the die was cast. They had much to lose—their lives and their fortunes—but more to gain—the blessings of freedom for themselves and their posterity! A year later, Thomas Jefferson—a man whose reputation, integrity, and honesty were above reproach—was asked to pen the words of the Declaration of Independence.

A previous lecture noted Jefferson's character that was reflected in a letter of advice he wrote to his young nephew, Peter Carr, in which he wrote,

> Rather than do an immoral act, give up money, fame, and everything the world contains; and never suppose under any circumstances it is best for you to do a dishonorable thing. Whenever you are inclined to do it, ask yourself how you would act were all the world looking at you.[316]

And that is how Jefferson lived his life. Others noted his character. When it came time to write the Declaration of Independence, it was suggested that John Adams take the assignment. He declined, indicating that Jefferson should perform the duty. He noted the following reasons that justified his position: first, Jefferson was a Virginian, and Virginia should take the lead in the matter; second, John Adams recognized that he had a personality that often grated on others, making his positions unpopular; and third, he noted that Jefferson wrote ten times better than he did.

Thus, the assignment to write the Declaration fell to Thomas Jefferson.

The immortal words of the Declaration of Independence reflect eternal truths upon which the foundation of the United States of America is built:

> We hold these truths to be self-evident, that all men are created equal, that they are endowed by their Creator with certain unalienable rights, that among these are life, liberty, and the pursuit of happiness—that to secure these rights, governments are instituted among men, deriving their just powers from the consent of the governed, that whenever any form of government becomes destructive of these ends, it is the right of the people to alter or abolish it, and to institute new government, laying its foundation on such principles, and organizing its powers in such form, as to them shall seem most likely to effect their safety and happiness.
>
> And for the support of this Declaration, with a firm reliance on the protection of Divine Providence, we mutually pledge to each other our lives, our fortunes, and our sacred honor.

[316.] Bergh, *Thomas Jefferson*, 5:82-7.

OUR SACRED HONOR: OUR MODERN DUTY TO PRESERVE OUR LIBERTIES

These men who brought forth the American Declaration of Independence were not wild-eyed radicals bent on destroying society—they were men of sound understanding who had much to lose, but sought the blessings of liberty for themselves and their posterity.

John Hancock

John Hancock was the first to sign. After writing his name in large bold letters, he is said to have stated,

> There, his majesty can now read my name without spectacles, and can now double his reward of 500 pounds for my head. That is my defiance. We must be unanimous. There must be no pulling different ways; we must all hang together.[317]

---

[317]. James Parton, "The Drafting of the Declaration of Independence," *Great Epochs in American History*, 3:136.

TO PRESERVE THE NATION

To which, the witty Ben Franklin, who was the oldest delegate at age seventy, is said to have responded, "Yes, we must all hang together, or most assuredly we shall all hang separately."

Interestingly, Edward Rutledge was the youngest delegate at age twenty-six.

Edward Rutledge

The brave men who stepped forward and signed the Declaration became instant traitors and subject to the king's vengeance and execution if captured. They became hunted criminals with a price on their heads. Many of their families were also hunted. True to their pledge made at the close of the Declaration of Independence, many of these men lost their lives, almost all lost their fortunes, but none of them lost their sacred honor!

Disaster and ruin was the lot of many of the signers. Nine died of wounds or hardships during the war. Five were jailed and brutally treated. One lost all thirteen

OUR SACRED HONOR: OUR MODERN DUTY TO PRESERVE OUR LIBERTIES

of his children. The wives, sons, and daughters of others were killed, imprisoned, harassed, or deprived of all material possessions. Seventeen signers lost everything they owned, and all of them were hunted as traitors, with most separated from their homes and families.

But none of the signers ever betrayed his pledged word. There were no defectors. No one changed his mind. Lives and fortunes were lost, but their sacred honor was never sacrificed.

Stephen Hopkins

At the signing, Stephen Hopkins, the second-oldest signer, was afflicted with palsy. As he signed, he said, "My hand trembles, but my heart does not."

When Charles Carroll, one of the newest delegates and one of the wealthiest men in America signed, one of the delegates is said to have whispered, "There go a few millions!"

TO PRESERVE THE NATION

Charles Carroll of Carrolton

And so it went through the rest of the states.

Philip Livingston

OUR SACRED HONOR: OUR MODERN DUTY TO PRESERVE OUR LIBERTIES

Philip Livingston lost two homes and much of his business property. He died in 1778, separated from his family by the war.

Francis Lewis was away when the British came to capture him, so his wife was seized and treated brutally and thrown into prison under foul conditions. She died shortly after being released on a prisoner exchange in 1778.

Francis Lewis

Lewis Morris

Lewis Morris lost his magnificent estate, which was sacked and burned. He lived in poverty for years.

John Hart

As British troops approached their home, John Hart's dying wife insisted that he leave her bedside so he could escape. He was hunted by soldiers and dogs and was forced to hide in the woods and caves of the Sourland Mountains during icy December weather. By the time he returned, his wife had died. His health soon failed, and he died within three years.

Richard Stockton

Richard Stockton was betrayed and seized and subjected to frequent beatings and starvation. He was released as an invalid and died shortly thereafter at age fifty-one.

OUR SACRED HONOR: OUR MODERN DUTY TO PRESERVE OUR LIBERTIES

Abraham Clark

Abraham Clark had two sons who were army officers and who were captured and accorded barbarous treatment on the hell ship *Jersey*. The British offered to free his sons if he would renounce the Declaration of Independence. He refused, stating that he had pledged his sacred honor to the cause of American independence. When Congress heard of the brutal treatment that was being inflicted on Abraham Clark's sons, they ordered George Washington to throw a British officer into a hole and starve him to death. When the British heard of the order, they began to treat the sons better. They survived their captivity, and Washington did not starve the British officer.

Thomas Nelson Jr

TO PRESERVE THE NATION

Thomas Nelson Jr. sacrificed his beautiful mansion and died in poverty. During the 1781 siege of Yorktown, the British had occupied Thomas Nelson Jr.'s mansion in Yorktown and were using it as a headquarters. As the American artillery pounded British targets in the city, Thomas Nelson Jr. noticed that they were not firing upon his home. When he asked them why, they replied that it was out of respect for him. Nelson assumed command of a cannon and promptly fired a round into his home, destroying it and killing some British officers.

Joseph Hewes

Joseph Hewes was a Quaker with a long pacifist heritage. He died a lonely man ostracized by principle from his Quaker friends and family. He died in 1779, having worked himself to death in the effort to establish a navy for the nation.

Arthur Middleton

OUR SACRED HONOR: OUR MODERN DUTY TO PRESERVE OUR LIBERTIES

Thomas Heyward Jr.   Edward Rutledge

Thomas Heyward Jr., Arthur Middleton, and Edward Rutledge, all of South Carolina, were captured and shipped to the Crown stockade in Florida. They were offered their freedom if they would renounce the Declaration. They refused. They were freed in 1781 through a prisoner exchange. During his captivity, Thomas Heyward's wife had died.

John Morton

John Morton was the first of the signers to die. He fell ill early in 1777 and died, rejected by his Tory friends and family.

TO PRESERVE THE NATION

"Tell them," he is said to have noted, "that they will live to see the hour when they shall acknowledge it to have been the most glorious service that I ever rendered to my country."

Such was the caliber of the men who signed the Declaration of Independence to guarantee the nation's rights to life, liberty, and the pursuit of happiness.

But *declaring* their independence did not automatically make it so! There were seven more arduous years of battles and struggle before victory was recognized.

The ink was hardly dry on the Declaration of Independence when twenty-five thousand British soldiers landed on New York's Long Island and laid waste most of the countryside.

There were many dark times wherein the outcome was not sure. Victories were too few and defeats too many. Men, arms, and resources were often scarce, and the agonies of Valley Forge and Morristown had to be faced.

And those who did not love freedom stood on the sidelines and watched.

Thomas Paine

Thomas Paine, whose fiery pen was worth a hundred thousand men in the field, captured the vision of the day with the following words:

These are the times that try men's souls. The summer soldier and the sunshine patriot will, in this crisis, shrink from the service of their country, but he that stands it now deserves the love and thanks of man and woman. Tyranny, like hell, is not easily conquered; yet we have this consolation with us that, the harder the conflict, the more glorious the triumph. What we obtain too cheap, we esteem too lightly; it is dearness only that gives everything its value. Heaven knows how to put a proper price upon its goods; and it would be strange, indeed, if so celestial an article as freedom should not be highly rated.[318]

Samuel Adam

Unfortunately, then, as always, there were many summer soldiers and sunshine patriots. Samuel Adams expressed his disdain for these poor creatures, saying,

> If ye love wealth better than liberty, the tranquility of servitude better than the animating contest of freedom, go home from us in peace. We ask not your counsels or arms. Crouch down and lick the hands which feed you. May your chains set lightly upon you, and may posterity forget that ye were our countrymen.[319]

[318.] Thomas Paine, *Common Sense*, 23 December 1776.
[319.] Samuel Adams, "On American Independence," *The World's Famous Orations*, 1:118.

TO PRESERVE THE NATION

Nathan Hale

There were others, however, like the young captain Nathan Hale, who, as the noose was tightened around his neck, in the moment before his death, cried out, "I only regret that I have but one life to lose for my country!"[320] He died a hero at age twenty-one, and his words live on as an inspiration for generations.

Washington Crossing the Deleware

---

[320]. William Jackson, *History of the American Nation*, 2:499.

OUR SACRED HONOR: OUR MODERN DUTY TO PRESERVE OUR LIBERTIES

The year 1776 did not see many military victories. But Washington's perilous crossing of the ice-choked Delaware during a howling night storm in prelude to his surprise Christmas Day attack on Trenton, New Jersey, led to a monumental and badly needed victory.

And in December of 1777, Washington entered Valley Forge, with his ten thousand men. As spring came, he wrote,

> No history now extant can furnish an instance of an army's suffering such uncommon hardships as ours has done. To see men without sufficient clothes to cover their nakedness, without blankets to lie on, without shoes (for the want of which their marches might be traced by the blood from their feet), and almost as often without provisions as with them, marching through the frost and snow, and at Christmas taking up their winter quarters within a day's march of the enemy, without a house or hut to cover them, with hard duty to perform and little or no strength to perform it with, and submitting to it without a murmur, is a proof of patience and obedience which in my opinion can scarce be paralleled.[321]

Washington and Lafayette at Valley Forge

Many of those who suffered and died during the conflict were buried in common graves that do not recognize the names of those interred there. The ground was hallowed by their service and their last full measure of sacrifice.

Washington pled in vain with the local population and with Congress for support during their struggles, so he took the matter to God. Often retiring to a quiet grove where he could be alone, he pled repeatedly, seeking relief for his suffering men.

In spite of all the cold, in spite of all the hunger and pain, in spite of all the difficulties, the victory is finally won—the nation was free!

Now there was a government to be established.

[321.] Valley Forge letter to John Banister, 21 April 1778, in Fitzpatrick, *George Washington*, 11:291.

TO PRESERVE THE NATION

The founders knew all too well the dangers of a charter that authorized excessive power to the government.

Throughout the hot summer of 1787, the noble delegates to the constitutional convention met in an effort to bring the wisdom of the ages to bear in order to form an entirely new government, based upon a new concept.

That concept was that mankind's rights were sacred gifts from God. That it was the purpose of government to protect and preserve those individual God-given rights.

The founders of this great nation clearly understood that a government that considers itself the source of rights is powerful enough to destroy those rights, so they sought most diligently to establish a government whose powers are few and well defined, a government whose powers are enumerated and limited to the specific powers granted to it by the people and the states.

The debates throughout that hot summer of 1787 were arduous, challenging, and often frustrating. During the heat of the debates, the wise Benjamin Franklin admonished the convention to seek the help of heaven, saying,

> Gentlemen, gentlemen!! The small progress we have made in these last weeks is monumental proof of the imperfections of human understanding. During the conflict with Great Britain we many times offered prayers for help in this very room. And our prayers were graciously answered. "I have lived, sir, a long time; and the longer I live, the more convincing proofs I see of this truth, that God governs in the affairs of men. And if a sparrow cannot fall to the ground without His notice, is it probable that an empire can rise without His aid? We have been assured, sir, in the sacred writings that 'except the Lord build the house, they labor in vain that build it.' I firmly believe this; and I also believe that, without his concurring aid, we shall succeed in this political building no better than the builders of Babel . . . .

Benjamin Franklin

I therefore beg leave to move that, henceforth, prayers imploring the assistance of heaven and its blessings on our deliberations be held in this assembly every morning before we proceed to business.[322]

The founders of this nation recognized that their prayers were answered, and many noted the hand of God in the successful completion of the new United States constitution. And they saw in this new constitution a great hope for mankind and an enduring liberty. Their vision was large, even expansive!

And as part of that vision, it was their hope to solve the great challenge of slavery that vexed the nation so that the vision could include all who dwell here. The slavery issue was a problem that many had hoped to resolve during the Constitutional Convention of 1787. The issue is one that received impassioned discussion during the convention. In an effort to emphasis the importance of resolving slavery, George Mason made the following comment in regard to the matter:

> As nations cannot be rewarded or punished in the next world, they must be in this. By an inevitable chain of causes and effects, Providence punishes national sins by national calamities.[323]

In spite of this understanding, the issue was not easily solved because of a great dilemma. While slavery had been prohibited in England, slavery had been encouraged in the colonies under the impression that slavery in America could result in greater economic benefit to investors in England. Large plantations, particularly in the South, had borrowed large sums of money from the Bank of England to purchase slaves to work the plantations. The plantation owners, in many instances, had mortgaged their land to the Bank of England as collateral for the slave loans. If the new constitution abolished slavery, and thereby the slaves were set free, plantation loans would default, and the Bank of England would repossess the plantations—thereby resulting in England again taking possession of the South.

It was recognized that with that risk, the states that held slaves would not ratify the new constitution, and the effort to create the "more perfect union" they sought to bring into existence would fail. Thereby, without the ratification of the new constitution, the nation would fail, and slavery would never be abolished because the national framework would not exist to bring the abolition about.

The hope was that within a relatively short period—twenty years—the nation would be able to take action and rid the nation of this scourge. The twenty-year delay would give the current slaveholders time to pay off their mortgages, releasing them from their ties to England, and allow them to prepare to run their farms with hired help, rather than slaves.

The first step, however, was the creation of the nation under the new constitution; then the step could be taken to stop slavery.

---

[322]. Madison, *Journal*, 1:259-60.
[323]. Madison, *Journal*, Vol. 2, Wednesday August 22, 1787.

In the interim, the Constitution briefly touched upon the issue of slavery in regard to the matters of representation in the House of Representatives and the matter of taxation.

The Constitution specified that states were to be represented in the United States House of Representative based upon population, and the people were to directly elect their congressmen. Of course, the states with large slave populations desired to count the slaves as part of the base that would determine the number of representatives they would have in the U.S. House of Representatives. This would give them a proportionally larger number in the House.

On the other hand, as originally established (before the Sixteenth Amendment and income tax), states were to be taxed by the national government based upon population.[324]

The argument became this: If slaves were to be counted toward representation, they naturally must be counted toward tax obligations. Of course, the states with large numbers of slaves wanted to count them toward representation, but were opposed to the larger tax obligation (arguing that slaves had no economic means to contribute to the retirement of the tax obligation). States with few slaves did not want to dilute their representation by allowing slave states full representation including the slave numbers and argued that if slaves brought economic means to their masters, the tax burden should be borne by the state that counted slaves.

To address this dilemma, the following clause was added into the Constitution:

> Representatives and direct Taxes shall be apportioned among the several States which may be included within this Union, according to their respective Numbers, which shall be determined by adding to the whole Number of free Persons, including those bound to Service for a Term of Years, and excluding Indians not taxed, three fifths of all other Persons.[325]

The decision to count slaves toward both the representation issue and the taxation issue was a compromise that arbitrarily picked the number of three-fifths as the basis by which each was established to be counted. It had nothing to do with the worth of a soul, but simply addressed the taxation/representation issue.

In addition, the convention established a date twenty years out, after which the nation could address and correct the slave issue. Article 1, section 9 of the U.S. Constitution says,

> The Migration or Importation of such Persons as any of the States now existing shall think proper to admit, shall not be prohibited by the Congress prior to the Year one thousand eight hundred and eight, but a Tax or duty may be imposed on such Importation, not exceeding ten dollars for each Person.

[324.] See U.S. Constitution, article 1, section 9, clause 4.

[325.] U.S. Constitution, article 1, section 2; this was later changed by section 2 of the Fourteenth Amendment.

Action could be taken after this period.

Many lamented that this abominable practice of slavery had not been corrected by the convention, but recognized that the way to correct it was to *first* establish a constitution that bound the nation together and *then* correct it. It appeared that this was the only feasible way to bring it to resolution. In many ways, it was like the dilemma of a bill of rights. Many initially refused to ratify the Constitution because it did not have a bill of rights. It appeared that ratification would fail. To solve this problem, it was agreed that if the Constitution were first ratified, the desired bill of rights would be added. Without the Constitution, however, there would not have been a nation that could have lived under a bill of rights. The first step was binding the nation under the Constitution, the second step was the creation of the Bill of Rights. Similarly, the national problem of slavery could not be solved without a nation bound together by the Constitution, so the first intended step was to create the Constitution, then solve slavery within the nation.

The founders clearly understood that mankind's wickedness in this practice was thousands of years old and that slavery had been practiced by contending tribes and nations since almost the beginning of mortality. Indeed, tragically, slavery continues to be practiced in many nations across the world even today. Peoples of all races have suffered under it, and it stands as a testimony of how debauched man's inhumanity to man can become.

While disappointed that immediate resolution was not possible at the signing of the Constitution, some of the Founding Fathers were thrilled to hope that the way had been made through the new constitution and the conditions that it would create to finally correct this problem.

James Madison wrote,

> It were doubtless to be wished that the power of prohibiting the importation of slaves had not been postponed until the year 1808, or rather that it had been suffered to have immediate operation. But it is not difficult to account either for this restriction on the general government, or for the manner in which the whole clause is expressed. It ought to be considered as a great point gained in favor of humanity that a period of twenty years may terminate forever, within these States, a traffic which has so long and so loudly upbraided the barbarism of modern policy; that within that period it will receive a considerable discouragement from the federal government, and may be totally abolished, by a concurrence of the few States which continue the unnatural traffic in the prohibitory example which has been given by so great a majority of the Union. Happy would it be for the unfortunate Africans if an equal prospect lay before them of being redeemed from the oppressions of their European brethren![326]

James Madison looked back over the long history of slavery throughout the nations of the earth and rejoiced "that a period of twenty years may terminate forever, within these States" this barbaric practice.

---

[326]. Federalist no. 42

TO PRESERVE THE NATION

Unfortunately, during the preparatory twenty-year period in which the nation was to work the matter to closure, there were developments that further entrenched slavery, but the "original intent" of the founders was to rid the nation of this terrible practice and truly create a land wherein all mankind were free to enjoy their vision of *all* individuals being privileged to enjoy their God-given individual rights.

In 1786, John Adams wrote that it was his hope "to see rising in America an empire of liberty, and the prospect of two or three hundred millions of freemen, without one noble or king among them."[327]

Such was their vision of a free and independent nation—governed under principles ordained of God and miraculously established. And it must be remembered that as this nation's founders set forth this new nation upon its course of liberty, they did what they did largely for their posterity—even when they knew that they personally may not live to enjoy the full blessings of liberty they sought to establish.

And of course, since the founding era, there have been countless good and noble souls who have faithfully sought to preserve those blessings of liberty and the proper government that was originally established.

Individuals today would do well to consider what their posterity will say of them if they fail to preserve for them these great blessings of liberty!

To make the point, consider the words spoken in May 1962 at the United States Military Academy at West Point by General Douglas MacArthur in what has come to be termed his farewell address (or valedictory remarks). It was a talk given to men who were tasked with the duty of defending this great nation. Perhaps there is wisdom in these words that modern freedom-loving Americans may apply to their duty to seek the preservation of the divinely established principles of liberty upon which this nation was established and that are embodied in the United States Constitution, the Bill of Rights, and other sacred documents that capture the essence of all that we cherish.

General MacArthur

[327.] Cited in Koch, *American Enlightenment*, 191.

OUR SACRED HONOR: OUR MODERN DUTY TO PRESERVE OUR LIBERTIES

While MacArthur's entire address is not reviewed herein, it is recommended for review. The words apply to those who have taken an oath to uphold the Constitution or have a hope to restore, uphold, and sustain the cause of liberty and the United States Constitution. Consider the words and apply them if appropriate. Early in his address, MacArthur said,

> "Duty," "Honor," "Country"—those three hallowed words reverently dictate what you ought to be, what you can be, what you will be. They are your rallying point to build courage when courage seems to fail, to regain faith when there seems to be little cause for faith, to create hope when hope becomes forlorn.

Later, he speaks of the individual sacrifices of those who have borne the burdens of the cause of liberty, saying,

> In twenty campaigns, on a hundred battlefields, around a thousand campfires, I have witnessed that enduring fortitude, that patriotic self-abnegation, and that invincible determination which have carved his statue in the hearts of his people.

> From one end of the world to the other, he has drained deep the chalice of courage . . . in memory's eye I could see those staggering columns of the First World War, bending under soggy packs on many a weary march, from dripping dusk to drizzling dawn, slogging ankle deep through mire of shell-pocked roads; to form grimly for the attack, blue-lipped, covered with sludge and mud, chilled by the wind and rain, driving home to their objective, and for many, to the judgment seat of God.

> I do not know the dignity of their birth, but I do know the glory of their death. They died unquestioning, uncomplaining, with faith in their hearts, and on their lips the hope that we would go on to victory. Always for them: Duty, Honor, Country. Always their blood, and sweat, and tears, as they saw the way and the light.

Skipping ahead, he said,

> Their resolute and determined defense, their swift and sure attack, their indomitable purpose, their complete and decisive victory—always victory, always through the bloody haze of their last reverberating shot, the vision of gaunt, ghastly men, reverently following your password of Duty, Honor, Country.

> The code which those words perpetuate embraces the highest moral laws and will stand the test of any ethics or philosophies ever promulgated for the uplift of mankind. Its requirements are for the things that are right, and its restraints are from the things that are wrong . . . No physical courage and no brute instinct can take the place of the Divine help which alone can sustain him.

TO PRESERVE THE NATION

And he urgently reminds his hearers, and may modern America hear it in their hearts and minds and souls as a message to the nation today,

> There is no substitute for victory, that if you lose, the Nation will be destroyed, that the very obsession of your public service must be Duty, Honor, Country . . . .

> . . . Your guidepost stands out like a tenfold beacon in the night: Duty, Honor, Country.

> The long gray line has never failed us. Were you to do so, a million ghosts in olive drab, in brown khaki, in blue and gray, would rise from their white crosses, thundering those magic words: Duty, Honor, Country.

The reader is admonished to consider *your* duty, *your* honor, *your* country. To those that went before—to the Pilgrim/Puritan fathers, to the signers of the Declaration of Independence, to the unknown soldiers who gave their all in the cause of liberty and lie buried with their fellow countrymen in common graves, to the men who received the inspiration of God as He engraved the words of the United States Constitution upon their hearts and minds, to those who brought the word forward to us and defended them with the vigor of valiant warriors, to the thousands of faithful unknown patriots who have sought to preserve these blessings—the nation owes an undying debt of gratitude.

But today it is a new generation. Generations yet unborn look to this generation to preserve these great blessings of liberty and proper government. There is much at stake. The threat of utter destruction that hangs so precariously over the nation cannot be overstated at this moment. Powerful, prominent forces hold sway in the nation and the world today. There has never been a time of greater risk. It is the duty of freedom-loving Americans to stand in the gap. Each must all do their part in the preservation of the cause of liberty.

Perhaps many may feel like Frodo, saying,

> I wish it need not have happened in my time!

To which one may respond, as did Gandalf:

> So do I, and so do all who live to see such times. But that is not for them to decide. All we have to decide is what to do with the time that is given us."[328]

And care must be taken to prevent being deceived by the many false philosophies of government that are so cleverly disguised and powerfully promoted today. These destructive

---

[328]. Tolkien, *Fellowship of the Ring*, 50.

OUR SACRED HONOR: OUR MODERN DUTY TO PRESERVE OUR LIBERTIES

deceptions have received such prominence through the media, political promoters, and educational sources for so long that many have embraced them as sound doctrine. To counter these pernicious concepts, Americans must return to the pure wellsprings of government as established by our noble Founding Fathers.

The nation must return to the "original intent" that has been presented throughout this lecture series.

Proper government was instituted to preserve the God-given rights of mankind. Its powers are few and well defined. Those powers are specific and enumerated and may not be modified except by the process defined within article 5 of the United States Constitution. Until modified by that authentic act, they are sacredly obligatory upon all this nation, and all who hold office are bound by their sacred oath to live within the constraints of the Constitution.

To understand these things, students of proper government are obligated to study carefully the words of the Founding Fathers so they may clearly understand the original intent of those who established, under the inspiration of God, this marvelous constitutional republic.

In conclusion, consider the powerful words of an inspired patriot, former United States secretary of agriculture Ezra Taft Benson. These words capture the vision of the modern patriot's duty:

Ezra Taft Benson

> I reverence the Constitution of the United States as a sacred document. To me its words are akin to the revelations of God, for God has placed His stamp of approval upon it.
>
> I testify that the God of heaven sent some of His choicest spirits to lay the foundation of this government, and He has now sent other choice spirits to help preserve it.
>
> We, the blessed beneficiaries of the Constitution, face difficult days in America, 'a land which is choice above all other lands'.
>
> May God give us the faith and the courage exhibited by those patriots who pledged their lives, their fortunes, and their sacred honor.
>
> May we be equally as valiant and as free, I pray.[329]

So said that inspired patriot Ezra Taft Benson.

No longer are there oceans to navigate whereby the Pilgrims/Puritans could gain the privilege of worshiping God according to the dictates of their conscience. No longer are there frontiers to cross in order to establish a haven wherein God may be recognized publicly in the affairs of man.

The line of demarcation has been drawn. Those who desire liberty may no longer retreat and find havens of safety wherein they may worship their god, cherish their individual liberties, and enjoy government constrained within its proper bounds. It is here and now wherein they must make their stand and make sure the nation's freedom and peace and ensure that their wives and children, indeed their unborn posterity, may enjoy these blessings and continue to abide in truth and proper principle.

All that the nation has cherished is at stake. Those that went before recognized what the stakes were. They drew upon their faith in God and upon their courage and stepped forward in the cause of liberty.

To this end, the founders willingly pledged (before God) their lives, their fortunes, and their sacred honor.

Perhaps that pledge and devotion may be renewed in modern America!

---

[329]. "Our Divine Constitution," *Ensign*, November 1987, 4-7.

Appendix A

PLEDGE OF ALLEGIANCE

I pledge allegiance to the flag of the United States of America and to the Republic for which it stands, one Nation under God, indivisible, with liberty and justice for all.

Appendix B

THE MAYFLOWER COMPACT

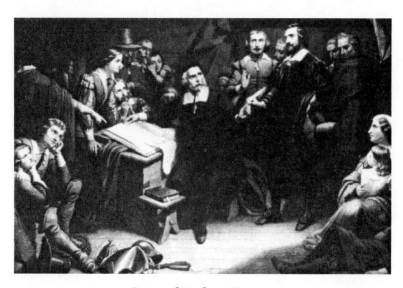

Signing of Mayflower Compact

We whose names are underwritten, the loyal subjects of our dread Sovereign Lord King James, by the Grace of God of Great Britain, France and Ireland, King, Defender of the Faith, etc.

Having undertaken, for the Glory of God and advancement of the Christian Faith and Honour of our King and Country, a Voyage to plant the First Colony in the Northern Parts of Virginia, do by these presents solemnly and mutually in the presence of God and one of another, Covenant and Combine ourselves together into a Civil Body Politic, for our better ordering and preservation and furtherance of the ends aforesaid; and by virtue hereof to enact, constitute and frame such just and equal Laws, Ordinances, Acts, Constitutions and Offices, from time to time, as shall be thought most meet and convenient for the general good of the Colony, unto which we promise all due submission

APPENDIX B: MAYFLOWER COMPACT

and obedience. In witness whereof we have hereunder subscribed our names at Cape Cod, the 11th of November, in the year of the reign of our Sovereign Lord King James, of England, France and Ireland the eighteenth, and of Scotland the fifty-fourth. Anno Domini 1620.

Appendix C

Signing of Declaration of Independence

THE DECLARATION OF INDEPENDENCE

IN CONGRESS, JULY 4, 1776
The unanimous Declaration of the thirteen united States of America

When in the Course of human events it becomes necessary for one people to dissolve the political bands which have connected them with another and to assume among the powers of the earth, the separate and equal station to which the Laws of Nature and of Nature's God entitle them, a decent respect to the opinions of mankind requires that they should declare the causes which impel them to the separation.

We hold these truths to be self-evident, that all men are created equal, that they are endowed by their Creator with certain unalienable Rights, that among these are Life, Liberty and the pursuit of Happiness.—That to secure these rights, Governments are instituted among Men, deriving their just powers from the consent of the governed,—That whenever any Form of Government becomes destructive of these ends, it is the Right of the People to alter or to abolish it, and to institute new Government, laying its foundation on such principles and organizing its powers in such form, as to them shall seem most likely to effect their Safety and Happiness. Prudence, indeed, will dictate that Governments long established should not be changed for light and transient causes; and accordingly all experience hath shewn that mankind are more disposed to suffer, while evils are sufferable than to right themselves by abolishing the forms to which they are accustomed. But when a long train of abuses and usurpations, pursuing invariably the same Object evinces a design to reduce them under absolute Despotism, it is their right, it is their duty, to throw off such Government, and to provide new Guards for their future security.—Such has been the patient sufferance of these Colonies; and such is now the necessity which constrains them to alter their former Systems of Government. The history of the present King of Great Britain is a history of repeated injuries and usurpations, all having in direct object the establishment of an absolute Tyranny over these States. To prove this, let Facts be submitted to a candid world.

He has refused his Assent to Laws, the most wholesome and necessary for the public good.

He has forbidden his Governors to pass Laws of immediate and pressing importance, unless suspended in their operation till his Assent should be obtained; and when so suspended, he has utterly neglected to attend to them.

He has refused to pass other Laws for the accommodation of large districts of people, unless those people would relinquish the right of Representation in the Legislature, a right inestimable to them and formidable to tyrants only.

He has called together legislative bodies at places unusual, uncomfortable, and distant from the depository of their Public Records, for the sole purpose of fatiguing them into compliance with his measures.

He has dissolved Representative Houses repeatedly, for opposing with manly firmness his invasions on the rights of the people.

He has refused for a long time, after such dissolutions, to cause others to be elected, whereby the Legislative Powers, incapable of Annihilation, have returned to the People at large for their exercise; the State remaining in the mean time exposed to all the dangers of invasion from without, and convulsions within.

He has endeavoured to prevent the population of these States; for that purpose obstructing the Laws for Naturalization of Foreigners; refusing to pass others to encourage their migrations hither, and raising the conditions of new Appropriations of Lands.

> **TO PRESERVE THE NATION**

He has obstructed the Administration of Justice by refusing his Assent to Laws for establishing Judiciary Powers.

He has made Judges dependent on his Will alone for the tenure of their offices, and the amount and payment of their salaries.

He has erected a multitude of New Offices, and sent hither swarms of Officers to harass our people and eat out their substance.

He has kept among us, in times of peace, Standing Armies without the Consent of our legislatures.

He has affected to render the Military independent of and superior to the Civil Power.

He has combined with others to subject us to a jurisdiction foreign to our constitution, and unacknowledged by our laws; giving his Assent to their Acts of pretended Legislation:

For quartering large bodies of armed troops among us:

For protecting them, by a mock Trial from punishment for any Murders which they should commit on the Inhabitants of these States:

For cutting off our Trade with all parts of the world:

For imposing Taxes on us without our Consent:

For depriving us in many cases, of the benefit of Trial by Jury:

For transporting us beyond Seas to be tried for pretended offences:

For abolishing the free System of English Laws in a neighbouring Province, establishing therein an Arbitrary government, and enlarging its Boundaries so as to render it at once an example and fit instrument for introducing the same absolute rule into these Colonies

For taking away our Charters, abolishing our most valuable Laws and altering fundamentally the Forms of our Governments:

For suspending our own Legislatures, and declaring themselves invested with power to legislate for us in all cases whatsoever.

He has abdicated Government here, by declaring us out of his Protection and waging War against us.

He has plundered our seas, ravaged our coasts, burnt our towns, and destroyed the lives of our people.

He is at this time transporting large Armies of foreign Mercenaries to compleat the works of death, desolation, and tyranny, already begun with circumstances of Cruelty & Perfidy scarcely paralleled in the most barbarous ages, and totally unworthy the Head of a civilized nation.

He has constrained our fellow Citizens taken Captive on the high Seas to bear Arms against their Country, to become the executioners of their friends and Brethren, or to fall themselves by their Hands.

He has excited domestic insurrections amongst us, and has endeavoured to bring on the inhabitants of our frontiers, the merciless Indian Savages whose known rule of warfare, is an undistinguished destruction of all ages, sexes and conditions.

In every stage of these Oppressions We have Petitioned for Redress in the most humble terms: Our repeated Petitions have been answered only by repeated injury. A Prince, whose character is thus marked by every act which may define a Tyrant, is unfit to be the ruler of a free people.

Nor have We been wanting in attentions to our British brethren. We have warned them from time to time of attempts by their legislature to extend an unwarrantable jurisdiction over us. We have reminded them of the circumstances of our emigration and settlement here. We have appealed to their native justice and magnanimity, and we have conjured them by the ties of our common kindred to disavow these usurpations, which would inevitably interrupt our connections and correspondence. They too have been deaf to the voice of justice and of consanguinity. We must, therefore, acquiesce in the necessity, which denounces our Separation, and hold them, as we hold the rest of mankind, Enemies in War, in Peace Friends.

We, therefore, the Representatives of the United States of America, in General Congress, Assembled, appealing to the Supreme Judge of the world for the rectitude of our intentions, do, in the Name, and by Authority of the good People of these Colonies, solemnly publish and declare, That these United Colonies are, and of Right ought to be Free and Independent States, that they are Absolved from all Allegiance to the British Crown, and that all political connection between them and the State of Great Britain, is and ought to be totally dissolved; and that as Free and Independent States, they have full Power to levy War, conclude Peace, contract Alliances, establish Commerce, and to do all other Acts and Things which Independent States may of right do.—And for the support of this Declaration, with a firm reliance on the protection of Divine Providence, we mutually pledge to each other our Lives, our Fortunes, and our sacred Honor.

—John Hancock

TO PRESERVE THE NATION

New Hampshire: Josiah Bartlett, William Whipple, Matthew Thornton

Massachusetts: John Hancock, Samuel Adams, John Adams, Robert Treat Paine, Elbridge Gerry

Rhode Island: Stephen Hopkins, William Ellery

Connecticut: Roger Sherman, Samuel Huntington, William Williams, Oliver Wolcott

New York: William Floyd, Philip Livingston, Francis Lewis, Lewis Morris

New Jersey: Richard Stockton, John Witherspoon, Francis Hopkinson, John Hart, Abraham Clark

Pennsylvania: Robert Morris, Benjamin Rush, Benjamin Franklin, John Morton, George Clymer, James Smith, George Taylor, James Wilson, George Ross

Delaware: Caesar Rodney, George Read, Thomas McKean

Maryland: Samuel Chase, William Paca, Thomas Stone, Charles Carroll of Carrollton

Virginia: George Wythe, Richard Henry Lee, Thomas Jefferson, Benjamin Harrison, Thomas Nelson, Jr., Francis Lightfoot Lee, Carter Braxton

North Carolina: William Hooper, Joseph Hewes, John Penn

South Carolina: Edward Rutledge, Thomas Heyward, Jr., Thomas Lynch, Jr., Arthur Middleton

Georgia: Button Gwinnett, Lyman Hall, George Walton

Appendix D

THE PREAMBLE TO THE UNITED STATES CONSTITUTION

Signing of the United States Constitution

We the People of the United States, in Order to form a more perfect Union, establish Justice, insure domestic Tranquility, provide for the common defense, promote the general Welfare, and secure the Blessings of Liberty to ourselves and our Posterity, do ordain and establish this Constitution for the United States of America.

Appendix E

THE UNITED STATES CONSTITUTION

ARTICLE 1.—THE LEGISLATIVE BRANCH

Section 1—The Legislature
All legislative Powers herein granted shall be vested in a Congress of the United States, which shall consist of a Senate and House of Representatives.

Section 2—The House
The House of Representatives shall be composed of Members chosen every second Year by the People of the several States, and the Electors in each State shall have the Qualifications requisite for Electors of the most numerous Branch of the State Legislature.

No Person shall be a Representative who shall not have attained to the Age of twenty five Years, and been seven Years a Citizen of the United States, and who shall not, when elected, be an Inhabitant of that State in which he shall be chosen.

(Representatives and direct Taxes shall be apportioned among the several States which may be included within this Union, according to their respective Numbers, which shall be determined by adding to the whole Number of free Persons, including those bound to Service for a Term of Years, and excluding Indians not taxed, three fifths of all other Persons.) (The previous sentence in parentheses was modified by the 14th Amendment, section 2.) The actual Enumeration shall be made within three Years after the first Meeting of the Congress of the United States, and within every subsequent Term of ten Years, in such Manner as they shall by Law direct. The Number of Representatives shall not exceed one for every thirty Thousand, but each State shall have at Least one Representative; and until such enumeration shall be made, the State of New Hampshire shall be entitled to chuse three, Massachusetts eight, Rhode Island and Providence Plantations one, Connecticut five, New York six, New Jersey four, Pennsylvania eight, Delaware one, Maryland six, Virginia ten, North Carolina five, South Carolina five and Georgia three.

When vacancies happen in the Representation from any State, the Executive Authority thereof shall issue Writs of Election to fill such Vacancies.

The House of Representatives shall chuse their Speaker and other Officers; and shall have the sole Power of Impeachment.

Section 3—The Senate
The Senate of the United States shall be composed of two Senators from each State, (chosen by the Legislature thereof,) (The preceding words in parentheses superseded by 17th Amendment, section 1.) for six Years; and each Senator shall have one Vote.

Immediately after they shall be assembled in Consequence of the first Election, they shall be divided as equally as may be into three Classes. The Seats of the Senators of the first Class shall be vacated at the Expiration of the second Year, of the second Class at the Expiration of the fourth Year, and of the third Class at the Expiration of the sixth Year, so that one third may be chosen every second Year; (and if Vacancies happen by Resignation, or otherwise, during the Recess of the Legislature of any State, the Executive thereof may make temporary Appointments until the next Meeting of the Legislature, which shall then fill such Vacancies.) (The preceding words in parentheses were superseded by the 17th Amendment, section 2.)

No person shall be a Senator who shall not have attained to the Age of thirty Years, and been nine Years a Citizen of the United States, and who shall not, when elected, be an Inhabitant of that State for which he shall be chosen.

The Vice President of the United States shall be President of the Senate, but shall have no Vote, unless they be equally divided.

The Senate shall chuse their other Officers, and also a President pro tempore, in the absence of the Vice President, or when he shall exercise the Office of President of the United States.

The Senate shall have the sole Power to try all Impeachments. When sitting for that Purpose, they shall be on Oath or Affirmation. When the President of the United States is tried, the Chief Justice shall preside: And no Person shall be convicted without the Concurrence of two thirds of the Members present.

Judgment in Cases of Impeachment shall not extend further than to removal from Office, and disqualification to hold and enjoy any Office of honor, Trust or Profit under the United States: but the Party convicted shall nevertheless be liable and subject to Indictment, Trial, Judgment and Punishment, according to Law.

Section 4—Elections, Meetings

The Times, Places and Manner of holding Elections for Senators and Representatives, shall be prescribed in each State by the Legislature thereof; but the Congress may at any time by Law make or alter such Regulations, except as to the Place of Chusing Senators.

The Congress shall assemble at least once in every Year, and such Meeting shall (be on the first Monday in December,) (The preceding words in parentheses were superseded by the 20th Amendment, section 2.) unless they shall by Law appoint a different Day.

Section 5—Membership, Rules, Journals, Adjournment

Each House shall be the Judge of the Elections, Returns and Qualifications of its own Members, and a Majority of each shall constitute a Quorum to do Business; but a smaller number may adjourn from day to day, and may be authorized to compel the Attendance of absent Members, in such Manner, and under such Penalties as each House may provide.

Each House may determine the Rules of its Proceedings, punish its Members for disorderly Behavior, and, with the Concurrence of two-thirds, expel a Member.

Each House shall keep a Journal of its Proceedings, and from time to time publish the same, excepting such Parts as may in their Judgment require Secrecy; and the Yeas and Nays of the Members of either House on any question shall, at the Desire of one fifth of those Present, be entered on the Journal.

Neither House, during the Session of Congress, shall, without the Consent of the other, adjourn for more than three days, nor to any other Place than that in which the two Houses shall be sitting.

Section 6—Compensation

(The Senators and Representatives shall receive a Compensation for their Services, to be ascertained by Law, and paid out of the Treasury of the United States.) (The preceding words in parentheses were modified by the 27th Amendment.) They shall in all Cases, except Treason, Felony and Breach of the Peace, be privileged from Arrest during their Attendance at the Session of their respective Houses, and in going to and returning from the same; and for any Speech or Debate in either House, they shall not be questioned in any other Place.

No Senator or Representative shall, during the Time for which he was elected, be appointed to any civil Office under the Authority of the United States which shall have been created, or the Emoluments whereof shall have been increased during such time; and no Person holding any Office under the United States, shall be a Member of either House during his Continuance in Office.

APPENDIX E: THE UNITED STATES CONSTITUTION

Section 7—Revenue Bills, Legislative Process, Presidential Veto

All bills for raising Revenue shall originate in the House of Representatives; but the Senate may propose or concur with Amendments as on other Bills.

Every Bill which shall have passed the House of Representatives and the Senate, shall, before it become a Law, be presented to the President of the United States; If he approve he shall sign it, but if not he shall return it, with his Objections to that House in which it shall have originated, who shall enter the Objections at large on their Journal, and proceed to reconsider it. If after such Reconsideration two thirds of that House shall agree to pass the Bill, it shall be sent, together with the Objections, to the other House, by which it shall likewise be reconsidered, and if approved by two thirds of that House, it shall become a Law. But in all such Cases the Votes of both Houses shall be determined by Yeas and Nays, and the Names of the Persons voting for and against the Bill shall be entered on the Journal of each House respectively. If any Bill shall not be returned by the President within ten Days (Sundays excepted) after it shall have been presented to him, the Same shall be a Law, in like Manner as if he had signed it, unless the Congress by their Adjournment prevent its Return, in which Case it shall not be a Law.

Every Order, Resolution, or Vote to which the Concurrence of the Senate and House of Representatives may be necessary (except on a question of Adjournment) shall be presented to the President of the United States; and before the Same shall take Effect, shall be approved by him, or being disapproved by him, shall be repassed by two thirds of the Senate and House of Representatives, according to the Rules and Limitations prescribed in the Case of a Bill.

Section 8—Powers of Congress

The Congress shall have Power To lay and collect Taxes, Duties, Imposts and Excises, to pay the Debts and provide for the common Defence and general Welfare of the United States; but all Duties, Imposts and Excises shall be uniform throughout the United States;

To borrow money on the credit of the United States;

To regulate Commerce with foreign Nations, and among the several States, and with the Indian Tribes;

To establish an uniform Rule of Naturalization, and uniform Laws on the subject of Bankruptcies throughout the United States;

To coin Money, regulate the Value thereof, and of foreign Coin, and fix the Standard of Weights and Measures;

To provide for the Punishment of counterfeiting the Securities and current Coin of the United States;

TO PRESERVE THE NATION

To establish Post Offices and Post Roads;

To promote the Progress of Science and useful Arts, by securing for limited Times to Authors and Inventors the exclusive Right to their respective Writings and Discoveries;

To constitute Tribunals inferior to the supreme Court;

To define and punish Piracies and Felonies committed on the high Seas, and Offenses against the Law of Nations;

To declare War, grant Letters of Marque and Reprisal, and make Rules concerning Captures on Land and Water;

To raise and support Armies, but no Appropriation of Money to that Use shall be for a longer Term than two Years;

To provide and maintain a Navy;

To make Rules for the Government and Regulation of the land and naval Forces;

To provide for calling forth the Militia to execute the Laws of the Union, suppress Insurrections and repel Invasions;

To provide for organizing, arming, and disciplining the Militia, and for governing such Part of them as may be employed in the Service of the United States, reserving to the States respectively, the Appointment of the Officers, and the Authority of training the Militia according to the discipline prescribed by Congress;

To exercise exclusive Legislation in all Cases whatsoever, over such District (not exceeding ten Miles square) as may, by Cession of particular States, and the acceptance of Congress, become the Seat of the Government of the United States, and to exercise like Authority over all Places purchased by the Consent of the Legislature of the State in which the Same shall be, for the Erection of Forts, Magazines, Arsenals, dock-Yards, and other needful Buildings; And

To make all Laws which shall be necessary and proper for carrying into Execution the foregoing Powers, and all other Powers vested by this Constitution in the Government of the United States, or in any Department or Officer thereof.

Section 9—Specific Limits on Congress Noted
   The Migration or Importation of such Persons as any of the States now existing shall think proper to admit, shall not be prohibited by the Congress prior to the Year one thousand eight

hundred and eight, but a tax or duty may be imposed on such Importation, not exceeding ten dollars for each Person.

The privilege of the Writ of Habeas Corpus shall not be suspended, unless when in Cases of Rebellion or Invasion the public Safety may require it.

No Bill of Attainder or ex post facto Law shall be passed.

(No capitation, or other direct, Tax shall be laid, unless in Proportion to the Census or Enumeration herein before directed to be taken.) (Section in parentheses modified by the 16th Amendment.)

No Tax or Duty shall be laid on Articles exported from any State.

No Preference shall be given by any Regulation of Commerce or Revenue to the Ports of one State over those of another: nor shall Vessels bound to, or from, one State, be obliged to enter, clear, or pay Duties in another.

No Money shall be drawn from the Treasury, but in Consequence of Appropriations made by Law; and a regular Statement and Account of the Receipts and Expenditures of all public Money shall be published from time to time.

No Title of Nobility shall be granted by the United States: And no Person holding any Office of Profit or Trust under them, shall, without the Consent of the Congress, accept of any present, Emolument, Office, or Title, of any kind whatever, from any King, Prince or foreign State.

Section 10—Powers prohibited of States
No State shall enter into any Treaty, Alliance, or Confederation; grant Letters of Marque and Reprisal; coin Money; emit Bills of Credit; make any Thing but gold and silver Coin a Tender in Payment of Debts; pass any Bill of Attainder, ex post facto Law, or Law impairing the Obligation of Contracts, or grant any Title of Nobility.

No State shall, without the Consent of the Congress, lay any Imposts or Duties on Imports or Exports, except what may be absolutely necessary for executing it's inspection Laws: and the net Produce of all Duties and Imposts, laid by any State on Imports or Exports, shall be for the Use of the Treasury of the United States; and all such Laws shall be subject to the Revision and Controul of the Congress.

No State shall, without the Consent of Congress, lay any duty of Tonnage, keep Troops, or Ships of War in time of Peace, enter into any Agreement or Compact with another State, or with a foreign Power, or engage in War, unless actually invaded, or in such imminent Danger as will not admit of delay.

TO PRESERVE THE NATION

Article 2.—The Executive Branch

Section 1—The President

The executive Power shall be vested in a President of the United States of America. He shall hold his Office during the Term of four Years, and, together with the Vice-President chosen for the same Term, be elected, as follows:

Each State shall appoint, in such Manner as the Legislature thereof may direct, a Number of Electors, equal to the whole Number of Senators and Representatives to which the State may be entitled in the Congress: but no Senator or Representative, or Person holding an Office of Trust or Profit under the United States, shall be appointed an Elector.

(The Electors shall meet in their respective States, and vote by Ballot for two persons, of whom one at least shall not be an Inhabitant of the same State with themselves. And they shall make a List of all the Persons voted for, and of the Number of Votes for each; which List they shall sign and certify, and transmit sealed to the Seat of the Government of the United States, directed to the President of the Senate. The President of the Senate shall, in the Presence of the Senate and House of Representatives, open all the Certificates, and the Votes shall then be counted. The Person having the greatest Number of Votes shall be the President, if such Number be a Majority of the whole Number of Electors appointed; and if there be more than one who have such Majority, and have an equal Number of Votes, then the House of Representatives shall immediately chuse by Ballot one of them for President; and if no Person have a Majority, then from the five highest on the List the said House shall in like Manner chuse the President. But in chusing the President, the Votes shall be taken by States, the Representation from each State having one Vote; a quorum for this Purpose shall consist of a Member or Members from two-thirds of the States, and a Majority of all the States shall be necessary to a Choice. In every Case, after the Choice of the President, the Person having the greatest Number of Votes of the Electors shall be the Vice President. But if there should remain two or more who have equal Votes, the Senate shall chuse from them by Ballot the Vice-President.) (This clause in parentheses was superseded by the 12th Amendment.)

The Congress may determine the Time of chusing the Electors, and the Day on which they shall give their Votes; which Day shall be the same throughout the United States.

No person except a natural born Citizen, or a Citizen of the United States, at the time of the Adoption of this Constitution, shall be eligible to the Office of President; neither shall any Person be eligible to that Office who shall not have attained to the Age of thirty-five Years, and been fourteen Years a Resident within the United States.

(In Case of the Removal of the President from Office, or of his Death, Resignation, or Inability to discharge the Powers and Duties of the said Office, the same shall devolve on the Vice President, and the Congress may by Law provide for the Case of Removal, Death, Resignation or Inability, both of the President and Vice President, declaring what Officer shall then act as President, and such Officer shall act accordingly, until the Disability be removed, or a President shall be elected.) (This clause in parentheses has been modified by the 20th and 25th Amendments.)

The President shall, at stated Times, receive for his Services, a Compensation, which shall neither be increased nor diminished during the Period for which he shall have been elected, and he shall not receive within that Period any other Emolument from the United States, or any of them.

Before he enter on the Execution of his Office, he shall take the following Oath or Affirmation:

"I do solemnly swear (or affirm) that I will faithfully execute the Office of President of the United States, and will to the best of my Ability, preserve, protect and defend the Constitution of the United States."

Section 2—Civilian Power over Military, Cabinet, Pardon Power, Appointments
   The President shall be Commander in Chief of the Army and Navy of the United States, and of the Militia of the several States, when called into the actual Service of the United States; he may require the Opinion, in writing, of the principal Officer in each of the executive Departments, upon any subject relating to the Duties of their respective Offices, and he shall have Power to Grant Reprieves and Pardons for Offenses against the United States, except in Cases of Impeachment.

He shall have Power, by and with the Advice and Consent of the Senate, to make Treaties, provided two thirds of the Senators present concur; and he shall nominate, and by and with the Advice and Consent of the Senate, shall appoint Ambassadors, other public Ministers and Consuls, Judges of the supreme Court, and all other Officers of the United States, whose Appointments are not herein otherwise provided for, and which shall be established by Law: but the Congress may by Law vest the Appointment of such inferior Officers, as they think proper, in the President alone, in the Courts of Law, or in the Heads of Departments.

The President shall have Power to fill up all Vacancies that may happen during the Recess of the Senate, by granting Commissions which shall expire at the End of their next Session.

Section 3—State of the Union, Convening Congress
   He shall from time to time give to the Congress Information of the State of the Union, and recommend to their Consideration such Measures as he shall judge necessary and expedient; he may, on extraordinary Occasions, convene both Houses, or either of them, and in Case of Disagreement between them, with Respect to the Time of Adjournment, he

may adjourn them to such Time as he shall think proper; he shall receive Ambassadors and other public Ministers; he shall take Care that the Laws be faithfully executed, and shall Commission all the Officers of the United States.

Section 4—Disqualification
The President, Vice President and all civil Officers of the United States, shall be removed from Office on Impeachment for, and Conviction of, Treason, Bribery, or other high Crimes and Misdemeanors.

ARTICLE 3.—THE JUDICIAL BRANCH

Section 1—Judicial powers
The judicial Power of the United States, shall be vested in one supreme Court, and in such inferior Courts as the Congress may from time to time ordain and establish. The Judges, both of the supreme and inferior Courts, shall hold their Offices during good Behavior, and shall, at stated Times, receive for their Services a Compensation which shall not be diminished during their Continuance in Office.

Section 2—Trial by Jury, Original Jurisdiction, Jury Trials
(The judicial Power shall extend to all Cases, in Law and Equity, arising under this Constitution, the Laws of the United States, and Treaties made, or which shall be made, under their Authority; to all Cases affecting Ambassadors, other public Ministers and Consuls; to all Cases of admiralty and maritime Jurisdiction; to Controversies to which the United States shall be a Party; to Controversies between two or more States; between a State and Citizens of another State; between Citizens of different States; between Citizens of the same State claiming Lands under Grants of different States, and between a State, or the Citizens thereof, and foreign States, Citizens or Subjects.) (This section in parentheses is modified by the 11th *Amendment*.)

In all Cases affecting Ambassadors, other public Ministers and Consuls, and those in which a State shall be Party, the supreme Court shall have original Jurisdiction. In all the other Cases before mentioned, the supreme Court shall have appellate Jurisdiction, both as to Law and Fact, with such Exceptions, and under such Regulations as the Congress shall make.

The Trial of all Crimes, except in Cases of Impeachment, shall be by Jury; and such Trial shall be held in the State where the said Crimes shall have been committed; but when not committed within any State, the Trial shall be at such Place or Places as the Congress may by Law have directed.

Section 3—Treason
Treason against the United States, shall consist only in levying War against them, or in adhering to their Enemies, giving them Aid and Comfort. No Person shall be convicted of Treason unless on the Testimony of two Witnesses to the same overt Act, or on Confession in open Court.

The Congress shall have power to declare the Punishment of Treason, but no Attainder of Treason shall work Corruption of Blood, or Forfeiture except during the Life of the Person attainted.

ARTICLE 4.—THE STATES

Section 1—Each State to Honor all others
Full Faith and Credit shall be given in each State to the public Acts, Records, and judicial Proceedings of every other State. And the Congress may by general Laws prescribe the Manner in which such Acts, Records and Proceedings shall be proved, and the Effect thereof.

Section 2—State citizens, Extradition
The Citizens of each State shall be entitled to all Privileges and Immunities of Citizens in the several States.

A Person charged in any State with Treason, Felony, or other Crime, who shall flee from Justice, and be found in another State, shall on demand of the executive Authority of the State from which he fled, be delivered up, to be removed to the State having Jurisdiction of the Crime.

(No Person held to Service or Labour in one State, under the Laws thereof, escaping into another, shall, in Consequence of any Law or Regulation therein, be discharged from such Service or Labour, But shall be delivered up on Claim of the Party to whom such Service or Labour may be due.) (This clause in parentheses is superseded by the 13th *Amendment*.)

Section 3—New States
New States may be admitted by the Congress into this Union; but no new States shall be formed or erected within the Jurisdiction of any other State; nor any State be formed by the Junction of two or more States, or parts of States, without the Consent of the Legislatures of the States concerned as well as of the Congress.

The Congress shall have Power to dispose of and make all needful Rules and Regulations respecting the Territory or other Property belonging to the United States; and nothing in this Constitution shall be so construed as to Prejudice any Claims of the United States, or of any particular State.

Section 4—Republican government
The United States shall guarantee to every State in this Union a Republican Form of Government, and shall protect each of them against Invasion; and on Application of the Legislature, or of the Executive (when the Legislature cannot be convened) against domestic Violence.

Article 5.—Amendment Process

The Congress, whenever two thirds of both Houses shall deem it necessary, shall propose Amendments to this Constitution, or, on the Application of the Legislatures of two thirds of the several States, shall call a Convention for proposing Amendments, which, in either Case, shall be valid to all Intents and Purposes, as part of this Constitution, when ratified by the Legislatures of three fourths of the several States, or by Conventions in three fourths thereof, as the one or the other Mode of Ratification may be proposed by the Congress; Provided that no Amendment which may be made prior to the Year One thousand eight hundred and eight shall in any Manner affect the first and fourth Clauses in the Ninth Section of the first Article; and that no State, without its Consent, shall be deprived of its equal Suffrage in the Senate.

Article 6.—Debts, Supremacy, Oaths

All Debts contracted and Engagements entered into, before the Adoption of this Constitution, shall be as valid against the United States under this Constitution, as under the Confederation.

This Constitution, and the Laws of the United States which shall be made in Pursuance thereof; and all Treaties made, or which shall be made, under the Authority of the United States, shall be the supreme Law of the Land; and the Judges in every State shall be bound thereby, any Thing in the Constitution or Laws of any State to the Contrary notwithstanding.

The Senators and Representatives before mentioned, and the Members of the several State Legislatures, and all executive and judicial Officers, both of the United States and of the several States, shall be bound by Oath or Affirmation, to support this Constitution; but no religious Test shall ever be required as a Qualification to any Office or public Trust under the United States.

Article 7.—Ratification Documents

The Ratification of the Conventions of nine States, shall be sufficient for the Establishment of this Constitution between the States so ratifying the Same.

Done in Convention by the Unanimous Consent of the States present the Seventeenth Day of September in the Year of our Lord one thousand seven hundred and Eighty seven and of the Independence of the United States of America the Twelfth. In Witness whereof We have hereunto subscribed our Names.

Go. Washington—President and deputy from Virginia

APPENDIX E: THE UNITED STATES CONSTITUTION

New Hampshire—John Langdon, Nicholas Gilman

Massachusetts—Nathaniel Gorham, Rufus King

Connecticut—Wm Saml Johnson, Roger Sherman

New York—Alexander Hamilton

New Jersey—Wil Livingston, David Brearley, Wm Paterson, Jona. Dayton

Pensylvania—B Franklin, Thomas Mifflin, Robt Morris, Geo. Clymer, Thos FitzSimons, Jared Ingersoll, James Wilson, Gouv Morris

Delaware—Geo. Read, Gunning Bedford jun, John Dickinson, Richard Bassett, Jaco. Broom

Maryland—James McHenry, Dan of St Tho Jenifer, Danl Carroll

Virginia—John Blair, James Madison Jr.

North Carolina—Wm Blount, Richd Dobbs Spaight, Hu Williamson

South Carolina—J. Rutledge, Charles Cotesworth Pinckney, Charles Pinckney, Pierce Butler

Georgia—William Few, Abr Baldwin

Attest: William Jackson, Secretary

Appendix F

THE BILL OF RIGHTS

The first ten Amendments collectively are commonly known as the Bill of Rights.

PREAMBLE

CONGRESS OF THE UNITED STATES
BEGUN AND HELD AT THE CITY OF NEW YORK, ON WEDNESDAY THE FOURTH OF MARCH, ONE THOUSAND SEVEN HUNDRED AND EIGHTY NINE.

THE Conventions of a number of the States having at the time of their adopting the Constitution, expressed a desire, in order to prevent misconstruction or abuse of its powers, that further declaratory and restrictive clauses should be added: And as extending the ground of public confidence in the Government, will best insure the beneficent ends of its institution

RESOLVED by the Senate and House of Representatives of the United States of America, in Congress assembled, two thirds of both Houses concurring, that the following Articles be proposed to the Legislatures of the several States, as Amendments to the Constitution of the United States, all or any of which Articles, when ratified by three fourths of the said Legislatures, to be valid to all intents and purposes, as part of the said Constitution; viz.:

ARTICLES in addition to, and Amendment of the Constitution of the United States of America, proposed by Congress, and ratified by the Legislatures of the several States, pursuant to the fifth Article of the original Constitution.

Amendment 1—Freedom of Religion, Press, Expression.

Congress shall make no law respecting an establishment of religion, or prohibiting the free exercise thereof; or abridging the freedom of speech, or of the press; or the right of the people peaceably to assemble, and to petition the Government for a redress of grievances.

APPENDIX F: THE BILL OF RIGHTS

Amendment 2—Right to Bear Arms.

A well regulated Militia, being necessary to the security of a free State, the right of the people to keep and bear Arms, shall not be infringed.

Amendment 3—Quartering of Soldiers.

No Soldier shall, in time of peace be quartered in any house, without the consent of the Owner, nor in time of war, but in a manner to be prescribed by law.

Amendment 4—Search and Seizure.

The right of the people to be secure in their persons, houses, papers, and effects, against unreasonable searches and seizures, shall not be violated, and no Warrants shall issue, but upon probable cause, supported by Oath or affirmation, and particularly describing the place to be searched, and the persons or things to be seized.

Amendment 5—Trial and Punishment, Compensation for Takings.

No person shall be held to answer for a capital, or otherwise infamous crime, unless on a presentment or indictment of a Grand Jury, except in cases arising in the land or naval forces, or in the Militia, when in actual service in time of War or public danger; nor shall any person be subject for the same offense to be twice put in jeopardy of life or limb; nor shall be compelled in any criminal case to be a witness against himself, nor be deprived of life, liberty, or property, without due process of law; nor shall private property be taken for public use, without just compensation.

Amendment 6—Right to Speedy Trial, Confrontation of Witnesses.

In all criminal prosecutions, the accused shall enjoy the right to a speedy and public trial, by an impartial jury of the State and district wherein the crime shall have been committed, which district shall have been previously ascertained by law, and to be informed of the nature and cause of the accusation; to be confronted with the witnesses against him; to have compulsory process for obtaining witnesses in his favor, and to have the Assistance of Counsel for his defence.

Amendment 7—Trial by Jury in Civil Cases.

In Suits at common law, where the value in controversy shall exceed twenty dollars, the right of trial by jury shall be preserved, and no fact tried by a jury shall be otherwise reexamined in any Court of the United States, than according to the rules of the common law.

TO PRESERVE THE NATION

Amendment 8—Cruel and Unusual Punishment.

Excessive bail shall not be required, nor excessive fines imposed, nor cruel and unusual punishments inflicted.

Amendment 9—Construction of Constitution—Enumerated Powers.

The enumeration in the Constitution of certain rights shall not be construed to deny or disparage others retained by the people.

Amendment 10—Powers of the States and People. National Government Denied Powers Not Specifically Delegated.

The powers not delegated to the United States by the Constitution, nor prohibited by it to the States, are reserved to the States respectively, or to the people.

Appendix G

U.S. CONSTITUTION AMENDMENTS 11-27

Amendment 11—Judicial Limits.
Ratified 2/7/1795.

The Judicial power of the United States shall not be construed to extend to any suit in law or equity, commenced or prosecuted against one of the United States by Citizens of another State, or by Citizens or Subjects of any Foreign State.

Amendment 12—Choosing the President, Vice-President.
Ratified 6/15/1804.

The Electors shall meet in their respective states, and vote by ballot for President and Vice-President, one of whom, at least, shall not be an inhabitant of the same state with themselves; they shall name in their ballots the person voted for as President, and in distinct ballots the person voted for as Vice-President, and they shall make distinct lists of all persons voted for as President, and of all persons voted for as Vice-President and of the number of votes for each, which lists they shall sign and certify, and transmit sealed to the seat of the government of the United States, directed to the President of the Senate;

The President of the Senate shall, in the presence of the Senate and House of Representatives, open all the certificates and the votes shall then be counted;

The person having the greatest Number of votes for President, shall be the President, if such number be a majority of the whole number of Electors appointed; and if no person have such majority, then from the persons having the highest numbers not exceeding three on the list of those voted for as President, the House of Representatives shall choose immediately, by ballot, the President. But in choosing the President, the votes shall be taken by states, the representation from each state having one vote; a quorum for this purpose shall consist of a member or members from two-thirds of the states, and a majority of all the states shall be necessary to a choice. And if the House of Representatives shall not choose a President whenever the right of choice shall devolve upon them, before the fourth day of March next following, then the Vice-President shall act as President, as in the case of the death or other constitutional disability of the President.

The person having the greatest number of votes as Vice-President, shall be the Vice-President, if such number be a majority of the whole number of Electors appointed, and if no person have a majority, then from the two highest numbers on the list, the Senate shall choose the Vice-President; a quorum for the purpose shall consist of two-thirds of the whole number of Senators, and a majority of the whole number shall be necessary to a choice. But no person constitutionally ineligible to the office of President shall be eligible to that of Vice-President of the United States.

Amendment 13—Slavery Abolished.
Ratified 12/6/1865.

1. Neither slavery nor involuntary servitude, except as a punishment for crime whereof the party shall have been duly convicted, shall exist within the United States, or any place subject to their jurisdiction.
2. Congress shall have power to enforce this article by appropriate legislation.

Amendment 14—Citizenship Rights.
Ratified 7/9/1868.

1. All persons born or naturalized in the United States, and subject to the jurisdiction thereof, are citizens of the United States and of the State wherein they reside. No State shall make or enforce any law which shall abridge the privileges or immunities of citizens of the United States; nor shall any State deprive any person of life, liberty, or property, without due process of law; nor deny to any person within its jurisdiction the equal protection of the laws.
2. Representatives shall be apportioned among the several States according to their respective numbers, counting the whole number of persons in each State, excluding Indians not taxed. But when the right to vote at any election for the choice of electors for President and Vice-President of the United States, Representatives in Congress, the Executive and Judicial officers of a State, or the members of the Legislature thereof, is denied to any of the male inhabitants of such State, being twenty-one years of age, and citizens of the United States, or in any way abridged, except for participation in rebellion, or other crime, the basis of representation therein shall be reduced in the proportion which the number of such male citizens shall bear to the whole number of male citizens twenty-one years of age in such State.
3. No person shall be a Senator or Representative in Congress, or elector of President and Vice-President, or hold any office, civil or military, under the United States, or under any State, who, having previously taken an oath, as a member of Congress, or

as an officer of the United States, or as a member of any State legislature, or as an executive or judicial officer of any State, to support the Constitution of the United States, shall have engaged in insurrection or rebellion against the same, or given aid or comfort to the enemies thereof. But Congress may by a vote of two-thirds of each House, remove such disability.
4. The validity of the public debt of the United States, authorized by law, including debts incurred for payment of pensions and bounties for services in suppressing insurrection or rebellion, shall not be questioned. But neither the United States nor any State shall assume or pay any debt or obligation incurred in aid of insurrection or rebellion against the United States, or any claim for the loss or emancipation of any slave; but all such debts, obligations and claims shall be held illegal and void.
5. The Congress shall have power to enforce, by appropriate legislation, the provisions of this article.

Amendment 15—Race No Bar to Vote.
Ratified 2/3/1870.

1. The right of citizens of the United States to vote shall not be denied or abridged by the United States or by any State on account of race, color, or previous condition of servitude.
2. The Congress shall have power to enforce this article by appropriate legislation.

Amendment 16—Income Tax.
Ratified 2/3/1913.

The Congress shall have power to lay and collect taxes on incomes, from whatever source derived, without apportionment among the several States, and without regard to any census or enumeration.

Amendment 17—Senators Elected by Popular Vote.
Ratified 4/8/1913.

The Senate of the United States shall be composed of two Senators from each State, elected by the people thereof, for six years; and each Senator shall have one vote. The electors in each State shall have the qualifications requisite for electors of the most numerous branch of the State legislatures.

When vacancies happen in the representation of any State in the Senate, the executive authority of such State shall issue writs of election to fill such vacancies: Provided, That the legislature of any State may empower the executive thereof to make temporary appointments until the people fill the vacancies by election as the legislature may direct.

This amendment shall not be so construed as to affect the election or term of any Senator chosen before it becomes valid as part of the Constitution.

Amendment 18—Liquor Abolished.
Ratified 1/16/1919. Repealed by Amendment 21, 12/5/1933.

1. After one year from the ratification of this article the manufacture, sale, or transportation of intoxicating liquors within, the importation thereof into, or the exportation thereof from the United States and all territory subject to the jurisdiction thereof for beverage purposes is hereby prohibited.
2. The Congress and the several States shall have concurrent power to enforce this article by appropriate legislation.
3. This article shall be inoperative unless it shall have been ratified as an amendment to the Constitution by the legislatures of the several States, as provided in the Constitution, within seven years from the date of the submission hereof to the States by the Congress.

Amendment 19—Women's Suffrage.
Ratified 8/18/1920.

The right of citizens of the United States to vote shall not be denied or abridged by the United States or by any State on account of sex.

Congress shall have power to enforce this article by appropriate legislation.

Amendment 20—Presidential, Congressional Terms.
Ratified 1/23/1933.

1. The terms of the President and Vice President shall end at noon on the 20th day of January, and the terms of Senators and Representatives at noon on the 3d day of January, of the years in which such terms would have ended if this article had not been ratified; and the terms of their successors shall then begin.
2. The Congress shall assemble at least once in every year, and such meeting shall begin at noon on the 3d day of January, unless they shall by law appoint a different day.
3. If, at the time fixed for the beginning of the term of the President, the President elect shall have died, the Vice President elect shall become President. If a President shall not have been chosen before the time fixed for the beginning of his term, or if the President elect shall have failed to qualify, then the Vice President elect shall act as President until a President shall have qualified; and the Congress may by law provide for the case wherein neither a President elect nor a Vice President elect shall have qualified, declaring who shall then act as President, or the manner

in which one who is to act shall be selected, and such person shall act accordingly until a President or Vice President shall have qualified.
4. The Congress may by law provide for the case of the death of any of the persons from whom the House of Representatives may choose a President whenever the right of choice shall have devolved upon them, and for the case of the death of any of the persons from whom the Senate may choose a Vice President whenever the right of choice shall have devolved upon them.
5. Sections 1 and 2 shall take effect on the 15th day of October following the ratification of this article.
6. This article shall be inoperative unless it shall have been ratified as an amendment to the Constitution by the legislatures of three-fourths of the several States within seven years from the date of its submission.

Amendment 21—Amendment 18 Repealed.
Ratified 12/5/1933.

1. The eighteenth article of amendment to the Constitution of the United States is hereby repealed.
2. The transportation or importation into any State, Territory, or possession of the United States for delivery or use therein of intoxicating liquors, in violation of the laws thereof, is hereby prohibited.
3. The article shall be inoperative unless it shall have been ratified as an amendment to the Constitution by conventions in the several States, as provided in the Constitution, within seven years from the date of the submission hereof to the States by the Congress.

Amendment 22—Presidential Term Limits.
Ratified 2/27/1951.

1. No person shall be elected to the office of the President more than twice, and no person who has held the office of President, or acted as President, for more than two years of a term to which some other person was elected President shall be elected to the office of the President more than once. But this Article shall not apply to any person holding the office of President, when this Article was proposed by the Congress, and shall not prevent any person who may be holding the office of President, or acting as President, during the term within which this Article becomes operative from holding the office of President or acting as President during the remainder of such term.
2. This article shall be inoperative unless it shall have been ratified as an amendment to the Constitution by the legislatures of three-fourths of the several States within seven years from the date of its submission to the States by the Congress.

Amendment 23—Presidential Electoral Vote for District of Columbia.
Ratified 3/29/1961.

1. The District constituting the seat of Government of the United States shall appoint in such manner as the Congress may direct: A number of electors of President and Vice President equal to the whole number of Senators and Representatives in Congress to which the District would be entitled if it were a State, but in no event more than the least populous State; they shall be in addition to those appointed by the States, but they shall be considered, for the purposes of the election of President and Vice President, to be electors appointed by a State; and they shall meet in the District and perform such duties as provided by the twelfth article of amendment.
2. The Congress shall have power to enforce this article by appropriate legislation.

Amendment 24—Poll Tax Barred.
Ratified 1/23/1964.

1. The right of citizens of the United States to vote in any primary or other election for President or Vice President, for electors for President or Vice President, or for Senator or Representative in Congress, shall not be denied or abridged by the United States or any State by reason of failure to pay any poll tax or other tax.
2. The Congress shall have power to enforce this article by appropriate legislation.

Amendment 25—Presidential Disability and Succession.
Ratified 2/10/1967.

1. In case of the removal of the President from office or of his death or resignation, the Vice President shall become President.
2. Whenever there is a vacancy in the office of the Vice President, the President shall nominate a Vice President who shall take office upon confirmation by a majority vote of both Houses of Congress.
3. Whenever the President transmits to the President pro tempore of the Senate and the Speaker of the House of Representatives his written declaration that he is unable to discharge the powers and duties of his office, and until he transmits to them a written declaration to the contrary, such powers and duties shall be discharged by the Vice President as Acting President.
4. Whenever the Vice President and a majority of either the principal officers of the executive departments or of such other body as Congress may by law provide, transmit to the President pro tempore of the Senate and the Speaker of the House of Representatives their written declaration that the President is unable to discharge the powers and duties of his office, the Vice President shall immediately assume the powers and duties of the office as Acting President.

Thereafter, when the President transmits to the President pro tempore of the Senate and the Speaker of the House of Representatives his written declaration that no inability exists, he shall resume the powers and duties of his office unless the Vice President and a majority of either the principal officers of the executive department or of such other body as Congress may by law provide, transmit within four days to the President pro tempore of the Senate and the Speaker of the House of Representatives their written declaration that the President is unable to discharge the powers and duties of his office. Thereupon Congress shall decide the issue, assembling within forty eight hours for that purpose if not in session. If the Congress, within twenty one days after receipt of the latter written declaration, or, if Congress is not in session, within twenty one days after Congress is required to assemble, determines by two thirds vote of both Houses that the President is unable to discharge the powers and duties of his office, the Vice President shall continue to discharge the same as Acting President; otherwise, the President shall resume the powers and duties of his office.

Amendment 26—Voting Age Set to 18 Years.
Ratified 7/1/1971.

1. The right of citizens of the United States, who are eighteen years of age or older, to vote shall not be denied or abridged by the United States or by any State on account of age.
2. The Congress shall have power to enforce this article by appropriate legislation.

Amendment 27—Limiting Congressional Pay Increases.
Ratified 5/7/1992.

No law, varying the compensation for the services of the Senators and Representatives, shall take effect, until an election of Representatives shall have intervened.

Appendix H

GEORGE WASHINGTON'S FAREWELL ADDRESS

George Washington

UNITED STATES, September 17, 1796.
Messages and Papers of the Presidents, George Washington, Vol. 1, Pg.205-216

Friends and Fellow—Citizens:

The period for a new election of a citizen to administer the Executive Government of the United States being not far distant, and the time actually arrived when your thoughts must be employed in designating the person who is to be clothed with that important trust, it appears to me proper, especially as it may conduce to a more distinct expression of the public voice, that I should now apprise you of the resolution I have formed to decline being considered among the number of those out of whom a choice is to be made.

I beg you at the same time to do me the justice to be assured that this resolution has not been taken without a strict regard to all the considerations appertaining to the relation which binds a dutiful citizen to his country; and that in withdrawing the tender of service, which silence in my Situation might imply, I am influenced by no diminution of zeal for your future interest, no deficiency of grateful respect for your past kindness, but am supported by a full conviction that the step is compatible with both.

The acceptance of and continuance hitherto in the office to which your suffrages have twice called me have been a uniform sacrifice of inclination to the opinion of duty and to a deference for what appeared to be your desire. I constantly hoped that it would have been much earlier in my power, consistently with motives which I was not at liberty to disregard, to return to that retirement from which I had been reluctantly drawn. The strength of my inclination to do this previous to the last election had even led to the preparation of an address to declare it to you; but mature reflection on the then perplexed and critical posture of our affairs with foreign nations and the unanimous advice of persons entitled to my confidence impelled me to abandon the idea. I rejoice that the state of your concerns, external as well as internal, no longer renders the pursuit of inclination incompatible with the sentiment of duty or propriety, and am persuaded, whatever partiality may be retained for my services, that in the present circumstances of our country you will not disapprove my determination to retire.

The impressions with which I first undertook the arduous trust were explained on the proper occasion. In the discharge of this trust I will only say that I have, with good intentions, contributed toward the organization and administration of the Government the best exertions of which a very fallible judgment was capable, Not unconscious in the outset of the inferiority of my qualifications, experience in my own eyes, perhaps still more in the eyes of others, has strengthened the motives to diffidence of myself; and every day the increasing weight of years admonishes me more and more that the shade of retirement is as necessary to me as it will be welcome. Satisfied that if any circumstances have given peculiar value to my services they were temporary, I have the consolation to believe that, while choice and prudence invite me to quit the political scene, patriotism does not forbid it.

In looking forward to the moment which is intended to terminate the career of my political life my feelings do not permit me to suspend the deep acknowledgment of that debt of gratitude which I owe to my beloved country for the many honors it has conferred upon me; still more for the steadfast confidence with which it has supported me, and for the opportunities I have thence enjoyed of manifesting my inviolable attachment by services faithful and persevering, though in usefulness unequal to my zeal. If benefits have resulted to our country from these services, let it always be remembered to your praise and as an instructive example in our annals that under circumstances in which the passions, agitated in every direction, were liable to mislead; amidst appearances sometimes dubious; vicissitudes of fortune often discouraging; in situations in which not unfrequently want of success has countenanced the spirit of criticism, the constancy of your support was the essential prop of the efforts and a guaranty of the plans by which they were effected. Profoundly penetrated with this idea, I shall carry it with me to my grave as a strong incitement to unceasing vows that Heaven may continue to you the choicest tokens of its beneficence; that your union and brotherly affection may be perpetual; that the free Constitution which is the work of your hands may be sacredly maintained; that its administration in every department may be stamped with wisdom and virtue; that, in fine, the happiness of the people of these States, under the auspices of liberty, may be made complete by so careful a preservation and so prudent a use of this blessing as will acquire to them the glory of recommending it to the applause, the affection, and adoption of every nation which is yet a stranger to it.

Here, perhaps, I ought to stop. But a solicitude for your welfare which can not end but with my life, and the apprehension of danger natural to that solicitude, urge me on an occasion like the present to offer to your solemn contemplation and to recommend to your frequent review some sentiments which are the result of much reflection, of no inconsiderable observation, and which appear to me all important to the permanency of your felicity as a people. These will be offered to you with the more freedom as you can only see in them the disinterested warnings of a parting friend, who can possibly have no personal motive to bias his counsel. Nor can I forget as an encouragement to it your indulgent reception of my sentiments on a former and not dissimilar occasion.

Interwoven as is the love of liberty with every ligament of your hearts, no recommendation of mine is necessary to fortify or confirm the attachment.

The unity of government which constitutes you one people is also now dear to you. It is justly so, for it is a main pillar in the edifice of your real independence, the support of your tranquillity at home, your peace abroad, of your safety, of your prosperity, of that very liberty which you so highly prize. But as it is easy to foresee that from different causes and from different quarters much pains will be taken, many artifices employed, to weaken in your minds the conviction of this truth, as this is the point in your political fortress against which the batteries of internal and external enemies will be most constantly and actively (though often covertly and insidiously) directed, it is of infinite moment that you should properly estimate the immense value of your national union to your collective and individual happiness; that you should cherish a cordial, habitual, and immovable attachment to it; accustoming yourselves to think and speak of it as of the palladium of your political safety and prosperity; watching for its preservation with jealous anxiety; discountenancing whatever may suggest even a suspicion that it can in any event be abandoned, and indignantly frowning upon the first dawning of every attempt to alienate any portion of our country from the rest or to enfeeble the sacred ties which now link together the various parts.

For this you have every inducement of sympathy and interest. Citizens by birth or choice of a common country, that country has a right to concentrate your affections. The name of American, which belongs to you in your national capacity, must always exalt the just pride of patriotism more than any appellation derived from local discriminations. With slight shades of difference, you have the same religion, manners, habits, and political principles. You have in a common cause fought and triumphed together. The independence and liberty you possess are the work of joint councils and joint efforts, of common dangers, sufferings, and successes.

But these considerations, however powerfully they address themselves to your sensibility, are greatly outweighed by those which apply more immediately to your interest. Here every portion of our country finds the most commanding motives for carefully guarding and preserving the union of the whole.

The North, in an unrestrained intercourse with the South, protected by the equal laws of a common government, finds in the productions of the latter great additional resources of maritime and commercial enterprise and precious materials of manufacturing industry. The South, in the same intercourse, benefiting by the same agency of the North, sees its agriculture grow and its commerce expand. Turning partly into its own channels the seamen of the North, it finds its particular navigation invigorated; and while it contributes in different ways to nourish and increase the general mass of the national navigation, it looks forward to the protection of a maritime strength to which itself is unequally adapted. The East, in a like intercourse with the West, already finds, and in the progressive improvement of interior communications by land and water will more and more find, a valuable vent for the commodities which it brings from abroad or manufactures at home. The West derives from the East supplies requisite to its growth and comfort, and what is perhaps of still greater consequence, it must of necessity owe the secure enjoyment of indispensable outlets for its own productions to the weight, influence, and the future maritime strength of the Atlantic side of the Union, directed by an indissoluble community of interest as one nation. Any other tenure by which the West can hold this essential advantage, whether derived from its own separate strength or from an apostate and unnatural connection with any foreign power, must be intrinsically precarious.

While, then, every part of our country thus feels an immediate and particular interest in union, all the parts combined can not fail to find in the united mass of means and efforts greater strength, greater resource, proportionably greater security from external danger, a less frequent interruption of their peace by foreign nations, and what is of inestimable value, they must derive from union an exemption from those broils and wars between themselves which so frequently afflict neighboring countries not tied together by the same governments, which their own rivalships alone would be sufficient to produce, but which opposite foreign alliances, attachments, and intrigues would stimulate and imbitter. Hence, likewise, they will avoid the necessity of those overgrown military establishments which, under any form of government, are inauspicious to liberty, and which are to be regarded as particularly hostile to republican liberty. In this sense it is that your union ought to be considered as a main prop of your liberty, and that the love of the one ought to endear to you the preservation of the other.

These considerations speak a persuasive language to every reflecting and virtuous mind, and exhibit the continuance of the union as a primary object of patriotic desire. Is there a doubt whether a common government can embrace so large a sphere? Let experience solve it. To listen to mere speculation in such a case were criminal. We are authorized to hope that a proper organization of the whole, with the auxiliary agency of governments for the respective subdivisions, will afford a happy issue to the experiment. It is well worth a fair and full experiment. With such powerful and obvious motives to union affecting all parts of our country, while experience shall not have demonstrated its impracticability, there will always be reason to distrust the patriotism of those who in any quarter may endeavor to weaken its bands.

In contemplating the causes which may disturb our union it occurs as matter of serious concern that any ground should have been furnished for characterizing parties by geographical discriminations—Northern and Southern, Atlantic and Western—whence designing men may endeavor to excite a belief that there is a real difference of local interests and views. One of the expedients of party to acquire influence within particular districts is to misrepresent the opinions and aims of other districts. You can not shield yourselves too much against the jealousies and heartburnings which spring from these misrepresentations; they tend to render alien to each other those who ought to be bound together by fraternal affection. The inhabitants of our Western country have lately had a useful lesson on this head. They have seen in the negotiation by the Executive and in the unanimous ratification by the Senate of the treaty with Spain, and in the universal satisfaction at that event throughout the United States, a decisive proof how unfounded were the suspicions propagated among them of a policy in the General Government and in the Atlantic States unfriendly to their interests in regard to the Mississippi. They have been witnesses to the formation of two treaties that with Great Britain and that with Spain—which secure to them everything they could desire in respect to our foreign relations toward confirming their prosperity. Will it not be their wisdom to rely for the preservation of these advantages on the union by which they were procured? Will they not henceforth be deaf to those advisers, if such there are, who would sever them from their brethren and connect them with aliens?

To the efficacy and permanency of your union a government for the whole is indispensable. No alliances, however strict, between the parts can be an adequate substitute. They must inevitably experience the infractions and interruptions which all alliances in all times have experienced. Sensible of this momentous truth, you have improved upon your first essay by the adoption of a Constitution of Government better calculated than your former for an intimate union and for the efficacious management of your common concerns. This Government, the offspring of our own choice, uninfluenced and unawed, adopted upon full investigation and mature deliberation, completely free in its principles, in the distribution of its powers, uniting security with energy, and containing within itself a provision for its own amendment, has a just claim to your confidence and your support. Respect for its authority, compliance with its laws, acquiescence in its measures, are duties enjoined by the fundamental maxims of true liberty. The basis of our political systems is the right of the people to make and to alter their constitutions of government. But the constitution which at any time exists till changed by an explicit and authentic act of the whole people is sacredly obligatory upon all. The very idea of the power and the right of the people to establish government presupposes the duty of every individual to obey the established government.

All obstructions to the execution of the laws, all combinations and associations, under whatever plausible character, with the real design to direct, control, counteract, or awe the regular deliberation and action of the constituted authorities, are destructive of this fundamental principle and of fatal tendency. They serve to organize faction; to give it an artificial and extraordinary force; to put in the place of the delegated will of the nation the will of a party, often a small but artful and enterprising minority of the community, and, according to the alternate triumphs of different parties, to snake the public administration the mirror of the ill-concerted and incongruous projects of faction rather than the organ of consistent and wholesome plans, digested by common counsels and modified by mutual interests.

However combinations or associations of the above description may now and then answer popular ends, they are likely in the course of time and things to become potent engines by which cunning, ambitious, and unprincipled men will be enabled to subvert the power of the people, and to usurp for themselves the reins of government, destroying, afterwards the very engines which have lifted them to unjust dominion.

Toward the preservation of your Government and the permanency of your present happy state, it is requisite not only that you steadily discountenance irregular oppositions to its acknowledged authority, but also that you resist with care the spirit of innovation upon its principles, however specious the pretexts. One method of assault may be to effect in the forms of the Constitution alterations which will impair the energy of the system, and thus to undermine what can not be directly overthrown. In all the changes to which you may be invited remember that time and habit are at least as necessary to fix the true character of governments as of other human institutions; that experience is the surest standard by which to test the real tendency of the existing constitution of a country; that facility in changes upon the credit of mere hypothesis and opinion exposes to perpetual change, from the endless variety of hypothesis and opinion; and remember especially that for the efficient management of your common interests in a country so extensive as ours a government of as much vigor as is consistent with the perfect security of liberty is indispensable. Liberty itself will find in such a government, with powers properly distributed and adjusted, its surest guardian. It is, indeed, little else than a name where the government is too feeble to withstand the enterprises of faction, to confine each member of the society within the limits prescribed by the laws, and to maintain all in the secure and tranquil enjoyment of the rights of person and property.

I have already intimated to you the danger of parties in the State, with particular reference to the founding of them on geographical discriminations. Let me now take a more comprehensive view, and warn you in the most solemn manner against the baneful effects of the spirit of party generally.

This spirit, unfortunately, is inseparable from our nature, having its root in the strongest passions of the human mind. It exists under different shapes in all governments, more or less stifled, controlled, or repressed; but in those of the popular form it is seen in its greatest rankness and is truly their worst enemy.

The alternate domination of one faction over another, sharpened by the spirit of revenge natural to party dissension, which in different ages and countries has perpetrated the most horrid enormities, is itself a frightful despotism. But this leads at length to a more formal and permanent despotism. The disorders and miseries which result gradually incline the minds of men to seek security and repose in the absolute power of an individual, and sooner or later the chief of some prevailing faction, more able or more fortunate than his competitors, turns this disposition to the purposes of his own elevation on the ruins of public liberty.

Without looking forward to an extremity of this kind (which nevertheless ought not to be entirely out of sight), the common and continual mischiefs of the spirit of party are sufficient to make it the interest and duty of a wise people to discourage and restrain it.

It serves always to distract the public councils and enfeeble the public administration. It agitates the community with ill-rounded jealousies and false alarms; kindles the animosity of one part against another; foments occasionally riot and insurrection. It opens the door to foreign influence and corruption, which find a facilitated access to the government itself through the channels of party passion. Thus the policy and the will of one country are subjected to the policy and will of another.

There is an opinion that parties in free countries are useful checks upon the administration of the government, and serve to keep alive the spirit of liberty. This within certain limits is probably true; and in governments of a monarchical cast patriotism may look with indulgence, if not with favor, upon the spirit of party. But in those of the popular character, in governments purely elective, it is a spirit not to be encouraged. From their natural tendency it is certain there will always be enough of that spirit for every salutary purpose; and there being constant danger of excess, the effort ought to be by force of public opinion to mitigate and assuage it. A fire not to be quenched, it demands a uniform vigilance to prevent its bursting into a flame, lest, instead of warming, it should consume.

It is important, likewise, that the habits of thinking in a free country should inspire caution in those intrusted with its administration to confine themselves within their respective constitutional spheres, avoiding in the exercise of the powers of one department to encroach upon another. The spirit of encroachment tends to consolidate the powers of all the departments in one, and thus to create, whatever the form of government, a real despotism. A just estimate of that love of power and proneness to abuse it which predominates in the human heart is sufficient to satisfy us of the truth of this position. The necessity of reciprocal checks in the exercise of political power, by dividing and distributing it into different depositories, and constituting each the guardian of the public weal against invasions by the others, has been evinced by experiments ancient and modern, some of them in our country and under our own eyes. To preserve them must be as necessary as to institute them. If in the opinion of the people the distribution or modification of the constitutional powers be in any particular wrong, let it be corrected by an amendment in the way which the Constitution designates. But let there be no change by usurpation; for though this in one instance may be the instrument of good, it is the customary weapon by which free governments are destroyed. The precedent must always greatly overbalance in permanent evil any partial or transient benefit which the use can at any time yield.

Of all the dispositions and habits which lead to political prosperity, religion and morality are indispensable supports. In vain would that man claim the tribute of patriotism who should labor to subvert these great pillars of human happiness—these firmest props of the duties of men and citizens. The mere politician, equally with the pious man, ought to respect and to cherish them. A volume could not trace all their connections with private and public felicity. Let it simply be asked, Where is the security for property, for reputation, for life, if the sense of religious obligation desert the oaths which are the instruments of investigation in courts of justice? And let us with caution indulge the supposition that morality can be maintained without religion. Whatever may be conceded to the influence of refined education on minds of peculiar structure, reason and experience both forbid us to expect that national morality can prevail in exclusion of religious principle.

It is substantially true that virtue or morality is a necessary spring of popular government. The rule indeed extends with more or less force to every species of free government. Who that is a sincere friend to it can look with indifference upon attempts to shake the foundation of the fabric? Promote, then, as an object of primary importance, institutions 'for the general diffusion of knowledge. In proportion as the structure of a government gives force to public opinion, it is essential that public opinion should be enlightened.

As a very important source of strength and security, cherish public credit. One method of preserving it is to use it as sparingly as possible, avoiding occasions of expense by cultivating peace, but remembering also that timely disbursements to prepare for danger frequently prevent much greater disbursements to repel it; avoiding likewise the accumulation of debt, not only by shunning occasions of expense, but by vigorous exertions in time of peace to discharge the debts which unavoidable wars have occasioned, not ungenerously throwing upon posterity the burthen which we ourselves ought to bear. The execution of these maxims belongs to your representatives; but it is necessary that public opinion should cooperate. To facilitate to them the performance of their duty it is essential that you should practically bear in mind that toward the payment of debts there must be revenue; that to have revenue there must be taxes; that no taxes can be devised which are not more or less inconvenient and unpleasant; that thee intrinsic embarrassment inseparable from the selection of the proper objects (which is always a choice of difficulties), ought to be a decisive motive for a candid construction of the conduct of the Government in making it, and for a spirit of acquiescence in the measures for obtaining revenue which the public exigencies may at any time dictate.

Observe good faith and justice toward all nations. Cultivate peace and harmony with all. Religion and morality enjoin this conduct. And can it be that good policy does not equally enjoin it? It will be worthy of a free, enlightened, and at no distant period a great nation to give to mankind the magnanimous and too novel example of a people always guided by an exalted justice and benevolence. Who can doubt that in the course of time and things the fruits of such a plan would richly repay any temporary advantages which might be lost by a steady adherence to it? Can it be that Providence has not connected the permanent felicity of a nation with its virtue? The experiment, at least, is recommended by every sentiment which ennobles human nature. Alas! is it rendered impossible by its vices?

In the execution of such a plan nothing is more essential than that permanent, inveterate antipathies against particular nations and passionate attachments for others should be excluded, and that in place of them just and amicable feelings toward all should be cultivated. The nation which indulges toward another an habitual hatred or an habitual fondness is in some degree a slave. It is a slave to its animosity or to its affection, either of which is sufficient to lead it astray from its duty and its interest. Antipathy in one nation against another disposes each more readily to offer insult and injury, to lay hold of slight causes of umbrage, and to be haughty and intractable when accidental or trifling occasions of dispute occur.

Hence frequent collisions, obstinate, envenomed, and bloody contests. The nation prompted by ill will and resentment sometimes impels to war the government contrary to the best calculations of policy. The government sometimes participates in the national propensity, and adopts through passion what reason would reject. At other times it makes the animosity of the nation subservient to projects of hostility, instigated by pride, ambition, and other sinister and pernicious motives. The peace often, sometimes perhaps the liberty, of nations has been the victim.

So, likewise, a passionate attachment of one nation for another produces a variety of evils. Sympathy for the favorite nation, facilitating the illusion of an imaginary common interest in cases where no real common interest exists, and infusing into one the enmities of the other, betrays the former into a participation in the quarrels and wars of the latter without adequate inducement or justification. It leads also to concessions to the favorite nation of privileges denied to others, which is apt doubly to injure the nation making the concessions by unnecessarily parting with what ought to have been retained, and by exciting jealousy, ill will, and a disposition to retaliate in the parties from whom equal privileges are withheld; and it gives to ambitions, corrupted, or deluded citizens (who devote themselves to the favorite nation) facility to betray or sacrifice the interests of their own country without odium, sometimes even with popularity, gilding with the appearances of a virtuous sense of obligation, a commendable deference for public opinion, or a laudable zeal for public good the base or foolish compliances of ambition, corruption, or infatuation.

As avenues to foreign influence in innumerable ways, such attachments are particularly alarming to the truly enlightened and independent patriot. How many opportunities do they afford to tamper with domestic factions, to practice the arts of seduction, to mislead public opinion, to influence or awe the public councils! Such an attachment of a small or weak toward a great and powerful nation dooms the former to be the satellite of the latter. Against the insidious wiles of foreign influence (I conjure you to believe me, fellow-citizens) the jealousy of a free people ought to be constantly awake, since history and experience prove that foreign influence is one of the most baneful foes of republican government. But that jealousy, to be useful, must be impartial, else it becomes the instrument of the very influence to be avoided, instead of a defense against it. Excessive partiality for one foreign nation and excessive dislike of another cause those whom they actuate to see danger only on one side, and serve to veil and even second the arts of influence on the other. Real patriots who may resist the intrigues of the favorite are liable to become suspected and odious, while its tools and dupes usurp the applause and confidence of the people to surrender their interests.

The great rule of conduct for us in regard to foreign nations is, in extending our commercial relations to have with them as little political connection as possible. So far as we have already formed engagements let them be fulfilled with perfect good faith. Here let us stop.

Europe has a set of primary interests which to us have none or a very remote relation. Hence she must be engaged in frequent controversies, the causes of which are essentially foreign to our concerns. Hence, therefore, it must be unwise in us to implicate ourselves by artificial ties in the ordinary vicissitudes of her politics or the ordinary combinations and collisions of her friendships or enmities.

Our detached and distant situation invites and enables us to pursue a different course. If we remain one people, under an efficient government, the period is not far off when we may defy material injury from external annoyance; when we may take such an attitude as will cause the neutrality we may at any time resolve upon to be scrupulously respected; when belligerent nations, under the impossibility of making acquisitions upon us, will not lightly hazard the giving us provocation; when we may choose peace or war, as our interest, guided by justice, shall counsel.

Why forego the advantages of so peculiar a situation? Why quit our own to stand upon foreign ground? Why, by interweaving our destiny with that of any part of Europe, entangle our peace and prosperity in the toils of European ambition, rivalship, interest, humor, or caprice?

It is our true policy to steer clear of permanent alliances with any portion of the foreign world, so far, I mean, as we are now at liberty to do it; for let me not be understood as capable of patronizing infidelity to existing engagements. I hold the maxim no less applicable to public than to private affairs that honesty is always the best policy. I repeat, therefore, let those engagements be unwise to extend them.

Taking care always to keep ourselves by suitable establishments on a respectable defensive posture, we may safely trust to temporary alliances for extraordinary emergencies.

Harmony, liberal intercourse with all nations are recommended by policy, humanity, and interest. But even our commercial policy should hold an equal and impartial hand, neither seeking nor granting exclusive favors or preferences; consulting the natural course of things; diffusing and diversifying by gentle means the streams of commerce, but forcing nothing; establishing with powers so disposed, in order to give trade a stable course, to define the rights of our merchants, and to enable the Government to support them, conventional rules of intercourse, the best that present circumstances and mutual opinion will permit, but temporary and liable to be from time to time abandoned or varied as experience and circumstances shall dictate; constantly keeping in view that it is folly in one nation to look for disinterested favors from another; that it must pay with a portion of its independence for whatever it may accept under that character; that by such acceptance it may place itself in the condition of having given equivalents for nominal favors, and yet of being reproached with ingratitude for not giving more. There can be no greater error than to expect or calculate upon real favors from nation to nation. It is an illusion which experience must cure, which a just pride ought to discard.

In offering to you, my countrymen, these counsels of an old and affectionate friend I dare not hope they will make the strong and lasting impression I could wish—that they will control the usual current of the passions or prevent our nation from running the course which has hitherto marked the destiny of nations. But if I may even flatter myself that they may be productive of some partial benefit, some occasional good—that they may now and then recur to moderate the fury of party spirit, to warn against the mischiefs of foreign intrigue, to guard against the impostures of pretended patriotism—this hope will be a full recompense for the solicitude for your welfare by which they have been dictated.

How far in the discharge of my official duties I have been guided by the principles which have been delineated the public records and other evidences of my conduct must witness to you and to the world. To myself, the assurance of my own conscience is that I have at least believed myself to be guided by them.

In relation to the still subsisting war in Europe my proclamation of the 22d of April, 1793, is the index to my plan. Sanctioned by your approving voice and by that of your representatives in both Houses of Congress, the spirit of that measure has continually governed me, uninfluenced by any attempts to deter or divert me from it.

After deliberate examination, with the aid of the best lights I could obtain, I was well satisfied that our country, under all the circumstances of the case, had a right to take, and was bound in duty and interest to take, a neutral position. Having taken it, I determined as far as should depend upon me to maintain it with moderation, perseverance, and firmness.

The considerations which respect the right to hold this conduct it is not necessary on this occasion to detail. I will only observe that, according to my understanding of the matter, that right, so far from being denied by any of the belligerent powers, has been virtually admitted by all.

The duty of holding a neutral conduct may be inferred, without anything more, from the obligation which justice and humanity impose on every nation, in cases in which it is free to act, to maintain inviolate the relations of peace and amity toward other nations.

The inducements of interest for observing that conduct will best be referred to your own reflections and experience. With me a predominant motive has been to endeavor to gain time to our country to settle and mature its yet recent institutions, and to progress without interruption to that degree of strength and consistency which is necessary to give it, humanly speaking, the command of its own fortunes.

Though in reviewing the incidents of my Administration I am unconscious of intentional error, I am nevertheless too sensible of my defects not to think it probable that I may have committed many errors. Whatever they may be, I fervently beseech the Almighty to avert or mitigate the evils to which they may tend. I shall also carry with me the hope that my country will never cease to view them with indulgence, and that, after forty-five years of my life dedicated to its service with an upright zeal, the faults of incompetent abilities will be consigned to oblivion, as myself must soon be to the mansions of rest.

Relying on its kindness in this as in other things, and actuated by that fervent love toward it which is so natural to a man who views in it the native soil of himself and his progenitors for several generations, I anticipate with pleasing expectation that retreat in which I promise myself to realize without alloy the sweet enjoyment of partaking in the midst of my fellow-citizens the benign influence of good laws under a free government—the ever-favorite object of my heart, and the happy reward, as I trust, of our mutual cares, labors, and dangers.

GO. WASHINGTON.

Appendix I

GEORGE WASHINGTON'S
FAREWELL ADDRESS
VOCABULARY

ALL VOCABULARY WORD DEFINITIONS ARE TAKEN FROM THE
1828 NOAH WEBSTER PUBLICATION:
AN AMERICAN DICTIONARY OF THE ENGLISH LANGUAGE

UNLESS OTHERWISE NOTED, EXAMPLE SENTENCES

by
Scott N. Bradley

The definitions apply to the context in which the words are used in the address.

abandon. One who totally forsakes or deserts. (God will not *abandon* those who truly love and serve Him.)

abandoned. Wholly forsaken or deserted. (A righteous people can be assured that they will never be *abandoned* by God.)

abroad. At large; widely; not confined to narrow limits; beyond the bounds of a country; in foreign countries. (Americans who travel *abroad* often return to this country with a greater appreciation for the liberties enjoyed in this nation.)

absolute. Free, independent of any thing extraneous; complete in itself; positive, as an absolute declaration; unconditional, as an absolute promise; existing independent of any other cause, as God is absolute; unlimited by extraneous power or control, as an absolute government or prince; not relative, as absolute space. (God is the *absolute* power in the universe.)

acceptance. A receiving with approbation or satisfaction; favorable reception; as work done to acceptance. (They shall come up with *acceptance* on my altar [Is. 60:7].)

access. A coming to; near approach; means of approach. (The right to petition our leaders gives us *access* to the halls of government.)

accumulation. The act of accumulation; a collecting together. (The national government for years has sought the *accumulation* of powers never envisioned by the Founding Fathers.)

accustoming. Making familiar by practice. (Repeated review of correct principles is necessary in *accustoming* a people to truth.)

acknowledged. To own, avow or admit to be true, by a declaration of assent; as to acknowledge the being of a God. (I *acknowledge* my transgressions, and my sin is ever before me [Ps. 51]. The faithful *acknowledged* their dependence upon God for all good things [Ps. 32].)

acquiescence. A quiet assent; a silent submission, or submission with apparent content; distinguished from avowed consent on the one hand, and on the other, from opposition or open discontent. As an acquiescence in the decisions of a court, or in the allotments of providence. (*Acquiescence* is often mistaken for concurrence. If politicians do not hear of our concerns, they may assume our *acquiescence*.)

acquire. To seek; to gain. (Plants *acquire* a green color from the solar rays. You may *acquire* a testimony of God's truth through diligent study, prayer, and fasting.)

APPENDIX I: GEORGE WASHINGTON'S FAREWELL ADDRESS VOCABULARY WORDS

acquisitions. The act of acquiring; as, a man takes pleasure in the acquisition of property, as well as in the possession; The thing acquired, or gained; as, learning is an acquisition; It is used for intellectual attainments, as well as for external things, property, or dominion. (It is a natural tendency of most men in authority to seek *acquisition* of additional power.)

actuate. To put in action; to move or incite to action; as, men are actuated by motives, or passions. (Our love of God and our fellow man will *actuate* us to uphold proper principle.)

actuated. Put in action; incited to action. (A remembrance of his responsibility to his God, his family and his country *actuated* the patriot to defend the principles of righteousness.)

adapted. Suited; made suitable; fitted. (The U.S. Constitution is *adapted* only for a righteous people.)

adequate. Equal; proportionate; correspondent to; fully sufficient; as, means adequate to the object. (We have no *adequate* understanding of infinite power.)

adherence. The quality or state of sticking or adhering; steady attachment; as, an adherence to a party or opinions. (*Adherence* to the Constitution is a lost philosophy for most Americans and their leaders.)

adjusted. Made exact or conformable; reduced to a right form or standard; settled. (A properly *adjusted* government will not improperly infringe upon the God-given rights of mankind.)

administer. To contribute; to add something; to perform the office of administrator. (A shade *administers* to our comfort. The Bishop *administers* to the congregation.)

admonishes. To warn or notify of a fault; to reprove with mildness. (Count him not as an enemy, but *admonish* him as a brother [2 Thes. 3]. A wise son will listen and heed as his mother *admonishes* him.)

advantages. Any state, condition, or circumstance, favorable to success, prosperity, interest, or reputation; benefit; gain; profit. (The enemy had the *advantage* of elevated ground. There exists, in the economy and course of nature, an indissoluble union between virtue and happiness between duty and *advantage* [Washington]. The General took *advantage* of his enemy's negligence.)

affection. Passion; a bent of mind towards a particular object, holding a middle place between disposition which is natural, and passion, which excited by the presence of its exciting object. (Love of family is a natural *affection*.)

affections. A passion; but more generally a bent of mind towards a particular object, a settled good will, love or zealous attachment; as, the affection of a parent for his child. (The *affections* of a people who know God will be to please Him.)

afflict. To trouble; to harass; to distress. (The thorns and thistles of life seem to *afflict* and torment mortal mankind.)

agitated. Tossed from side to side; shaken; moved violently and irregularly; disturbed; discussed; considered. (The peace of the people is *agitated* by tyrants who undermine the freedom of the land.)

agitates. To disturb, or excite into tumult; to discuss; to debate; to controvert; to stir violently; to move or force into violent irregular action; as to agitate the mind or passions, as to agitate a question, as politicians agitate desperate designs (King Charles). (An impassioned speaker *agitates* those who hear to take action.)

alien. Estranged; foreign; not belonging to the same country, land or government. (*Aliens* to this country often bring their incorrect ideas of government with them.)

alienate. To estrange; withdrawn from; stranger to. (When we *alienate* ourselves from God, we remove the power of salvation from our lives.)

alliance. To tie or unite; the union between nations, contracted by compact, treaty or league; any union or connection of interests between persons, families, states or corporations. (An improper *alliance* between nations can undermine the sovereignty of each nation.)

alliances. The union between nations, contracted by compact, treaty or league. (A nation must carefully choose its *alliances*, lest the nation become embroiled in controversies not of her own.)

alloy. Evil mixed with good; as, no happiness is without alloy. (Most politicians create an *alloy* in the mistaken belief that compromise is the only way a law may be passed.)

alter. To make some change; to make different in some particular; to vary in some degree, without an entire change. (It is not possible to *alter* eternal truth by popular whim.)

alterations. The act of making different, or of varying in some particular. (Thus a cold substance suffers an *alteration* when it becomes hot. In this century, unconstitutional *alterations* of the processes of government have undermined individual liberties.)

APPENDIX I: GEORGE WASHINGTON'S FAREWELL ADDRESS VOCABULARY WORDS

alternate. Being by turns; one following the other in succession of time or place; hence reciprocal. (Contending parties often offer *alternate* solutions without sound principles.)

ambition. As desire of excellence or superiority; it is used in a good sense; it also denotes an inordinate desire of power, or eminence, often accompanied with illegal means to obtain the object. (George Washington led the people of his day based upon his love of them; he was devoid of personal *ambition* for power.)

ambitious. Desirous of power, honor, office, superiority or excellence; aspiring; eager for fame. (Beware of those *ambitious* to lead.)

amendment. An alteration or change for the better; correction of a fault or faults. (Experience has demonstrated that care must be taken to prevent the amendment process from changing the original intent of the Constitution of 1787.)

amicable. Friendly; peaceable; harmonious in social or mutual transactions; usually applied to the dispositions of men who have business with each other, or to their intercourse and transactions; disposed to peace and friendship; as, an amicable temper (but rarely applied to a single person); as, nations or men have come to an amicable adjustment of their differences. (The principles of the Constitution are *amicable* to religious liberty.)

amity. Friendship, in a general sense, between individuals, societies or nations; harmony; good understanding; as, our nation is in amity with all the world; a treaty of amity and commerce. (The Constitution facilitated *amity* between the states.)

animosity. Violent hatred accompanied with active opposition; active enmity. Animosity differs from enmity which may be secret and inactive; and it expresses a less criminal passion than malice. Animosity seeks to gain a cause or destroy an enemy or rival, from hatred or private interest; malice seeks revenge for the sake of giving pain. (Tyrants have *animosity* against the rights of the individual.)

annals. A species of history digested in order of time, or a relation of events in chronological order, each event being recorded under the year in which it happened. Annals differ from history, in merely relating events, without observations on the motives, causes and consequences, which, in history, are more diffusively illustrated. (The *annals* of this nation are devoid of characters superior to the Founding Fathers.)

annoyance. That which annoys, or injures; the act of annoying; the state of being annoyed. (Those who seek power are an *annoyance* to the cause of individual liberty.)

anticipate. To foretaste or foresee; to have a previous view or impression of something future. (If we abide in correct principles, we may *anticipate* the ultimate triumph.)

antipathies. Natural aversion; instinctive contrariety or opposition in feeling. This word literally denotes a natural aversion, which may be of different degrees, and in some cases may excite terror or horror at the presence of an object. Such is the aversion of animals for their natural enemies, as the antipathy of a mouse to a cat, or a weasel. (Sometimes persons have an insuperable constitutional *antipathy* to certain kinds of food. Inveterate *antipathies* against particular nations, and passionate attachments to others, are to be avoided [Washington]. Those who have a love of the Constitution in the tradition of the Founding Fathers have extreme *antipathies* toward socialism and expansive government.)

antipathy. Natural aversion; see antipathies. (We should have an *antipathy* to soul-destroying temptations.)

anxiety. Concern or solicitude respecting some event, future or uncertain, which disturbs the mind, and keeps it in a state of painful uneasiness. It expresses more than uneasiness or disturbance, and even more than trouble or solicitude. (Washington had *anxiety* that we would apostatize from the Constitution they had labored so hard to create.)

apostate. One who has forsaken the church, sect or profession to which he before adhered. (The power of position and office has turned many a previously good man into an *apostate* from proper government.)

appellation. The word by which a thing is called and known. (We should be pleased to be called by the *appellation* Christian.)

appertaining. Belonging. (All things *appertaining* to the kingdom of God speak of His perfection and love.)

applicable. That may be applied; fit to be applied, as related to a thing; that may have relation to something else; as this observation is applicable to the case under consideration. (The limits of power in government established by the Constitution are *applicable* to all elected officials.)

apprehension. Fear; suspicion; the prospect of future evil, accompanied with uneasiness of mind. (Claudius was in no small *apprehension* for his own life. Washington's great *apprehension* was that the nation would stray from the pure principles upon which it was founded and lose the liberty with which it had been blessed.)

APPENDIX I: GEORGE WASHINGTON'S FAREWELL ADDRESS VOCABULARY WORDS

apprize. To inform; to give notice, verbal or written. (We will *apprize* the general of an intended attack. He *apprized* the commander of what he had done.)

apt. Fit; suitable; inclined; qualified. (George Washington was an *apt* leader of the new nation.)

arduous. Difficult; attended with great labor, like the ascending of acclivities; as, an arduous employment, task, or enterprise. (Preserving liberty is an *arduous* task which can never be safely ignored.)

artful. Performed with art or skill; cunning; stratagem; crafty. (Politicians are *artful* in their ability to subvert principle in their quest for power.)

artifices. Stratagem; an artful or ingenious device, in a good or bad sense. In a bad sense, it corresponds with trick, or fraud. (Those seeking to undermine good government will employ every *artifice* of deception.)

artificial. Made or contrived by art, or by human skill and labor, in opposition to natural. (By *artificial* expressions of concern for mankind, tyrants are often granted powers by which they enslave the people they pretend to protect.)

assault. An attack or violent onset, whether by an individual, a company, or an army; an attack by hostile words or measures; to attack or fall upon by violence, or with a hostile intention. (The *assault* on our liberties can be overt or covert, but must be guarded against.)

associations. The act of associating; union; connection of persons. (People of like mind who seek a common goal often organize into *associations*.)

assuage. Soften; to allay, mitigate, ease or lessen, as pain or grief; to appease or pacify, as passion or tumult; to abate or subside; in strictness, it signifies rather to moderate, than to quiet, tranquilize or reduce to perfect peace or ease. (Soft words and music *assuage* the savage beast.)

assurance. The act of assuring, or of making a declaration in terms that furnish ground of confidence. (Whereof he hath given *assurance* to all men, in that he hath raised him from the dead [Acts 17]. Let us draw near with a true heart, in full *assurance* of faith [Heb. 10]. Obedience to God's will brings the *assurance* of His approval.)

assured. Certain; indubitable; not doubting; bold to excess. (We may be *assured* of God's love.)

astray. Out of the right way or proper place, both in literal and figurative sense; In morals and religion, it signifies wandering from the path of rectitude, from duty and happiness. (Before I was afflicted, I went *astray* [Ps. 119]. Cattle go *astray* when they leave their proper owners or inclosures [Deut. 22].)

attachment. Close adherence or affection; fidelity; regard; any passion or affection that binds a person; as, an attachment to a friend, or to a party. (The taking of marriage vows should create a devoted and unending *attachment* to each other.)

auspices. Protection; favor shown; patronage; influence. (Those who dwell under the *auspices* of a loving God owe Him their allegiance.)

authentic. Having a genuine original or authority, in opposition to that which is false, fictitious, or counterfeit; being what it purports to be; genuine; true; applied to things; as, an authentic paper or register. (Belief in Christ gives us an *authentic* hope of eternal life.)

auxiliary. Helping; aiding; assisting; subsidiary; conferring aid or support by joint exertion, influence or use; as auxiliary troops. (*Auxiliary* organizations of government are absolutely bound by the limits defined by the Constitution.)

avenues. A passage; a way or opening for entrance into a place; any opening or passage by which a thing is or may be introduced. (The gospel of Jesus Christ provides the *avenues* to peace, freedom, and eternal life.)

avert. To turn from; to turn off or away; as, to avert the eyes from an object. (If we are to *avert* the downfall of this nation, we must reenthrone God in our lives.)

awe. Fear mingled with admiration or reverence; reverential fear; to strike with fear and reverence. (Stand in *awe* and sin not [Ps. 4]. We stand in *awe* of the goodness, greatness, and glory of God. Congress must not be kept from their sworn duty by an *awe* for the office of the president.)

baneful. Poisonous; pernicious; destructive. (A leader's love of power has proven *baneful* to the freedom of the nation.)

base. Low in place; mean; vile; worthless; that is, low in value or estimation; of low station. (The *base* shall behave proudly against the honorable [Is. 3]. The thieves basic motive is *base* greed.)

batteries. Instrument of battering or beating. (Evil, greed, and desire for power are *batteries* of destruction used against a freedom loving people.)

belligerent. Waging war; carrying on war; as a belligerent nation. (The nation's defenses must be strong and sure enough to prevent attack by a *belligerent* nation.)

beneficence. The practice of doing good; active goodness, kindness, or charity. (The *beneficence* of God is unending.)

benefitting. Doing good to; profiting; gaining advantage. (The *benefitting* effect of a good law will be felt by all people.)

benevolence. The disposition to do good; good will; kindness; charitableness; the love of mankind, accompanied with a desire to promote their happiness. (The *benevolence* of God is one of his moral attributes; the attribute which delights in the happiness of intelligent beings. "God is love" [1 John 4]. A righteous leader will exercise the power of his office with great *benevolence*.)

benign. Kind; gracious; generous; favorable; wholesome; not pernicious (The *benign* light of revelation [Washington]. The *benign* love of our Heavenly Father will sustain us in our times of trial.)

beseech. To implore; to ask or pray with urgency. (We must *beseech* God for forgiveness of our sins and seek to obey His will.)

bias. A leaning of the mind; inclination. (Education gives *bias* to the mind; thus, the foundation of the education must be based upon proper principle.)

broils. A tumult; a noisy quarrel; contention; discord, wither between individuals or in the state. (When the true brotherhood of mankind is revealed, the *broils* of war will cease.)

burden. That which is borne with labor or difficulty; that which is grievous, wearisome or oppressive. (The government should never become an oppressive *burden* upon a righteous people.)

calculated. To make a computation; computed; reckoned. (We *calculate* better for ourselves than for others. The laws of God are *calculated* to bring us to eternal joy.)

calculations. Estimate formed in the mind by comparing the various circumstances and facts which influence its determination. (All of the *calculations* of the Founding Fathers were to find a way to obtain their liberty.)

candid. Frank; open; fair; ingenuous; free from undue bias; disposed to think and judge according to truth and justice, or without partiality or prejudice; just; impartial. (A *candid* review of the words of the founders will bring understanding of their original intent.)

capable. Possessing mental powers; intelligent; able to understand, or receive into the mind; having a capacious mind; as a capable judge; a capable instructor. (God's assistance and guidance make us *capable* of achievement beyond our natural ability.)

capacity. Passive power; the power of containing, or holding; extent of room or space. (Heavenly Father's children have the *capacity* to achieve eternal life and exaltation.)

caprice. A sudden start of the mind; a sudden change of opinion, or humor; a whim, freak, or particular fancy. (Government policy is never to be based upon *caprice* but upon sound principles.)

cast. To throw, fling or send; that is, to drive from, by force; to sow; to scatter seed. (Hagar *cast* the child under a shrub [Gen. 21]. Uzziah prepared slings to *cast* stones [2 Ch.]. If a man should *cast* seed into the ground [Mk 4]. Tyrants *cast* those who oppose them into prisons.)

channels. In a general sense, a passage; a place of passing or flowing; that through which any thing passes; means of passing, conveying, or transmitting. (If a family is to succeed, *channels* of caring communication must remain open.)

characterizing. Describing or distinguishing by peculiar qualities. (Bad men have a habit of *characterizing* good as evil and evil as good.)

circumstances. Something attending, appendant, or relative to a fact, or case; a particular thing, which, though not essential to an action, in some way affects it; the same to a moral action, as accident to a natural substance; as, the circumstances of time, place and persons, are to be considered. (*Circumstances* may vary, but principles must be firm and pure.)

collective. Gathered into a mass, sum, or body. (The *collective* power of the people must never be used to violate correct principles.)

collisions. The act of striking together; the state of being struck together; a clashing; opposition; interference. (The *collisions* of nations results in death and destruction.)

commanding. Bidding; ordering; directing with authority; governing. (The will of God must be the *commanding* motivation in our lives.)

commendable. That may be commended or praised; worthy of approbation or praise; laudable. (Seeking eternal life and exaltation by obedience to God and His commandments is a most *commendable* desire.)

commerce. An interchange or mutual change of goods, wares, productions or property of any kind, between nations or individuals, whether by barter, or by purchase and sale; trade. (Foreign *commerce* is the trade that one nation carries on with another. The ability to exercise free *commerce* between and among the states of the United States has contributed greatly to our prosperity and abundance.)

commercial. Pertaining to commerce or trade; as commercial concerns; commercial relations. (The powers of government were intended by the Founding Fathers to be very limited in matters concerning *commercial* trade.)

commodities. That which affords ease, convenience or advantage; any thing that is useful, but particularly in commerce, including every thing movable that is bought and sold, goods, wares, merchandise, produce of land and manufactures. (Political and economic freedom have created an environment in which *commodities* of every conceivable type are general available.)

compatible. Consistent; that may exist with; suitable; not incongruous; agreeable; followed by with; sometimes by to, but less properly. (The poets have joined qualities which by nature are the most *compatible* [Broome]. The office of a legislator and of a judge are deemed not *compatible*. To pardon offenders is not always *compatible* with public safety.)

compliance. The act of complying; a yielding, as to a request, wish, desire, demand or proposal; concession; submission. (We should be always willing to bring ourselves into *compliance* with God's will.)

comprehensive. Having the quality of comprising much, or including a great extent; extensive; having the power to comprehend or understand many things at once. (A test that covers everything that has been learned in a class is called a *comprehensive* exam.)

conceded. Yielded; admitted; granted. (God's infallible wisdom is *conceded* by the faithful.)

concessions. The act of granting or yielding; usually implying a demand, claim, or request from the party to whom it is made, and thus distinguished from giving, which is voluntary or spontaneous; the thing yielded. (A tyrant grants rights to his people as a *concession* to gain their favor.)

conduce. To lead or tend; to contribute. (They may *conduce* to further discoveries for completing the theory of light. Virtue *conduces* to the welfare of society. Religion *conduces* to temporal happiness. Temperance *conduces* to health and long life.)

conduct. In a general sense, personal behavior; course of actions. (Our *conduct* must reflect the highest principle and our commitment to God.)

confidence. A trusting, or reliance; an assurance of mind or firm belief in the integrity, stability or veracity of another, or in the truth and reality of a fact. (It is better to trust in the Lord, than to put *confidence* in man [Ps. 118]. I rejoice that I have *confidence* in you in all things [2 Cor. 7]. We must never place our *confidence* in leaders who oppose the things of God.)

confine. To bound or limit; to restrain within limits; hence, to imprison; to shut up; to restrain from escape by force or insurmountable obstacles, in a general sense (as to *confine* horses or cattle to an inclosure; as a man *confines* himself to his studies or to his house. The Constitution of the United States *confines* to the states the exercise of powers of a local nature.)

confirm. To make firm or certain; to give new assurance of truth or certainty; to put past doubt. (The testimony of Christ was *confirmed* in you.)

confirming. Making firm or more firm; strengthening; ratifying; giving additional evidence or proof; establishing. (God's *confirming* hand was universally recognized in the foundation of the nation.)

conjure. To call on or summon by a sacred name, or in a solemn manner; to implore with solemnity. (The Founding Fathers would daily *conjure* their Heavenly Father in the hope to obtain His guidance in the critical matters of beginning a new nation.)

consequence. That which follows from any act, cause, principle, or series of actions. Hence, an event or effect produced by some preceding act or cause. (The *consequences* of intemperance are disgrace, poverty, disease, and premature death.)

consigned. Delivered; committed for keeping, or management; deposited in trust. (We will be *consigned* to a state of misery if we violate the commandments of God.)

consistently. In a consistent manner; in agreement; agreeably; as, to command confidence, a man must act consistently. (A *consistently* honest man demonstrates a worthy trait.)

consolation. Comfort; alleviation of misery, or distress of mind; refreshment of mind or spirits; a comparative degree of happiness in distress or misfortune, springing from any circumstance that abates the evil, or supports and strengthens the mind, as hope, joy, courage and the like. (Knowing their children have chosen correctly is a great *consolation* to parents.)

consolidate. To make solid; to unite or press together loose or separate parts, and from a compact mass; to harden or make dense and firm. (He fixed and *consolidated* the earth above the waters. Tyrants seek to *consolidate* powers into their hands.)

constancy. Fixedness; a standing firm; hence, applied to God or His works, immutability; unalterable continuance; a permanent state; unshaken determination; particularly applicable to firmness of mind under sufferings, to steadiness in attachments, and to perseverance in enterprise. Lasting affection; stability in love or friendship. (Dedicated *constancy* in support of timeless principles is required if freedom is to be preserved.)

constituted. Set; fixed; established; made; elected; appointed. (Tyrants seek to act beyond the scope of the *constituted* limits of proper government.)

constitutes. To enact; to establish; to form or compose; to appoint. (Truth and reason *constitute* that intellectual gold that defies destruction [Johnson]. A sheriff is *constituted* a conservator of the peace. The principle of God-given rights *constitutes* the basis of correct government.)

consulting. Asking advice; seeking information; deliberating and enquiring mutually; regarding. (Choices are best made after *consulting* with Heavenly Father through prayer.)

contemplating. Considering with continued attention, meditating on. (*Contemplating* the gospel will bring peace of mind and happiness.)

contemplation. The act of mind in considering with attention; meditation; study; continued attention of the mind to a particular subject. (*Contemplation* is keeping the idea, brought into the mind, some time actually in view [Locke]. The truths of eternity elude all but those who are willing to spend time in *contemplation* of them.)

continuance. A particular holding on or remaining in a particular state, or in a course or series. Applied to time, duration; a state of lasting; as the continuance or rain or fair weather for a day or a week. (Sensual pleasure is of short *continuance*. By patient continuance in well doing [Rom. 2].)

contrary. Opposite; adverse; moving against or in an opposite direction; contradictory. (The flesh lusteth against the spirit, and the spirit against the flesh; and these are *contrary*, the one to the other [Gal. 5]. The thought that government is the source of rights is *contrary* to the principle taught by both the prophets and our conscience.)

contributes. To impart a portion or share to a common purpose; to pay a share. (England *contributes* much more than any other of the allies [Addison]. It is a duty of Christians to *contribute* a portion of their substance for the propagation of the gospel.)

controversies. Dispute; debate; agitation of contrary opinions. (A dispute is commonly oral, and a *controversy* in writing [Johnson]. In *controversies* regarding the extent of power granted to the national government, the original intent of the Founding Fathers must be considered.)

conviction. The act of convincing or compelling one to admit the truth. (A *conviction* that Christ is the Savior and Redeemer of the world causes the convert to change his life to conform to the teachings of Christ.)

cooperate. To act or operate jointly with another or others, to the same end; to work or labor with mutual efforts to promote the same object; to act together. (Russia *cooperated* with Great Britain, Austria, and Prussia to reduce the power of Bonaparte. Natural and moral events *cooperate* in illustrating the wisdom of the Creator.)

cordial. Proceeding from the heart; hearty; sincere; warm; affectionate. (We give our friends a *cordial* reception.)

corrupted. Putrefied; vitiated; depraved; spoiled; marred; bribed; infected with errors. (Long years of neglect by a people that are not vigilant has resulted in a *corrupted* state of government.)

councils. An assembly of men summoned or convened for consultation, deliberation and advice. (The kings of England were formerly assisted by a grand *council* of peers. The *councils* of government have the responsibility to uphold correct principles at all times.)

counsel. Advice; opinion or instruction, given upon request or otherwise, for directing the judgment or conduct of another; opinion given upon deliberation or consultation. (Every purpose is established by *counsel* [Prob. 20]. Thou hast not hearkened to my *counsel* [2 Chron. 25]. Listen only to the *counsel* of worthy teachers.)

countenanced. Favored; encouraged; supported. (The continuous efforts of the Founding Fathers *countenanced* the blessing of liberty for themselves and their posterity.)

counteract. To act in opposition to; to hinder, defeat or frustrate by contrary agency. (Good precepts will sometimes *counteract* the effects of evil example; but more generally good precepts are *counteracted* by bad examples.)

covertly. Secretly; closely; in private; insiduously. (The power hungry seek to *covertly* destroy the principles of our liberty.)

credit. Belief; faith; a reliance or resting of the mind on the truth of something said or done; honor; reputation. (We give *credit* to a man's declaration, when the mind rests on the truth of it, without doubt or suspicion, which is attended with wavering. We give *credit* to testimony or to a report, when we rely on its truth and certainty. The *credit* of a man depends on his virtues; the credit of his writings, on their worth.)

critical. Decisive, noting a time or state on which the issue of things depends; important, as regards the consequences; as a critical time or moment; a critical juncture. (The negotiations reached a *critical* state and required the most careful diplomacy.)

cultivate. To improve by labor or study; to advance the growth of; to refine and improve by correction of faults, and enlargement of powers or good qualities; as, to cultivate talents. (We may *cultivate* righteousness as we study the scriptures.)

cultivated. To improve by labor or study; to advance the growth of; to refine and improve by correction of faults, and enlargement of powers or good qualities; as, to cultivate talents; to cultivate a taste for poetry. (The leaders *cultivated* a peaceful, prosperous nation by obedience to proper principle.)

cultivating. Tilling; preparing for crops; improving in worth or good qualities; fostering. (*Cultivating* a knowledge of truth with strength of character and high moral standards should be the goal of each student.)

cunning. Knowing; skillful; experienced; well-instructed. Wrought with skill; curious, ingenious; shrewd; sly; crafty; astute; designing. (Beware a *cunning* man, for his intentions are rarely truly displayed.)

current. Flowing, running, passing; hence, passing from person to person, or from hand to hand; circulating; as current opinions. (*Current* events often influence lawmakers to legislate without analysis regarding the correctness of the principles involved.)

customary. According to custom, or to established or common usage; as a customary dress; customary compliments; in common practice; habitual. (It was formerly *customary* for the Supreme Court to adhere to the words and intent of the founders in their decisions.)

declare. To make a declaration; to proclaim or avow some opinion or resolution in favor or in opposition; to make known explicitly some determination; with for or against; as, the prince declared for the allies; the Allied powers declared against France. (Like fawning courtiers, for success they wait; / And then come smiling, and *declare* for fate [Dryden]. Rarely will a tyrant *declare* his truthful intentions.)

decline. A leaning from; a falling off; a tendency to a worse state; deterioration. (The *decline* of virtue and religion.)

deference. A yielding in opinion; submission of judgment to the opinion or judgment of another; complaisance; condescension; submission. (We often decline acting in opposition to those for whose wisdom we have a great *deference*. When questions of doctrine arise, one must give *deference* to the prophet of God.)

deficiency. A failing; a falling short; imperfection; as a deficiency in moral duties. (Mortality implies the existence of *deficiency* to some degree.)

defy. To dare; to brave; to provoke to combat or strife, by appealing to courage of another; to challenge. (Goliath *defied* the armies of Israel. Were we to abolish the common law, it would rise triumphant above its own ruins, deriding and *defying* its impotent enemies [Duponceau]. Logic cannot explain how the colonies were able to *defy* the power of England and gain their liberty. The hand of God must be recognized in the matter.)

delegated. Deputed; sent with a trust or commission to act for another; appointed a judge; committed, as authority. (*Delegated* authority must not exceed the scope of the appointment.)

deliberate. To weigh in the mind; to consider and examine the reasons for and against a measure. (Let us use proper principle as we *deliberate* the course we shall follow.)

deliberation. The act of deliberating; the act of weighing and examining the reasons for and against a choice or measure; consideration. We say, a measure has been taken with deliberation. (*Deliberation* will result in good decisions if proper principle is given full consideration and is followed.)

delineated. Drawn; marked with lines exhibiting the form or figure; sketched; designed; painted; described. (The proper form and function of government is *delineated* within the United States Constitution.)

deluded. Deceived; misled; led into error. (The people were *deluded* to believing that giving up their God-given rights would bring them peace, security and happiness.)

depository (depositories). A place where anything is lodged for safekeeping. (A warehouse is a *depository* for goods; a clerk's office, for records.

derived. Drawn, as from a source. (The government *derived* its just powers from the consent of the people.)

derives. To draw from, as in a regular course or channel; to receive from a source by a regular conveyance. (A nation *derives* its just powers from the consent of the governed.)

APPENDIX I: GEORGE WASHINGTON'S FAREWELL ADDRESS VOCABULARY WORDS

desert. To forsake; to leave utterly; to abandon; to quit with a view not to return. (For decades it has been the tenancy for political leaders and citizens alike to *desert* sound principles put forth in the Constitution of the United States.)

design. Purpose, intention; aim; implying a scheme or plan in the mind. (The hearts of evil men have as their *design* the destruction of good.)

designates. Marked out; indicated; shown; pointed out; appointed. (The Constitution *designates* and defines the powers obligated to the branches of the national government.)

designating. Pointing out; indicating; appointing. (Thank you for *designating* the problem.)

designing. Forming a design; planning. (*Designing* men are always liable to suspicion.)

despotism. Absolute rule; authority unlimited and uncontrolled by men, constitution or laws, and depending alone on the will of the prince; as, the despotism of a Turkish sultan. (One of the primary roots of *despotism* is a desire for power.)

destiny. State or condition appointed or predetermined; ultimate fate; as, men are solicitous to know their future destiny, which is however happily concealed from them; the fates, or supposed powers which preside over human life, spin it out and determine it. (It is the *destiny* of this nation to endure in glory if it holds true to principles of righteousness.)

detached. Separated; parted from; disunited. (In an attempt to exercise what they perceived as states rights, the states of the Confederacy *detached* themselves from the Union.)

deter. To discourage and stop by fear; to stop or prevent from acting or proceeding, by danger, difficulty or other consideration which disheartens, or countervails the motive for an act. (We are often *deterred* from our duty by trivial difficulties. The state of the road or a cloudy sky may *deter* a man from undertaking a journey.)

determination. The act of determining or deciding. Decision of a question in the mind; firm resolution; settled purpose; as, they have acquainted me with their determination. (To remain free, the people must exhibit a firm *determination* to resist experimentation upon their liberties.)

devote. To appropriate by vow; to set apart or dedicate by a solemn act; to consecrate; to give up wholly; to direct attention wholly or chiefly. (No *devoted* thing that a man shall *devote* to the Lord shall be sold or redeemed. Every *devoted* thing is most holy to the Lord [Lev. 27]. We should *devote* our lives to following Christ and doing His will.)

dictate. To tell with authority; to suggest; to admonish. (We say, the spirit of God *dictated* the messages of the prophets to Israel. Conscience often *dictates* to men the rules by which they are to govern their conduct.)

diffidence. Distrust; want of confidence; any doubt of the power, ability or disposition of others. It is said there was a general diffidence of the strength and resources of the nation, and of the sincerity of the king. (His lack of experience created an attitude of *diffidence* toward his abilities.)

diffusing. To spread; to send out or extend in all directions; to disperse. (Flowers *diffuse* their odors. The fame of Washington is *diffused* over Europe. The knowledge of the true God will be *diffused* over the earth.)

diffusion. A spreading or scattering; dispersion; as the diffusion of water; the diffusion of air or light; the diffusion of knowledge, or of good principles. (We may become instruments of the *diffusion* of the gospel when we become missionaries.)

digested. Reduced to method; arranged in due order; received without rejection; borne; disposed for use. (The Founding Fathers *digested* the natural tendencies of mankind and established a government, which was designed to keep evil designs in check.)

diminution. The act of lessening; a making smaller; opposed to augmentation; as the diminution of size, of wealth, of power, of safety. (Unrighteousness brings a *diminution* of faith and spiritual light.)

disbursements. The act of paying out, as money from a public or private chest. (The public heart has purchased and embraced socialism through the *disbursement* of public funds.)

discard. To dismiss from service or employment, or from society; to cast off; to thrust away, to reject. (Many modern-day political leaders are trying to *discard* our Constitution.)

discharge. To perform or execute, as a duty or office considered as a charge. (One man *discharges* the office of a sheriff; another that of a priest. We are all bound to *discharge* the duties of piety, of benevolence, and of charity. Good men are bound by duty for the faithful *discharge* of all of their responsibilities.)

discountenance. To abash; to ruffle or discompose the countenance; to put to shame; to put out of countenance. (How would one look from his majestic brow / *Discountenance* her despised [Milton]. A evil act will *discountenance* your good family name.)

discountenancing. Abashing; discouraging. (It is *discountenancing* to think how far we have strayed from the ideals proposed by Washington, Jefferson, and Madison.)

APPENDIX I: GEORGE WASHINGTON'S FAREWELL ADDRESS VOCABULARY WORDS

discrimination. Separating; distinguishing; marking with notes of difference; characterized by peculiar differences; the act of making or observing a difference; distinction. (*Discrimination* between right and wrong is made easier if one listens to the whisperings of the Holy Ghost.)

discriminations. The act of distinguishing; the act of making or observing a difference; distinction. (The *discrimination* between right and wrong allows a people to choose to serve God.)

disorders. Want of order; tumult; disturbance of the peace of society; irregularity; as, the troops were thrown into disorder. (The papers are in *disorder*. The city is sometimes troubled with the *disorders* of its citizens.)

disposed. Set in order; arranged; placed; adjusted; applied; bestowed; inclined. (A nation *disposed* to recognizing the hand of God in its affairs will reap great blessings.)

disposes. To set; to place or distribute; to arrange. (The general *disposed* his troops in three lines. The ships were *disposed* in the from of a crescent. The trees are *disposed* in the form of a quincunx. Understanding the Constitution in the tradition of the Founding Fathers *disposes* us to preserve our liberty.)

disposition. The act of disposing, or state of being disposed; manner in which things or the part of a complex body are placed or arranged; order; method; distribution; arrangement; natural fitness or tendency, as the disposition in plants to grow in a direction upwards; temper or natural constitution of the mind; as a disposition in bodies to putrefaction; as an amiable or an irritable disposition. (We speak of the *disposition* of a person to undertake a particular work. The *dispositions* of men toward one another; a *disposition* friendly to any design. The Constitution acts as a restraint upon those whose *disposition* would lead to tyranny.)

dispositions. Temper or natural constitution of the mind; inclination; propensity; the temper or frame of mind, as directed to particular objects. (Cheerful and happy *dispositions* create a pleasant atmosphere.)

disregard. To omit to take notice of; to neglect to observe; to slight as unworthy of regard or notice. (Studious of good, man *disregarded* fame [Blackmore]. We are never to *disregard* the wants of the poor, nor the admonitions of conscience.)

dissension. Disagreement in opinion, usually a disagreement which is violent, producing warm debates or angry words; contention in words; strife; discord; quarrel; breach of friendship and union. (Debates, *dissensions*, uproars are thy joy [Dryden]. Paul and Barnabas had no small *dissension* with them [Acts 15]. *Dissension* in a family destroys their peace and happiness.)

dissimilar. Unlike, either in nature, properties or external form; not similar; not having the resemblance of; heterogeneous. (The tempers of men are as *dissimilar* as their features. The principles upon which this nation was founded are *dissimilar* to the current alien philosophies that are fostered among our people.)

distinct. Literally, having the difference marked; separated by a visible sign, or by a note or mark. (He holds two *distinct* offices. He is known by *distinct* titles.)

distract. To draw apart; to pull in different directions, and separate; to turn or draw from any object; to divert from any point, towards another point or toward various other objects. (Contradictory or mistaken orders may *distract* an army. Petty issues are often used to *distract* the attention of the citizens from more ominous threats.)

distribution. The act of dividing among a number; a dealing in parts or portions. (As the *distribution* of an estate among heirs or children.)

diversifying. Making various in form or qualities; giving variety to; variegating. (*Diversifying* one's business allows one to take advantage of a broader marketplace.)

divert. To turn off from any course, direction or intended application; to turn the mind from business or study. (Politicians often *divert* the nation's attention from principle by using emotion.)

domestic. Belonging to the house, or home; pertaining to one's place of residence, and to the family; as domestic concerns; domestic life; domestic duties; domestic affairs; domestic contentions; domestic happiness; domestic worship; pertaining to a nation considered as a family, or to one's own country. (Proper government should have minimal power over the *domestic* affairs of the people.)

domination. The exercise of power in ruling; dominion; arbitrary authority; tyranny; one highly exalted in power; or the fourth order of angelic beings. (*Domination* of the world was the mad tyrant's greatest desire.)

dominion. Sovereign or supreme authority; the power of governing and controlling. Territory under a government; right of governing. (Whether they be thrones, or *dominions*, or principalities, or powers [Col. 1]. A tyrant seeks to enlarge his *dominion* by force or other nefarious means.)

dooms. To judge; to condemn to any punishment; to consign by a decree or sentence; as, the criminal is doomed to chains; condemnation; sentence. (Hence, the final *doom* is the last judgment. To toil for subsistence is the *doom* of most men. Ignorance, greed, and laziness have brought *doom* to many a free nation.)

dubious. Doubtful; wavering or fluctuating in opinion; not settled; not determined; as, the mind is in a dubious state; uncertain; that which the truth is not ascertained or known; as a dubious question; not clear; not plain. (Frivolous tampering with the original intent of the Constitution results in *dubious* outcome.)

dupes. A person who is deceived; or one easily led astray by his credulity. (Enemies of the Constitution make use of *dupes* who embrace their rhetoric and philosophies.)

dutiful. Expressive of respect or a sense of duty; respectful; reverential; required by duty; as dutiful reverence; dutiful attentions. (A *dutiful* son will always be considerate of his mother.)

edifice. A building; a structure; the word is not applied to a mean building, but to temples, churches or elegant mansion—houses, and to other great structures. (The *edifice* of sound government is based upon correct principles.)

effect. Consequence; event; purpose; general intent. (Poverty, disease, and disgrace are the natural *effects* of immorality.)

efficacious. Effectual; producing the effect intended; as an efficacious remedy for disease. (Limiting the power of government to its proper bounds is *efficacious* in preserving individual liberty.)

efficacy. Power to produce effects (as the *efficacy* of the gospel in converting men from sin; the *efficacy* of medicine in counteracting disease; and the *efficacy* of manure in fertilizing land.)

efficient. Causing effects; producing; that causes any thing to be what it is. (The most *efficient* efforts of man fall far short of the perfection of God.)

elevation. The act of raising or conveying from a lower or deeper place to a higher; the act of exalting in rank, degree or condition; as, the elevation of a man to a throne (Angels, in their several degrees of *elevation* above us, may be endowed with more comprehensive faculties [Locke]. Noble acts bring *elevation* to one's soul.)

embitter. To make bitter; painful; afflicted; distressed; hurtful; mourning. (That which will *embitter* the soul is often destructive of the peace of the soul.)

embrace. To seize eagerly; to lay hold on; to receive or take with willingness that which is offered; as, to embrace the Christian religion; to embrace the opportunity of doing a favor. (Truly good men will *embrace* and live by proper principles.)

employed. Occupied; applied in business. (A portion of time should be daily *employed* in reading the scriptures.)

enable. To make able; to supply with power, physical or moral. (Fortitude *enables* us to bear pain without murmuring. The law enables us to dispose of our property by will.)

encouragement. The act of giving courage, or confidence of success; incitement to action or to practice; incentive. (We ought never to neglect the *encouragement* of youth in generous deeds. The praise of good men serves as an *encouragement* to virtue and heroism.)

encroach. To enter on the rights and possessions of another; to intrude; to take possession of what belongs to another, by gradual advances into his limits or jurisdiction, and usurping a part of his rights or prerogatives; to creep on gradually without right. (The farmer who runs a fence on his neighbor's land, and encloses a piece with his own, *encroaches* on his neighbor's property. The sea is said to *encroach* on the land, when it wears it away gradually; and the land encroaches on the sea, when it is extended into it by alluvion. It is important to prevent one branch of government from *encroaching* on the jurisdiction of another. For many years, it has been the tendency of the national government to *encroach* on the proper spheres of state and local government, as well as the rights of the individual.)

encroachment. The entering gradually on the rights or possessions of another, and taking possession; unlawful intrusion; advance into the territories or jurisdiction of another, by silent means, or without right. (In law, if a tenant owes two shillings rent service to the Lord, and the Lord takes three, it is an *encroachment* [Cowel]. The issuing of executive orders by the president is an *encroachment* upon the legislative powers of Congress.)

endeavor. An effort; an essay; an attempt; an exertion of physical strength, to the intellectual powers, towards the attainment of an object. (The bold and sufficient pursue their game with more passion, *endeavor*, and application, and therefore often succeed [Temple]. The vigor with which one *endeavors* to press his point is not a sure indication of truth.)

enfeeble. To deprive of strength; to reduce the strength or force of; to weaken. (Excessive grief and melancholy *enfeeble* the mind. Long wars *enfeeble* a state.)

APPENDIX I: GEORGE WASHINGTON'S FAREWELL ADDRESS VOCABULARY WORDS

engagements. The act of pawning, pledging or making liable for debt; obligation by agreement or contract. (Men are often more ready to make *engagements* than to fulfill them.)

engines. A military machine; as a battering ram, &c. Means; any thing used to effect a purpose. (Despots often foster popular uprisings as effective *engines* in their quest for power.)

enjoin. To join. (Husbands and wives *enjoin* in an effort to raise their children in righteousness.)

enlightened. Rendered light; illuminated; instructed; informed; furnished with clear views. (One's mind may be *enlightened* to the truth through the study of the word of God, prayer, fasting, and service to mankind.)

enmities. The quality of being an enemy; the opposite of friendship; ill will; hatred; unfriendly dispositions; malevolence; it expresses more than aversion and less than malice, and differs from displeasure in denoting a fixed or rooted hatred, whereas displeasure is more transient. (I will put *enmity* between thee and the woman [Gen. 3]. The carnal mind is *enmity* against God [Rom. 8]. The friendship of the world is *enmity* with God [James 4]. Satan has an undying *enmity* against Christ and His plan. The *enmities* of Satan against righteousness are expressed in countless ways.)

ennobles. To make noble; to raise to nobility; to dignify; to exalt; to aggrandize; to elevate in degree, qualities or excellence; to make famous or illustrious. (What can *ennoble* sots, or slaves, or cowards? The gospel of Jesus Christ *ennobles* the souls of mankind and brings them to greatness.)

enormities. Literally, the transgression of a rule, or deviation from right. Hence, any wrong, irregular, vicious or sinful act, either in government or morals. (We shall speak of the *enormities* of the government [Spenser]. This law will not restrain the *enormity* [Hooker].)

entangle. To twist or interweave in such a manner as not to be easily separated; to make confused or disordered; to involve in any thing complicated, and from which it is difficult to extricate one's self; to involve in difficulties. (The Pharisees took counsel how they might *entangle* him in his talk. It is not our right to *entangle* our nation in the internal affairs of other nations.)

enterprise. That which is undertaken, or attempted to be performed. (An *enterprise* that detracts from principle is unworthy of support.)

enterprising. Undertaking, especially bold design; bold or forward to undertake; resolute, active, or prompt to attempt great or untried schemes. (*Enterprising* men often succeed beyond all human probability.)

entitled. Dignified or distinguished by a title; having a claim; as, every good man is entitled to respect. (Modern and mere politicians are rarely *entitled* to the respect of principled statesmen.)

envenomed. Tainted or impregnated with venom or poison; embittered; exasperated. (O what a world is this, when what is comely / *Envenoms* him that bears it! [Shakespeare]. The tyrant spoke *envenomed* words against those who sought to uphold their liberty.)

equivalents. Equal in value or worth; equal in force, power or effect. (In barter, the goods given are supposed to be *equivalent* to the goods received. A steam engine may have force or power *equivalent* to that of thirty horses. It is folly to assume that recent interpretations of constitutional principles are *equivalent* to the sound understanding of correct principles put forth by the Founding Fathers.

essay. Seek; to try; to attempt; endeavor. (In spite of opposition, it is proper to *essay* upholding correct principles.)

essential. Necessary to the constitution or existence of a thing; important in the highest degree. (Piety and good works are *essential* to the Christian character. Judgement is more *essential* to a general than courage [Denham].)

essentially. In essence; as, minerals and plants are essentially different; in an important degree; in effect. (There is *essentially* no difference in the effect on individual liberty between communism, fascism, and Nazism.)

estimate. A valuing or rating in the mind; a judgment or opinion of the value, degree, extent or quantity of any thing, without ascertaining it. (We form *estimates* of the expenses of a war, of the probable outfits of a voyage, of the comparative strength or merits of two men, of the extent of a kingdom or its population.)

evinced. Made evident; proved. (The character of a leader is *evinced* by his actions, rather than his words.)

exalt. To raise high; to elevate; to raise in pride; to elevate in power; to elevate with joy or confidence. (He is my father's God, and I will *exalt* him [Ex. 15:2]. Heavenly Father's plan and the atonement of Christ allow us to be *exalted*.)

exalted. Raised to a lofty height; elevated; honored with office or rank; extolled; magnified; refined; dignified; sublime. (Time never fails to bring every *exalted* reputation to a strict scrutiny [Ames]. True principles will eventually be *exalted* in the hearts and minds of the people.)

excessive. Beyond any given degree, measure or limit, or beyond the common measure or proportion. (*Excessive* bail shall not be required [Bill of Rights]. The movement toward the welfare state by those in power has placed an *excessive* burden upon all citizens of the nation.)

excluded. Thrust out; shut out; hindered or prohibited from entrance or admission; debarred; not included or comprehended. (The principles of communism are *excluded* as a potential form of government by the Constitution established by the Founding Fathers.)

exclusion. The act of excluding, or of thrusting out; ejection; the act of denying entrance or admission; a shutting out; rejection. (Supreme Court decisions have resulted in the *exclusion* of the God of Israel from public schools and much of our public life.)

exclusive. Having the power of preventing entrance; debarring from participation; possessed and enjoyed to the exclusion of others; as an exclusive privilege. (Government-mandated monopoly provides an *exclusive* market for favored businesses.)

execution. Performance; the act of completing or accomplishing. (The excellence of the subject contributed much to the happiness of the *execution* [Dryden]. The *execution* of our responsibilities to uphold correct principles should be carried out after seeking the inspiration of God.)

executive. The officer, whether king, president or other chief magistrate, who superintends the execution of the laws; the person who administers the government; executive power or authority in government. (An honorable *executive* will lead the nation using proper principle.)

exemption. Freedom from any service, charge, burden, tax, evil or requisition, to which others are subject; immunity; privilege. (Many cities of Europe purchased or obtained *exemptions* from feudal servitude. No man can claim an *exemption* from pain, sorrow, or death.)

exertions. The act of exerting or straining; the act of putting into motion or action; effort. (The ship was saved by great *exertions* of the crew. No *exertions* will suppress a vice that great men countenance. Politicians exercise great *exertions* to make reasonable improper forms of government appear reasonable.)

exhibit. To offer or present to view; to present for inspection; to show; to display; to manifest publicly; as, to exhibit a noble example of bravery or generosity. (A man without guile will *exhibit* his true intentions.)

exigencies. Demand, urgency; urgent need or want; We speak of the exigence of the case; the exigence of the times, or of business. Pressing necessity; distress; any case which demands immediate action, supply or remedy. (A wise man adapts his measures to his *exigencies*. In the present *exigency*, no time is to be lost.)

expectation. The act of expecting or looking forward to a future event with at least some reason to believe the event will happen. (My soul, wait thou only on God, for my *expectation* is from Him [Ps. 62:5]. We obey God's commandments with the *expectation* of receiving His approval.)

expedients. Literally hastening; urging forward; that which serves to promote or advance; any means which may be employed to accomplish an end; useful; profitable. (Many things may be lawful, which are not *expedient* to mortality.)

explicit. Plain; open; clear. (He was *explicit* in his terms. His description of the situation was *explicit*.)

exposes. To lay open; to set to public view; to disclose; to uncover or draw from concealment. (Teaching the gospel *exposes* the false and foolish doctrines of men and devils.)

extend. To stretch in any direction; to carry forward, or continue in length; to enlarge; to widen; to continue; to prolong. (He hath *extended* mercy to me before the king [Ezra 7]. I will *extend* peace to her like a river [Is. 66]. Let our charities *extend* to the heathen.)

extensive. Wide; large; having great enlargement or extent. (As an *extensive* farm, an *extensive* lake, *extensive* benevolence. The achievement of good and noble works is most *extensive* among a people that love and serve God and each other in righteousness.)

external. Outward; exterior; as the external surface of a body; opposed to internal. (*External* appearance often does not reflect the heart of the men.)

extraordinary. Beyond or out of the common order or method; not in the usual, customary or regular course; not ordinary. (*Extraordinary* evils require extraordinary remedies. The temple of Solomon was *extraordinarily* magnificent [Wilkins]. This nation's Founding Fathers were, almost to a man, *extraordinary* men.)

APPENDIX I: GEORGE WASHINGTON'S FAREWELL ADDRESS VOCABULARY WORDS

extremity. The utmost point or side; the verge; the point or border that terminates a thing; the utmost parts; extreme or utmost distress, straits or difficulties; the utmost rigor or violence; the most aggravated state. (As the *extremities* of a country. The *extremities* of the body, in painting and sculpture, are the head, hands, and feet. Even charity and forbearance may be carried to *extremity*. The Greeks have endured oppression in its utmost *extremity*. The world is running after farce, the *extremity* of bad poetry [Dryden].)

fabric. The structure of any thing; the manner in which the parts of a thing are united by art and labor; workmanship; the frame or structure of a building; any system composed of connected parts. (The *fabric* of our nation has unraveled as we have violated the laws of God and strayed from His path.)

facilitate. To make easy or less difficult; to free from difficulty or impediment, or to diminish it; difficulty or impediment, or to diminish it; to lessen the labor of. (The greed of the people will *facilitate* the purposes of a tyrant.)

facilitating. Rendering easy or easier. (It seems common for men in power to use their office in *facilitating* their personal wealth.)

facility. Easiness to be performed; freedom from difficulty; ease. (He performed the work or operation with great *facility*. Though *facility* and hope of success might invite some other choice. Practice gives a wonderful *facility* in executing works of art.)

faction. A party, in political society, combined or acting in union, in opposition to the prince, government or state; usually applied to a minority, but it may be applied to a majority. (Sometimes a state is divided into *factions* nearly equal. Rome was almost always disturbed by *factions*. A feeble government produces more *factions* than an oppressive one [Ames]. By a *faction*, I understand a number of citizens, whether amounting to a majority or minority of the whole, who are united and actuated by some common impulse of passion, or of interest, adverse to the rights of other citizens, or to the permanent and aggregate interests of the community [Madison, *The Federalist*].)

fallible. Liable to fail or mistake; that may err or be deceived in judgment. (All mortal men are *fallible*.)

fatal. Destructive; calamitous. (Rejecting the counsel of God is *fatal* to one's spirituality.)

feeble. Weak; destitute of much physical strength; sickly. (A nation becomes *feeble* as it strays from proper principle.)

felicity. Happiness, or rather great happiness; blessedness; blissfulness; the joys of heaven. (A just and principled people has a greater hope of *felicity*.)

fervent. Ardent; very warm; earnest; excited; animated; glowing; as fervent zeal; fervent piety. (Let us call upon God in *fervent* prayer.)

fervently. Earnestly; eagerly; vehemently; with great warmth; with pious ardor; with earnest zeal. (Epaphras—saluted you, laboring *fervently* for you in prayers [Col. 4]. We must *fervently* pray for the preservation of the correct principles upon which this nation was founded.)

foes. An enemy; an opponent; one who opposes any thing in principle. (Those who seek to alter our constitutional form of government may be viewed as the *foes* of liberty.)

folly. Weakness on intellect; imbecility of mind; want of understanding. (A fool layeth open his *folly* [Prov. 13]. It is *folly* for a nation to believe that it may be ignorant of correct principles and maintain its liberty.)

foments. To encourage; to abet; to cherish and promote by excitements. (Civil unrest *foments* a government to suppress proper government and impose tyranny.)

forbid. To prohibit; to interdict; to command to forbear or not to do. (The laws of God *forbid* us to swear. Good manners also *forbid* us to use profane language.)

forego. To give up; to renounce; to resign; voluntarily to avoid the enjoyment of good; to forbear to possess or enjoy. (Let us *forego* the pleasures of sense, to secure immortal bliss. The wise will *forego* a transitory pleasure to preserve a future blessing.)

foresee. To see beforehand; to see or know an event before it happens. (A prudent man *foreseeth* the evil and hideth himself [Prov. 22]. If we abide in correct principles I *foresee* a happy people.)

formation. The act of making or forming; the act of creating or causing to exist; or more generally, the operation of composing, by bringing materials together, or of shaping and giving form; as the formation of the earth; the formation of a state or constitution. (The hand of God in the *formation* of the government under the U.S. Constitution was widely admitted by the founders.)

former. Before in time; preceding another or something else in order of time. (The *former* friends, Adams and Jefferson, again renewed their association.)

APPENDIX I: GEORGE WASHINGTON'S FAREWELL ADDRESS VOCABULARY WORDS

fortify. Strengthen. (To *fortify* the mind against sudden calamity, to *fortify* an opinion or resolution, to *fortify* hope or desire)

fortress. To guard; to fortify. (Abiding in the Constitution in the tradition of the Founding Fathers is a *fortress* by which correct government may be preserved.)

foundation. The basis or groundwork of any thing; that on which any thing stands, and by which it is supported. (A free government has its *foundation* in the choice and consent of the people to be governed. Christ is the *foundation* of the church.)

fraternal. Brotherly; pertaining to brethren; becoming brothers. (As *fraternal* love or affection, a *fraternal* embrace)

frequent. Often seen or done; often happening at short intervals; often repeated or occurring. (We made *frequent* visits to the hospital. *Frequent* review of the Constitution is required if we are to maintain its viability.)

fundamental. Pertaining to the foundation or basis; serving for the foundation. Hence, essential; important; as a fundamental truth or principle. (Individual and national righteousness are *fundamental* to liberty.)

fury. Rage; a storm of anger; madness; turbulence. (I do oppose my patience to his *fury* [Shakespeare]. Can a nation long offend God and not experience His *fury*?)

generally. In general; commonly; extensively, though not universally; most frequently, but not without exceptions. (A hot summer *generally* follows a cold winter. Men are *generally* more disposed to censure than to praise, as they generally suppose it easier to depress excellence in others than to equal or surpass it by elevating themselves.)

genuine. Native; belonging to the original stock; hence, real; natural; true; pure; not spurious, false or adulterated. (The Gaels are supposed to be *genuine* descendants of the Celts. Vices and crimes are the *genuine* effects of depravity, as virtue and piety are the *genuine* fruits of holiness.)

gilding. The art or practice of overlaying things with gold leaf or liquid. That which is laid on in overlaying with gold. (A pompous leader is often guilty of *gilding* his character for public display.)

gratitude. An emotion of the heart, excited by a favor of benefit received; a sentiment of kindness or good will towards a benefactor; thankfulness. Gratitude is an agreeable emotion, consisting in or accompanied with good will to a benefactor, and a disposition to make a suitable return can be made, with a desire to see the benefactor prosperous and happy. Gratitude is a virtue of the highest excellence, as it implies a feeling and generous heart, and a proper sense of duty. (The love of God is the sublimest *gratitude* [Paley]. *Gratitude* expressed is one of the most noble sentiments. It is a duty and an honor to express *gratitude* to God for blessings received.)

guardian. Protecting; performing the office of a protector. (The people of the nation are to be the *guardian* of the Constitution.)

habitual. Formed to acquired by habit; frequent use or custom. (Abusive power is the *habitual* means by which tyrants destroy liberty.)

harmony. Concord or agreement in views, sentiments or manners, interests, etc.; agreement; concord. (The citizens live in *harmony*. To become a Zion, people we must live in *harmony* with righteousness and become of one heart and one mind.)

haughty. Proud and disdainful; having a opinion of one's self, with some contempt for others; lofty and arrogant; supercilious. (His wife was a woman of a *haughty* and imperious nature [Clarendon]. A *haughty* spirit goeth before a fall [Prov. 16]. Our leaders have become *haughty* and unteachable.)

hazard. Chance; accident; casualty; a fortuitous event; that which falls or comes suddenly or unexpectedly, the cause of which is unknown, or whose operation is unforeseen or unexpected; danger; peril; risk. (We cannot allow the preservation of our liberties to be left to *hazard* or happenstance. We must vigorously preserve them.)

hence. From this place; from this time; in the future; from this cause or reason. (The Founding Fathers intended that the form of government they established was to be the "law of the land" from *hence* forth.)

hitherto. In any time, or every time till now; in time preceding the present. (The principles embodied in the United States Constitution were *hitherto* unknown in any modern government.)

hostile. Belonging to a public enemy; designating enmity, particularly public enmity, or a state of war. (*Hostile* invading forces must be repulsed by effective and immediate defenses.)

hostility. The state of war between nations or states; the actions of an open enemy; aggression; attacks of an enemy. (*Hostility* being thus suspended with France [Hayward]. We have carried on even our *hostilities* with humanity [Atterbury]. Satan and his minions have operated for generations with open *hostility* against the God-given principle of agency.)

humanity. Mankind collectively; the human race. (It is a debt we owe to *humanity* [S. S. Smith]. It is God's desire that *humanity* live in peace and freedom.)

hypothesis. A supposition; a proposition or principle which is supposed or taken for granted, in order to draw a conclusion or inference for proof of the point in question; something not proved, but assumed for the purpose of argument. (Many concepts that are taught as truth in school are in actuality based merely upon *hypothesis*.)

ill-concerted. Wrongly acting together. (Majority actions which destroy God-given rights are *ill-concerted*, regardless of popularity.)

ill-will. Enmity; malevolence. (*Ill-will* is often generated in a political system, which fosters party over principle. Bearing of *ill-will* begats unhappiness for one who holds it in his heart.)

illusion. Deceptive appearance; false show, by which a person is or may be deceived, or his expectations disappointed; mockery. (Freedom of the press is an *illusion* in the Soviet Union because the government owns and controls the means of printing.)

immense. Unlimited; unbounded; infinite. (This nation has *immense* power to do good if it abides in correct principles.)

impair. To make worse; to diminish in quantity, value or excellence; to weaken; to enfeeble. (The force of evidence may be *impaired* by the suspicion of interest in the witness. Power-seeking leaders *impair* proper government.)

impartial. Not partial; not biased in favor of one party more than another; indifferent; unprejudiced. (The laws of the nation should be *impartial* to the station and position of each citizen.)

impelled. Driven forward; urged on; moved by any force or power, physical or moral. (One is *impelled* toward God when motivated by righteous, noble principles.)

impels. To drive or urge forward; to press on; to excite to action or to move forward, by the application of physical force, or moral suasion or necessity. (Our love of God *impels* our righteousness.)

implicate. To involve; connected; concerned; proved to be concerned or to have had a part. (In an attempt to prove the existence of a conspiracy, the attorneys sought to *implicate* others as codefendants.)

imply. Literally, to enfold or involve; to wrap up. To involve or contain in substance or essence, or by fair inference, or by construction of law, when not expressed in words.

(Where a malicious act is proved, a malicious intention is *implied* [Sherlock]. When a man employs a laborer to work for him, or an agent to transact business for him, the act of hiring *implies* an obligation, and a promise that he shall pay him a reasonable reward for his services. Contracts are express or *implied*; express contracts are those in which an agreement or promise is expressed by words or in writing; *implied* contracts are such as arise from the presumption of law, or the justice and reason of the transaction [Blackstone].)

impostures. Deception practiced under a false or assumed character; fraud or imposition practiced by a false pretender. (Many modern organizations *imposture* as friends of liberty, but they have only assumed the slogans of liberty and have not embraced the principles of freedom.)

impracticability. The state or quality of being beyond human power, or the means proposed; infeasibility; that cannot be done or performed. (It is *impracticable* for a man to lift a ton by his unassisted strength; but not *impracticable* for a man aided by a mechanical power.)

impression. The effect which objects produce on the mind. (The truths of the gospel make an *impression* on the mind. The heart is *impressed* with love or gratitude. We lie open to the *impressions* of flattery.)

inauspicious. Ill-omened; unfortunate; unlucky; evil; unfavorable. (The war commenced at an *inauspicious* time, and its issue was *inauspicious*. The counsels of a bad man have an *inauspicious* influence on society.)

incidents. Happening, apt to happen. (The *incidents* of our lives and our reaction to them define our character.)

incitement. That which incites the mind or mover to action; motive; incentive; impulse. (From the long records of a distant age, / Derive *incitements* to renew thy rage [Pope]. The role of prophets has ever been to provide the *incitement* necessary to focus the people on behavior pleasing to God.)

inclination. A leaning of the mind or will; propension or propensity; a disposition more favorable to one thing than to another. (The prince has no *inclination* to peace. The bachelor has manifested no *inclination* to marry. Men have a natural *inclination* to pleasure. A mere *inclination* to a thing is not properly a willing of that thing.)

incline. To lean, in a moral sense; to be disposed; to have some wish or desire; to give a tendency or propension to the will or affections; to bend; to cause to stoop or bow. (As, to be inclined to eat. A road *inclines* to the north or south. The Connecticut river runs

APPENDIX I: GEORGE WASHINGTON'S FAREWELL ADDRESS VOCABULARY WORDS

south, *inclining* in some part of its course to the west, and below Middletown, it *inclines* to the east. Incline our hearts to keep this law [Common Prayer].)

incompatible. Inconsistent; that cannot subsist with something else. Thus, truth and falsehood are essentially incompatible, as are virtue and vice. (Redistribution of private property by government agency is *incompatible* with the principles upon which this nation was founded.)

incompetent. Wanting adequate powers of mind or suitable faculties; as an incompetent judge; infancy, derangement, want of learning or dotage may render a person incompetent to fill an office or to transact business; wanting the legal or constitutional qualifications; inadequate; insufficient; unfit. (A person convicted of a crime is an *incompetent* witness in a court of law or equity.)

incongruous. Not congruous; unsuitable; not fitting; inconsistent; improper. (The dress of a seaman on a judge would be deemed *incongruous* with his character and station. A tendency to abuse power is *incongruous* to the character of one who truly loves liberty.)

inconsiderable. Not worthy of consideration or notice; unimportant; small; trivial. (No sin is *inconsiderable* in the sight of a holy God.)

inconvenient. Incommodious; unsuitable; disadvantageous; giving trouble or uneasiness; increasing the difficulty of progress or success. (Those who find it *inconvenient* to preserve freedom shall lose their freedom.)

index. That which points out; that which shows or manifests. (The *index* to freedom is measured by individual liberty.)

indifference. A state in which the mind is not inclined to one side more than the other; impartiality. (No person of humanity can behold the wretchedness of the poor with *indifference*. The indifference to the cause of liberty has caused the nation to lose many of the promises offered under proper government.)

indignantly. Affected at once with anger and disdain; feeling the mingled emotions of wrath and scorn or contempt, as when a person is exasperated at one despised, or by a mean action, or by the charge of a dishonorable act. (Goliath was *indignant* at the challenge of David.)

indispensable. Not to be dispensed with; that cannot be omitted, remitted or spared; absolutely necessary or requisite. (Air and water are *indispensable* to the life of man. Our duties to God and to our fellow men are of *indispensable* obligation. Integrity, honesty, and virtue are *indispensable* traits of proper character.)

indissoluble. That cannot be broken or rightfully violated; perpetually binding or obligatory; as an indissoluble league or covenant. (The marriage covenant is *indissoluble*, except in certain specified cases.)

inducement. Motive; any thing that leads the mind to will or to act; any argument, reason or fact that tends to persuade or influence the mind. (The love of ease is an *inducement* to idleness. The love of money is an *inducement* to industry in good men and to the perpetration of crimes in the bad.)

indulge. To permit to be or to continue; to gratify, negatively; not to check or restrain the will, appetite or desire; to gratify, positively; to permit to enjoy or practice. (Most men are more willing to *indulge* in easy vices, than to practice laborious virtues [Johnson]. It has become the practice of politicians to *indulge* themselves in power at the expense of principle.)

indulgence. To permit to enjoy or practice; or to yield to the enjoyment or practice of, without restraint or control; as, to indulge in sin, or in sensual pleasure. (Most men are more willing to *indulge* in easy vices, than to practice laborious virtues [Johnson]. *Indulgence* in vices that remove virtue from our lives will lead to great sorrow.)

indulgent. Yielding to the wishes, desires, humor or appetites of those under one's care; compliant; not opposing or restraining; as an indulgent parent. (One who is *indulgent* to dissipating desires will reap the whirlwind of sorrow.)

inestimable. That cannot be estimated or computed; as an estimable sum of money. (The value of truth and its worth to mankind in *inestimable*.)

inevitably. Without possibility of escape or evasion; unavoidably; certainly. (Sin *inevitably* leads to sorrow.)

infatuation. A state of mind in which the intellectual powers are weakened, either generally, or in regard to particular objects, so that the person affected acts without his usual judgement, and contrary to the dictates of reason. (All men who waste their substance in gaining, intemperance, or any other vice are chargeable with *infatuation*. Love of socialism breeds an *infatuation* with government and an abuse of the powers of government.)

infidelity. Unfaithfulness; breach of trust; treachery; deceit. (*Infidelity* will destroy the most sacred of relationships.)

APPENDIX I: GEORGE WASHINGTON'S FAREWELL ADDRESS VOCABULARY WORDS

infinite. Without limits; unbounded. (God is *infinite* in duration, having neither beginning nor end of existence.)

influenced. Moved; excited; affected; persuaded; induced. (His decision was *influenced* by a dedication to truth and principle.)

infractions. The act of breaking; breach; violation; nonobservance (As an *infraction* of a treaty, compact, agreement, or law. *Infractions* of God's law can have eternal consequences.)

infusing. Pouring in; instilling; steeping. (Ones efforts should be spent in *infusing* a love of God in their own heart and the hearts of their children.)

innovation. Change made by the introduction of something new; change in established laws, customs, rites or practices. (*Innovation* is expedient, when it remedies an evil, and safe, when men are prepared to receive it. *Innovation* is often used in an ill sense, for a change that disturbs settled opinions and practices without an equivalent advantage. An *innovation* by a creative person can often solve difficult problems. *Innovation* without principle invites disaster.)

innumerable. Not to be counted; that cannot be enumerated or numbered for multitude; in a loose sense, very numerous. (To many to be counted or numbered; *innumerable* [Milton]. The creations of God in all eternity are *innumerable* [Pope].)

insidious. Lying in wait; hence, watching an opportunity to ensnare or entrap; deceitful; sly; treacherous. (Politicians lay *insidious* plans to gather (arrogate) power to themselves.)

insidiously. With intention to ensnare; deceitfully; treacherously. (Wicked men *insidiously* seek the power to enslave.)

instigated. Incited or persuaded, as to evil. (Power-hungry men have *instigated* the overthrow of the principles of freedom.)

institutions. Establishment; that which is appointed, prescribed or founded by authority, and intended to be permanent; a system plan or society established, either by law or by the authority of individuals for promoting any object, public or social. (God originally established government as an *institution* to protect the God-given rights of all mankind.)

insurrection. A rising against civil or political authority; the open and active opposition of a number of persons to the execution of law in a city or state. (*Insurrection* differs from rebellion, for the latter expresses a revolt, or an attempt to overthrow the government, to establish a different one or to place the country under another jurisdiction. *Insurrection* differs from mutiny, as it respects the civil or political government; whereas a mutiny is an open opposition to law in the army or navy. It is found that this city of old time hath made *insurrection* against kings, and that rebellion and sedition have been made therein [Ezra 4].)

intentional. Intended; designed done with design or purpose. (The act was *intentional*, not accidental.)

intercourse. Communication; commerce; connection by reciprocal dealings between persons or nations, either in common affairs and civilities, in trade, or correspondence by letters. (We have an *intercourse* with neighbors and friends in mutual visits and in social concerns. Nations and individuals have *intercourse* with foreign nations or individuals by an interchange of commodities, by purchase and sale, by treaties, contracts, etc.)

internal. Inward; interior. (The *internal* peace of man is peace of mind or conscience.)

interruption. The act of interrupting, or breaking in upon progression. (Individual progress suffers *interruption* as personal righteousness ceases.)

interwoven. To weave together; to intermix or unite; intermingle. (To *interweave* truth with falsehood; as threads of silk and cotton *interwoven*. Our efforts must be to ensure that God's eternal truths are *interwoven* within our souls.)

intimate. Near; close; close in friendship or acquaintance. (An *intimate* knowledge of the scriptures helps one keep an eternal perspective.)

intimated. Hinted; slightly mentioned or signified. (The farmer quietly *intimated* that he would like to sell his farm.)

intractable. Not to be governed or managed; violent; stubborn; obstinate; refractory; as an intractable temper; not to be taught; indocile. (Many children today are *intractable* because of the false principles they are taught in school, and the media.)

intrigue. A plot or scheme of a complicated nature, intended to effect some purpose by secret artifices. (An *intrigue* may be formed and prosecuted by an individual, and we often hear of the *intrigues* of a minister or a courtier, but often several projectors are concerned in an *intrigue*. The destruction of a nation's freedom in often accomplished through the *intrigue* of conspirators.)

intrigues. A plot or scheme of a complicated nature, intended to effect some purpose by secret artifices. (The nation's internal security and national defense has been put at risk by the *intrigues* of enemies [foreign and domestic] who seek to over throw the Constitution of the nation.)

intrinsic. Inward; internal; hence, true; genuine; real; essential; inherent; not apparent or accidental; as the intrinsic value of gold or silver; the intrinsic merit of an action, the intrinsic worth or goodness of a person. (The *intrinsic* value of gold has contributed to its recognition as money throughout the world [Prior].)

intrinsically. Internally; in its nature; really; truly. (A lie is a thing absolutely and *intrinsically* evil [South].)

inveterate. Old; long established; deep rooted; firmly established by long continuance. (It is an *inveterate* and received opinion [Bacon]. The *principle* of liberty is *inveterate* to God's plan of happiness.)

invigorated. Strengthened; animated. (A nation may be *invigorated* by righteousness.)

inviolable. Not to be profaned; that ought not to be injured, polluted or treated with irreverence; as, a sacred place and sacred things should be considered inviolable. Not to be broken; as an inviolable league, covenant, agreement, contract, vow or promise. (Our covenants must be *inviolable*.)

irregular. Not regular; not according to common form or rules; not according to established principles or customs; not comfortable to nature or the usual operation of natural laws; not conformity to laws, human or divine. (The *irregular* soldiers fought a very successful guerilla warfare.)

issue. Event; consequence; end or ultimate result. (A return to God is the *issue* of mortal life.)

justice. The virtue which consists in giving to every one what is his due; practical conformity to the laws and to principles of rectitude in the dealings of men with each other; honesty; integrity in commerce or mutual intercourse. (The king was accused of the obstruction of *justice*.)

justifications. The act of justifying; a showing to be just or conformable to law, rectitude or propriety; vindication; defense. (The court listened to the evidence and arguments in *justification* of the prisoner's conduct. Our disobedience to God's commands admits no *justification*. I hope, for my brother's *justification*, he wrote this but as an essay of my virtue [Shakespeare]. Evil men use any *justification* available to usurp power.)

latter. Coming or happening after something else; mentioned the last of two. (The difference between reason and revelation and in what sense the *latter* is superior [Watts]. The days approaching the millennial advent of the Savior are considered the *latter* days.)

laudable. Praiseworthy; commendable; as laudable motives; laudable actions. (His efforts to restore the Constitution and the principles defined by the Founding Fathers were *laudable*.)

liable. Bound; obliged in law or equity; responsible; answerable. The surety is liable for the debt of his principal. (The parent is not *liable* for debts contracted by a son who is a minor, 4except for necessaries. A people who do not understand the proper principles of government are *liable* to be convinced to give up liberty for security.)

liberal. Of free heart; free to give or bestow; bountiful; generous; ample; it expresses less than profuse or extravagant; as a liberal donor or the liberal founders of a college or hospital; free; open; candid; as a liberal communication of thoughts. (Heavenly Father has been *liberal* in His bestowal of marvelous blessings upon His children.)

ligament. Any thing that ties or unites one thing or part to another. (Interwoven is the love of liberty with every *ligament* of your hearts [Washington]. The *ligaments* of the nation are strained by dissension.)

local. Pertaining to a place, or to a fixed or limited portion of space. (*Local* interests must never cause us to set aside correct principles.)

magnanimous. Greatness of mind; elevated in soul or in sentiment; brave. (There is an indissoluble union between a *magnanimous* policy and the solid rewards of public prosperity and felicity [Washington]. George Washington's life reflected a *magnanimous* dedication to his fellow countrymen.)

mansions. Any place of residence; a house; a habitation. (Thy *mansion* wants thee, Adam, rise [Milton]. In my Father's house are many *mansions* [John 14].)

maritime. Relating or pertaining to the sea or ocean; performed on the sea; naval; as maritime service. (The *maritime* powers of the United States have helped keep the nation free from foreign invasions.)

mass. Gross body of things considered collectively; the body ; the bulk; as the mass of people in a nation. (A *mass* of people may be misled by a skillful and unprincipled speaker.)

maxims. An established principle or proposition; a principle generally received or admitted as true. ("Wickedness never was happiness" is a *maxim* to live by.)

mere. This or that only; distinct from anything else. (*Mere* mortals seek to lead us and, therefore, must be bound down by the chains of the Constitution.)

APPENDIX I: GEORGE WASHINGTON'S FAREWELL ADDRESS VOCABULARY WORDS

minority. The smaller number; as the minority of the senate or house of representatives; opposed to majority. (The concept of republican government preserves the God-given rights of the *minority*.)

mirror. A pattern; an exemplar; that on which men ought to fix their eyes; that which gives a true representation, or in which a true image may be seen. (In a free nation, the government is largely a *mirror* of the moral standard of the people.)

mischiefs. To hurt; to harm; to injure. (Tyrants are forever indulging in *mischiefs* against the rights of liberty.)

misrepresent. To represent falsely or incorrectly; to give a false or erroneous representation, either maliciously, ignorantly or carelessly. (Widely distributed reports that *misrepresent* the truth destroy the peace of the nation.)

mitigate. To alleviate, as suffering; to assuage; to lessen; to make less severe; to abate; to make less rigorous; to moderate; to temper to calm; to appease; to diminish. (Government is to *mitigate* the oppression of the weak by the strong.)

moderate. Not extreme; restrained in passion. (Shall we be *moderate* in our love of God and obedience to His will?)

moderation. The state of being moderate, or of keeping a due mean between extremes or excess of violence. (*Moderation* in temper is always a virtue, but *moderation* in principle is always a vice [Thomas Paine].)

modification. The act of modifying or giving to any thing new forms, or differences of external qualities or modes. (The *modification* of the Constitution is to occur by the process outlined in article 5, not by usurpation or interpretation.)

modified. Changed in form or external qualities; varied; diversified. (Article 5 of the Constitution defines the process by which the Constitution may be *modified*.)

momentous. Important; weighty; of consequence. (Let no false step be made in the *momentous* concerns of the soul. Decisions made during one's youth can have *momentous* consequences.)

monarchical. Ruler; pertaining to monarchy (As *monarchical* government to power. *Monarchical* powers of the king are generally considered absolute.)

morality. The doctrine or system of moral duties, or the duties of men in the social character; ethics; the practice of the moral duties; virtue; the quality of an action which renders it good. (The system of *morality* to be gathered from the writings of ancient sages, falls very short of that delivered in the gospel [Swift]. We often admire the politeness of men whose *morality* we question. *Morality* is essential to please God.)

motive. That which incites to action; that which determines the choice, or moves the will. (Thus, we speak of good motives and bad *motives*, strong and weak *motives*. While a *motive* may be pure, it must be based upon proper principles if it is to be acceptable before God.)

mutual. Reciprocal; interchanged; each acting in return or correspondence to the other; given and received. Mutual love is that which is entertained by two persons each for the other; mutual advantage is that which is conferred by one person on another, and received by him in return. (And, what should most excite a *mutual* flame, / Your rural cares and pleasures are the same [Pope]. The relationship of husband and wife should be based upon a *mutual* love and respect.)

navigation. The art of conducting ships or vessels from one place to another. (The successful *navigation* of the Ship of State requires close adherence to the national charter, the Constitution.)

negotiation. The act of negotiating; the transacting of business in traffic; the treating with another respecting sale or purchase. The transaction of business between nations; the mutual intercourse of governments by their agents, in making treaties and the like. (In *negotiation*, principle must never be compromised.)

neutral. Not engaged on either side; not taking an active part with either of contending parties. (It is policy for a nation to be *neutral* when other nations are at war. Belligerents often obtain supplies from *neutral* states.)

neutrality. The state of being unengaged in disputes or contests between others; the state of taking no part on either side. (George Washington admonished the United States to maintain an official position of *neutrality* in the contests between nations and to avoid entangling alliances that would subvert our ability to choose our own path.)

nominal. Titular; existing in name only; as, a nominal distinction or difference is a difference in name and not in reality. (The actual differences created in the market place by selecting either gold or silver as the coinage of the nation would be *nominal*.)

novel. New; of recent origin or introduction; not ancient. (The proceedings of the court were *novel*. It would be *novel* today to find a politician imbued in the principles of the Constitution in the tradition of the Founding Fathers.)

APPENDIX I: GEORGE WASHINGTON'S FAREWELL ADDRESS VOCABULARY WORDS

obligation. The binding power of a vow, promise, oath or contract, or of law, civil, political or moral, independent of a promise; that which constitutes legal or moral duty, and which renders a person liable to coercion and punishment for neglecting it; the binding force or civility, kindness or gratitude, when the performance of a duty cannot be enforced by law; any act by which a person becomes bound to do something to or for another, or to forbear something. (Moral *obligation* binds men without promise or contract. Every citizen is under an *obligation* to obey the laws of the state. The laws and commands of God impose on us an *obligation* to love him supremely, and our neighbor as ourselves.)

obligatory. Binding in law or conscience; imposing duty; requiring performance or forbearance of some act. (As long as law is *obligatory*, so long our obedience is due. Adherence to the Constitution of the United States is *obligatory* upon all officers of the government.)

oblivion. Forgetfulness; cessation of remembrance; a forgetting of offenses, or remission of punishment. (Among our crimes *oblivion* may be set [Dryden]. An act of *oblivion* is an amnesty, or general pardon of crimes and offenses, granted by a sovereign, by which punishment is remitted. A nation that indulges in acts based upon improper principles is ultimately consigned to *oblivion*.)

obstinate. Stubborn; pertinaciously adhering to an opinion or purpose; fixed firmly in resolution; not yielding to reason, arguments or other mean; not yielding or not easily subdued or removed; as an obstinate cough or fever. (I have known great cures done by *obstinate* resolutions of drinking no wine [Temple]. No ass so meek, no ass so *obstinate* [Pope]. We must be *obstinate* in our defense of truth and righteousness.)

obstructions. Obstacle; impediment; any thing that stops or closes a way or channel. (A lack of personal righteousness is one of the great *obstructions* to spirituality.)

obvious. Plain; evident; easily discovered, seen or understood; readily perceived by the eye or the intellect. (We say, a phenomenon *obvious* to the sight, or a truth obvious to the mind [Dryden]. To an honest heart God's great works are obvious [Milton].)

occasion. Properly, a falling, happening or coming to; an occurrence, casualty, incident; something distinct from the ordinary course or regular order of things. (Remembrance of the establishment of this nation should be an *occasion* for rejoicing [Hooker].)

occasioned. Caused incidentally; caused; produced. (Our laziness as a people in politics has *occasioned* the destruction of our God-given liberties.)

odious. Hateful; deserving hatred; it expresses something less than detestable and abominable; as an odious name. (All wickedness is *odious*. He rendered himself *odious* to the parliament [Clarendon]. As the government has expanded its powers beyond the original intent of the Founding Fathers, the burden of government has become more *odious* to the citizens of the nations.)

odium. The quality that provokes hatred; offensiveness. (She threw the *odium* of the fact on me [Dryden]. Tyrants exhibit an undying *odium* against the individual rights granted by God.)

opposition. The act of opposing; attempt to check, restrain or defeat; Contrariety or diversity of meaning; as one term used in opposition to another. (He makes *opposition* to the measure. The bill passed without *opposition*. The two parties are in *opposition* to each other.)

outweighed. To exceed in value, influence or importance. (The consensus of the majority must, as necessary, be *outweighed* by proper principle.

palladium. Something that affords effectual defense protection and safety. (The trial by jury is the *palladium* of our civil rights [Blackstone].)

partiality. Inclination to favor one party or one side of a question more than the other; an undue bias of mind towards one party or side, which is apt to warp the judgment. (*Partiality* springs from the will and affections, rather than from a love of truth and justice. Special interest groups seek to influence the agencies of government to act with *partiality* toward their cause.)

passionate. Expressing strong emotion; animated; with strong feeling; easily moved to anger; easily excited or agitated by injury or insult; highly excited; vehement; warm; applied to things; as passionate affection; passionate desire; passionate concern. (Homer's Achilles is haughty and *passionate* [Prior]. The prophets have a *passionate* love for principles that uphold the agency of man.)

passions. The feeling of the mind, or the sensible effect of impression; excitement, perturbation or agitation of mind; as desire, fear, hope, joy, grief, love, hatred. The eloquence of the orator is employed to move the passions. (The noble *passions* of the heart lift the soul to greater achievement.)

patronizing. Defending; supporting; favoring; promoting. (*Patronizing* and defending proper principles should be encouraged.)

APPENDIX I: GEORGE WASHINGTON'S FAREWELL ADDRESS VOCABULARY WORDS

peculiar. Belonging to a person and to him only; particular; special; belonging to a nation, system or other thing, and not to others. (The founders recognized that they had established a *peculiar* form of government, different from any then in existence.)

penetrated. Entered; pierced; understood; fathomed. (The prayers of the people *penetrated* the heavens and God heard their pleas.)

permanency. Continuance in the same state, or without a change that destroys the form or nature of a thing. (The *permanency* of a government or state. The *permanency* of a system of principles.)

pernicious. Destructive; having the quality of killing, destroying or injuring; very injurious or mischievous; destructive; tending to injure or destroy. (Food, drink, or air may be *pernicious* to life or health. Evil examples are *pernicious* to morals. Intemperance is a *pernicious* vice. *Pernicious* actions over many generations by those in power have greatly eroded the proper role of government.)

perpetrated. Done; committed; an evil act. (Unconstitutional acts are often *perpetrated* by those claiming good intentions.)

perpetual. Never ceasing; continuing forever in future time; destined to be eternal; continuing or continued without intermission; uninterrupted. (The *perpetual* action of the heart and arteries. Destructions are come to a *perpetual* end [Ps.9]. The works of God are *perpetual*.)

perplexed. Made intricate; embarrassed; puzzled. (The people are *perplexed* if a leader's actions contradict his words.)

perseverance. Persistence in any thing undertaken; continued pursuit or prosecution of any business or enterprise begun. (*Perseverance* keeps honor bright [Shakespeare]. Patience and *perseverance* overcome the greatest difficulties [Clarissa]. Through *perseverance* we may resolve most challenges.)

persevering. Persisting in any business or course begun. Constant in the execution of a purpose or enterprise; as a persevering student. (In spite of opposition, Columbus obtained his goal by *persevering* the course he had set.)

persuaded. Influenced or drawn to an opinion or determination by argument, advice or reasons suggested; convinced; induced. (Many a good man has been *persuaded* into false paths by the flattery of prominent men.)

persuasive. Having the power of persuading; influencing the mind or passions; as persuasive eloquence; persuasive evidence. (The principles behind a *persuasive* argument must be examined before a decision is made.)

pillar. Foundation; support. (The Constitution is the *pillar* of good government in our nation.)

pillars. A supporter; that which sustains or upholds; foundation; support. (Faithfulness and love are *pillars* of a marriage.)

pious. Godly; reverencing and honoring the Supreme Being in heart and in the practice of the duties he has enjoined; having due veneration and affection for the character of God, and habitually obeying his commands; religious; devoted to the service of God; having due respect and affection for parents or other relatives. (This people should be a *pious* people. A *pious* people seek to know and do the will of God.)

plausible. That may be applauded; that may gain favor or approbation; hence, superficially pleasing; apparently right; specious; popular; as a plausible argument. (Many tyrants foster ideas which appear *plausible*, but which undermine proper government.)

policy. The art, prudence or wisdom of individuals in the management of their private or social concerns. (It has been the *policy* of Great Britain to encourage her navy, by keeping her carrying trade in her own hands. It has been the *policy* of France to preclude females from the throne. The *policy* of all laws has made some forms necessary in the wording of last wills and testaments [Blackstone]. All violent *policy* defeats itself. [Hamilton]. It should be our *policy* to seek the restoration of proper government.)

posterity. Descendants; children, children's children &c. indefinitely. (The whole human race is the *posterity* of Adam. We do ordain and establish this Constitution for ourselves and our *posterity*. The Founding Fathers' actions were closely aligned with their concern and consideration for their *posterity*, even at their own expense. The American tradition today is to place burdens upon our *posterity* by our violation of principle and the growth of our debt.)

posture. Situation; condition; particular state with regard to something else; as the posture of public affairs before or after a war. (Our *posture* before God must always be one of humility and love.)

potent. Powerful; physically strong; forcible; efficacious; as a potent medicine. (Moses once more his *potent* rod extends [Milton]. The military might of the nation is *potent*, but subject to constitutional constraint.)

APPENDIX I: GEORGE WASHINGTON'S FAREWELL ADDRESS VOCABULARY WORDS

precarious. Depending on the will or pleasure of another; held by courtesy; liable to be changed or lost at the pleasure of another. (A privilege depending on another's will is *precarious*, or held by a *precarious* tenure [Addison].)

precedent. Going before in time; anterior; antecedent; something done or said, that may serve or be adduced as an example to authorize a subsequent act of the like kind. (The world, or any part thereof, could not be *precedent* to the creation of man [Hole]. A *precedent* condition, in law, is a condition which must happen or be performed before an estate or some right can vest, and on failure of which the estate or right is defeated [Blackstone]. The establishment of the Constitution of the United States was a necessary *precedent* to a free and prosperous people.)

predominant. Prevalent over others; superior in strength, influence or authority; ascendant; ruling; controlling; as a predominant color; predominant beauty or excellence; a predominant passion. (The *predominant* purpose of government is to preserve God-given rights.)

predominate. To prevail; to surpass in strength, influence or authority; to be superior; to have controlling influence; to rule over. (In some persons, the love of money *predominates* over all other passions; in others, ambition or the love of fame *predominates*; in most men, self-interest *predominates* over patriotism and philanthropy.)

preferences. The act of preferring one thing before another. (The knowledge of things alone gives a value to our reasonings, and *preference* of one man's knowledge over another's [Locke]. In the market place consumers express their *preference* for good by the choices they make as they purchase products.)

prescribed. Directed; ordered. (The Founding Fathers, under God's inspiration, *prescribed* the proper role of government.)

preservation. The act of preserving or keeping safe; the act of keeping from injury, destruction or decay. (When a thing is kept entirely from decay, or nearly in its original state, we say it is in a high state of *preservation*.)

presuppose. To suppose as previous; to imply as antecedent. (The existence of created things *presupposes* the existence of a Creator. Each kind of knowledge *presupposes* many necessary things learned in other sciences and known beforehand [Hooker].)

pretext. Pretense; false appearance; ostensible reason or motive assigned to assumed as a color or cover for the real reason or votive. (He gave plausible reasons for his conduct, but these were only a *pretext* to conceal his real motives. They suck the blood of those they depend on, under a *pretext* of service and kindness [L'Estrange].)

prevail. To overcome; to gain the victory or superiority; to gain the advantage. (When Moses held up his hand, Israel *prevail*ed; when he let down his hand, Amalek prevailed [Ex. 17]. David *prevailed* over the Philistine with a sling and with a stone [Sam. 17]. Truth will ultimately *prevail*.)

prevailing. Gaining advantage, superiority or victory; having effect; persuading; succeeding; predominant; having more influence; prevalent; superior in power; efficacious. (As a *prevailing* disease, as a *prevailing* opinion. The love of money and the love of power are the *prevailing* passions of men. Saints shall assist thee with *prevailing* prayers [Rowe]. Intemperance is the prevailing vice of many countries.)

previous. Going before in time; being or happening before something else; antecedent; prior; as a previous intimation of a design; a previous notion; a previous event. (Sound from the mountain, *previous* to the storm, / Rolls o'er the muttering earth [Thomson]. *Previous* actions are often an indication of future behavior.)

primary. First in dignity or importance; first in order of time; chief; principal. (Our ancestors considered the education of youth of *primary* importance.)

principle. A general truth; a law comprehending many subordinate truths; as the principles of morality, of law, of government, &c. (Preservation of private property is a fundamental *principle* necessary to freedom.)

privileges. A particular and peculiar benefit or advantage enjoyed by a person, company or society, beyond the common advantages of other citizens. (A nation despicable by its weakness, forfeits even the *privilege* of being neutral [Hamilton, *The Federalist*]. Writ of *privilege* is a writ to deliver a privileged person from custody when arrested in a civil suit [Blackstone]. We should rejoice in the *privileges* bestowed upon us by a loving and benevolent God.)

proclamation. Publication by authority; official notice given to the public. (Leaders often declare their purposes by *proclamation*.)

procured. Obtained; caused to be done; effected; brought on. (Peace is often *procured* by a strong defense.)

productions. The act or process of producing, bringing forth or exhibiting to view. (Perhaps the most valuable of all of the *productions* of the United States has been the Constitution of 1787.)

progenitors. An ancestor in the direct line; a forefather. (Adam was the *progenitor* of the human race. Our *progenitors* had a keen interest in preserving for their posterity the blessings of life, liberty, and property.)

progressive. Moving forward; proceeding onward; advancing; as progressive motion or course; opposed to retrograde. (Many today who call themselves "*progressive*" are, in reality, proposing the destruction of the nation's foundation principles.)

promote. To forward; to advance; to contribute to the growth, enlargement or excellence of any thing valuable, or to the increase of any thing evil; to exalt; to elevate; to raise. (I will *promote* thee to very great honors [Num. 22]. We must *promote* principles of righteousness and truth at every opportunity.)

prompted. Incited; moved to action; instigated; assisted in speaking or learning. (Good men are *prompted* to assist those in need.)

proneness. The state of bending downward; inclination of mind, heart or temper; propension, disposition; as the proneness of the Israelites to idolatry; proneness to self—gratification or to self—justification. (Mankind suffers from a *proneness* to use power unrighteously.)

prop. To support; to sustain; in a general sense; as, to prop a declining state. (I *prop* myself upon the few supports that are left me [Pope]. The only sure *prop* of a nation is its righteousness before God.)

propagated. Continued or multiplied by generation or production of the same kind; spread; extended. (Lies, however widely *propagated*, remain lies.)

propensity. Bent of mind, natural or acquired; inclination; in a moral sense; disposition to any thing good or evil, particularly to evil; as a propensity to sin; the corrupt propensity of the will; natural tendency. (It requires critical nicety to find out the genius of *propensions* of a child [L'Estrange]. A truly righteous and moral person has no *propensity* to do evil.)

proper. Naturally or essentially belonging; particularly suited to; correct; just. (Every animal has his *proper* instincts and inclinations, appetites, and habits. Every muscle and vessel of the body has its *proper* office. Every art has its *proper* rules. Creation is the *proper* work of an Almighty Being.)

proportion. The comparative relation of any one thing to another. (Let a man's exertions be in *proportion* to his strength. The national government has exceeded the *proportion* assigned to it by the Founding Fathers.)

proportionably. According to proportion or comparative relation. (A nation's peace, prosperity, and joy diminish *proportionably* as it strays from God's commands.)

propriety. Fitness; suitableness; appropriateness; consonance with established principles, rules or customs; justness; accuracy. (*Propriety* dictates a measure of humility in a leader who respects God.)

props. That which sustains an incumbent weight; that on which any thing rests for support; a support; a stay. (An affectionate child is the *prop* of declining age. A righteous and a moral people are necessary *props* to sustain the Constitution in the tradition of the Founding Fathers.)

prosperity. Advance or gain in anything good or desirable; successful progress in any business or enterprise; success; attainment of the object desired. (The *prosperity* of fools shall destroy them [Prov. 1]. The *prosperity* of this nation came about because of God's blessings upon a people that sought to obey His will.)

Providence. The care and superintendence which God exercises over His creatures. (A belief in divine *providence* is a source of great consolation to good men.)

provision. Previous stipulation; terms or agreement made, or measures taken for a future exigency. (An all wise and loving God, knowing of the weakness of mortality, made *provision* for the salvation of mankind through the atonement of the Savior.)

provocation. Anything that excites anger; the cause of resentment. (Often the slightest *provocation* is used by a nation as an excuse to enter improper areas.)

prudence. Implies caution in deliberating and consulting on the most suitable means to accomplish valuable purposes, and the exercise of sagacity in discerning and selecting them. Prudence differs from wisdom in this, that prudence implies more caution and reserve than wisdom, or is exercised more in foreseeing and avoiding evil, than in devising and executing that which is good. It is sometimes mere caution or circumspection. (*Prudence* is principally in reference to actions to be done, and due means, order, season and method of doing or not doing [Hale]. *Prudence* dictates the careful exercise of the war-making powers of a nation.)

prudent. Cautious; circumspect; practically wise; careful of the consequences of enterprises, measures or actions; cautious not to act when the end is of doubtful utility, or probably impracticable. (The *prudent* course of the nation is found in adherence to its foundation principles.)

pursue. To follow; to go or proceed after or in a like direction. (The captain *pursued* the same course as former navigators have taken. A subsequent legislature *pursued* the course of their predecessors. He that *pursueth* evil, *pursueth* it to his own death [Prov. 11]. We must *pursue* a course of righteousness in our efforts to prepare to be with our God.)

APPENDIX I: GEORGE WASHINGTON'S FAREWELL ADDRESS VOCABULARY WORDS

pursuit. A following with a view to reach, accomplish or obtain; endeavor to attain to or gain; as the pursuit of knowledge; the pursuit of happiness or pleasure; the pursuit of power, of honor, of distinction, of a phantom. (America's *pursuit* of Christian principles is tied to her greatness.)

quenched. Extinguished; allayed; repressed. (A desire for righteousness *quenched* the tendency to evil.)

rankness. Rancidness. (His sense of smell was offended by the *rankness* of the rotting fish.)

ratification. The act of ratifying; confirmation; the act of giving sanction and validity to something done by another; as the ratification of a treaty by the senate of the United States. (The *ratification* of a treaty by the Senate does not nullify the original intent of the Constitution.)

reception. The act of receiving. (The *reception* of truth is a cause for rejoicing.)

reciprocal. Mutual; done by each to the other; mutually interchangeable. (Treaties between nations should bring *reciprocal* value to both nations.)

recommend. To praise to another; to offer or commend to another's notice, confidence or kindness by favorable representations. (We may with confidence *recommend* the cause of liberty to all peoples and nations.)

recommendation. The act of recommending or of commending. (We introduce a friend to a stranger by a *recommendation* of his virtues or accomplishments.)

recompense. To compensate; to make return of an equivalent for any thing given, done or suffered; as, to recompense a person for services, for fidelity or for sacrifices of time, for loss or damages. (*Recompense* to no man evil for evil [Rom. 12]. The labor of man is *recompensed* by the fruits of the earth. Peace of mind is the *recompense* for a moral life.)

recur. To return to the thought or mind. (When any word has been used to signify an idea, the old idea will *recur* in the mind, when the word is heard [Watts]. The return of tyranny upon a newly freed people is a *recurring* plague throughout the world's history.)

refined. Purified; separated from extraneous matter; separated from what is coarse, rude or improper. (Those that love and serve God will be *refined* and become pure before Him.)

reflecting. Turning back, as thought upon themselves or upon past events. (The honorable man has peace when *reflecting* upon the actions of his life.)

reflection. The operation of the mind by which it turns its views back upon itself and its operations; the review or reconsideration of past thought, opinions or decisions of the mind, or of past events. (Job's *reflections* on his once flourishing estate, at the same time afflicted and encouraged him [Atterbury]. Most often, our actions are a *reflection* of our motivation.)

reluctantly. With opposition of heart; unwillingly. What is undertaken reluctantly is seldom well performed. (The nation *reluctantly* accepted the retirement of Washington.)

relying. Reposing on something, as the mind; confiding in; trusting in; depending. (*Relying* upon the mercies of God, His wisdom, and His strength, let us go forward seeking to do His will.)

remote. Distant in place; not near; distant in time; not immediate. (It is not all *remote* and even apparent good that affects us [Locke]. Many actions of the national government no longer bear a *remote* resemblance to the intentions of the Founding Fathers.)

render. A surrender; a giving up; a payment of rent. (In those early times, the king's household was supported by specific *renders* of corn and other victuals from the tenants of the domains [Blackstone]. We *render* thanks to God for our bounteous blessings.)

rendered. Returned; paid back; given; assigned; making; translating; surrendering; affording. (If we *rendered* all the thanks it were possible to give we still could not pay adequate thanks to our Savior for His atonement.)

renders. To make a cause to be, by some influence upon a thing, or by some change. (A trying circumstance often *renders* a change of heart.)

repel. To drive back; to force to return; to resist; to oppose. (Americans should *repel* the encroachment of government from areas of individual liberty and responsibility.)

repose. To lay at rest; to sleep; to rest in confidence. (At Flanders field the warriors all *repose* in neat rows beneath white crosses.)

repressed. Crushed; subdued. (His hope for success was *repressed* as he recognized the difficulty of the task.)

reputation. Good name; the credit, honor or character which is derived from a favorable public opinion or esteem; character by report; in a good or bad sense. (The best evidence of *reputation* is a man's whole life [Ames]. Many modern authors seek to destroy the *reputation* of the Founding Fathers.)

APPENDIX I: GEORGE WASHINGTON'S FAREWELL ADDRESS VOCABULARY WORDS

requisite. Required by the nature of things or by circumstances; necessary; so needful that it cannot be dispensed with. (Repentance and faith are *requisite* to salvation. Air is *requisite* to support life.)

resentment. The excitement of passion which proceeds from a sense of wrong offered to ourselves, or to those who are connected with us; anger. This word usually expresses less excitement than anger, though it is often synonymous with it. It expresses much less than wrath, exasperation and indignation. In this use, resent is not the sense or perception of injury, but the excitement which is the effect of it. (Many who have come to embrace the socialistic principles express *resentment* against those who wish to return to the original intent of the Founding Fathers.)

resolution. The act or process of unraveling or disentangling perplexities, or of dissipating obscurity in moral subjects; as the resolution of difficult questions in moral science; fixed purpose or determination of mind; as a resolution to reform our lives; a resolution to undertake an expedition. (It was his firm *resolution* to obey all of God's commandments.)

resolve. To fix in opinion or purpose; to determine in mind; to determine by vote. (He *resolved* to abandon his vicious course of life. The legislature *resolved* to receive no petitions after a certain day. With greatest *resolve*, let us go forward in our commitment to proper principle.)

resource. Any source of aid or support. (Under the many forms of socialism, a *resource* is placed under government control.)

respective. Relative; having relation to something else; not absolute; as the respective connections of society; particular; relating to a particular person or thing. (Let each give according to his *respective* proportion. Each branch of government should be required to act only within their *respective* constitutionally defined spheres.)

restrain. To hold back; to check; to hold from action, proceeding or advancing, either by physical or moral force, or by any interposing obstacle. (We *restrain* a horse by a bridle. We *restrain* water by dams and dikes. We *restrain* men from crimes and trespasses by laws.)

retained. Held; kept in possession. (Our liberties may be *retained* only by constant vigilance.)

retaliate. To return like for like; to repay or requite by an act of the same kind as has been received. (In war, enemies often *retaliate* the death or inhuman treatment of prisoners, the burning of towns, or the plunder of goods. In regard to the desire to *retaliate*, the Lord has said, "Vengeance is mine.")

retire. To withdraw; to retreat; to go from company or from a public place into privacy; as, to retire from the world; to retire from notice. (We must never *retire* from the principles of righteousness and the foundation of truth.)

retirement. The act of withdrawing from company or from public notice or station. (*Retirement* is as necessary tome as it will be welcome [Washington].)

retreat. The act of retiring; a withdrawing of one's self from any place. (We must not *retreat* from responsibilities we bear in order to achieve a life of ease.)

revenge. To inflict pain or injury in return for an injury received. (The gods are just and will *revenge* our cause [Dryden]. Seeking *revenge* damages the peace of one's soul.)

revenue. The annual produce of taxes, excise, customs, duties, rents, &c. which a nation or state collects and receives into the treasury for public use. (All bills for raising *revenue* shall originate in the House of Representatives [U.S. Constitution I, 7].)

rival. One who is in pursuit of the same object as another; one striving to reach or obtain something which another is attempting to obtain, and which one only can possess; a competitor. (Love will not patiently bear a *rival*. *Rival* parties seek our support, but principle must determine our allegiance, not party.)

rivalship. The state or character of a rival; strife; contention for superiority; emulation; rivalry. (In the affairs of government, a system of political parties often creates a *rivalship* of philosophies, none of which are based upon proper principle.)

ruins. Destruction; fall; overthrow; defeat; that change of any thing which destroys it, or entirely defeats its object, or unfits it for use; the remains of a natural object; the remains of a decayed or demolished city, house, fortress ore any work of art or other thing. (As the *ruins* of a wall, as a castle in *ruins*. The errors of young men are the *ruin* of business [Bacon]. The labor of a day will not build up a virtuous habit on the *ruins* of an old and vicious character [Buckminster].)

sacrifice. To offer to God in homage or worship, by killing and consuming, as victims on an altar; to immolate, either as an atonement for sin, or to procure favor, or to express thankfulness; as, to sacrifice an ox or a lamb (2 Sam. 6). (A mother's sacrifice on behalf of her children cannot be adequately measured.)

salutary. Wholesome; healthful; promoting health; promotion of public safety; contributing to some beneficial purpose. (The strict discipline of youth has a *salutary* affect on society. Diet and exercise are *salutary* to men of sedentary habits.)

APPENDIX I: GEORGE WASHINGTON'S FAREWELL ADDRESS VOCABULARY WORDS

sanctioned. Ratified; confirmed; authorized. (Beliefs *sanctioned* by popularity are not necessarily based upon proper principle.)

satellite. A follower; an obsequious attendant or dependant. (For many years the conquered and subjugated countries of eastern Europe have been considered *satellites* of the Soviet Union.)

scrupulously. With a nice, regard to minute particulars or to exact propriety. (Henry was *scrupulously* careful not to ascribe the success to himself [Addison]. We must *scrupulously* adhere to the Constitution in the tradition of the Founding Fathers.)

secure. Free from danger of being taken by an enemy; that may resist assault or attack. (Liberty is only *secure* under the watchful eye of an informed people.)

seduction. The act of seducing, or of enticing from the path of duty. (Love of power and greed have often proved the *seduction* of leaders.)

sensibility. Susceptibility of impressions; the capacity of feeling or perceiving the impressions of external objects; capacity or acuteness of perception; that quality of the soul which renders it susceptible of impressions. (The *sensibility* of a moral people will cause them to reject that which debases purity.)

sentiment. Properly, a thought prompted by passion or feeling; opinion; notion. (Our *sentiment* toward the high and noble, the godly and the pure, will be reflected in our national policies.)

sever. To part or divide by violence; to separate by cutting or rending. (Acts that *sever* our relationship with God will not be blessed by Him.)

shunning. Avoiding; keeping clear from; declining. (By *shunning* evil and seeking righteousness, we become a godly people.)

sinister. Evil; bad; corrupt; perverse; dishonest. (He scorns to undermine another's interest by any *sinister* or inferior arts [South]. The people must beware of leaders who seek office for the *sinister* purpose of obtaining power for their vain ambition.)

situation. State; condition; circumstances; position; seat. (The *situation* of a stranger among people of habits differing from his own, cannot be pleasant. While a *situation* and circumstance may vary, principle is firm.)

solemn. Serious; grave; religiously serious. (A *solemn* face; a *solemn* oath. There reign'd a *solemn* silence over all [Spenser].)

solicitude. Carefulness; concern; anxiety; uneasiness of mind occasioned by the fear of evil or the desire of good. (A man feels *solicitude* when his friend is sick. We feel *solicitude* for the success of an enterprise. With what *solicitude* should men seek to secure future happiness?)

sparingly. Not abundantly; frugally; moderately; seldom. (Christians are obliged to taste even the innocent pleasures of life but *sparingly* [Atterbury]. The power of government should be used *sparingly* and only under the correct circumstances.)

species. Sort; kind; in a loose sense; as a species of generosity; a species of cloth; in logic, a special idea, corresponding to the specific distinctions of things in nature. (Communism, fascism, Nazism, and Fabian socialism are all *species* of collectivism.)

specious. Showy; pleasing to the view; apparently right; superficially fair, just or correct; plausible; appearing well at first view (As *specious* reasoning, a *specious* argument, a *specious* objection, *specious* deeds. Temptation is of greater danger because it is covered with the *specious* names of good nature, good manners, nobleness of mind, etc. The scribes and pharisees and hypocrites of Christ's day were *specious* in their obedience to the law.)

speculation. Mental view of any thing in its various aspects and relations; contemplation; intellectual examination. (*Speculation* upon a topic does not necessarily bring a truthful understanding.)

sphere. Circuit of action, knowledge or influence. (The *sphere* of God's graces is infinite in scope and magnitude.)

spring. To arise; to appear; to begin to appear or exist; to break forth; to proceed or issue, as from a fountain or source; to proceed, as from a cause, reason, principle or other original. (The noblest title *springs* from virtue. Aaron and Moses *sprung* from Levi. The love of liberty must begin to *spring* forth in the hearts of mankind.)

stifled. To suffocate; to stop; to oppress; to extinguish; to deaden; to quench; to suppress; to hinder from transpiring or spreading. (His criticism of her efforts *stifled* her desire to complete the project.)

stimulate. To excite, rouse or animate to action or more vigorous exertion by some pungent motive or by persuasion. (It is amazing how a skillful orator may *stimulate* national passions and foment the destruction of war.)

structure. Manner of building; form; make; construction. (The *structure* of the nation is founded upon God-given principles recognized and embodied in the Constitution of the United States.)

subdivisions. The act of subdividing or separating a part into smaller parts. (*Subdivisions* of a great truth cannot contradict the greater truth.)

subjected. Reduced to the dominion of another; enslaved; exposed; submitted; made to undergo. (The conquered people were *subjected* to the whims of their conquerors.)

subservient. Useful as an instrument to promote a purpose; serving to promote some end; subordinate; acting as a subordinate instrument. (These are the creatures of God, subordinate to him, and *subservient* to his will. These ranks of creatures are *subservient* one to another [Ray]. The leaders of our nation have taken an oath to be *subservient* to the principles enshrined in the Constitution of the United States.)

subsist. To feed; to maintain; to support with provisions. (By our daily work, we may *subsist* and prosper.)

substantially. Strongly; solidly; truly; solidly; really. (The laws of this religion would make men, if they would truly observe them, *substantially* religious towards God, chaste and temperate [Tillotson]. The founder's of the United States were *substantially* men of firm religious conviction.)

subvert. To overthrow from the foundation; to overturn; to ruin utterly; to corrupt; to confound; to pervert the mind, and turn it from the truth. (The northern nations of Europe *subverted* the Roman Empire. He is the worst enemy of man, who endeavors to *subvert* the Christian religion. The elevation of corrupt men to office will slowly, but surely, *subvert* a republican government.)

sufficient. Enough; equal to the end proposed; adequate to wants; competent. (My grace is *sufficient* for thee [2 Cor. 12]. The U.S. Constitution contains principles *sufficient* to bring peace, happiness and good government to all who will abide in them.)

suffrages. A vote; a voice given in deciding a controverted question, or in the choice of a man for an office or trust. (Nothing can be more grateful to a good man than to be elevated to office by the unbiased *suffrages* of free enlightened citizens. Lactantius and St. Austin confirm by their *suffrages* the observation made by heathen writers [Atterbury]. By our *suffrages* let us select good and wise men to be our rulers.)

suitable. Fitting; according with; agreeable to; proper; becoming; adequate. (We cannot make *suitable* returns for divine mercies.)

supposition. The act of laying down, imagining or admitting as true or existing, what is known not to be true, or what is not proved; the position of something known not to be true or not proved; hypothesis; belief without full evidence. (This is only an infallibility upon *supposition* that if a thing be true, it is impossible to be false [Tillotson]. The nation has been deceived to operate under the *supposition* that the Constitution is what the Supreme Court says it is.)

suspend. To cause to cease for a time from operation or effect. (The fierceness of the battle caused the soldier to *suspend* his hope of delivery.)

suspicion. The act of suspecting; the imagination of the existence of something without proof, or upon very slight evidence, or upon no evidence at all. (*Suspicions* among thoughts, are like bats among birds; they ever fly by twilight [Bacon]. Tyrants have great *suspicion* about freedom loving people.)

sympathy. Fellow feeling the quality of being affected by the affection of another, with feeling correspondent in kind, if not in degree. (We feel *sympathy* for another when we see him in distress, or when we are informed of his distresses. I value myself upon *sympathy*; I hate and despise myself for envy [Kames]. To such associations may be attributed most of the *sympathies* and antipathies of our nature [Anon.].)

tamper. To meddle; to be busy; to try little experiments; as, to tamper with a disease; to have to do with without fitness or necessity; to practice secretly. (Those who *tamper* with false and foolish philosophies of government undermine the God-given blessing of liberty vouched safe by the Constitution.)

tendency. Drift; direction or course towards any place, object, effect or result. (Read such books only as have a good moral *tendency*. Mild language has a *tendency* to allay irritation.)

tender. To offer in words; or to exhibit or present for acceptance. (As the magnitude of his misdeeds became apparent, he resolved to *tender* his resignation in an effort to correct the wrongs done.)

tenure. Manner of holding in general. (In a free country, *tenure* of office is defined by law.)

terminate. To end; to close; to come to a limit in time. (The session of Congress, every second year, must *terminate* on the third of March. The wisdom of this world, its designs and efficacy, *terminate* on this side heaven [South].)

toils. To labor; to work; to exert strength with pain and fatigue of body or mind, particularly of the body. (Master, we have *toiled* all night and caught nothing [Luke 5]. A righteous leader *toils* on behalf of his people, not for his own glory.)

APPENDIX I: GEORGE WASHINGTON'S FAREWELL ADDRESS VOCABULARY WORDS

tranquil. Quiet; calm; undisturbed; peaceful; not agitated. (The atmosphere is *tranquil*. The state is *tranquil*. A *tranquil* retirement is desirable; but a *tranquil* mind is essential to happiness. If we know our actions please God, our minds may be *tranquil*.)

tranquility. Quietness; a calm state; freedom from disturbance or agitation. (We speak of the *tranquillity* of public affairs, of the state, of the world, the *tranquillity* of a retired life, the *tranquillity* of mind proceeding from conscious rectitude. Peace and *tranquility* abide in the soul of a righteous person.)

transient. Passing; not stationary; hence, of short duration; not permanent; not lasting or durable; hasty; momentary. (How *transient* are the pleasures of this life!)

treaty. An agreement, league or contract between two or more nations or sovereigns, formally signed by commissioners properly authorized, and solemnly ratified by the several sovereigns or the supreme power of each state. (Under the Constitution, the U.S. Senate must ratify each *treaty* before it becomes effective.)

tribute. A personal contribution; something given or contributed. (God gives *tribute* to His prophets as He fulfills their words.)

trifling. Acting or talking with levity, or without seriousness or being in earnest; being of small value or importance; trivial. (For a nation to exercise its war-making powers is not a *trifling* event.)

umbrage. Suspicion of injury; offense; resentment. (The court of France took *umbrage* at the conduct of Spain. The king of England took *umbrage* at his colonies as they sought to be free.)

unanimous. Being of one mind; agreeing in opinion or determination; as, the house of assembly was unanimous; the members of the council were unanimous. (The people were always *unanimous* in their selection of Washington as their leader.)

unavoidable. Not avoidable; not to be shunned; inevitable; in a manner that prevents failure or escape. (Unrighteousness brings an *unavoidable* consequence if repentance is not complete.)

unawed. Not awed; not restrained by fear; undaunted. (Young David was *unawed* by Goliath.)

undermine. To remove the foundation or support of any thing by clandestine means; as, to undermine reputation; to undermine the constitution of the state. (He should be warned who are like to *undermine* him [Locke]. Ignorant voters and conspiring leaders *undermine* the soul of a nation.)

undertook. To engage in; to enter upon; to take in hand; to begin to perform. (When I *undertook* this work, I had a very inadequate knowledge of the extent of my labors. By our labors we *undertook* to preserve our liberty.

ungenerously. Unkindly; dishonorably. (Historians in recent years have *ungenerously* viewed the lives and accomplishments of great and noble men.)

uniform. Having always the same form or manner; not variable; consistent with itself; not different; of the same form. (It is the duty of a Christian to observe a *uniform* course of piety and religion. How far churches are bound to be *uniform* in their ceremonies, is doubted [Hooker]. The leaders of the nation should have a *uniform* understanding of the Constitution, and it must abide in the principles of the founders.)

uninfluenced. Not influenced; not persuaded or moved by others, or by foreign considerations; not biased; acting freely. (A completely righteous person is *uninfluenced* by temptation.)

union. The act of joining two or more things. (One kingdom, joy and *union* without end [Milton]. The *union* of the states under the Constitution brought great peace and prosperity to this nation.)

unity. The state of being one; oneness. (The *unity* we seek is a oneness with God.)

unprincipled. Not having settled principles; as souls unprincipled in virtue. (*Unprincipled* men believe the ends justify the means.)

unrestrained. Not restrained; not controlled; not confined; not hindered. (A people *unrestrained* by moral discipline will soon be oppressed by tyranny.)

usurp. To seize and hold in possession by force or without right; as, to usurp a throne; to usurp the prerogatives of the crown; to usurp power. (To *usurp* the right of a patron, is to oust or dispossess him. Vice sometimes *usurps* the place of virtue [Denham].)

usurpation. The act of seizing or occupying and enjoying the property of another, with right; as the usurpation of a throne; the usurpation of the supreme power. (*Usurpation* of private property was never condoned by the Founding Fathers.)

varied. Altered; partially changed; changed. (We have found that as we *varied* from the principles set forth in the founding documents of this nation that we suffered increasing hardship.)

veil. To cover; to disguise. (Tyrants often attempt to *veil* their efforts to expand their powers by relying upon high sounding calls to support their government.)

vices. Properly, a spot or defect; a fault; a blemish. (One of the *vices* of mankind is to seek to use power unrighteously and exercise unrighteous dominion.)

vicissitudes. Regular change or succession of one thing to another; as the vicissitudes of day and night, and of winter and summer; the vicissitudes of the seasons; change; revolution; as in human affairs. (We are exposed to continual *vicissitudes* of fortune. The *vicissitudes* of life can bring challenges as well as joys.)

vigilance. Forbearance of sleep; a state of being awake; watchfulness; circumspection; attention of the mind in discovering and guarding against danger, or providing for safety. (*Vigilance* is a virtue of prime importance in a general. The *vigilance* of the dog is no less remarkable than his fidelity. Constant *vigilance* is required if we are to maintain our liberty.)

vigor. Active strength or force of body in animals; physical force; strength of mind; intellectual force; energy. (We say, a man possesses *vigor* of mind or intellect.)

vigorous. Full of physical strength or active force; powerful; strong. (We must be *vigorous* in our efforts to maintain the Constitution in the tradition of the Founding Fathers.)

virtue. Strength; bravery; valor; moral goodness; excellence. (The practice of moral duties from sincere love to God and his laws, is *virtue* and religion.)

virtuous. Morally good; acting in conformity to the moral law; practicing the moral duties, and abstaining from vice; as a virtuous man. Being in conformity to the moral or divine law; as a virtuous action; a virtuous life. (The mere performance of *virtuous* actions does not denominate an agent *virtuous* [Price]. A *virtuous* heart is a priceless possession.)

volume. A book; a collection of sheets of paper usually printed or written paper, folded and bound or covered. (An odd *volume* of a set of books, bears not the value of its proportion to the set [Franklin]. The words of the Founding Fathers fill many *volumes* and clarify their intent.)

vows. A solemn promise made to God, or by a pagan to his deity. (When thou vowest a *vow*, defer not to pay it [Eccles. 5]. The *vows* of marriage are sacred and holy.)

weal. To be strong; to avail, to prevail; the primary sense of weal is strength, soundness, from the sense of straining, stretching or advancing; a sound state of a person or thing; a state which is prosperous, or at least not unfortunate, not declining; prosperity; happiness. (As we love the *weal* of our souls and bodies [Bacon]. So we say, the public *weal*, the general weal, the weal of the nation or state [B. Trumball]. Righteousness is the *weal* of a nation.)

welfare. Exemption from misfortune, sickness, calamity or evil; the enjoyment of health and the common blessings of life; prosperity; happiness; applied to person. Exemption from any unusual evil or calamity; the enjoyment of peace and prosperity, or the ordinary blessings of society and civil government; applied to states. (The Founding Father's understanding of *welfare* did not include redistribution of private property by government compulsion.)

whence. From what place; from what source. (*Whence* shall we derive hope? *Whence* comes this honor? *Whence* hath this man this wisdom? [Matt. 13:54].)

wiles. A trick or stratagem practiced for ensnaring or deception; a sly, insidious artifice; to deceive; to beguile. (That ye may be able to stand against the *wiles* of the devil [Eph. 6]. For a people to be free, they must constantly guard against the *wiles* of those who seek power.)

yield. To produce; to allow; to concede; to contribute; to give up ; to submit; to surrender; to comply. (Most vegetable juices *yield* a salt. The flowers in spring *yield* a beautiful sight. We *yield* that there is a God. He saw the fainting Grecians *yield* [Dryden].)

zeal. Passionate ardor in the pursuit of any thing; in general, zeal is an eagerness of desire to accomplish or obtain some object, and it may be manifested either in favor of any person or thing, or in opposition to it, and in a good or bad cause. (Excessive *zeal* may rise to enthusiasm. They have a *zeal* of God, but not according to knowledge [Rom. 10]. A *zeal* for liberty is sometimes an eagerness to subvert, with little care what shall be established [Johnson].)

Appendix J

Frederick Engels

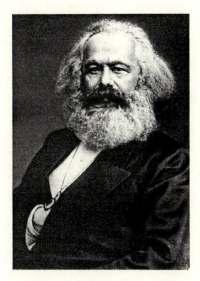
Karl Marx

THE COMMUNIST MANIFESTO—1848

Karl Marx and Frederick Engels

PREFACE

The Manifesto was published as the platform of the Communist League, a working men's association, first exclusively German, later on international, and under the political conditions of the Continent before 1848, unavoidably a secret society. At a Congress of the League, held in November 1847, Marx and Engels were commissioned to prepare a complete theoretical and practical party programme. Drawn up in German, in January 1848, the manuscript was sent to the printer in London a few weeks before the French Revolution of February 24. A French translation was brought out in Paris shortly before the insurrection of June 1848. The first English translation, by Miss Helen Macfarlane, appeared in George Julian Harney's *Red Republican*, London, 1850. A Danish and a Polish edition had also been published.

TO PRESERVE THE NATION

The defeat of the Parisian insurrection of June 1848—the first great battle between proletariat and bourgeoisie—drove again into the background, for a time, the social and political aspirations of the European working class. Thenceforth, the struggle for supremacy was, again, as it had been before the Revolution of February, solely between different sections of the propertied class; the working class was reduced to a fight for political elbow-room, and to the position of extreme wing of the middle-class Radicals. Wherever independent proletarian movements continued to show signs of life, they were ruthlessly hunted down. Thus the Prussian police hunted out the Central Board of the Communist League, then located in Cologne. The members were arrested and, after eighteen months' imprisonment, they were tried in October 1852. This celebrated "Cologne Communist Trial" lasted from October 4 till November 12; seven of the prisoners were sentenced to terms of imprisonment in a fortress, varying from three to six years. Immediately after the sentence, the League was formally dissolved by the remaining members. As to the Manifesto, it seemed henceforth doomed to oblivion.

When the European workers had recovered sufficient strength for another attack on the ruling classes, the International Working Men's Association sprang up. But this association, formed with the express aim of welding into one body the whole militant proletariat of Europe and America, could not at once proclaim the principles laid down in the Manifesto. The International was bound to have a programme broad enough to be acceptable to the English trade unions, to the followers of Proudhon in France, Belgium, Italy, and Spain, and to the Lassalleans in Germany.

[ENGEL'S FOOTNOTE: Lassalle personally, to us, always acknowledged himself to be a disciple of Marx, and, as such, stood on the ground of the Manifesto. But in his first public agitation, 1862-1864, he did not go beyond demanding co-operative workshops supported by state credit.]

Marx, who drew up this programme to the satisfaction of all parties, entirely trusted to the intellectual development of the working class, which was sure to result from combined action and mutual discussion. The very events and vicissitudes in the struggle against capital, the defeats even more than the victories, could not help bringing home to men's minds the insufficiency of their various favorite nostrums, and preparing the way for a more complete insight into the true conditions for working-class emancipation. And Marx was right. The International, on its breaking in 1874, left the workers quite different men from what it found them in 1864. Proudhonism in France, Lassalleanism in Germany, were dying out, and even the conservative English trade unions, though most of them had long since severed their connection with the International, were gradually advancing towards that point at which, last year at Swansea, their president could say in their name: "Continental socialism has lost its terror for us." In fact, the principles of the Manifesto had made considerable headway among the working men of all countries.

The Manifesto itself came thus to the front again. Since 1850, the German text had been reprinted several times in Switzerland, England, and America. In 1872, it was translated into English in New York, where the translation was published in *Woorhull and Claflin's Weekly*.

APPENDIX J: COMMUNIST MANIFESTO

From this English version, a French one was made in *Le Socialiste* of New York. Since then, at least two more English translations, moer or less mutilated, have been brought out in America, and one of them has been reprinted in England. The first Russian translation, made by Bakunin, was published at Herzen's Kolokol office in Geneva, about 1863; a second one, by the heroic Vera Zasulich, also in Geneva, in 1882. A new Danish edition is to be found in *Socialdemokratisk Bibliothek*, Copenhagen, 1885; a fresh French translation in *Le Socialiste*, Paris, 1886. From this latter, a Spanish version was prepared and published in Madrid, 1886. The German reprints are not to be counted; there have been twelve altogether at the least. An Armenian translation, which was to be published in Constantinople some months ago, did not see the light, I am told, because the publisher was afraid of bringing out a book with the name of Marx on it, while the translator declined to call it his own production. Of further translations into other languages I have heard but had not seen. Thus the history of the Manifesto reflects the history of the modern working-class movement; at present, it is doubtless the most wide spread, the most international production of all socialist literature, the common platform acknowledged by millions of working men from Siberia to California.

Yet, when it was written, we could not have called it a *socialist* manifesto. By Socialists, in 1847, were understood, on the one hand the adherents of the various Utopian systems: Owenites in England, Fourierists in France, both of them already reduced to the position of mere sects, and gradually dying out; on the other hand, the most multifarious social quacks who, by all manner of tinkering, professed to redress, without any danger to capital and profit, all sorts of social grievances, in both cases men outside the working-class movement, and looking rather to the "educated" classes for support. Whatever portion of the working class had become convinced of the insufficiency of mere political revolutions, and had proclaimed the necessity of total social change, called itself Communist. It was a crude, rough-hewn, purely instinctive sort of communism; still, it touched the cardinal point and was powerful enough amongst the working class to produce the Utopian communism of Cabet in France, and of Weitling in Germany. Thus, in 1847, socialism was a middle-class movement, communism a working-class movement. Socialism was, on the Continent at least, "respectable"; communism was the very opposite. And as our notion, from the very beginning, was that "the emancipation of the workers must be the act of the working class itself," there could be no doubt as to which of the two names we must take. Moreover, we have, ever since, been far from repudiating it.

The Manifesto being our joint production, I consider myself bound to state that the fundamental proposition which forms the nucleus belongs to Marx. That proposition is: That in every historical epoch, the prevailing mode of economic production and exchange, and the social organization necessarily following from it, form the basis upon which it is built up, and from that which alone can be explained the political and intellectual history of that epoch; that consequently the whole history of mankind (since the dissolution of primitive tribal society, holding land in common ownership) has been a history of class struggles, contests between exploiting and exploited, ruling and oppressed classes; That the history of these class struggles forms a series of evolutions in which, nowadays, a stage has been reached where the exploited and oppressed class—the proletariat—cannot attain its emancipation from the sway of the exploiting and ruling class—the bourgeoisie—without, at the same time, and once and for all, emancipating society at large from all exploitation, oppression, class distinction, and class struggles.

This proposition, which, in my opinion, is destined to do for history what Darwin's theory has done for biology, we both of us, had been gradually approaching for some years before 1845. How far I had independently progressed towards it is best shown by my *Conditions of the Working Class in England*. But when I again met Marx at Brussels, in spring 1845, he had it already worked out and put it before me in terms almost as clear as those in which I have stated it here.

From our joint preface to the German edition of 1872, I quote the following:

> "However much that state of things may have altered during the last twenty-five years, the general principles laid down in the Manifesto are, on the whole, as correct today as ever. Here and there, some detail might be improved. The practical application of the principles will depend, as the Manifesto itself states, everywhere and at all times, on the historical conditions for the time being existing, and, for that reason, no special stress is laid on the revolutionary measures proposed at the end of Section II. That passage would, in many respects, be very differently worded today. In view of the gigantic strides of Modern Industry since 1848, and of the accompanying improved and extended organization of the working class, in view of the practical experience gained, first in the February Revolution, and then, still more, in the Paris Commune, where the proletariat for the first time held political power for two whole months, this programme has in some details been antiquated. One thing especially was proved by the Commune, viz., that "the working class cannot simply lay hold of ready-made state machinery, and wield it for its own purposes." (See *The Civil War in France: Address of the General Council of the International Working Men's Assocation* 1871, where this point is further developed.) Further, it is self-evident that the criticism of socialist literature is deficient in relation to the present time, because it comes down only to 1847; also that the remarks on the relation of the Communists to the various opposition parties (Section IV), although, in principle still correct, yet in practice are antiquated, because the political situation has been entirely changed, and the progress of history has swept from off the Earth the greater portion of the political parties there enumerated.
>
> "But then, the Manifesto has become a historical document which we have no longer any right to alter."

The present translation is by Mr Samuel Moore, the translator of the greater portion of Marx's *Capital*. We have revised it in common, and I have added a few notes explanatory of historical allusions.

FREDERICK ENGELS
January 30, 1888 London

Manifesto of the Communist Party

by Karl Marx

Karl Marx

A spectre is haunting Europe—the spectre of communism. All the powers of old Europe have entered into a holy alliance to exorcise this spectre: Pope and Tsar, Metternich and Guizot, French Radicals and German police-spies.

Where is the party in opposition that has not been decried as communistic by its opponents in power? Where is the opposition that has not hurled back the branding reproach of communism, against the more advanced opposition parties, as well as against its reactionary adversaries?

Two things result from this fact:

  I. Communism is already acknowledged by all European powers to be itself a power.
  II. It is high time that Communists should openly, in the face of the whole world, publish their views, their aims, their tendencies, and meet this nursery tale of the spectre of communism with a manifesto of the party itself.

To this end, Communists of various nationalities have assembled in London and sketched the following manifesto, to be published in the English, French, German, Italian, Flemish and Danish languages.

I–BOURGEOIS AND PROLETARIANS [1]

The history of all hitherto existing society [2] is the history of class struggles.

Freeman and slave, patrician and plebian, lord and serf, guild-master [3] and journeyman, in a word, oppressor and oppressed, stood in constant opposition to one another, carried on an uninterrupted, now hidden, now open fight, a fight that each time ended, either in a revolutionary reconstitution of society at large, or in the common ruin of the contending classes.

In the earlier epochs of history, we find almost everywhere a complicated arrangement of society into various orders, a manifold gradation of social rank. In ancient Rome we have patricians, knights, plebians, slaves; in the Middle Ages, feudal lords, vassals, guild-masters, journeymen, apprentices, serfs; in almost all of these classes, again, subordinate gradations.

The modern bourgeois society that has sprouted from the ruins of feudal society has not done away with class antagonisms. It has but established new classes, new conditions of oppression, new forms of struggle in place of the old ones.

Our epoch, the epoch of the bourgeoisie, possesses, however, this distinct feature: it has simplified class antagonisms. Society as a whole is more and more splitting up into two great hostile camps, into two great classes directly facing each other—bourgeoisie and proletariat.

From the serfs of the Middle Ages sprang the chartered burghers of the earliest towns. From these burgesses the first elements of the bourgeoisie were developed.

The discovery of America, the rounding of the Cape, opened up fresh ground for the rising bourgeoisie. The East-Indian and Chinese markets, the colonization of America, trade with the colonies, the increase in the means of exchange and in commodities generally, gave to commerce, to navigation, to industry, an impulse never before known, and thereby, to the revolutionary element in the tottering feudal society, a rapid development.

The feudal system of industry, in which industrial production was monopolized by closed guilds, now no longer suffices for the growing wants of the new markets. The manufacturing system took its place. The guild-masters were pushed aside by the manufacturing middle class; division of labor between the different corporate guilds vanished in the face of division of labor in each single workshop.

Meantime, the markets kept ever growing, the demand ever rising. Even manufacturers no longer sufficed. Thereupon, steam and machinery revolutionized industrial production. The place of manufacture was taken by the giant, MODERN INDUSTRY; the place of the industrial middle class by industrial millionaires, the leaders of the whole industrial armies, the modern bourgeois.

Modern industry has established the world market, for which the discovery of America paved the way. This market has given an immense development to commerce, to navigation, to communication by land. This development has, in turn, reacted on the extension of industry; and in proportion as industry, commerce, navigation, railways extended, in the same proportion the bourgeoisie developed, increased its capital, and pushed into the background every class handed down from the Middle Ages.

We see, therefore, how the modern bourgeoisie is itself the product of a long course of development, of a series of revolutions in the modes of production and of exchange.

Each step in the development of the bourgeoisie was accompanied by a corresponding political advance in that class. An oppressed class under the sway of the feudal nobility, an armed and self-governing association of medieval commune [4]: here independent urban republic (as in Italy and Germany); there taxable "third estate" of the monarchy (as in France); afterward, in the period of manufacturing proper, serving either the semi-feudal or the absolute monarchy as a counterpoise against the nobility, and, in fact, cornerstone of the great monarchies in general—the bourgeoisie has at last, since the establishment of Modern Industry and of the world market, conquered for itself, in the modern representative state, exclusive political sway. The executive of the modern state is but a committee for managing the common affairs of the whole bourgeoisie.

The bourgeoisie, historically, has played a most revolutionary part.

The bourgeoisie, wherever it has got the upper hand, has put an end to all feudal, patriarchal, idyllic relations. It has pitilessly torn asunder the motley feudal ties that bound man to his "natural superiors", and has left no other nexus between people than naked self-interest, than callous "cash payment". It has drowned out the most heavenly ecstasies of religious fervor, of chivalrous enthusiasm, of philistine sentimentalism, in the icy water of egotistical calculation. It has resolved personal worth into exchange value, and in place of the numberless indefeasible chartered freedoms, has set up that single, unconscionable freedom—Free Trade. In one word, for exploitation, veiled by religious and political illusions, it has substituted naked, shameless, direct, brutal exploitation.

The bourgeoisie has stripped of its halo every occupation hitherto honored and looked up to with reverent awe. It has converted the physician, the lawyer, the priest, the poet, the man of science, into its paid wage laborers.

The bourgeoisie has torn away from the family its sentimental veil, and has reduced the family relation into a mere money relation.

The bourgeoisie has disclosed how it came to pass that the brutal display of vigor in the Middle Ages, which reactionaries so much admire, found its fitting complement in the most slothful indolence. It has been the first to show what man's activity can bring about. It has accomplished wonders far surpassing Egyptian pyramids, Roman aqueducts, and Gothic cathedrals; it has conducted expeditions that put in the shade all former exoduses of nations and crusades.

The bourgeoisie cannot exist without constantly revolutionizing the instruments of production, and thereby the relations of production, and with them the whole relations of society. Conservation of the old modes of production in unaltered form, was, on the contrary, the first condition of existence for all earlier industrial classes. Constant revolutionizing of production, uninterrupted disturbance of all social conditions, everlasting uncertainty and agitation distinguish the bourgeois epoch from all earlier ones. All fixed, fast frozen relations, with their train of ancient and venerable prejudices and opinions, are swept away, all new-formed ones become antiquated before they can ossify. All that is solid melts into air, all that is holy is profaned, and man is at last compelled to face with sober senses his real condition of life and his relations with his kind.

The need of a constantly expanding market for its products chases the bourgeoisie over the entire surface of the globe. It must nestle everywhere, settle everywhere, establish connections everywhere.

The bourgeoisie has, through its exploitation of the world market, given a cosmopolitan character to production and consumption in every country. To the great chagrin of reactionaries, it has drawn from under the feet of industry the national ground on which it stood. All old-established national industries have been destroyed or are daily being destroyed. They are dislodged by new industries, whose introduction becomes a life and death question for all civilized nations, by industries that no longer work up indigenous raw material, but raw material drawn from the remotest zones; industries whose products are consumed, not only at home, but in every quarter of the globe. In place of the old wants, satisfied by the production of the country, we find new wants, requiring for their satisfaction the products of distant lands and climes. In place of the old local and national seclusion and self-sufficiency, we have intercourse in every direction, universal inter-dependence of nations. And as in material, so also in intellectual production. The intellectual creations of individual nations become common property. National one-sidedness and narrow-mindedness become more and more impossible, and from the numerous national and local literatures, there arises a world literature.

The bourgeoisie, by the rapid improvement of all instruments of production, by the immensely facilitated means of communication, draws all, even the most barbarian, nations into civilization. The cheap prices of commodities are the heavy artillery with which it forces the barbarians' intensely obstinate hatred of foreigners to capitulate. It compels all nations, on pain of extinction, to adopt the bourgeois mode of production; it compels them to introduce what it calls civilization into their midst, i.e., to become bourgeois themselves. In one word, it creates a world after its own image.

The bourgeoisie has subjected the country to the rule of the towns. It has created enormous cities, has greatly increased the urban population as compared with the rural, and has thus rescued a considerable part of the population from the idiocy of rural life. Just as it has made the country dependent on the towns, so it has made barbarian and semi-barbarian countries dependent on the civilized ones, nations of peasants on nations of bourgeois, the East on the West.

The bourgeoisie keeps more and more doing away with the scattered state of the population, of the means of production, and of property. It has agglomerated population, centralized the means of production, and has concentrated property in a few hands. The necessary consequence of this was political centralization. Independent, or but loosely connected provinces, with separate interests, laws, governments, and systems of taxation, became lumped together into one nation, with one government, one code of laws, one national class interest, one frontier, and one customs tariff.

The bourgeoisie, during its rule of scarce one hundred years, has created more massive and more colossal productive forces than have all preceding generations together. Subjection of nature's forces to man, machinery, application of chemistry to industry and agriculture, steam navigation, railways, electric telegraphs, clearing of whole continents for cultivation, canalization or rivers, whole populations conjured out of the ground—what earlier century had even a presentiment that such productive forces slumbered in the lap of social labor?

We see then: the means of production and of exchange, on whose foundation the bourgeoisie built itself up, were generated in feudal society. At a certain stage in the development of these means of production and of exchange, the conditions under which feudal society produced and exchanged, the feudal organization of agriculture and manufacturing industry, in one word, the feudal relations of property became no longer compatible with the already developed productive forces; they became so many fetters. They had to be burst asunder; they were burst asunder.

Into their place stepped free competition, accompanied by a social and political constitution adapted in it, and the economic and political sway of the bourgeois class.

A similar movement is going on before our own eyes. Modern bourgeois society, with its relations of production, of exchange and of property, a society that has conjured up such gigantic means of production and of exchange, is like the sorcerer who is no longer able to control the powers of the nether world whom he has called up by his spells. For many a decade past, the history of industry and commerce is but the history of the revolt of modern productive forces against modern conditions of production, against the property relations that are the conditions for the existence of the bourgeois and of its rule. It is enough to mention the commercial crises that, by their periodical return, put the existence of the entire bourgeois society on its trial, each time more threateningly. In these crises, a great part not only of the existing products, but also of the previously created productive forces, are periodically destroyed. In these crises, there breaks out an epidemic that, in all earlier epochs, would have seemed an absurdity—the epidemic of over-production. Society suddenly finds itself put back into a state of momentary barbarism; it appears as if a famine, a universal war of devastation, had cut off the supply of every means of subsistence; industry and commerce seem to be destroyed. And why? Because there is too much civilization, too much means of subsistence, too much industry, too much commerce. The productive forces at the disposal of society no longer tend to further the development of the conditions of bourgeois property; on the contrary, they have become too powerful for these conditions, by which they are fettered, and so soon as they overcome these fetters, they bring disorder into the whole of bourgeois society, endanger the existence of bourgeois property. The conditions of bourgeois society are too narrow to comprise the wealth created by them. And how does the bourgeoisie get over these crises? On the one hand, by enforced destruction of a mass of productive forces; on the other, by the conquest of new markets, and by the more thorough exploitation of the old ones. That is to say, by paving the way for more extensive and more destructive crises, and by diminishing the means whereby crises are prevented.

The weapons with which the bourgeoisie felled feudalism to the ground are now turned against the bourgeoisie itself.

But not only has the bourgeoisie forged the weapons that bring death to itself; it has also called into existence the men who are to wield those weapons—the modern working class—the proletarians.

In proportion as the bourgeoisie, i.e., capital, is developed, in the same proportion is the proletariat, the modern working class, developed—a class of laborers, who live only so long as they find work, and who find work only so long as their labor increases capital. These laborers, who must sell themselves piecemeal, are a commodity, like every other article of commerce, and are consequently exposed to all the vicissitudes of competition, to all the fluctuations of the market.

Owing to the extensive use of machinery, and to the division of labor, the work of the proletarians has lost all individual character, and, consequently, all charm for the workman. He becomes an appendage of the machine, and it is only the most simple, most monotonous, and most easily acquired knack, that is required of him. Hence, the cost of production of a workman is restricted, almost entirely, to the means of subsistence that he requires for maintenance, and for the propagation of his race. But the price of a commodity, and therefore also of labor, is equal to its cost of production. In proportion, therefore, as the repulsiveness of the work increases, the wage decreases. What is more, in proportion as the use of machinery and division of labor increases, in the same proportion the burden of toil also increases, whether by prolongation of the working hours, by the increase of the work exacted in a given time, or by increased speed of machinery, etc.

Modern Industry has converted the little workshop of the patriarchal master into the great factory of the industrial capitalist. Masses of laborers, crowded into the factory, are organized like soldiers. As privates of the industrial army, they are placed under the command of a perfect hierarchy of officers and sergeants. Not only are they slaves of the bourgeois class, and of the bourgeois state; they are daily and hourly enslaved by the machine, by the overlooker, and, above all, in the individual bourgeois manufacturer himself. The more openly this despotism proclaims gain to be its end and aim, the more petty, the more hateful and the more embittering it is.

The less the skill and exertion of strength implied in manual labor, in other words, the more modern industry becomes developed, the more is the labor of men superseded by that of women. Differences of age and sex have no longer any distinctive social validity for the working class. All are instruments of labor, more or less expensive to use, according to their age and sex.

No sooner is the exploitation of the laborer by the manufacturer, so far at an end, that he receives his wages in cash, than he is set upon by the other portion of the bourgeoisie, the landlord, the shopkeeper, the pawnbroker, etc.

The lower strata of the middle class—the small tradespeople, shopkeepers, and retired tradesmen generally, the handicraftsmen and peasants—all these sink gradually into the proletariat, partly because their diminutive capital does not suffice for the scale on which Modern Industry is carried on, and is swamped in the competition with the large capitalists, partly because their specialized skill is rendered worthless by new methods of production. Thus, the proletariat is recruited from all classes of the population.

The proletariat goes through various stages of development. With its birth begins its struggle with the bourgeoisie. At first, the contest is carried on by individual laborers, then by the work of people of a factory, then by the operative of one trade, in one locality, against the individual bourgeois who directly exploits them. They direct their attacks not against the bourgeois condition of production, but against the instruments of production themselves; they destroy imported wares that compete with their labor, they smash to pieces machinery, they set factories ablaze, they seek to restore by force the vanished status of the workman of the Middle Ages.

At this stage, the laborers still form an incoherent mass scattered over the whole country, and broken up by their mutual competition. If anywhere they unite to form more compact bodies, this is not yet the consequence of their own active union, but of the union of the bourgeoisie, which class, in order to attain its own political ends, is compelled to set the whole proletariat in motion, and is moreover yet, for a time, able to do so. At this stage, therefore, the proletarians do not fight their enemies, but the enemies of their enemies, the remnants of absolute monarchy, the landowners, the non-industrial bourgeois, the petty bourgeois. Thus, the whole historical movement is concentrated in the hands of the bourgeoisie; every victory so obtained is a victory for the bourgeoisie.

But with the development of industry, the proletariat not only increases in number; it becomes concentrated in greater masses, its strength grows, and it feels that strength more. The various interests and conditions of life within the ranks of the proletariat are more and more equalized, in proportion as machinery obliterates all distinctions of labor, and nearly everywhere reduces wages to the same low level. The growing competition among the bourgeois, and the resulting commercial crises, make the wages of the workers ever more fluctuating. The increasing improvement of machinery, ever more rapidly developing, makes their livelihood more and more precarious; the collisions between individual workmen and individual bourgeois take more and more the character of collisions between two classes. Thereupon, the workers begin to form combinations (trade unions) against the bourgeois; they club together in order to keep up the rate of wages; they found permanent associations in order to make provision beforehand for these occasional revolts. Here and there, the contest breaks out into riots.

Now and then the workers are victorious, but only for a time. The real fruit of their battles lie not in the immediate result, but in the ever expanding union of the workers. This union is helped on by the improved means of communication that are created by Modern Industry, and that place the workers of different localities in contact with one another. It was just this contact that was needed to centralize the numerous local struggles, all of the same character, into one national struggle between classes. But every class struggle is a political struggle. And that union, to attain which the burghers of the Middle Ages, with their miserable highways, required centuries, the modern proletarian, thanks to railways, achieve in a few years.

This organization of the proletarians into a class, and, consequently, into a political party, is continually being upset again by the competition between the workers themselves. But it ever rises up again, stronger, firmer, mightier. It compels legislative recognition of particular interests of the workers, by taking advantage of the divisions among the bourgeoisie itself. Thus, the Ten-Hours Bill in England was carried.

Altogether, collisions between the classes of the old society further in many ways the course of development of the proletariat. The bourgeoisie finds itself involved in a constant battle. At first with the aristocracy; later on, with those portions of the bourgeoisie itself, whose interests have become antagonistic to the progress of industry; at all time with the bourgeoisie of foreign countries. In all these battles, it sees itself compelled to appeal to the proletariat, to ask for help, and thus to drag it into the political arena. The bourgeoisie itself, therefore, supplies the proletariat with its own elements of political and general education, in other words, it furnishes the proletariat with weapons for fighting the bourgeoisie.

Further, as we have already seen, entire sections of the ruling class are, by the advance of industry, precipitated into the proletariat, or are at least threatened in their conditions of existence. These also supply the proletariat with fresh elements of enlightenment and progress.

Finally, in times when the class struggle nears the decisive hour, the progress of dissolution going on within the ruling class, in fact within the whole range of old society, assumes such a violent, glaring character, that a small section of the ruling class cuts itself adrift, and joins the revolutionary class, the class that holds the future in its hands. Just as, therefore, at an earlier period, a section of the nobility went over to the bourgeoisie, so now a portion of the bourgeoisie goes over to the proletariat, and in particular, a portion of the bourgeois ideologists, who have raised themselves to the level of comprehending theoretically the historical movement as a whole.

Of all the classes that stand face to face with the bourgeoisie today, the proletariat alone is a genuinely revolutionary class. The other classes decay and finally disappear in the face of Modern Industry; the proletariat is its special and essential product.

The lower middle class, the small manufacturer, the shopkeeper, the artisan, the peasant, all these fight against the bourgeoisie, to save from extinction their existence as fractions of the middle class. They are therefore not revolutionary, but conservative. Nay, more, they are reactionary, for they try to roll back the wheel of history. If, by chance, they are revolutionary, they are only so in view of their impending transfer into the proletariat; they thus defend not their present, but their future interests; they desert their own standpoint to place themselves at that of the proletariat.

The "dangerous class", the social scum, that passively rotting mass thrown off by the lowest layers of the old society, may, here and there, be swept into the movement by a proletarian revolution; its conditions of life, however, prepare it far more for the part of a bribed tool of reactionary intrigue.

In the condition of the proletariat, those of old society at large are already virtually swamped. The proletarian is without property; his relation to his wife and children has no longer anything in common with the bourgeois family relations; modern industry labor, modern subjection to capital, the same in England as in France, in America as in Germany, has stripped him of every trace of national character. Law, morality, religion, are to him so many bourgeois prejudices, behind which lurk in ambush just as many bourgeois interests.

All the preceding classes that got the upper hand sought to fortify their already acquired status by subjecting society at large to their conditions of appropriation. The proletarians cannot become masters of the productive forces of society, except by abolishing their own previous mode of appropriation, and thereby also every other previous mode of appropriation. They have nothing of their own to secure and to fortify; their mission is to destroy all previous securities for, and insurances of, individual property.

All previous historical movements were movements of minorities, or in the interest of minorities. The proletarian movement is the self-conscious, independent movement of the immense majority, in the interest of the immense majority. The proletariat, the lowest stratum of our present society, cannot stir, cannot raise itself up, without the whole superincumbent strata of official society being sprung into the air.

Though not in substance, yet in form, the struggle of the proletariat with the bourgeoisie is at first a national struggle. The proletariat of each country must, of course, first of all settle matters with its own bourgeoisie.

In depicting the most general phases of the development of the proletariat, we traced the more or less veiled civil war, raging within existing society, up to the point where that war breaks out into open revolution, and where the violent overthrow of the bourgeoisie lays the foundation for the sway of the proletariat.

Hitherto, every form of society has been based, as we have already seen, on the antagonism of oppressing and oppressed classes. But in order to oppress a class, certain conditions must be assured to it under which it can, at least, continue its slavish existence. The serf, in the period of serfdom, raised himself to membership in the commune, just as the petty bourgeois, under the yoke of the feudal absolutism, managed to develop into a bourgeois. The modern laborer, on the contrary, instead of rising with the process of industry, sinks deeper and deeper below the conditions of existence of his own class. He becomes a pauper, and pauperism develops more rapidly than population and wealth. And here it becomes evident that the bourgeoisie is unfit any longer to be the ruling class in society, and to impose its conditions of existence upon society as an overriding law. It is unfit to rule because it is incompetent to assure an existence to its slave within his slavery, because it cannot help letting him sink into such a state, that it has to feed him, instead of being fed by him. Society can no longer live under this bourgeoisie, in other words, its existence is no longer compatible with society.

The essential conditions for the existence and for the sway of the bourgeois class is the formation and augmentation of capital; the condition for capital is wage labor. Wage labor rests exclusively on competition between the laborers. The advance of industry, whose involuntary promoter is the bourgeoisie, replaces the isolation of the laborers, due to competition, by the revolutionary combination, due to association. The development of Modern Industry, therefore, cuts from under its feet the very foundation on which the bourgeoisie produces and appropriates products. What the bourgeoisie therefore produces, above all, are its own grave-diggers. Its fall and the victory of the proletariat are equally inevitable.

FOOTNOTES

[1] By bourgeoisie is meant the class of modern capitalists, owners of the means of social production and employers of wage labor.

By proletariat, the class of modern wage laborers who, having no means of production of their own, are reduced to selling their labor power in order to live. [Note by Engels—1888 English edition]

[2] That is, all written history. In 1847, the pre-history of society, the social organization existing previous to recorded history, all but unknown. Since then, August von Haxthausen (1792-1866) discovered common ownership of land in Russia, Georg Ludwig von Maurer proved it to be the social foundation from which all Teutonic races started in history, and, by and by, village communities were found to be, or to have been, the primitive form of society everywhere from India to Ireland. The inner organization of this primitive communistic society was laid bare, in its typical form, by Lewis Henry Morgan's (1818-1861) crowning discovery of the true nature of the gens and its relation to the tribe. With the dissolution of the primeaval communities, society begins to be differentiated into separate and finally antagonistic classes. I have attempted to retrace this dissolution in _Der Ursprung der

Familie, des Privateigenthumus und des Staats_, second edition, Stuttgart, 1886. [Engels, 1888 English edition]

[3] Guild-master, that is, a full member of a guild, a master within, not a head of a guild. [Engels: 1888 English edition]

[4] This was the name given their urban communities by the townsmen of Italy and France, after they had purchased or conquered their initial rights of self-government from their feudal lords. [Engels: 1890 German edition]

"Commune" was the name taken in France by the nascent towns even before they had conquered from their feudal lords and masters local self-government and political rights as the "Third Estate". Generally speaking, for the economical development of the bourgeoisie, England is here taken as the typical country, for its political development, France. [Engels: 1888 English edition]

II—PROLETARIANS AND COMMUNISTS

In what relation do the Communists stand to the proletarians as a whole? The Communists do not form a separate party opposed to the other working-class parties.

They have no interests separate and apart from those of the proletariat as a whole.

They do not set up any sectarian principles of their own, by which to shape and mold the proletarian movement.

The Communists are distinguished from the other working-class parties by this only:

(1) In the national struggles of the proletarians of the different countries, they point out and bring to the front the common interests of the entire proletariat, independently of all nationality.
(2) In the various stages of development which the struggle of the working class against the bourgeoisie has to pass through, they always and everywhere represent the interests of the movement as a whole.

The Communists, therefore, are on the one hand practically, the most advanced and resolute section of the working-class parties of every country, that section which pushes forward all others; on the other hand, theoretically, they have over the great mass of the proletariat the advantage of clearly understanding the lines of march, the conditions, and the ultimate general results of the proletarian movement.

The immediate aim of the Communists is the same as that of all other proletarian parties: Formation of the proletariat into a class, overthrow of the bourgeois supremacy, conquest of political power by the proletariat.

The theoretical conclusions of the Communists are in no way based on ideas or principles that have been invented, or discovered, by this or that would-be universal reformer.

They merely express, in general terms, actual relations springing from an existing class struggle, from a historical movement going on under our very eyes. The abolition of existing property relations is not at all a distinctive feature of communism.

All property relations in the past have continually been subject to historical change consequent upon the change in historical conditions.

The French Revolution, for example, abolished feudal property in favor of bourgeois property.

APPENDIX J: COMMUNIST MANIFESTO

The distinguishing feature of communism is not the abolition of property generally, but the abolition of bourgeois property. But modern bourgeois private property is the final and most complete expression of the system of producing and appropriating products that is based on class antagonisms, on the exploitation of the many by the few.

In this sense, the theory of the Communists may be summed up in the single sentence: Abolition of private property.

We Communists have been reproached with the desire of abolishing the right of personally acquiring property as the fruit of a man's own labor, which property is alleged to be the groundwork of all personal freedom, activity and independence.

Hard-won, self-acquired, self-earned property! Do you mean the property of petty artisan and of the small peasant, a form of property that preceded the bourgeois form? There is no need to abolish that; the development of industry has to a great extent already destroyed it, and is still destroying it daily.

Or do you mean the modern bourgeois private property?

But does wage labor create any property for the laborer? Not a bit. It creates capital, i.e., that kind of property which exploits wage labor, and which cannot increase except upon conditions of begetting a new supply of wage labor for fresh exploitation. Property, in its present form, is based on the antagonism of capital and wage labor. Let us examine both sides of this antagonism.

To be a capitalist, is to have not only a purely personal, but a social STATUS in production. Capital is a collective product, and only by the united action of many members, nay, in the last resort, only by the united action of all members of society, can it be set in motion.

Capital is therefore not only personal; it is a social power.

When, therefore, capital is converted into common property, into the property of all members of society, personal property is not thereby transformed into social property. It is only the social character of the property that is changed. It loses its class character.

Let us now take wage labor.

The average price of wage labor is the minimum wage, i.e., that quantum of the means of subsistence which is absolutely requisite to keep the laborer in bare existence as a laborer. What, therefore, the wage laborer appropriates by means of his labor merely suffices to prolong and reproduce a bare existence. We by no means intend to abolish this personal appropriation of the products of labor, an appropriation that is made for the maintenance and reproduction of human life, and that leaves no surplus wherewith to command the labor of others. All that we want to do away with is the miserable character of this appropriation, under which the laborer lives merely to increase capital, and is allowed to live only in so far as the interest of the ruling class requires it.

In bourgeois society, living labor is but a means to increase accumulated labor. In communist society, accumulated labor is but a means to widen, to enrich, to promote the existence of the laborer.

In bourgeois society, therefore, the past dominates the present; in communist society, the present dominates the past. In bourgeois society, capital is independent and has individuality, while the living person is dependent and has no individuality.

And the abolition of this state of things is called by the bourgeois, abolition of individuality and freedom! And rightly so. The abolition of bourgeois individuality, bourgeois independence, and bourgeois freedom is undoubtedly aimed at.

By freedom is meant, under the present bourgeois conditions of production, free trade, free selling and buying.

But if selling and buying disappears, free selling and buying disappears also. This talk about free selling and buying, and all the other "brave words" of our bourgeois about freedom in general, have a meaning, if any, only in contrast with restricted selling and buying, with the fettered traders of the Middle Ages, but have no meaning when opposed to the communist abolition of buying and selling, or the bourgeois conditions of production, and of the bourgeoisie itself.

You are horrified at our intending to do away with private property. But in your existing society, private property is already done away with for nine-tenths of the population; its existence for the few is solely due to its non-existence in the hands of those nine-tenths. You reproach us, therefore, with intending to do away with a form of property, the necessary condition for whose existence is the non-existence of any property for the immense majority of society.

In one word, you reproach us with intending to do away with your property. Precisely so; that is just what we intend.

From the moment when labor can no longer be converted into capital, money, or rent, into a social power capable of being monopolized, i.e., from the moment when individual property can no longer be transformed into bourgeois property, into capital, from that moment, you say, individuality vanishes.

APPENDIX J: COMMUNIST MANIFESTO

You must, therefore, confess that by "individual" you mean no other person than the bourgeois, than the middle-class owner of property. This person must, indeed, be swept out of the way, and made impossible.

Communism deprives no man of the power to appropriate the products of society; all that it does is to deprive him of the power to subjugate the labor of others by means of such appropriations.

It has been objected that upon the abolition of private property, all work will cease, and universal laziness will overtake us.

According to this, bourgeois society ought long ago to have gone to the dogs through sheer idleness; for those who acquire anything, do not work. The whole of this objection is but another expression of the tautology: There can no longer be any wage labor when there is no longer any capital.

All objections urged against the communistic mode of producing and appropriating material products, have, in the same way, been urged against the communistic mode of producing and appropriating intellectual products. Just as to the bourgeois, the disappearance of class property is the disappearance of production itself, so the disappearance of class culture is to him identical with the disappearance of all culture.

That culture, the loss of which he laments, is, for the enormous majority, a mere training to act as a machine.

But don't wrangle with us so long as you apply, to our intended abolition of bourgeois property, the standard of your bourgeois notions of freedom, culture, law, etc. Your very ideas are but the outgrowth of the conditions of your bourgeois production and bourgeois property, just as your jurisprudence is but the will of your class made into a law for all, a will whose essential character and direction are determined by the economical conditions of existence of your class.

The selfish misconception that induces you to transform into eternal laws of nature and of reason the social forms stringing from your present mode of production and form of property—historical relations that rise and disappear in the progress of production—this misconception you share with every ruling class that has preceded you. What you see clearly in the case of ancient property, what you admit in the case of feudal property, you are of course forbidden to admit in the case of your own bourgeois form of property.

Abolition of the family! Even the most radical flare up at this infamous proposal of the Communists.

TO PRESERVE THE NATION

On what foundation is the present family, the bourgeois family, based? On capital, on private gain. In its completely developed form, this family exists only among the bourgeoisie. But this state of things finds its complement in the practical absence of the family among proletarians, and in public prostitution.

The bourgeois family will vanish as a matter of course when its complement vanishes, and both will vanish with the vanishing of capital.

Do you charge us with wanting to stop the exploitation of children by their parents? To this crime we plead guilty.

But, you say, we destroy the most hallowed of relations, when we replace home education by social.

And your education! Is not that also social, and determined by the social conditions under which you educate, by the intervention direct or indirect, of society, by means of schools, etc.? The Communists have not intended the intervention of society in education; they do but seek to alter the character of that intervention, and to rescue education from the influence of the ruling class.

The bourgeois claptrap about the family and education, about the hallowed correlation of parents and child, becomes all the more disgusting, the more, by the action of Modern Industry, all the family ties among the proletarians are torn asunder, and their children transformed into simple articles of commerce and instruments of labor.

But you Communists would introduce community of women, screams the bourgeoisie in chorus.

The bourgeois sees his wife a mere instrument of production. He hears that the instruments of production are to be exploited in common, and, naturally, can come to no other conclusion that the lot of being common to all will likewise fall to the women.

He has not even a suspicion that the real point aimed at is to do away with the status of women as mere instruments of production.

For the rest, nothing is more ridiculous than the virtuous indignation of our bourgeois at the community of women which, they pretend, is to be openly and officially established by the Communists. The Communists have no need to introduce free love; it has existed almost from time immemorial.

Our bourgeois, not content with having wives and daughters of their proletarians at their disposal, not to speak of common prostitutes, take the greatest pleasure in seducing each other's wives.

Bourgeois marriage is, in reality, a system of wives in common and thus, at the most, what the Communists might possibly be reproached with is that they desire to introduce, in substitution for a hypocritically concealed, an openly legalized system of free love. For the rest, it is self-evident that the abolition of the present system of production must bring with it the abolition of free love springing from that system, i.e., of prostitution both public and private.

The Communists are further reproached with desiring to abolish countries and nationality.

The workers have no country. We cannot take from them what they have not got. Since the proletariat must first of all acquire political supremacy, must rise to be the leading class of the nation, must constitute itself the nation, it is, so far, itself national, though not in the bourgeois sense of the word.

National differences and antagonism between peoples are daily more and more vanishing, owing to the development of the bourgeoisie, to freedom of commerce, to the world market, to uniformity in the mode of production and in the conditions of life corresponding thereto.

The supremacy of the proletariat will cause them to vanish still faster. United action of the leading civilized countries at least is one of the first conditions for the emancipation of the proletariat.

In proportion as the exploitation of one individual by another will also be put an end to, the exploitation of one nation by another will also be put an end to. In proportion as the antagonism between classes within the nation vanishes, the hostility of one nation to another will come to an end.

The charges against communism made from a religious, a philosophical and, generally, from an ideological standpoint, are not deserving of serious examination.

Does it require deep intuition to comprehend that man's ideas, views, and conception, in one word, man's consciousness, changes with every change in the conditions of his material existence, in his social relations and in his social life?

What else does the history of ideas prove, than that intellectual production changes its character in proportion as material production is changed? The ruling ideas of each age have ever been the ideas of its ruling class.

When people speak of the ideas that revolutionize society, they do but express that fact that within the old society the elements of a new one have been created, and that the dissolution of the old ideas keeps even pace with the dissolution of the old conditions of existence.

When the ancient world was in its last throes, the ancient religions were overcome by Christianity. When Christian ideas succumbed in the eighteenth century to rationalist ideas, feudal society fought its death battle with the then revolutionary bourgeoisie. The ideas of religious liberty and freedom of conscience merely gave expression to the sway of free competition within the domain of knowledge.

"Undoubtedly," it will be said, "religious, moral, philosophical, and juridicial ideas have been modified in the course of historical development. But religion, morality, philosophy, political science, and law, constantly survived this change."

"There are, besides, eternal truths, such as Freedom, Justice, etc., that are common to all states of society. But communism abolishes eternal truths, it abolishes all religion, and all morality, instead of constituting them on a new basis; it therefore acts in contradiction to all past historical experience."

What does this accusation reduce itself to? The history of all past society has consisted in the development of class antagonisms, antagonisms that assumed different forms at different epochs.

But whatever form they may have taken, one fact is common to all past ages, viz., the exploitation of one part of society by the other. No wonder, then, that the social consciousness of past ages, despite all the multiplicity and variety it displays, moves within certain common forms, or general ideas, which cannot completely vanish except with the total disappearance of class antagonisms.

The communist revolution is the most radical rupture with traditional property relations; no wonder that its development involved the most radical rupture with traditional ideas.

But let us have done with the bourgeois objections to communism.

We have seen above that the first step in the revolution by the working class is to raise the proletariat to the position of ruling class to win the battle of democracy.

The proletariat will use its political supremacy to wrest, by degree, all capital from the bourgeoisie, to centralize all instruments of production in the hands of the state, i.e., of the proletariat organized as the ruling class; and to increase the total productive forces as rapidly as possible.

Of course, in the beginning, this cannot be effected except by means of despotic inroads on the rights of property, and on the conditions of bourgeois production; by means of measures, therefore, which appear economically insufficient and untenable, but which,

APPENDIX J: COMMUNIST MANIFESTO

in the course of the movement, outstrip themselves, necessitate further inroads upon the old social order, and are unavoidable as a means of entirely revolutionizing the mode of production.

These measures will, of course, be different in different countries.

Nevertheless, in most advanced countries, the following will be pretty generally applicable.

1. Abolition of property in land and application of all rents of land to public purposes.
2. A heavy progressive or graduated income tax.
3. Abolition of all rights of inheritance.
4. Confiscation of the property of all emigrants and rebels.
5. Centralization of credit in the hands of the state, by means of a national bank with state capital and an exclusive monopoly.
6. Centralization of the means of communication and transport in the hands of the state.
7. Extension of factories and instruments of production owned by the state; the bringing into cultivation of waste lands, and the improvement of the soil generally in accordance with a common plan.
8. Equal obligation of all to labor. Establishment of industrial armies, especially for agriculture.
9. Combination of agriculture with manufacturing industries; gradual abolition of all the distinction between town and country by a more equable distribution of the populace over the country.
10. Free education for all children in public schools. Abolition of children's factory labor in its present form. Combination of education with industrial production, etc.

When, in the course of development, class distinctions have disappeared, and all production has been concentrated in the hands of a vast association of the whole nation, the public power will lose its political character. Political power, properly so called, is merely the organized power of one class for oppressing another. If the proletariat during its contest with the bourgeoisie is compelled, by the force of circumstances, to organize itself as a class; if, by means of a revolution, it makes itself the ruling class, and, as such, sweeps away by force the old conditions of production, then it will, along with these conditions, have swept away the conditions for the existence of class antagonisms and of classes generally, and will thereby have abolished its own supremacy as a class.

In place of the old bourgeois society, with its classes and class antagonisms, we shall have an association in which the free development of each is the condition for the free development of all.

III—SOCIALIST AND COMMUNIST LITERATURE

1. REACTIONARY SOCIALISM

a. Feudal Socialism

Owing to their historical position, it became the vocation of the aristocracies of France and England to write pamphlets against modern bourgeois society. In the French Revolution of July 1830, and in the English reform agitation, these aristocracies again succumbed to the hateful upstart. Thenceforth, a serious political struggle was altogether out of the question. A literary battle alone remained possible. But even in the domain of literature, the old cries of the restoration period had become impossible. [1]

In order to arouse sympathy, the aristocracy was obliged to lose sight, apparently, of its own interests, and to formulate its indictment against the bourgeoisie in the interest of the exploited working class alone. Thus, the aristocracy took their revenge by singing lampoons on their new masters and whispering in his ears sinister prophesies of coming catastrophe.

In this way arose feudal socialism: half lamentation, half lampoon; half an echo of the past, half menace of the future; at times, by its bitter, witty and incisive criticism, striking the bourgeoisie to the very heart's core, but always ludicrous in its effect, through total incapacity to comprehend the march of modern history.

The aristocracy, in order to rally the people to them, waved the proletarian alms-bag in front for a banner. But the people, so often as it joined them, saw on their hindquarters the old feudal coats of arms, and deserted with loud and irreverent laughter.

One section of the French Legitimists and "Young England" exhibited this spectacle:

In pointing out that their mode of exploitation was different to that of the bourgeoisie, the feudalists forget that they exploited under circumstances and conditions that were quite different and that are now antiquated. In showing that, under their rule, the modern proletariat never existed, they forget that the modern bourgeoisie is the necessary offspring of their own form of society.

For the rest, so little do they conceal the reactionary character of their criticism that their chief accusation against the bourgeois amounts to this: that under the bourgeois regime a class is being developed which is destined to cut up, root and branch, the old order of society.

What they upbraid the bourgeoisie with is not so much that it creates a proletariat as that it creates a revolutionary proletariat.

In political practice, therefore, they join in all corrective measures against the working class; and in ordinary life, despite their highfalutin' phrases, they stoop to pick up the golden apples dropped from the tree of industry, and to barter truth, love, and honor, for traffic in wool, beetroot-sugar, and potato spirits. [2]

As the parson has ever gone hand in hand with the landlord, so has clerical socialism with feudal socialism.

Nothing is easier than to give Christian asceticism a socialist tinge. Has not Christianity declaimed against private property, against marriage, against the state? Has it not preached in the place of these, charity and poverty, celibacy and mortification of the flesh, monastic life and Mother Church? Christian socialism is but the holy water with which the priest consecrates the heart-burnings of the aristocrat.

b. Petty-Bourgeois Socialism

The feudal aristocracy was not the only class that was ruined by the bourgeoisie, not the only class whose conditions of existence pined and perished in the atmosphere of modern bourgeois society. The medieval burgesses and the small peasant proprietors were the precursors of the modern bourgeoisie. In those countries which are but little developed, industrially and commercially, these two classes still vegetate side by side with the rising bourgeoisie.

In countries where modern civilization has become fully developed, a new class of petty bourgeois has been formed, fluctuating between proletariat and bourgeoisie, and ever renewing itself a supplementary part of bourgeois society. The individual members of this class, however, as being constantly hurled down into the proletariat by the action of competition, and, as Modern Industry develops, they even see the moment approaching when they will completely disappear as an independent section of modern society, to be replaced in manufactures, agriculture and commerce, by overlookers, bailiffs and shopmen.

In countries like France, where the peasants constitute far more than half of the population, it was natural that writers who sided with the proletariat against the bourgeoisie should use, in their criticism of the bourgeois regime, the standard of the peasant and petty bourgeois, and from the standpoint of these intermediate classes, should take up the cudgels for the working class. Thus arose petty-bourgeois socialism. Sismondi was the head of this school, not only in France but also in England.

This school of socialism dissected with great acuteness the contradictions in the conditions of modern production. It laid bare the hypocritical apologies of economists. It proved, incontrovertibly, the disastrous effects of machinery and division of labor; the concentration of capital and land in a few hands; overproduction and crises; it pointed out the inevitable ruin of the petty bourgeois and peasant, the misery of the proletariat, the anarchy in production, the crying inequalities in the distribution of wealth, the industrial war of extermination between nations, the dissolution of old moral bonds, of the old family relations, of the old nationalities.

In it positive aims, however, this form of socialism aspires either to restoring the old means of production and of exchange, and with them the old property relations, and the old society, or to cramping the modern means of production and of exchange within the framework of the old property relations that have been, and were bound to be, exploded by those means. In either case, it is both reactionary and Utopian.

Its last words are: corporate guilds for manufacture; patriarchal relations in agriculture.

Ultimately, when stubborn historical facts had dispersed all intoxicating effects of self-deception, this form of socialism ended in a miserable hangover.

c. German or "True" Socialism

The socialist and communist literature of France, a literature that originated under the pressure of a bourgeoisie in power, and that was the expressions of the struggle against this power, was introduced into Germany at a time when the bourgeoisie in that country had just begun its contest with feudal absolutism.

German philosophers, would-be philosophers, and beaux esprits (men of letters), eagerly seized on this literature, only forgetting that when these writings immigrated from France into Germany, French social conditions had not immigrated along with them. In contact with German social conditions, this French literature lost all its immediate practical significance and assumed a purely literary aspect. Thus, to the German philosophers of the eighteenth century, the demands of the first French Revolution were nothing more than the demands of "Practical Reason" in general, and the utterance of the will of the revolutionary French bourgeoisie signified, in their eyes, the laws of pure will, of will as it was bound to be, of true human will generally.

The work of the German literati consisted solely in bringing the new French ideas into harmony with their ancient philosophical conscience, or rather, in annexing the French ideas without deserting their own philosophic point of view.

This annexation took place in the same way in which a foreign language is appropriated, namely, by translation.

It is well-known how the monks wrote silly lives of Catholic saints over the manuscripts on which the classical works of ancient heathendom had been written. The German literati reversed this process with the profane French literature. They wrote their philosophical nonsense beneath the French original. For instance, beneath the French criticism of the economic functions of money, they wrote "alienation of humanity", and beneath the French criticism of the bourgeois state they wrote "dethronement of the category of the general", and so forth.

The introduction of these philosophical phrases at the back of the French historical criticisms, they dubbed "Philosophy of Action", "True Socialism", "German Science of Socialism", "Philosophical Foundation of Socialism", and so on.

The French socialist and communist literature was thus completely emasculated. And, since it ceased, in the hands of the German, to express the struggle of one class with the other, he felt conscious of having overcome "French one-sidedness" and of representing, not true requirements, but the requirements of truth; not the interests of the proletariat, but the interests of human nature, of man in general, who belongs to no class, has no reality, who exists only in the misty realm of philosophical fantasy.

This German socialism, which took its schoolboy task so seriously and solemnly, and extolled its poor stock-in-trade in such a mountebank fashion, meanwhile gradually lost its pedantic innocence.

The fight of the Germans, and especially of the Prussian bourgeoisie, against feudal aristocracy and absolute monarchy, in other words, the liberal movement, became more earnest.

By this, the long-wished for opportunity was offered to "True" Socialism of confronting the political movement with the socialistic demands, of hurling the traditional anathemas against liberalism, against representative government, against bourgeois competition, bourgeois freedom of the press, bourgeois legislation, bourgeois liberty and equality, and of preaching to the masses that they had nothing to gain, and everything to lose, by this bourgeois movement. German socialism forgot, in the nick of time, that the French criticism, whose silly echo it was, presupposed the existence of modern bourgeois society, with its corresponding economic conditions of existence, and the political constitution adapted thereto, the very things whose attainment was the object of the pending struggle in Germany.

To the absolute governments, with their following of parsons, professors, country squires, and officials, it served as a welcome scarecrow against the threatening bourgeoisie.

It was a sweet finish, after the bitter pills of flogging and bullets, with which these same governments, just at that time, dosed the German working-class risings.

While this "True" Socialism thus served the government as a weapon for fighting the German bourgeoisie, it, at the same time, directly represented a reactionary interest, the interest of

German philistines. In Germany, the petty-bourgeois class, a relic of the sixteenth century, and since then constantly cropping up again under the various forms, is the real social basis of the existing state of things.

To preserve this class is to preserve the existing state of things in Germany. The industrial and political supremacy of the bourgeoisie threatens it with certain destruction—on the one hand, from the concentration of capital; on the other, from the rise of a revolutionary proletariat. "True" Socialism appeared to kill these two birds with one stone. It spread like an epidemic.

The robe of speculative cobwebs, embroidered with flowers of rhetoric, steeped in the dew of sickly sentiment, this transcendental robe in which the German Socialists wrapped their sorry "eternal truths", all skin and bone, served to wonderfully increase the sale of their goods amongst such a public. And on its part German socialism recognized, more and more, its own calling as the bombastic representative of the petty-bourgeois philistine.

It proclaimed the German nation to be the model nation, and the German petty philistine to be the typical man. To every villainous meanness of this model man, it gave a hidden, higher, socialistic interpretation, the exact contrary of its real character. It went to the extreme length of directly opposing the "brutally destructive" tendency of communism, and of proclaiming its supreme and impartial contempt of all class struggles. With very few exceptions, all the so-called socialist and communist publications that now (1847) circulate in Germany belong to the domain of this foul and enervating literature. [3]

2. CONSERVATIVE OR BOURGEOIS SOCIALISM

A part of the bourgeoisie is desirous of redressing social grievances in order to secure the continued existence of bourgeois society.

To this section belong economists, philanthropists, humanitarians, improvers of the condition of the working class, organizers of charity, members of societies for the prevention of cruelty to animals, temperance fanatics, hole-and-corner reformers of every imaginable kind. This form of socialism has, moreover, been worked out into complete systems.

We may cite Proudhon's Philosophy of Poverty as an example of this form.

The socialistic bourgeois want all the advantages of modern social conditions without the struggles and dangers necessarily resulting therefrom. They desire the existing state of society, minus its revolutionary and disintegrating elements. They wish for a bourgeoisie without a proletariat. The bourgeoisie naturally conceives the world in which it is supreme to be the best; and bourgeois socialism develops this comfortable conception into various more or less complete systems. In requiring the proletariat to carry out such a system, and thereby to march straightaway into the social New Jerusalem, it but requires in reality that the proletariat should remain within the bounds of existing society, but should cast away all its hateful ideas concerning the bourgeoisie.

A second, and more practical, but less systematic, form of this socialism sought to depreciate every revolutionary movement in the eyes of the working class by showing that no mere political reform, but only a change in the material conditions of existence, in economical relations, could be of any advantage to them. By changes in the material conditions of existence, this form of socialism, however, by no means understands abolition of the bourgeois relations of production, an abolition that can be affected only by a revolution, but administrative reforms, based on the continued existence of these relations; reforms, therefore, that in no respect affect the relations between capital and labor, but, at the best, lessen the cost, and simplify the administrative work of bourgeois government.

Bourgeois socialism attains adequate expression when, and only when, it becomes a mere figure of speech.

Free trade: for the benefit of the working class. Protective duties: for the benefit of the working class. Prison reform: for the benefit of the working class. This is the last word and the only seriously meant word of bourgeois socialism.

It is summed up in the phrase: the bourgeois is a bourgeois—for the benefit of the working class.

3. CRITICAL-UTOPIAN SOCIALISM AND COMMUNISM

We do not here refer to that literature which, in every great modern revolution, has always given voice to the demands of the proletariat, such as the writings of Babeuf [4] and others.

The first direct attempts of the proletariat to attain its own ends, made in times of universal excitement, when feudal society was being overthrown, necessarily failed, owing to the then undeveloped state of the proletariat, as well as to the absence of the economic conditions for its emancipation, conditions that had yet to be produced, and could be produced by the impending bourgeois epoch alone. The revolutionary literature that accompanied these first movements of the proletariat had necessarily a reactionary character. It inculcated universal asceticism and social leveling in its crudest form.

The socialist and communist systems, properly so called, those of Saint-Simon [5], Fourier [6], Owen [7], and others, spring into existence in the early undeveloped period, described above, of the struggle between proletariat and bourgeoisie (see Section 1. Bourgeois and Proletarians).

The founders of these systems see, indeed, the class antagonisms, as well as the action of the decomposing elements in the prevailing form of society. But the proletariat, as yet in its infancy, offers to them the spectacle of a class without any historical initiative or any independent political movement.

Since the development of class antagonism keeps even pace with the development of industry, the economic situation, as they find it, does not as yet offer to them the material conditions for the emancipation of the proletariat. They therefore search after a new social science, after new social laws, that are to create these conditions.

Historical action is to yield to their personal inventive action; historically created conditions of emancipation to fantastic ones; and the gradual, spontaneous class organization of the proletariat to an organization of society especially contrived by these inventors. Future history resolves itself, in their eyes, into the propaganda and the practical carrying out of their social plans.

In the formation of their plans, they are conscious of caring chiefly for the interests of the working class, as being the most suffering class. Only from the point of view of being the most suffering class does the proletariat exist for them.

The undeveloped state of the class struggle, as well as their own surroundings, causes Socialists of this kind to consider themselves far superior to all class antagonisms. They want to improve the condition of every member of society, even that of the most favored. Hence, they habitually appeal to society at large, without the distinction of class; nay, by preference, to the ruling class. For how can people when once they understand their system, fail to see in it the best possible plan of the best possible state of society?

Hence, they reject all political, and especially all revolutionary action; they wish to attain their ends by peaceful means, necessarily doomed to failure, and by the force of example, to pave the way for the new social gospel.

Such fantastic pictures of future society, painted at a time when the proletariat is still in a very undeveloped state and has but a fantastic conception of its own position, correspond with the first instinctive yearnings of that class for a general reconstruction of society.

But these socialist and communist publications contain also a critical element. They attack every principle of existing society. Hence, they are full of the most valuable materials for the enlightenment of the working class. The practical measures proposed in them—such as the abolition of the distinction between town and country, of the family, of the carrying on of industries for the account of private individuals, and of the wage system, the proclamation of social harmony, the conversion of the function of the state into a more superintendence of production—all these proposals point solely to the disappearance of class antagonisms which were, at that time, only just cropping up, and which, in these publications, are recognized in their earliest indistinct and undefined forms only. These proposals, therefore, are of a purely utopian character.

The significance of critical-utopian socialism and communism bears an inverse relation to historical development. In proportion as the modern class struggle develops and takes definite shape, this fantastic standing apart from the contest, these fantastic attacks on it, lose all practical value and all theoretical justifications. Therefore, although the originators of these systems were, in many respects, revolutionary, their disciples have, in every case, formed mere reactionary sects. They hold fast by the original views of their masters, in opposition to the progressive historical development of the proletariat. They, therefore, endeavor, and that consistently, to deaden the class struggle and to reconcile the class antagonisms. They still dream of experimental realization of their social utopias, of founding isolated phalansteres, of establishing "Home Colonies", or setting up a "Little Icaria" [8]—pocket editions of the New Jerusalem—and to realize all these castles in the air, they are compelled to appeal to the feelings and purses of the bourgeois. By degrees, they sink into the category of the reactionary conservative socialists depicted above, differing from these only by more systematic pedantry, and by their fanatical and superstitious belief in the miraculous effects of their social science.

They, therefore, violently oppose all political action on the part of the working class; such action, according to them, can only result from blind unbelief in the new gospel.

The Owenites in England, and the Fourierists in France, respectively, oppose the Chartists and the Reformistes.

FOOTNOTES

[1] NOTE by Engels to 1888 English edition: Not the English Restoration (1660-1689), but the French Restoration (1814-1830).

[2] NOTE by Engels to 1888 English edition: This applies chiefly to Germany, where the landed aristocracy and squirearchy have large portions of their estates cultivated for their own account by stewards, and are, moreover, extensive beetroot-sugar manufacturers and distillers of potato spirits. The wealthier British aristocracy are, as yet, rather above that; but they, too, know how to make up for declining rents by lending their names to floaters or more or less shady joint-stock companies.

[3] NOTE by Engels to 1888 German edition: The revolutionary storm of 1848 swept away this whole shabby tendency and cured its protagonists of the desire to dabble in socialism. The chief representative and classical type of this tendency is Mr. Karl Gruen.

[4] Francois Noel Babeuf (1760-1797): French political agitator; plotted unsuccessfully to destroy the Directory in revolutionary France and established a communistic system.

[5] Comte de Saint-Simon, Claude Henri de Rouvroy (1760-1825): French social philosopher; generally regarded as founder of French socialism. He thought society should be reorganized along industrial lines and that scientists should be the new spiritual leaders. His most important work is _Nouveau_Christianisme_ (1825).

[6] Charles Fourier (1772-1837): French social reformer; propounded a system of self-sufficient cooperatives known as Fourierism, especially in his work _Le_Nouveau_ Monde_industriel_ (1829-30)

[7] Richard Owen (1771-1858): Welsh industrialist and social reformer. He formed a model industrial community at New Lanark, Scotland, and pioneered cooperative societies. His books include _New_View_Of_Society_ (1813).

[8] NOTE by Engels to 1888 English edition: "Home Colonies" were what Owen called his communist model societies. _Phalansteres_ were socialist colonies on the plan of Charles Fourier; Icaria was the name given by Caber to his utopia and, later on, to his American communist colony.

IV—POSITION OF THE COMMUNISTS IN RELATION TO THE VARIOUS EXISTING OPPOSITION PARTIES

Section II has made clear the relations of the Communists to the existing working-class parties, such as the Chartists in England and the Agrarian Reformers in America.

The Communists fight for the attainment of the immediate aims, for the enforcement of the momentary interests of the working class; but in the movement of the present, they also represent and take care of the future of that movement. In France, the Communists ally with the Social Democrats* against the conservative and radical bourgeoisie, reserving, however, the right to take up a critical position in regard to phases and illusions traditionally handed down from the Great Revolution.

In Switzerland, they support the Radicals, without losing sight of the fact that this party consists of antagonistic elements, partly of Democratic Socialists, in the French sense, partly of radical bourgeois.

In Poland, they support the party that insists on an agrarian revolution as the prime condition for national emancipation, that party which fomented the insurrection of Krakow in 1846.

In Germany, they fight with the bourgeoisie whenever it acts in a revolutionary way, against the absolute monarchy, the feudal squirearchy, and the petty-bourgeoisie.

But they never cease, for a single instant, to instill into the working class the clearest possible recognition of the hostile antagonism between bourgeoisie and proletariat, in order that the German workers may straightway use, as so many weapons against the bourgeoisie, the social and political conditions that the bourgeoisie must necessarily introduce along with its supremacy, and in order that, after the fall of the reactionary classes in Germany, the fight against the bourgeoisie itself may immediately begin.

The Communists turn their attention chiefly to Germany, because that country is on the eve of a bourgeois revolution that is bound to be carried out under more advanced conditions of European civilization and with a much more developed proletariat than that of England was in the seventeenth, and France in the eighteenth century, and because the bourgeois revolution in Germany will be but the prelude to an immediately following proletarian revolution.

In short, the Communists everywhere support every revolutionary movement against the existing social and political order of things.

In all these movements, they bring to the front, as the leading question in each, the property question, no matter what its degree of development at the time.

Finally, they labor everywhere for the union and agreement of the democratic parties of all countries.

The Communists disdain to conceal their views and aims. They openly declare that their ends can be attained only by the forcible overthrow of all existing social conditions. Let the ruling classes tremble at a communist revolution. The proletarians have nothing to lose but their chains. They have a world to win.

Working men of all countries, unite!

FOOTNOTES

* NOTE by Engels to 1888 English edition: The party then represented in Parliament by Ledru-Rollin, in literature by Louis Blanc (1811-82), in the daily press by the *Reforme*. The name of Social-Democracy signifies, with these its inventors, a section of the Democratic or Republican Party more or less tinged with socialism.

Appendix K

BRIEF BIOGRAPHICAL AND PHILOSOPHICAL SKETCHES

JOHN LOCKE

BARON DE MONTESQUIEU

SIR WILLIAM BLACKSTONE

ST. GEORGE TUCKER

JOHN LOCKE

John Locke

John Locke (1632-1704) was an English philosopher. Born and raised within a Puritan family, he was educated in philosophy, logic, Hebrew, medicine, and natural science at Westminster School and Christ Church, Oxford. Due to the social and political circumstances of the day, many Puritans periodically relocated to Holland. Locke lived in Holland from 1683 to 1688. He returned to England at the accession to the throne of William of Orange. Shortly thereafter, he was appointed to commissioner of appeals and later as commissioner to the Board of Trade and Plantations.

Locke was an ardent advocate of civil liberties and encouraged religious toleration. He became a powerful voice in the advocacy of natural rights. He strongly supported these concepts through the application of reason and observation. While he wrote on a broad array of topics—including religion, political thought, education, and economics—two works stand out as exceptional and are considered his most important works: *An Essay Concerning Human Understanding* (1690) and *Two Treatises of Government* (1690). *Two Treatises of Government* was of particular importance in establishing many of the concepts that fired the imaginations of the men who were to later become known as the Founding Fathers of the United States of America.

In the first of the *Two Treatises of Government*, Locke debunked the concept of the divine right of kings and, in the second treatise, proposed (and eloquently supported) the precept that all mankind are born with and hold natural rights under the laws of nature. He tied the origins of natural law to God and to the knowledge and reason with which God has endowed mankind. He also defined many of the protocols associated with a people establishing a government by which they agree to be governed according to the laws of nature and the limits of power that a people may impose upon their government. The equality of all to be bound by the written and accepted law (including the selected governors) was a concept central to his philosophy regarding law and governance. He also proposed the logical extension that if a government violates the trust that it has received from the people, the government loses its claim upon the people, and the people are released from their obligation of obedience to that government.

The logic of Locke's view of the exercise of delegated power, as expressed in the second treatise, should be readily apparent to all who are willing to read and honestly consider:

> The legislative cannot transfer the power of making laws to any other hands, for it being but a delegated power from the people, they who have it cannot pass it over to others. The people alone can appoint the form of the commonwealth, which is by constituting the legislative, and appointing in whose hands that shall be. And when the people have said, "We will submit and be governed by laws made by such men, and in such forms," nobody else can say other men shall make laws for them; nor can they be bound by any laws but such as are enacted by those whom they have chosen and authorized to make laws for them.

Of course, these precepts were embraced within the founding documents that became the charters of the United States. The Declaration of Independence eloquently and succinctly captures the essence of many of these concepts in these words:

> When in the Course of human events, it becomes necessary for one people to dissolve the political bands which have connected them with another, and to assume among the Powers of the earth, the separate and equal station to which the Laws of Nature and of Nature's God entitle them, a decent respect to the opinions of mankind requires that they should declare the causes which impel them to the separation. We hold these truths to be self-evident, that all men are created equal, that they are endowed by their Creator with certain unalienable Rights, that among these are Life, Liberty and the pursuit of Happiness. That to secure these rights, Governments are instituted among Men, deriving their just powers from the consent of the governed, That whenever any Form of Government becomes destructive of these ends, it is the Right of the People to alter or to abolish it, and to institute new Government, laying its foundation on such principles and organizing its powers in such form, as to them shall seem most likely to effect their Safety and Happiness. Prudence, indeed, will dictate that Governments long established should not be changed for light and transient causes; and accordingly

all experience hath shown, that mankind are more disposed to suffer, while evils are sufferable, than to right themselves by abolishing the forms to which they are accustomed. But when a long train of abuses and usurpations, pursuing invariably the same Object evinces a design to reduce them under absolute Despotism, it is their right, it is their duty, to throw off such Government, and to provide new Guards for their future security.—Such has been the patient sufferance of these Colonies; and such is now the necessity which constrains them to alter their former Systems of Government. The history of the present King of Great Britain is a history of repeated injuries and usurpations, all having in direct object the establishment of an absolute Tyranny over these States.

Locke was also an eloquent advocate of private property and the right of mankind to retain the fruits of their labor, including the rights of exchange and inheritance.

Locke's philosophies were carefully studied by the Founding Fathers of the United States, and the application of many of his ideas can be clearly seen in the works and words of the nation's founders.

BARON DE MONTESQUIEU

Montesquieu

Many of the great political minds who founded the United States received marvelous insights into the different political philosophies and theories of government from early study of the French philosopher Baron de Montesquieu (1689-1755). It seems that his English translation of *The Spirit of Laws*[330] appeared most fortuitously during the formative years of those who were to lay the foundation of the nation that was to become the freest and most prosperous in modern history. In 1760, young John Adams noted in his diary that he had begun the study of *The Spirit of Laws* and that he planned to compile comprehensive marginal notes as he studied this great work. Thomas Jefferson was so impressed with Montesquieu's writings that he included twenty-eight pages of extracts from *The Spirit of Laws* in his *Commonplace Book*. And in 1792, in an essay entitled "Spirit of Governments," James Madison, the Father of the United States Constitution, heaped great praise upon Montesquieu and the political understandings he had brought forth.

[330.] The first English edition was Thomas Nugent's translation (London: Nourse, 1750). References to *The Spirit of Laws* found herein are taken from this original translation, and notation reflects the original format of the text: book, chapter, paragraph—i.e., V, 14, [30] denotes book V, chapter 14, paragraph 30.

BARON DE MONTESQUIEU

Rejected Philosophies

While the Founding Fathers of the United States studied Montesquieu and from his writings gained great insights into issues of law and government, they did not accept his theories carte blanc and with blind adoration. In fact, their collective actions in the *application* of political philosophy witness that they rejected large portions of his perspective. An example can be found in the fact that Montesquieu was completely enamored with monarchy as the best form of government (a position that was probably facilitated by the fact that he lived under the French monarchy, and it was not only a form of government he was most familiar with, but it was also a form in which he participated and with which he likely wished to curry favor). Those who we have come to term as the Founding Fathers of the United States, almost without exception, came to find monarchy absolutely repugnant as a form of government.

The Laws of Nature

In spite of this, many of Montesquieu's concepts resonated with the American love of liberty and found their way not only into the hearts of the American leadership, but also into their revolution and the formation of their political institutions. Montesquieu spoke eloquently and convincingly in regard to the perspective that laws, if they were to be proper, were to be based upon "natural law" or the "laws of nature." He promoted the idea that all men in all times are subject to natural law. Natural law, in Montesquieu's day, recognized law defined and declared by the God of the universe. This concept did not recognize law, or the nature of things, to be based upon a godless philosophy of random chance (as today's current crop of political and natural philosophers would have unsuspecting students believe). Order and purpose were observed in the nature of things, and the great effort was to bring man's law into conformance with God's ordained pattern. Montesquieu was a careful student and advocate of natural law, and his writings developed the concept into a viable philosophy that rang true to the future leaders of the American experiment. Students of the Declaration of Independence are familiar with Jefferson's application of these concepts. Montesquieu also enumerated many of the critically important concepts of freedom, including the necessity of due process of law, and many others.

Checking Power with Power

The Americans were exceptionally impressed and enlightened by Montesquieu's wisdom in the recommendation to separate and divide power to ensure that the considerable power inherent within government would not become abusive. Montesquieu's views of the division of the departments of government into different "competing" and power-checking arms thankfully found their way into the miraculous constitution that was brought into being during the Convention of 1787. The concepts of executive, legislative, and judicial elements were thoroughly introduced and reviewed in *The Spirit of Laws*. And the system of separated and balanced powers came to be one of the most highly valued concepts as the Americans established their government.

While Montesquieu did not originate the concept of separation of powers, he had observed it, particularly in the style exercised in the English system of government that was in existence during his lifetime. While Montesquieu found many faults within the English system of government, he had great praise for it because he perceived that the English had achieved freedom to a greater degree than most nations of that era had ever dreamed possible. In book 11, chapter 6 of *The Spirit of Laws*, he waxed eloquent in descriptions of freedom tied to the English system of government. He concluded that English freedom rested primarily on two pillars: the degree of separation that had been attained between executive, legislative, and judicial power and the satisfactory mixture of monarchy, aristocracy, and democracy in the Crown, the House of Lords, and the House of Commons.

Sir William Blackstone

Sir William Blackstone

The Laws of Nature and Nature's God

It would seem that even the most casual student of the founding era of the United States should have been exposed to the term "the Laws of Nature and of Nature's God" as found in the first paragraph of the Declaration of Independence. Many of today's historical revisionists who would deny the godly origins of the form of government established during the founding era of this nation attempt, in the most scurrilous manner, to subvert a true understanding of the remembrance of this nation's foundation. These revisionists promote the false concept that most of the nation's founders were, at best, agnostic in regard to their belief in God and that many of them were belligerent atheists who sought to promote their godless philosophies upon the new nation they were founding. Nothing could be farther from the truth, and, in fact, reality can be found in the exact opposite position.

The conscious decisions that the founders made to look to God as they laid the foundation stones that became the pillars of their new government were, in large measure, based upon their clear understanding of concepts put forth in the writings of Sir William Blackstone. The primary source of their references in this matter were taken from Blackstone's *Commentaries on the Laws of England*, which were written and published in England in 1765-1769 and which, fortuitously, were quickly imported to the colonies in America and thereafter became a foundational staple for the education of the rising class of statesmen who blossomed during these critical founding years. All references to Blackstone's *Commentaries on the Laws of England* found herein are taken from the original edition, and notation reflects the original volume and page of that original edition. The cover page of the original edition reads, "*Commentaries on the Laws of England. By William Blackstone, Esq. Vinerian Professor of Law, and Solicitor General to Her Majesty. Oxford, Printed at the Clarendon Press. M. DCC. LXV.*"

Blackstone approached the matter of proper law by examining a series of fundamental issues, addressing them through logic and observation.

Of the Nature of Laws in General

Blackstone begins by defining the terms—What is law? Who creates it? Who is bound by it? How is it applied?

Law as Order of the Universe

He looks back to the beginning, asking, How did the most elemental of all laws begin? Who originated them? How immutable are these laws? May the laws be universally applied? Did these laws come into existence through mere chance, or was there a guiding intelligence that set them in motion?

Law as a Rule of Human Action

Blackstone observes that, apparently, there are things to act and things to be acted upon. Those which are to be acted upon are bound by eternal decree to obediently abide in the law that has been placed upon them. But to mankind, the noblest and highest of God's creations, is given the agency or freedom to choose, which allows choice in their actions between themselves and their fellow man (but not freedom from the consequences that follow choices). But truly, God is superior to mankind, and mankind is ultimately dependant upon God. Therefore, mankind is obliged to be obedient to God's laws and conform to the laws that God has set forth.

Law of Nature

Blackstone proposes that the Maker (God) established the "law of nature." Mankind was endowed by God with a human nature. He gave mankind freewill and the ability to reason and discover human nature and the laws that would bring mankind into conformance with God's will. God, in His eternal wisdom, knows the circumstances and conditions that will bring the greatest joy to mankind. God's law is based upon His love, upon justice, and upon that which is good and right in God's eternal scheme. God's law is superior to and takes precedence over all other precepts.

Blackstone proposes that man is bound by God's laws, and by diligent application of his ability to think and reason, man may identify and come to understand God's laws. Blackstone then follows a number of logical steps that follow: God is just, good, and wise; therefore, His laws are just, good, and wise. His laws define good and evil. Happiness will follow obedience to God's law.

God's law is superior to, supersedes, and takes precedence over all other laws.

Revealed Law

God loves mankind enough to reveal to them the laws that will bring them freedom and happiness, as well as perfect order to society. Revelations of these great divine truths may be found in the Holy Scriptures.

Because of mankind's inherent weakness and his inability through his faulty reasoning to fully understand and comprehend the full measure of happiness that is possible through application of eternal laws, God has, in multiple ways, but particularly through the scriptures, helped mankind to come to a knowledge of His great laws of happiness.

Mankind's laws must never contradict God's laws. Mankind's laws are subordinate to God's declarations of law. If human laws contradict God's laws, the human laws must be disobeyed if we will not offend God. It would appear that Blackstone would reject the modern aphorism that morality cannot be legislated. If the revealed (superior) law supports a "moral" position, it would be appropriate to incorporate that "moral" position into human law.

Law of Nations

God's law is superior to the laws of all nations, and therefore, all nations are subject to it. Nations will exist in harmony if they will subject their actions to the superior law and comport themselves with other nations in accord with the higher law.

The Unalienable Rights

The second paragraph of the Declaration of Independence speaks of the "Creator" as being the source of certain unalienable rights. Those rights are mankind's by virtue of their creation and existence within God's great plan. Those unalienable rights predate government and arise from a source higher than government. Governments are instituted to secure these rights.

Right of Society to Control Debauchery

Modern revisionists who would alter the divinely decreed Laws of Nature and of Nature's God proclaim that licentiousness and debauchery fall within the realm of unalienable rights. Blackstone apparently believed there were limits and bounds within which society must operate if society is to be kept from unraveling. Society requires decorum in order to function and allow mankind in general to progress and succeed.

It should be noted that Blackstone did not presume to excuse or exempt private wicked, licentious, or debauched practices from ultimate review and judgment by God, only from control by society's laws. But it must be understood that by Blackstone's definition, *any* public revelation of such practices or *any* such practice which, by its nature or action, affects another person will bring the laws of society to force against the practice, and society's laws have jurisdiction.

Personal Security

The Declaration of Independence affirms that among the unalienable rights of mankind are the rights to life, liberty, and the pursuit of happiness. Blackstone was more specific and expansive in his definition of the elements that should be incorporated under life. It is interesting that Blackstone and his contemporaries, including those who were to become known as the Founding Fathers of the United States, clearly understood the matter of abortion as a practice that should be illegal in society and of the status of the unborn child before the law. This knowledge has somehow eluded the modern scholars of the law who currently sit upon the bench as judges.

Blackstone confirms that the unborn child was clearly understood to be a person, had standing before the law, and could expect the protection of the law. Blackstone notes that even the "ancient law" held such recognition. Of course, such a position was in conformance with the biblical record, to which men such as Blackstone looked in their efforts to comport mankind's legal system to the order defined by God.

As Blackstone noted the first of the unalienable rights, the right to life, and that which was associated with personal wholeness and security, he noted the second right as the right to personal liberty of individuals.

The right and control of private property were next on Blackstone's list of fundamental rights.

These fundamental principles of freedom were well understood by the American statesmen who established this nation, and these fundamental principles are under full assault by the modern socialist-humanist revisionists who have taken their own wisdom as the guide, rather than the divine law that was promoted by Blackstone and the founders of the nation.

The historical record, the written statements of the founders of the United States, and the legal heritage that forms the foundation of American jurisprudence testifies that Blackstone must be considered as a primary tutor of the men of the American founding era in regard to the principles of government. His writings were almost universally studied by the nation's founders, and much of what he wrote found its way into the foundation "enabling documents" of the nation.

Voluminous reviews of his dissertations on the importance of separating and balancing powers within government could be written, as could expansive reviews of other subjects he eloquently addressed, such as individual rights of free men—rights of property, habeas corpus, the rights of free men to be armed, freedom to travel and relocate, the right to not have bail set excessively high, protection against asset forfeiture, the right to due process of the law, the necessity of representation as relating to the subject of taxation, the right of trial by jury, the principle that judges are to be bound by the law (not creators of the law), the rights of petition for redress for government actions; as well as his logical assertion that edicts and directives of foreign powers are not enforceable upon a sovereign people!

These and many other elements that found their way into the United States Constitution and its marvelous Bill of Rights may be found within the powerful writings of Blackstone, but perhaps foremost of all the elements of proper government about which he wrote—or perhaps undergirding all of the other principles—were his concepts of the Laws of Nature and Nature's God. All Americans should be filled with gratitude for his eloquent exposition regarding the divine origin of mankind's rights and the recognition that the universe is governed by God's law and that God's law is an orderly plan that (if implemented and applied within government) would bring mankind to its premier state of happiness. Blackstone's writings greatly facilitated the effort to discover God's divine plan of proper government for mankind. The founders of the United States of America found in this concept the fundamental truths upon which they built a nation.

St. George Tucker

St. George Tucker

St. George Tucker was born in 1752 in Bermuda. In 1771, he migrated to Virginia Colony where he began his study of the law. For a year, he studied at the College of William and Mary under the tutelage of George Wythe (whom he succeeded in 1790 as a professor of law at the College of William and Mary). Tucker was admitted to the bar in 1775 and, shortly thereafter, became actively involved in the effort of the colonies to obtain their independence from Britain. Early in the revolution, he took part in an expedition to Bermuda to obtain military supplies for the Continental Army. Later he participated in the war effort as a colonel in the militia, serving under Nathaniel Greene in North Carolina, deporting himself bravely in that campaign. At the Battle of Yorktown, while serving under General Thomas Nelson, he was wounded.

After the war, Tucker enjoyed success in his law practice and was appointed to a committee charged with the revision of Virginia's laws. His prominence led him to be asked to be a Virginia commissioner to the Annapolis Convention (an early attempt to modify or correct the deficiencies of the then-current constitution—the Articles of Confederation).

As law professor at William and Mary, he used William Blackstone's *Commentaries on the Laws of England* (4 vols., published 1765-1769) as his text. While Blackstone's work was, and is, brilliant, it was based upon the British government and legal system, from which the Americans had so recently successfully gained their independence. Tucker felt compelled to undertake an effort to "Americanize" Blackstone's work to incorporate the advances in law, liberty, and government that were emerging in the United States. Tucker wrote numerous essays in this effort, the most detailed of which was titled *View of the Constitution of the United States*, which was published in 1803.

While Tucker's writings were ostensibly a review of Blackstone's *Commentaries* from an "Americanist" view, with the intent of demonstrating various convictions from the perspective of the new American Constitution and subsequent legal adaptations, Tucker's *View of the Constitution* is not a work solely focused on Blackstone's *Commentaries*. In this work, Tucker, an adopted Virginian, wrote often of the law and issues associated with the subjects he addressed in regard to the laws of Virginia, as well as comparisons between the United States Constitution and the previous constitution—the Articles of Confederation. The Federalist Papers are extensively quoted, as are other contemporary writings.

It is readily apparent to the reader that Tucker's positions on various issues closely parallel the positions held by fellow Virginians George Washington, Thomas Jefferson, and James Madison. References are made herein to writing of Washington, Jefferson, and Madison that reinforce Tucker's statements.

A primary volume used herein in this analysis is St. George Tucker's *View of the Constitution of the United States with Selected Writings*.[331] References to this specific edition of this publication are noted thus: Tucker, *View*, page number/s. While a primary focus of Tucker's *View of the Constitution* touches upon his stated and restated conviction that the new constitution of the United States incorporated a brilliant and unequivocal stipulation to the limited scope of the government established by the United States Constitution and to the dividing and subdividing of the power granted to the national government, other interesting nuances of the new government are touched upon, as are numerous fascinating perspectives on matters that received much debate during the era in which it was written.

An example of the scope of Tucker's discussion can be found in the debate regarding monarchy as a potential form of government in America. That such a debate was even deemed necessary seems truly inane today. During Tucker's lifetime, however, there were still many who held (particularly those who followed Alexander Hamilton's perverse logic for government) that monarchy was ultimately where the United States would end up—having "evolved" back to that after experimenting with the republic that the Constitution created. John Adams was perceived by many to be inclined to embrace the British form of monarchy and parliament—Jefferson was one who (at this period at the turn of the century—1800) accused Adams of this fault. Later in life, it appears that both Jefferson and Adams reconciled, and both were completely dedicated to the liberty the nation had won from England. Tucker sought fervently to debunk any perception that the British form of government was in any way superior to the new American government, and it would seem that a better understanding of the republican form of government came with experience with that form of government. Tucker's writings reflect the passionate disparity that existed in 1803 between the "King men" and those who jealously guarded the sovereignty of "the people." Tucker's fervent animosity against monarchy (and those who would foster it in America) reflects the debates that were current in America in 1800.

---

[331] Tucker, *View*.

Additionally, Tucker's writings emphasize the value and necessity of a written constitution that specifically and exactly delineates the scope and bounds of government and the fact that the people (and/or states) delegated only certain of their sovereign powers to the national government (retaining all others that are not delegated). Individual, God-given rights were the watchword of Tucker's political philosophy. Tucker viewed the written constitution to be a constraint on the natural tendency of government to metastasize over time into a leviathan.

Indeed, that perspective was the predominant view of the people and the states in Tucker's day. The skepticism with which the new constitution was received in 1787 and the debates that occurred in the ratifying conventions speak to that! The hue and cry for a bill of rights, which emanated from the state's ratifying conventions, and the recognition of that requirement by the First Congress after the ratification and establishment of the new government resulted in amendments being immediately presented to the states, which further constrained the power of the national government. The resolution that Congress passed (which became known as the Preamble to the Bill of Rights) as it forwarded the proposed amendments to the states for ratification succinctly stated the sentiments of the day:

Congress of the United States

> Begun and held at the City of New York, on Wednesday, the 4th of March, 1789.
>
> The conventions of a number of the states having, at the time of their adopting the Constitution, expressed a desire, in order *to prevent misconstruction or abuse of its powers, that further declaratory and restrictive clauses should be added;* and as extending the ground of public confidence in the government will best insure the beneficent ends of its institution.

Throughout his review, Tucker refers to the Bill of Rights as submitted to the states for ratification.

The proposed amendments were numbered Articles I to XII. The first two "articles" were not ratified at that time, and thus article 3 became the First Amendment. Numbered in sequence from the first amendment that was ratified, the Tenth Amendment that was ratified had been originally designated as article 12. Apparently Tucker was not aware of this circumstance as he wrote *View of the Constitution of the United States;* consequently, he makes reference within his writing to the original twelve articles as additions to the Constitution.

Tucker and others of the American founding era seemed to clearly understand mankind's natural tendency to accrue and then to begin to abuse power. Tucker's writings reinforced the concerns felt about this tendency of the natural man and sought to draw attention to the efforts that had been made within the United States Constitution to forestall power seekers within the new government.

Selected Bibliography

Acton, Lord. *Acton, Essays on Freedom and Power*. Editor Gertrude Himmelfarb. 1972.
Adams, Abigail. *Warren-Adams Letters*, vol. I, 1743-1777, Massachusetts Historical Society Collections
Adams, John. *The Works of John Adams*. Edited by Charles Francis Adams. 10 volumes. Boston: Little, Brown and Company, 1850-56.
Adams, John. *The American Enlightenment*. Adrienne Koch, editor. New York: George Braziller. 1965.
Adams, John. *The Political Writings of John Adams*, George A. Peek Jr., ed., Liberal Arts Press, New York, 1954
Adams, John Quincy. Address delivered at the request of the Committee of Arrangements for the Anniversary of Independence at The City of Washington on the Fourth of July 1821, while he served as U.S. Secretary of State. Published in pamphlet form, Cambridge: Printed at the Univ. Press, by Hilliard and Metcalf, sold by Cummings & Hilliard, No. 1 Cornhill, Boston. 1821
Adams, Samuel. *The Life and Public Services of Samuel Adams: Being a Narrative of His Acts and Opinions of His Agency in Producing and Forwarding the American Revolution, with Extracts from His Correspondence, State Papers, and Political Essays*. Contributors: William V. Wells—author. Boston: Little, Brown. 1888.
Adams, Samuel. *Debates and Proceedings in the Convention of the Commonwealth Of Massachusetts*. Boston: Pierce and Hale, editors. 1850.
Adams, Samuel. *Samuel Adams on American Independence, the World's Famous Orations*.
Barruel, A. *Memoirs Illustrating the History of Jacobinism [1798]*. Original in French. Translated into English by Robert Clifford. Printed for the translator, London: T. Burton. 1798. Republished 1995, 2002 by Real View Books. Introduction by Stanley K. Jakie.
Bastiat, Fredric. *The Law*. 1850. Irvington-on-Hudson, New York: Foundation for Economic Education, 1974, 1998.
Blackstone, William. *Commentaries on the Laws of England*. Four volumes. Written and published in England, 1765-1769. Oxford, printed at the Clarendon Press. M. DCC. LXV.
Burke, Edmund. *Reflections on the Revolution in France in a Letter* [1790]. The Harvard Classics. Volume 24. Pages 143-378. New York: P. F. Collier & Company. 1909.
Carson, Clarence B. *A Basic History of the United States*. Wadley, Alabama: American Textbook Committee. Six volumes. 1992.

Carson, Clarence B. *Basic Economics*. Watley, Alabama: American Textbook Committee. 1988.
Chesterton, G. K. *Tremendous Trifles*,(1909)
Clark, J. Reuben, Jr. *Selected Papers on International Affairs*. Editor David H. Yarn, Jr. Provo, Utah: Brigham Young University Press.
Clavell, James. *The Children's Story*. New York, New York: Dell Publishing. 1963.
Defoe, Daniel. The Kentish Petition. Addenda, 11. 1701.
Dewey, John, et al. *Humanist Manifestoes I, II, III*. Buffalo, New York: Prometheus Books. 1933, 1973, 2003.
Elliott, Jonathan, ed. *The Debates in the Several State Conventions on the Adoption of the Federal Constitution.* Five volumes. Philadelphia: J.B. Lippincott Co., 1901.
Franklin, Benjamin. *The Writings of Benjamin Franklin*. Edited by Albert Henry Smyth. 10 volumes. New York: Macmillan Company. 1905-7.
Griffin, G. Edward. *The Creature from Jekyll Island*. Appleton, Wisconsin. American Opinion Publishing, Inc. 1994.
Hamilton, Alexander; Madison, James; and Jay, John. *The Federalist Papers.*
Hancock, John. *Great Epochs*, James Parton, The Drafting of the Declaration of Independence
Henry, Patrick. William Wirt, Patrick Henry's Call to Arms, *Great Epics*.
Hazlitt, Henry. *Economics in One Lesson*. New York: Crown Publishing. 1946, 1962, 1979.
Hicks, Loral, et al. *American Government and Economics*. Pensacola Florida: Becka Book Publication. 1984.
Hodge, A. A. Dr. *Popular Lectures on Theological Themes*. Yale (1887)
House, Edward Mandell. *Philip Dru: Administrator*. New York: B. W. Huebsch. 1919.
Hyneman, Charles S., Lutz, Donald S., editors. *American Political Writing during the Founding Era 1760-1805*. Two volumes. Indianapolis: Liberty Fund. 1983.
Jackson, William. *History of the American Nation*.
Jay, John. *The Life of John Jay*, by William Jay [son]. New York: J. & J. Harper. Two Volumes [1833].
Jay, John. *The Correspondence and Public Papers of John Jay*, edited by Henry P. Johnston, A.M. Burt Franklin: New York, Four Volumes [1890]
Jefferson, Thomas. *The Writings of Thomas Jefferson*. Edited by Paul Leicester Ford. 10 volumes. New York: G. P. Putnam's Sons, 1892-99.
Jefferson, Thomas. *The Writings of Thomas Jefferson*. Edited by Albert Ellery Bergh. 20 volumes. Washington: Thomas Jefferson Memorial Association, 1907.
Kleck, Gary. *Point Blank: Guns and Violence in America*. New York: Aldine de Gruyter. 1991.
Lee, Richard Henry. *The Pennsylvania Gazette*, Feb. 20, 1788
Lee, Henry Gen. ("Lighthorse Harry Lee), *Eulogy in Memory of George Washington*, 26 December 1799, Philadelphia; also, Resolution prepared by General Lee and presented to the House of Representatives by John Marshall
Lenin, V.I. *A Contribution to the History of the Question of Dictatorship* (20 October, 1920); Lenin's Collected Works, 4th English Edition, Progress Publishers, Moscow, 1965

SELECTED BIBLIOGRAPHY

Lenin, V.I. *The Socialist Revolution and the Right of Nations to Self Determination* (Theses), Editorial Board of Social-Democrat, Central Organ of the R.S.D.L.P., Published in German in April 1916 in Vorbote, No. 2 Published in Russian in October 1916 in Sbornik Sotsial-Demokrata, No. 1 Printed according to the Sbornik text. Written in January-February 1916

Lincoln, Abraham. *The Collected Works of Abraham Lincoln*, Roy P. Basler, ed. (New Brunswick, N.J., 1953)

Locke, John. *Second Essay Concerning Civil Government.*

Lott, John R. Jr. *More Guns Less Crime.* The University Of Chicago Press. 1998.

Lutz, Donald S., editor. *Colonial Origins of the American Constitution.* Indianapolis: Liberty Fund, 1998.

MacArthur, Douglas, General. *Farewell Address (or Valedictory Remarks)* at the United States Military Academy at West Point. May 1962.

Madison, James *I Annals of Congress* 434, June 8, 1789

Madison, James. *The Complete Madison.* Paul K. Padover, ed. New York: Harper and Brothers. 1953.

Madison, James. *The Debates in the Federal Convention of 1787 Which Framed the Constitution of the United States of America.* Edited by Gaillard Hunt and James Brown Scott. New York: Oxford University Press, 1920.

Madison, James. *The Papers of James Madison.* Edited by Robert A. Rutland. 14 volumes. Chicago: University of Chicago press, 1962-.

Mao Tse-tung, *The Role of the Chinese Communist Party in the National War* (October 1938), Selected Works, Vol. II

Mao Tse-tung, *The Chinese Revolution and the Chinese Communist Party* (December 1939), Selected Works, Vol. II

Marx, Karl. *The Communist Manifesto.* Preface by Frederick Engels. Published 1848.

McGrath, Roger D. *Gunfighters, Highwaymen and Vigilantes: Violence on the Frontier.* University of California Press. 1984

McHenry, Dr. James, Papers on the Federal Convention of 1787, in Charles C. Tansill, comp. *Documents Illustrative of the Formation of the Union of the American States* (Washington: U.S. Printing Office, 1927)

Monroe, James President. *Messages and Papers of the Presidents*, James Monroe

Montesquieu. *The Spirit of Laws.* First English edition: Thomas Nugent's translation. London: Nourse, 1750.

Orwell, George. *1984.*

Paine, Thomas. *Common Sense, the Crisis.* 23 December 1776.

Perloff, James. *Tornado in a Junkyard.* Burlington, MA.: Refuge Books. 1999

The Right to Keep and Bear Arms. Report of the Senate Subcommittee on the Constitution. Washington: United States Government Printing Office, February 1982.

Robinson, John A. M. *Proofs of a Conspiracy [1798].* Republished, Boston, Los Angeles: Western Islands. 1967

Sandoz, Ellis, ed., *Political Sermons of the American Founding Era 1730-1805*. Indianapolis: Liberty Fund. 1990.

Santayana, George. *The Life of Reason*. 1905.

Shakespeare, *The Tempest*

Smith, Adam. *The Wealth of Nations*. Two volumes. New Rochelle, New York: Arlington House, n.d.

Tocqueville, Alexis de. *Democracy in America*. 1835, 1840. 12th edition. Two volumes. New York: Vintage Books, 1945.

Tolkien, J. R. R. *Lord of the Rings*. Harper Collins Publishers. 1994.

Tucker, St. George. *View of the Constitution of the United States (1803)*. Clyde N. Wilson, editor. Indianapolis: Liberty Fund. 1999.

Washington, George. *The Writings of George Washington*. Edited by John C. Fitzpatrick. 39 volumes. Washington: United States Government Printing Office, 1931-44.

Washington, George. *George Washington: a Collection*. Edited by W. B. Allen. Liberty Fund. Indianapolis.

Weaver, Henry Grady. *The Main Spring of Human Progress*. The Foundation for Economic Education, Irving-on-Hudson, New York. 1999.

Webster, Noah. *An America Dictionary of the English Language (1828)*. Republished in facsimile edition by Foundation for American Christian Education. Permission to reprint the 1828 edition granted by G. C. Merriam Company. San Francisco, California copyright 1967.

Webster, Noah. "An Examination of the Leading Principles of the Federal Constitution." [1787], Paul Leicester Ford, editor. *Pamphlets on the Constitution of the United States*. Chicago 1888.

Webster, *Noah. Letters to a Young Gentleman Commencing his Education. New Haven Conn: S. Converse. 1823.*

Index

A

Acton, 1st Baron (John Dalberg-Acton), 88, 309
Adams, Abigail (née Smith), 215
Adams, John, 33, 55, 116, 160, 215, 219, 283, 290, 337, 340, 358, 502, 510
Adams, John Quincy, 111, 175
Adams, Samuel, 105, 219, 234, 290, 338, 351
Afghanistan, 135
Alamo. *See* Battle of the Alamo
Alfred the Great, 229
Allen, W. B.
   George Washington\: A Collection, 312, 329
Al-Qaeda, 135
amendment process, 96, 141, 148, 152, 186, 191, 268, 361. *See also* Article V *under* U.S. Constitution
Amendments to the U.S. Constitution, 387. *See also* Bill of Rights
   First, 29, 40, 41, 153, 220, 237
   Second, 154, 194, 225, 227, 229, 232, 235, 237, 238, 239
   Third, 154
   Fourth, 154, 195, 196, 198, 237
   Fifth, 82, 155
   Sixth, 156
   Seventh, 158
   Eighth, 158, 160
   Ninth, 61, 159, 194
   Tenth, 61, 91, 159, 183, 194, 243
   Eleventh, 160
   Thirteenth, 160
   Fourteenth, 160, 356
   Fifteenth, 161
   Sixteenth, 161, 209, 212, 356
   Seventeenth, 57, 89, 120, 142, 162, 209, 212
   Eighteenth, 162
   Nineteenth, 162
   Twentieth, 162
   Twenty-first, 162
   Twenty-second, 162
   Twenty-three, 163
   Twenty-fourth, 163
   Twenty-fifth, 163
   Twenty-sixth, 163
   Twenty-seventh, 163
American Civil War, 120, 143
American Dictionary of the English Language, An (Webster), 57, 75, 76, 78, 167, 217, 259
American Revolutionary War, 9, 31, 107, 112, 137, 154, 195, 202, 232, 289, 291, 293, 310, 311, 316, 321, 330, 338
anarchy, 36, 44, 59, 72, 82, 283, 299
Annapolis Convention, 138, 509
aristocracy, 84, 504
arms, right to bear, 194
arms, the right to bear, 154, 225
Armstrong, John, 329
Articles of the Confederation, 78, 107, 137, 139, 148, 150, 151, 194, 265, 323, 509
Assize of Arms of 1181, 229
atheism, 249, 298
atomic bombing of Hiroshima and Nagasaki, 128
attainder of treason, 147
Austria, 121
Axis power, 129

B

bail, 158, 386, 508
barter, 201
Bastiat, Frederic
 Law, The, 45, 48, 49, 52, 284
Battle of Iwo Jima, 128
Battle of New Orleans, 112
Battle of Okinawa, 128
Battle of the Alamo, 113
Battle of Yorktown, 108, 348, 509
Battle Hymn of the Republic, The (Ward), 59
Beccaria, Cesare, 231
Benson, Ezra Taft, 361
bill of attainder, 144
bill of credit, 178, 201
Bill of Rights, 31, 110, 150, 194, 195, 225, 232, 233, 238, 289, 291, 357, 358, 384, 508. *See also* Amendments to the U.S. Constitution
Black Hand, 121
black-bag searches, 197
Blackstone, William, 79, 104, 505
 Commentaries on the Laws of England, 25, 26, 27, 81, 195, 216, 232, 505, 509
Bolsheviks, 301
Bonaparte, Napoleon, 298
Bosnia and Herzegovina, 121
bourgeoisie, 281, 282
Bowie, James, 113
Braddock, Edward, 311
Brady Handgun Act of 1993, 227
Bricker Amendment, 98
Bricker, John W., 98, 189
Burke, Edmund
 Reflections on the Revolution in France, 293
Burnside, Ambrose, 118
Bush, George H. W., 130, 134

C

CAFTA (Central American Free Trade Agreement), 135, 171
Cambodian Revolution, 303
capital punishment, 159

Carr, Peter, 40, 221, 236, 340
Carroll, Charles, 343
Castro, Fidel, 130, 302
Central American Free Trade Agreement, 135, 171
Central Intelligence Agency, 135, 198
CFR (Council on Foreign Relations), 52, 124
Charles II (king of England), 143
Charles-Louis de Secondat (baron de Montesquieu). *See* Montesquieu, Baron de
checks and balances, 16, 66, 77, 83, 84, 86, 140, 189, 190, 266, 291
Chesterton, G. K., 56
Children Story, The (Clavell), 15
China, 54, 135, 292, 302
Chinese Revolution, 54, 303
Chotek, Sophie. *See* Sophie (duchess of Hohenberg)
Christianity. *See also* religion
 abolishment of, 277, 279, 292, 301, 302
Church of England, 29
CIA (Central Intelligence Agency), 135, 198
citizenship, 148, 161
Clark, Abraham, 347
Clark, J. Reuben, Jr., 125, 131
Clavell, James
 Children Story, The, 15
Coinage Act of 1792, 159, 204
Columbus, Christopher, 102
Commentaries on the Laws of England (Blackstone), 25, 26, 27, 81, 195, 216, 232, 505, 509
Commerce Clause, 92, 170
committee of correspondence, 9, 105
Common Sense (Paine), 350
Commonplace Book (Jefferson), 502
communism, 15, 45, 53, 124, 127, 129, 156, 161, 275, 277, 279, 281, 282, 283, 285, 287, 292, 295, 299, 300, 302, 309
Communist League, 278, 281
Communist Manifesto, The (Marx and Engels), 19, 51, 53, 115, 144, 156, 159, 161, 210, 247, 253, 256, 275,

INDEX

292, 299, 301, 465
Communist Party of China (CPC), 54
Communist Party USA, 257
compound republic, 71
Constitution. *See* U.S. Constitution
Constitutional Convention of 1787, 29, 31, 39, 51, 57, 63, 64, 83, 87, 109, 139, 148, 150, 151, 180, 181, 194, 202, 224, 242, 305, 310, 311, 322, 354, 355, 503
constitutional republic, 51, 221, 223, 361
Continental Army, 107, 311, 313, 316, 509
Continental Congress, 28, 313
Cornwallis, 1st Marquis (Charles Cornwallis), 108
Council on Foreign Relations, 52, 124
courts, 189
Crockett, Davy, 113
Cuban Revolution, 303

D

Daedalus (Greek myth), 204
Darwin, Charles, 255, 281
death penalty. *See* capital punishment
debt, 171, 184, 206, 212, 260, 269
debts, 141, 149
Declaration of Independence, 10, 24, 29, 51, 78, 96, 106, 107, 151, 154, 157, 164, 166, 186, 231, 265, 290, 291, 340, 341, 350, 366, 500, 505, 507
Defoe, Daniel, 309
democracy, 44, 51, 53, 55, 56, 57, 59, 61, 63, 65, 67, 71, 74, 84, 253, 254, 287, 504. *See also* majority rule
Democracy in America (Tocqueville), 35, 36, 37, 42, 222
Dewey, John, 249
Dickens, Charles
  Tale of Two Cities, A, 293
District of Columbia, 143, 163
division of powers. *See* separation of powers
double jeopardy, 155
due process of law, 82, 155, 156, 503, 508
Dulles, John Foster, 98

Dwight, Timothy, 37

E

Eccles, Marriner, 211
education, 29, 35, 54, 62, 153, 162, 219, 240, 279, 286, 288, 292, 296
Eisenhower, Dwight D., 129
electoral college, 89, 145, 209, 311
Emancipation Proclamation, 119
Engels, Friedrich, 278
  Communist Manifesto, The, 19, 51, 53, 115, 144, 156, 159, 161, 210, 247, 253, 256, 275, 281, 292, 299, 301, 465
English Bill of Rights of 1689, 229
entangling alliances, 94, 110, 122, 123, 125, 133, 168, 172, 179, 269
enumerated powers, 62, 77, 140, 143, 291
Essay Concerning Human Understanding, An (Locke), 499
European common market, 172
European Union (EU), 172
evolution, theory of, 255, 281
Ex parte McCardle, 190
ex post facto, 144. *See also* law
Examination of the Leading Principles of the Federal Constitution, An (Webster), 234
executive, 77, 83, 84, 86, 87, 88, 89, 92, 93, 140, 141, 156, 168, 170, 171, 174, 176, 178, 181, 182, 189, 204, 309, 327, 334, 504

F

Fairfax, Bryan, 313
Farewell Address (Washington), 34, 37, 116, 172, 186, 192, 207, 218, 243, 259, 290, 298, 331, 332, 333, 394
Farewell Speech to the United States Military Academy at West Point (MacArthur), 358
fascism, 124
federal income tax, 161, 209
federal lands, 183
federal republic, 76
Federal Reserve System, 120, 210, 211

519

federalism, 75
Federalist Papers, 31, 65, 510
   no. 1, 66
   no. 9, 66
   no. 10, 64, 67
   no. 14, 67
   no. 32, 148
   no. 37, 31
   no. 39, 69, 89
   no. 42, 148, 202, 357
   no. 44, 202
   no. 45, 60, 170
   no. 46, 233
   no. 47, 88, 168
   no. 49, 70
   no. 51, 70, 88
   no. 57, 72
   no. 71, 73
   no. 73, 47, 82
   no. 79, 47, 82, 283
   no. 85, 73
Federation of the Just, 278
felonies, 93
Final Solution to the Jewish Problem, 129
Firearms Control Act of 1976 (Washington DC), 228
Fitzpatrick, John C.
   Writings of George Washington from the Original Manuscript Sources, 1745–1799, The, 312
foreign commerce. *See* Commerce Clause
Foster, William
   Toward Soviet America, 257
Franco-Prussian War, 292, 299
Franklin, Benjamin, 29, 41, 57, 198, 218, 290, 306, 342, 354
Franz Ferdinand (archduke of Austria), 121
Free Trade Areas of the Americas, 171
freedom of speech, 153, 237
freedom of the press, 152, 153
French and Indian War, 104, 311, 329

French Revolution, 279, 289, 292, 294, 296, 297, 302, 303
FTAA (Free Trade Areas of the Americas), 171
führerprinzip, 309

G

Gadsden Purchase, 115
GATT (General Agreement on Tariffs and Trade), 135, 171, 172
General Agreement on Tariffs and Trade, 135, 171, 172
general welfare, 78, 79
George Washington: A Collection (Allen), 312, 329
Germany, 122, 124, 125, 127, 129, 205, 276, 299
Give me liberty or give me death speech (Henry), 101, 106, 339
God of the Machine, The (Paterson), 50
government, 28, 29, 75, 76, 78, 81, 83, 85, 87, 89, 91, 94, 95, 120, 137, 139, 140, 141, 148, 151, 153, 154, 156, 157, 159, 161, 170, 177, 179, 180. *See also names of different types of government*
   abolishment of, 107, 115, 301
   branches of, 83
   limitations of, 58
   limits of, 61
   purpose of, 13, 15, 24, 29, 77, 164, 166
   regional, 171
   world, 122, 124, 129, 131, 135, 255
government, forms of, 43. *See also names of individual forms*
Graham, Catherine Macaulay, 330
Grant, Ulysses S., 118
Greene, Nathaniel, 509
Greenspan, Alan, 211
Griffin, G. Edward
   Creature from Jekyll Island, The, 211
guillotine, 297
Gulf War I, 134
Gulf War II, 134
gun control, 228
Gun Control Act of 1968, 226

INDEX

H

Hale, Nathan, 352
Hamilton, Alexander, 56, 60, 261, 330, 334, 510
   Federalist Papers, 47, 66, 73, 82, 148, 283
Hancock, John, 105, 290, 338, 341
Hargrove, John, 38
Hart, John, 346
Henry, Patrick, 151
   Give me liberty or give me death speech, 101, 106, 339
Hess, Moses, 278
Hewes, Joseph, 348
Heyward, Thomas, Jr., 349
Hiss, Alger, 126, 129
History of the United States (Webster), 244
Hitler, Adolf, 125, 127, 129
Ho Chi Minh, 303
Hodge, A. A., 248
Hooker, Joseph, 118
Hopkins, Harry, 126
Hopkins, Stephen, 343
House, Edward Mandell, 52, 122, 124
   Philip Dru: Administrator, 122
Howe, Julia Ward
   Battle Hymn of the Republic, The, 59
humanism, 240. *See also* religious humanism; secular humanism
Humanist Manifestos
   I, 249, 250
   II, 250
human nature, 47, 61, 82, 84, 87, 88, 95, 139, 251, 283, 308, 320, 506
Humphreys, David, 324
Hussein, Saddam, 135
hyperinflation, 123, 205

I

Icarus (Greek myth), 204
Illuminati, Order of the, 115, 279, 281, 291, 296, 302
immigration, 142, 176, 221
inflation, 79, 204, 211
international commerce, 170
Italian Social Republic, 124
Italy, 124, 127, 129

J

Jackson, Andrew, 206
Jackson, Thomas J. Stonewall, 117
Japan, 124, 127, 128, 129
Jay, John, 22, 60, 329
Jefferson, Thomas, 11, 28, 40, 41, 70, 88, 90, 97, 116, 135, 151, 157, 160, 167, 169, 173, 177, 181, 188, 199, 203, 204, 206, 207, 221, 223, 224, 234, 236, 240, 243, 274, 290, 293, 294, 320, 340, 503, 510
   Commonplace Book, 502
Johnson, Andrew, 161
Johnson, Lyndon B., 226
John (king of England), 143
Journal of the Federal Convention (Madison), 202
judicial, 77, 83, 87, 92, 140, 146, 156, 185, 189, 190, 504
judiciary, 88

K

Kennedy, John F., 226
Kennedy, Robert F., 226
Key, Francis Scott
   Star-Spangled Banner, The, 112
Khmer Rouge, 303
King, Martin Luther, 226
Knox, Henry, 324
Korean War, 134
kulaks, 127, 301

L

Lafayette, Marquis de, 330
law, 49, 58, 76, 84, 94, 96, 97, 157, 209, 216, 282. *See also* natural law
Law, The (Bastiat), 45, 48, 49, 52, 284
laws of nature. *See* natural law
Layton, Frank, 227
leader principle. *See führerprinzip*
League of Just Men, 278

League of Nations, 122, 123, 124, 129
Lee, Richard Henry, 233
Lee, Robert E., 116
legal plunder, 45, 49, 52, 284
legislative, 42, 77, 83, 84, 86, 87, 88, 92, 94, 140, 141, 147, 504
Lenin, Vladimir Ilyich, 53, 59, 300, 302, 309
Letters to a Young Gentleman Commencing His Education (Webster), 215
Lewis, Francis, 345
liberty, 139, 336
Life of Reason, The (Santayana), 136
Lincoln, Abraham, 116, 143, 311
Livingston, Philip, 345
Locke, John, 94, 499
  Essay Concerning Human Understanding, An, 499
  Second Essay Concerning Civil Government, 80
  Two Treatises of Government, 94, 168, 283, 499
Lord of the Rings, The (Tolkien), 336, 360

M

MacArthur, Douglas
  Douglas Farewell Speech to the United States Military Academy at West Point, 358
Madison, James, 29, 31, 60, 64, 83, 87, 92, 94, 98, 152, 180, 181, 188, 199, 213, 223, 290, 323
  Federalist Papers, 67, 68, 69, 70, 72, 88, 148, 168, 170, 202, 233, 357
  Journal of the Federal Convention, 202
  Spirit of Government, 502
Magna Carta, 143, 159
Mainspring of Human Progress (Weaver), 50
majority rule, 45, 52, 58, 63, 71. *See also* democracy
Making the World Safe for Democracy, 122
marriage, 214, 299
  abolishment of, 277, 279, 286, 292
Marx, Jenny (née von Westphaelen), 281
Marx, Karl, 276, 302, 309
  Communist Manifesto, The, 19, 51, 53, 115, 144, 156, 159, 161, 210, 247,
253, 256, 275, 292, 299, 301, 465
Mason, George, 39, 152, 224, 235, 305, 355
Mayflower Compact, 23, 103, 364
McCardle case. *See Ex parte McCardle*
McGuffey Readers (McGuffey), 247
McGuffey, William Holmes
  McGuffey Readers, 247
Mexican-American War, 114
Mexico, 112
Middleton, Arthur, 349
military imperialism, 124
militia, 143, 146, 180, 194, 226, 233, 235, 237, 238
Miller, Jack, 227
mob rule, 44, 58
monarchy, 44, 84, 169, 503, 504, 510
money, 79, 123, 141, 142, 144, 201, 202
Monroe, James, 111, 174, 175, 220
Monroe Doctrine, 111, 175
Montesquieu, Baron de, 67, 223, 502
  Spirit of Laws, The, 83, 87, 216, 502
morality, 17, 29, 34, 40, 42, 153, 214, 216, 218, 219, 220, 221, 222, 223, 240, 242, 256, 258, 260, 268, 269, 279, 282, 298, 326, 327. *See also* religion; virtue
  abolishment of, 287, 292
Morris, Lewis, 346
Morse, Jedidiah, 22
Morton, John, 349
mutilation, 159

N

NAFTA (North American Free Trade Agreement), 135, 171, 172
National Firearms Act of 1934, 226, 227
National Firearms Act of 1938, 226
National Security Agency, 198
NATO (North Atlantic Treaty Organization), 133, 134, 176, 270
  charter, 131
  handbook, 132
natural law, 24, 26, 27, 500, 503, 505, 506. *See also* law
naturalization, 142, 147, 176

INDEX

Nazism (National Socialism), 124, 309
Nelson, Thomas, Jr., 348, 509
New England Primer, The, 24, 241
Nicola, Lewis, 316
1917 October Revolution. *See* Russian Revolution
1984 (Orwell), 309
nonaggression pact, 125, 129
North American Free Trade Agreement, 135, 171, 172
North Atlantic Treaty Organization, 133, 134, 176, 270
  charter, 131
  handbook, 132
Northwest Ordinance of 1787, 29, 36, 153, 219, 220, 242
NSA (National Security Agency), 198

O

oligarchy, 44
Operation Keelhaul, 129
original intent, 9, 11, 29, 33, 51, 61, 74, 75, 110, 120, 121, 123, 149, 153, 156, 157, 159, 164, 166, 168, 170, 177, 184, 200, 202, 206, 225, 229, 358, 361
Orwell, George
  1984, 309
Oswald, Lee Harvey, 226

P

Paine, Thomas
  Common Sense, 350
Paterson, Isabell
  God of the Machine, The, 50
Patman, Wright, 211
Patriot Act. *See* USA PATRIOT Act
Pearl Harbor attack, 127
Peek, George A., Jr.
  Political Writings of John Adams, The, 82
Pentagon, The, 129
Philadelphia Convention.
    See Constitutional Convention of 1787

Philip Dru: Administrator (House), 122
Pilgrims, 23, 103, 285, 360, 362
Pledge of Allegiance, 59, 363
plunder. *See* legal plunder
Pol Pot, 303
Political Writings of John Adams, The (Peek), 82
Preamble to the U.S. Bill of Rights, 194, 511
Preamble to the U.S. Constitution, 78, 79, 200, 371
private property, 47, 79, 81, 82, 155, 156, 280, 285, 287
  abolishment of, 156, 277, 279, 283, 292, 295, 301, 302
Prohibition, 162
proletariat, 51, 53, 276, 279, 281, 282, 283, 287, 301, 302
Puritans, 24, 104, 360, 362

R

Randolph, Edmund, 64, 324
Reagan, Ronald, 227
Reflections on the Revolution in France (Burke), 293
regional government, 171
religion, 29, 33, 34, 35, 36, 40, 42, 61, 104, 153, 215, 219, 220, 221, 222, 223, 237, 242, 245, 258, 260, 268, 269, 282, 298, 499. *See also* Christianity; morality; virtue
  abolishment of, 107, 115, 287, 296
religious humanism, 250. *See also* humanism; secular humanism
republic, 45, 57, 58, 59, 61, 63, 64, 65, 76, 141, 148, 177, 184, 217, 326, 328
  constitutional, 51, 221, 223, 361
  federal, 76
Revere, Paul, 105, 232
Robespierre, Maximilien, 296
Roosevelt, Franklin Delano, 126, 129
Rousseau, Jean-Jacques, 295, 296
  Social Contract, The, 295
Ruby, Jack, 226

523

Rules of Civility and Decent Behaviour in Company and Conversation (Washington), 242
Russia. *See* Soviet Union
Russian Revolution, 124, 299, 303
Rutledge, Edward, 342, 349

S

Sabbath, 37
Santa Anna, Antonio Lopez de, 113
Santayana, George
  Life of Reason, The, 136
Saralof Decree of 1919, 286
scarcity doctrine, 254
SEATO (Southeast Asia Treaty Organization), 134, 176, 270
secret combinations, 121, 246
secular humanism, 38, 223, 256, 305.
  See also humanism; religious humanism
Security and Prosperity Partnership, 135, 171
separation of powers, 66, 77, 83, 85, 91, 96, 140, 168, 169, 266, 503
serfdom, 48
sex education, 252
Shakespeare, William
  Tempest, The, 101
Shaw, George Bernard, 280
Sherman, William T., 118
slavery, 116, 129, 160, 355, 357
Social Contract, The (Rousseau), 295
socialism, 45, 47, 53, 54, 74, 122, 130, 250, 254, 257, 277, 279, 280, 284, 285, 287, 295, 310
Socrates, 45
Soldier's Guide, The, 59
Sophie (duchess of Hohenberg), 121
Southeast Asia Treaty Organization, 134, 176, 270
Soviet Union, 53, 122, 124, 125, 127, 128, 134, 275, 285, 292
Spanish Civil War, 124
specie, 204
spheres of influence, 125

Spirit of Laws, The (Montesquieu), 83, 87, 216, 502
Spirit of Governments (Madison), 502
SPP (Security and Prosperity Partnership), 135, 171
Stalin, Joseph, 125, 127, 129, 300, 301, 302
Star-Spangled Banner, The, 112
Stockton, Richard, 346
Stuart, David, 331
Stuart, J. E. B., 117

T

Tale of Two Cities, The (Dickens), 293
Taney, Roger B., 143
Teheran, 129
Tempest, The (Shakespeare), 101
Ten Commandments, 27
Tet Offensive, 303
Texas Revolution, 112
Tocqueville, Alexis de
  Democracy in America, 35, 36, 37, 42, 222
Tolkien, J. R. R.
  Lord of the Rings, The, 336, 360
Tories, 291, 349
torture, 156, 159, 309
Toward Soviet America (Foster), 257
Travis, William Barrett, 113
treaties, 62, 94, 122, 144, 146, 148, 149, 168, 184, 185, 321. *See individual treaties by name*
Treaty of Guadalupe Hildalgo, 115
Treaty of Paris (1783), 108, 112
Treaty of Versailles, 123
Trotsky, Leon, 301
Tse-tung, Mao, 54, 59, 130, 135, 302, 303
Tucker, St. George, 509
  View of the Constitution of the United States, 83, 89, 91, 93, 94, 95, 96, 97, 133, 169, 179, 185, 187, 235, 238, 509
Two Treatises of Government (Locke), 94, 283, 499
Tytler, Alexander, 55

INDEX

tyranny, 10, 13, 16, 48, 56, 58, 61, 67, 77, 82, 87, 88, 107, 135, 144, 155, 165, 166, 168, 181, 190, 196, 198, 199, 209, 225, 248, 253, 254, 267, 268, 275, 283, 292, 294, 301, 304, 305, 306, 308, 310, 337, 338, 351
  of the masses, 45, 71

U

U.S. Army Training Manual, 58
U.S. Bill of Rights. *See* Bill of Rights
U.S. Constitution, 9, 11, 14, 29, 38, 51, 57, 58, 60, 63, 65, 70, 72, 73, 76, 77, 79, 83, 87, 89, 91, 93, 94, 96, 109, 120, 122, 123, 131, 135, 137, 139, 150, 152, 166, 168, 169, 170, 176, 177, 180, 184, 185, 188, 189, 191, 204, 213, 219, 220, 243, 254, 256, 264, 266, 267, 275, 289, 291, 308, 309, 310, 325, 329, 333, 356, 358, 361, 372, 508
  amendement of. (see amendment process *and specific amendments*)
  Article I, 90, 140, 141, 147, 170, 178, 180, 182, 184, 189, 190, 191, 201, 210, 356
  Article II, 96, 140, 325
  Article III, 140, 146, 189, 190, 191
  Article IV, 140, 147, 177, 183, 191
  Article V, 96, 141, 148, 152, 154, 176, 185, 191, 193, 265, 270, 361
  Article VI, 141, 149, 185, 291
  Article VII, 141, 149
unalienable rights, 507
Union Army, 116
Union or Death. *See* Black Hand
United Baptist Churches, 330
United Nations
  Charter, 131
United Nations (UN), 129, 134, 270
United States vs. Miller, 227

Uniting and Strengthening America by Providing Appropriate Tools Required to Intercept and Obstruct Terrorism Act of 2001, 195, 197, 198, 199
USA PATRIOT Act of 2001, 195, 197, 198, 199

V

Valley Forge, 107, 350, 353
veto, 86, 142
Vietnamese Revolution, 303
Vietnam War, 134
View of the Constitution of the United States (Tucker), 83, 89, 91, 93, 94, 95, 96, 97, 133, 169, 179, 185, 187, 235, 238, 509
virtue, 34, 40, 84, 203, 216, 219, 220, 221, 222, 223, 269, 326, 327.
  See also morality; religion

W

war, 93, 94, 97, 143, 168, 179, 269.
  See also individual wars by name
War of 1812, 112
Washington, George, 28, 31, 33, 41, 90, 104, 108, 203, 204, 206, 218, 242, 290, 291, 308, 347, 353
  Farewell Address, 34, 37, 116, 172, 186, 192, 207, 218, 243, 259, 290, 298, 331, 332, 333, 394
  Rules of Civility and Decent Behaviour in Company and Conversation, 242
Washington, Martha (née Dandridge), 314, 315
Weaver, Henry Grady
  Mainspring of Human Progress, 50
Webster, Noah, 238, 244, 246
  American Dictionary of the English Language, An, 57, 75, 76, 78, 167, 217, 259
  Examination of the Leading Principles of the Federal Constitution, An, 234

History of the United States, 244
Letters to a Young Gentleman Commencing His Education, 215
Weishaupt, Adam, 107, 279, 291, 292
welfare clause, 62
White, Harry Dexter, 126
William III (king of England), 501
Wilson, Woodrow, 52, 122
working class. *See* proletariat
world government, 122, 124, 129, 131, 135, 255
World Trade Organization, 135, 171, 172, 189
World War I, 121, 131, 205, 228, 299
World War II, 125, 130, 134, 302

writ of habeas corpus, 143, 508
Writings of George Washington from the Original Manuscript Sources, 1745–1799, The (Fitzpatrick), 312
writs of assistance, 155, 195, 196, 198
written constitution, 10, 62, 77, 97, 140, 188, 511
WTO (World Trade Organization), 135, 171, 172, 189
Wythe, George, 509

Y

Yalta, 129